REGULATING FOR COMPETITION

GOVERNMENT–INDUSTRY RELATIONS

Editors: Maurice Wright and Stephen Wilks

Volumes within this series incorporate original research into contemporary policy issues and policy-making processes in the UK, Western Europe, the United States, and South-East Asia.

ALREADY PUBLISHED

Comparative Government–Industry Relations: Western Europe, the United States, and Japan
edited by Stephen Wilks and Maurice Wright

Government and the Chemical Industry: A Comparative Study of Britain and West Germany
Wyn Grant, William Paterson, and Colin Whitston

Capitalism, Culture, and Economic Regulation
edited by Leigh Hancher and Michael Moran

Hostile Brothers: Competition and Closure in the European Electronics Industry
Alan Cawson, Kevin Morgan, Douglas Webber, Peter Holmes, and Anne Stevens

REGULATING FOR COMPETITION

Government, Law, and the Pharmaceutical
Industry in the United Kingdom
and France

LEIGH HANCHER

CLARENDON PRESS · OXFORD
1990

Oxford University Press, Walton Street, Oxford OX2 6DP
Oxford New York Toronto
Delhi Bombay Calcutta Madras Karachi
Petaling Jaya Singapore Hong Kong Tokyo
Nairobi Dar es Salaam Cape Town
Melbourne Auckland
and associated companies in
Berlin Ibadan

Oxford is a trade mark of Oxford University Press

Published in the United States
by Oxford University Press, New York

© Leigh Hancher 1990

British Library Cataloguing in Publication Data
Hancher, Leigh
Regulating for compensation: government, law and the
pharmaceutical industry in the United Kingdom and France.
– (Government-industry relations, ISSN 0955–9906; 5)
1. Europe. Pharmaceutical industries
I. Title II. Series
338.476151094
ISBN 0–19–827570–6

Library of Congress Cataloging in Publication Data
Hancher, Leigh, 1956–
Regulating for competition: government, law, and the
pharmaceutical industry in the United Kingdom and France / Leigh Hancher.
p. cm.—(Government-industry relations: 5)
Includes bibliographical references.
1. Pharmacy—Law and legislation—Great Britain. 2. Drugs—Law
and legislation—Great Britain. 3. Antitrust law—Great Britain.
4. Pharmacy—Law and legislation—Great Britain. 5. Drugs—Law and
legislation—France. 6. Antitrust law—France. I. Title.
II. Series.
KJC6191.H36 1990 344.41'0416—dc20 [344.104416] 90–7016
ISBN 0–19–827570–6

Typeset by Wyvern Typesetting Ltd, Bristol
Printed and bound in
Great Britain by Bookcraft (Bath) Ltd,
Midsomer Norton, Avon

For My Parents

Acknowledgements

THIS book forms part of the research on government–industry relations managed by the Economic and Social Research Council.

In the course of researching and writing this book I have received a great deal of support from numerous people in both France and the United Kingdom, and latterly in the Netherlands, where much of the final writing was done. I would particularly like to thank Professor Yves Meny, Professor George Viala, and Dr Catherine Maurain for their invaluable help with the French part of the research. Officials from the SNIP and from the French Ministries of Health, Industry, and the Economy supplied a great deal of information, assistance, and advice. Robert Hankin of DGIII of the Commission in Brussels has kindly helped me to keep up with developments in EC law and policy. Staff at the ABPI and at the Department of Health in the UK were always ready and willing to respond to my numerous requests for documentation, background information, and clarification.

In the UK, my colleagues at the School of Law of the University of Warwick permitted me a year of absence to undertake much of the early research, while Maurice Wright and Mick Moran at the University of Manchester ensured my brief term as Visiting Fellow there was a productive one. Finally, my colleagues at the University of Leiden have been prepared to suffer the final stages of the completion of the manuscript.

I would also like to acknowledge my gratitude to Stephen Wilks, Alan Page, Terence Daintith, and Piet Jan Slot for carefully reading the manuscript and commenting constructively upon it, and last but by no means least, I owe a great deal to Peter Mair for his continued support for, and forbearance with, this enterprise.

L.H.

Leiden
July, 1989

Contents

Abbreviations

ABPI	Association of the British Pharmaceutical Industry
All ER	All England Law Reports
AJDA	Actualité juridique (Droit administratif)
AMM	autorisation de mise sur le marché
API	Association of Pharmaceutical Importers
BEUC	Bureau of the European Union of Consumers
BMA	British Medical Association
BSM	brevet spéciale du médicament
BOCC	Bulletin officiel de la consommation et la concurrence
BOSP	Bulletin officiel du service du prix
Bull.Ordre pharm.	Bulletin du Conseil national de l'ordre des pharmaciens
CE	arrêt du Conseil d'État
CGP	Comptroller General of Patents
CMLR	Common Market Law Reports
C.M.L.Rev.	Common Market Law Review
CNAMTS	Caisse nationale de l'assurance maladie des travailleurs salariés
CNRS	Centre nationale de la recherche scientifique
CPA	Committee of Public Accounts
CPMP	Committee on Proprietary Medicinal Products
CRM	Committee on the Review of Medicines
CSD	Committee on the Safety of Drugs
CSM	Committee on the Safety of Medicines
CSP	Code de la santé publique
CSS	Code de la securité sociale
CTC	clinical trial certificate
CTX	clinical trial exemption certificate
DGCC	Direction générale de la consommation et de la concurrence
DICTD	Direction des industries chimiques, textiles et divers

DPHM	Direction de la pharmacie et du médicament
ECR	European Court Reports
EFPIA	European Federation of Pharmaceutical Industry Associations
E.L.Rev.	European Law Review
FDA	Food and Drug Administration
ICI	Imperial Chemical Industries
IIC	International Review of Industrial Property and Copyright Law
INPI	Institut national de la propriété industrielle
INSERM	Institut national de la santé et de la recherche médicale
JO	Journal officiel de la République française
MAIL	Medicine Act Information Letter
MMC	Monopolies and Mergers Commission
MLX	Medicine Act Consultation Letter
NCE	new chemical entity
NHS	National Health Service
OECD	Organisation for Economic Co-operation and Development
OFT	Office of Fair Trading
OJ	Official Journal of the European Communities
OTC	over-the-counter
PL	product licence
PL(PI)	product licence (parallel import)
PMA	Pharmaceutical Manufacturers Association
PPRS	Pharmaceutical Price Regulation Scheme
RCP	Royal College of Physicians
ROR	rate of return
RP	Rhone-Poulenc
RPC	Reports of Patent Cases
RTPC	Restrictive Trade Practices Court
TNC	transnational corporation
SNIP	Syndicat national de l'industrie pharmaceutique
SK&F	Smith, Kline & French
VPRS	Voluntary Price Regulation Scheme

1

The Legal Context of Government–Industry Relations

This study is concerned with the impact of regulation on competitive processes; that is, with an analysis of how government's regulatory goals conflict with market processes. More specifically, it examines the way in which law contributes to the development of mechanisms for the resolution of the recurring conflicts and tensions which, it will be argued, are inevitable in the process of regulating dynamic, market-based economies.

The problems confronting national governments in the regulation of one particular industrial sector—the pharmaceutical industry—are taken as a case-study of this process. In France and the United Kingdom, the two countries under study here, the pharmaceutical sector is, and always has been, economically buoyant. In terms of its current employment record, its contribution to exports and for-eign-currency earnings, as well as its future prospects as a high-technology or 'sunrise' industry, it is one of the most profitable and reputedly well-managed sectors of the economy. In contrast to developments in the 'sunset' sectors such as steel or shipbuilding, governments have not been required to intervene to support restructuring, or to contribute to large-scale programmes of modernization or investment; the industry has a good track record for investment and innovation, most of which is self-financed. Nor have pharmaceuticals featured as a key sector in national industrial policies or plans. In the United Kingdom official sponsorship of the industry rests not with the Department of Trade and Industry (DTI) but with the Department of Health. Even in France, where the process of plurien-niel planning permits, if nothing else, the public articulation of private ambitions, the pharmaceutical industry has received relatively little attention. A number of five-year plans have dealt with the industry indirectly, as a subsidiary to wider concerns about expenditure on social insurance or about national levels of innovation.

This study of regulation and competition is concerned not so much with the instruments of industrial policy but with the dilemmas faced by national governments who seek to reconcile their desire, as promoters of their home-based pharmaceutical firms, to maintain a strong, internationally competitive, research-based industry with their regulatory objectives in the area of health policy and, as the industry's major customer, with public-expenditure goals. While it may be safely assumed that the maximization of profitability is a goal equally espoused by the industry, the realization of that goal is dictated by the logic of the market, whereas the distribution of benefits by government is determined by the logic of the democratic political process.

Here regulation is approached from the perspective of competition. It is contended that the dominant logic informing the implementation of government regulation in the pharmaceutical sector is the maintenance of the efficient functioning of competitive market forces. In practice, although intervention in this sector has conventionally taken a highly legalistic form, its ultimate ends are not dissimilar to those which are taken to justify intervention elsewhere in the economy. In the case of pharmaceuticals, however, these broader policy goals must be mediated through complex and highly specific regulatory frameworks, which are designed primarily to fulfil the aims of policy on health or public expenditure rather than those of economic or industrial policy. It is contended that the process of regulatory intervention, whether directed at product safety, price control, or marketing, can only be understood if the constraints on regulation, imposed by the need to preserve effective competition, are recognized, and if the potential role of regulatory instruments as vehicles for the resolution of recurrent conflicts between government and industry is addressed.

Given that pharmaceutical regulation is examined here primarily in terms of the constraints imposed on regulators by the need to maintain effective competition, a central theme of this study will be the interrelated and cumulative effects of various regulatory regimes on the competitive process. As Chapter 2 will demonstrate in some detail, the pharmaceutical industry is best viewed as caught within a complex web of regulatory rules, which may be used, deliberately or incidentally, to restrict competition. Because prescription drugs are selected by medical practitioners but paid for, directly or indirectly, from public funds, industrial performance in this sector is traditionally viewed as based on *product* competition rather than *price* competition. Industrial success, nationally and internationally, and long-term profitability are founded on the ability to compete through the introduction of new products rather than on the ability to offer goods at lower prices. Innovation is the motor of product competition, but innovation has become increasingly expensive and time-consuming in this sector. Government regulation of prices and profits will obviously have a direct effect on the innovatory process where profits are held down, restricting the available financial resources for research and development. But other forms of regulation, including controls on pre-marketing and product safety, may also affect the process of innovation and indirectly impair product competition. Stricter regulation of product safety may not only make the development of new drugs more expensive but may also raise the barriers of entry into the market, effectively insulating the existing firms from further competition.

The chapters that follow do not seek to offer an exhaustive comparative account of the implementation of specific legislative programmes in France and the UK; they aim to provide a basis for understanding and comparing the role these intertwining regimes play in shaping the relations of the two governments with their respective industries.

The approach taken here to regulation is a functional one. On the basis of a comparative analysis of the development of pharmaceutical regulation over 40 years, three themes will be explored. First, the impact of government intervention, through regulation, on market structures and competitive processes will be investigated, with an emphasis on the recurrent nature of the tensions and conflicts which occur in the process of regulation. As will become obvious in later chapters, the same conflicts need not necessarily occur in each country: the structure of the pharmaceuticals market in fact differs in each country. Secondly, an attempt will be made to determine how regulation structures relations between government and industry. It is hoped that by adopting a comparative perspective the diversity in the legal form and content of regulatory instruments will be made apparent. This in turn will aid investigation of the third theme, namely the way in which regulatory processes may serve to institutionalize patterns of negotiation and bargaining between regulator and regulated.

The regulation of the pharmaceutical sector offers excellent material with which to develop and test these themes. Firstly, and largely as a result of the nature of the products involved, this is an industry which is subject to intensive regulation. Secondly, it is a sector which is currently undergoing a significant amount of structural change. The modern pharmaceutical industry dates from the large-scale commercialization of synthetic, chemically based drug substances in the early part of this century. The industry quickly developed into a sophisticated, globally organized but essentially oligopolistic industrial sector. In the last decade, however, significant changes have begun to occur in the structure of the pharmaceutical market, a number of which are explored in detail in this book. The industry world-wide is undergoing a period of adjustment. This process does not require active governmental support— for example, in the way in which declining sectors of national economies have required heavy injections of finance; but precisely because government regulation impinges so directly on the industry's competitive environment, the performance of existing regulatory mechanisms in a changed market structure must inevitably be addressed.

This brings me to the central question facing every analyst of contemporary regulation: how should economic regulation be approached and understood in a comparative perspective? In the following section I will examine a number of established approaches to economic regulation and will seek to demonstrate why these are inadequate for an exploration of the themes chosen for analysis here; I will then go on to suggest an alternative focus. The second section will examine, at a general level, divergences in the French and British styles of government intervention in the economy. The scope and structure of this specific case-study of the pharmaceutical sector, and the content of subsequent chapters of this book, are outlined in the third section.

Approaches to Regulation: Capture Theory, Cultural Variables, and Regulation

Analysis of economic and social regulation has become something of a growth industry in recent years, generating a vast body of specialist literature. Perhaps the most established and well-known critique of economic regulation is to be found in the work of so-called capture theorists, but more recently a significant body of comparative literature on policy implementation has also taken up the theme of regulation and its effectiveness. In this section I will critically appraise these different approaches to the study of regulation.

There are, broadly, three strands of capture theory. According to one version, regulations are enacted to serve the public interest but are subsequently subverted to serve the ends of those who are supposed to be regulated. The best-known example of this genre is the 'life cycle' theory, which argues that the institutions set up to administer regulation go through various stages, taking a proactive and vigorous approach to implementation in their youth but, as old age sets in, lapsing into a reactive mode as the recognized protector of their clients.[1] A second variant of capture theory contends that regulation is designed initially to serve private, as opposed to public, interests. It argues that the 'bounded rationality' of regulators prevents a rational analysis of the market failures which regulation is supposed to remedy, and so a coherent articulation of public goals is not feasible. Private goals therefore predominate.[2]

Neither of these approaches appears particularly suited to our purposes, for a number of reasons. Firstly, I have suggested that there is, between the origins of the various pharmaceutical regulatory schemes and their implementation in practice, a certain disjuncture, which neither the 'public interest' nor 'private interest' theory can address. At some critics have suggested, 'a theory of regulatory origin may not explain regulatory output'.[3] Secondly, neither approach appears to fit the empirical reality of pharmaceutical regulation. In subsequent chapters, particularly Chapter 4, which deals with the regulation of product safety, I will argue that the pharmaceutical industry has consistently been the target of more rather than less regulation. Thirdly, both versions concentrate exclusively on the influence of the regulated industry, to the exclusion of the influence of other political actors. In the case of pharmaceutical regulation, the medical and pharmacy professions, as well as consumer groups, are obvious and important sources of pressure on regulators. Fourthly, each version is insufficiently disaggregated to allow for a comparative analysis of the way in which different countries evolve diverse techniques to reach shifting compromises over continuing conflicts between regulation and market processes. Capture theory tends to take a static view of the situation: regulatory authorities are either captured or not captured. The subsequent chapters of this study will argue that in reality the capacity of industry to influence the regulatory process is in a constant state of flux. A more nuanced approach to the study of regulation is therefore required.

A fifth and final problem with capture theory concerns the various assumptions that underpin it. Much of the capture literature is American in origin and has in turn been influenced by the historical, legal, and political development of regulation in the USA. It also reflects certain implicit assumptions about the proper place of regulation in modern democratic systems. In consequence, an almost instinctive belief that 'private' influence over regulatory processes is illegitimate pervades this literature. The very idea of 'capture', moreover, is based upon an assumption that there is a sphere of public regulatory authority which ought to be inviolate from private influence. One of the most influential political critiques of the interventionist regulatory state, Lowi's *End of Liberalism*, rests on the argument that there once existed, and should exist again, an inviolable public core, bounded by law and clearly distinct from the private sphere.[4] If regulation is assumed to be an activity in which some ideal of the public interest is pursued at the expense of the private, any evidence that private interests influence the regulatory process or derive benefit from it is treated as an indication that the purpose of the activity has been distorted. Hence capture theorists rarely go on to consider whether private participation serves a useful, or even a necessary, function in the process of modern economic regulation.

To couch analysis in terms which suggest the necessity of identifying and defending a clearly delimited sphere of public authority is clearly unhelpful to our analysis here. Furthermore, such an approach rests on a culturally restricted assumption that the roles of 'public' and 'private' in the regulatory process can be clearly distinguished. In subsequent chapters it will be made clear that there are significant national variations in how the public–private dividing-line is conventionally drawn. It is these very variations which should be of central concern to anyone engaged in a comparative study of regulation. An appraisal of the diversity of legal mechanisms and of the scope which such mechanisms may or may not allow pharmaceutical companies as regards gaining influence over the regulatory process is, in consequence, the second major theme of this study.

In this context, a more promising approach to economic regulation is to consider it from a functional perspective, as a potential resource for a variety of competing interests. This is the approach adopted by the third, and more sophisticated, variation on the capture theme: interest-group theory. One version of this approach to regulation, advocated by theorists working on 'rational choice' assumptions about political behaviour, is to conceptualize the regulatory process as a form of market-place where rational, self-interested or egotistical actors maximize their utilities.[5] The different utilities of varying actors are reflected in differing proxy measures: for politicians introducing and monitoring regulation, utilities are measured in votes; for business, in profits; for bureaucrats, in income, promotion, and prestige. The content of regulatory outcomes is a function of the varying capacities of different actors to exert power in the regulatory process. Power is a function of the resources available to these actors and of the alliances formed between them. In the regulation of business activities, especially in sectors such as pharmaceuticals, where large, usually multinational firms predominate, the predicted outcome is that regulation will be practised in the interests of the regulated. The regulated industry enjoys a monopoly of important resources to secure this outcome: an obvious expertise in its own daily affairs, a monopoly of legitimate expertise in the workings of the market, and capacity for unified action, all of which may be deployed to secure influence over the creation and implementation of regulatory schemes.

Interest intermediation and interdependence

Accounts of regulation that are based on rational-choice theories rely largely on predictive models of individual and collective behaviour which abstract regulation from its social, and indeed its legal, setting. A second version of the interest-group theory is based on extrapolation from empirical studies of the organization and institutionalization of interest 'intermediation'. This approach seeks to identify and analyse the interactions or linkages between key actors or groups who attempt to influence regulatory outcomes. Such relationships are conceived of in terms of mutual but asymmetric dependence, reflecting the distribution of resources between players. These resources are similar to those identified by rational-choice theorists and include finance, legislative power, information, and so on, which are similarly perceived as unevenly distributed between the different actors.

In this respect, a distinction is drawn between social and economic regulation in advanced capitalist societies. The traditional resources of government, derived mainly from its monopoly over the legitimate exercise of legal and administrative powers, are perceived to be at their weakest in the implementation of economic regulation:

Virtually all the other main areas of state activity, from law and order and social security to education and housing, are able to call upon mandatory legislation and administrative hierarchies in order to achieve (however imperfectly) their goals. Such uncomplicated mechanisms are not, however, available in the field of industrial policy, and are not the dominant element in the government–industry relationship.[6]

It is argued that, because of the ideological and technical difficulties involved in the systematic formal or legal regulation of decisions about, for example, prices and investment levels, which are normally taken by autonomous actors in response to market signals, governments must ultimately rely on co-operation, as opposed to coercion, in its dealings with industry. Given this state of affairs, business and businessmen enjoy a privileged relationship with government in formulating and implementing economic regulation. This does not, however, imply that large firms either necessarily or consistently exercise a level of dominance amounting to capture.[7] The relation between regulator and regulated is a more subtle, complex one and is based on *interdependence*. The relevant issues for study then become not whether influence does or does not amount to capture but whether and why interdependence between regulators and regulated emerges and persists, and whether and why, if at all, patterns of interdependence vary as between nations and legal systems or between industrial sectors.

The increased prevalence of interdependent relationships between government and industry, and its consequences on the legal form of this relationship, has in fact been a dominant theme in an important body of theoretical legal work which seeks to explain the phenomenon of regulation rather than its function. This literature examines perceived changes in the role of law and state in late capitalist societies. One particularly influential strand of literature starts with the contention that the scale, level, and form of state intervention in economic matters takes on wholly new dimensions as the state strives to replace the market mechanism and to support the private accumulation of capital. The resultant 'compenetration'[8] of state and civil society has a number of consequences for the role and form of law. As a result of increased political intervention in private spheres of economic life, the forms of political and legal legitimation which thrived under *laissez-faire* capitalism are displaced. The state can no longer function within the rule-based confines of Weberian formal rationality if it is to meet the demands which are seen to flow from the politicization of hitherto private relations. Formal, or abstract and general law is used as a shield to conceal what are 'effectively *ad hoc* measures of an intrinsically administrative nature'.[9] Law has become instrumental, goal-oriented, and purposive.[10] The state is now responsible for stimulating economic growth and is forced to incorporate major private-interest groups in order to do so.[11] The resulting, often informal 'corporatist' arrangements between state and industry displace formal legal rules.

As general theories on the changing role of law and state, these writings offer valuable and provocative insights, but they are at once too broad and too narrow for the purposes of a comparative study of specific regulations. On the one hand, while suggesting possible causes for patterns of increased interdependence between regulator and regulated, such theories operate at too high a level of abstraction to be of help in understanding why patterns of interdependence assume different forms in different countries, or might even fail to emerge at all. Thus they cannot offer any observations on the significance of institutional diversity for the development of substantive policy. On the other hand, they are overly reductionist: law and legal order are examined only in terms of their form and never of their content. Yet such factors are of equal concern in a comparative study of specific regulatory programmes, and are issues which this study seeks to address.

The interest-intermediation variation on the capture theme, developed primarily in the literature of political science, therefore appears to be a more suitable basis from which to approach the themes of this study. The interest-intermediation approach to government-industry relations, with its emphasis on bargaining and interdependence, potentially offers a fruitful way of understanding the evolution and development of regulatory programmes from the more 'global' and functional perspective of their effect on competitive processes. As the following chapters will suggest, the pharmaceuticals sector is one in which, despite a seemingly high level of formal regulation, substantial interest intermediation and bargaining does in fact take place.

There are three dominant characteristics of pharmaceutical regulation which are indicative, prima facie, of why bargained solutions to regulatory problems might be preferred. In the first place, a predisposition to bargaining over regulatory goals is suggested by the conflicting roles which governments are forced to adopt in relation to this sector, as the industry's regulator, sponsor, and eventual customer. Secondly, as Chapter 2 will argue, in seeking to promote efficient or effective competition in an essentially oligopolistic market, and in attempting to suppress its wasteful or unwanted aspects, governments are drawn into a complex demarcation process which invariably cannot be implemented through formal, detailed rules. For example, as will be explained in greater detail in Chapter 8, which deals with advertising and promotion, it is difficult to lay down a priori rules on where wasteful promotional expenditure begins and where the advertising necessary to stimulate product competition ends. There is, rather, a preference for loosely drafted, open-ended rules, the specific application of which is a matter for negotiation. Thirdly, for the very reason that the competitive processes in this sector are governed by a complex, interlinking web of regulations, considerable potential for *trade-offs* between different types of regulation exists. In other words, the industry may be prepared to co-operate with government in implementing stricter standards on product safety in exchange, for example, for a relaxation in the rules applying to the promotion or commercialization of their products, if this readjustment of the 'regulatory web' will help it secure its long-term profitability goals.

In addition to these features of regulation, the pharmaceutical sector itself, in both the UK and France, exhibits certain *organizational* features which have been identified by interest-group theorists as important variables in relationships of so-called 'power dependence'.[12] Firstly, the sector is oligopolistic in structure; it is dominated by a small number of large, usually transnationally organized and economically powerful firms. Secondly, the interests of these firms are represented by well-organized, politically active interest associations, which may negotiate over the formulation of regulation or may act as agents of implementation and control. The Association of the British Pharmaceutical Industry (ABPI) and the Syndicat national de l'industrie pharmaceutique (SNIP), it will be argued in later chapters, have played an important role in shaping the course of regulatory policy in their respective countries. Thirdly, as Chapters 3 and 4 illustrate, the government organs entrusted with the implementation and enforcement of regulatory programmes operate within a defined legal and regulatory framework which would seem to provide for a certain amount of unilateral coercion and, therefore, of state autonomy from regulated groups. This in turn encourages powerful private actors to pursue strategies of negotiation and accommodation with regulatory bodies.[13]

Despite these promising beginnings, the question of the legal dimension of government–industry relations and its impact on processes of interest intermediation has been more or less neglected. Not only has it been underresearched, it has also been underconceptualized. The existing literature on interest intermediation has undoubtedly identified the potential relevance of law and legal factors to an analysis of patterns of interest intermediation, but from a somewhat narrow perspective. Legal authority, for example, is perceived as a resource available, to a greater or lesser extent, to government actors or regulators. The lawyer would immediately qualify this rather 'top-down' or instrumental view of law by expanding the notion of legal resources to include the subjective legal rights of, and remedies available to, different actors in the policy process to challenge and even frustrate government policy.[14] As Chapters 5 and 6 will illustrate, as the pharmaceutical industry's competitive environment alters, legal resources are becoming increasingly important, both for potential market-entrants seeking to challenge the dominant patterns of interdependence between government and established firms and as a weapon with which the latter attempt to defend their existing privileged bargaining positions.

Indeed, interest-intermediation theorists have not really addressed the question of why a variety of resources, legal or otherwise, are at the disposal of different actors in the first place. Their main concerns are first to identify internal 'networks' of actors within organizations or institutions within which resources are exchanged, and secondly to examine their implications for policy outcomes.[15] In other words, they are concerned primarily to establish *who* participates in policy networks and why, and what impact this has on policy implementation. The wider context in which these networks operate, and in particular the relationship between their surrounding legal and political environments or cultures, and the influence of such factors on the structural characteristics of these networks are, for the most part, left unexplored.[16]

Policy studies

The wider legal environment or surrounding 'legal culture' in which regulatory policies are formulated and implemented is, however, perceived as an important determinant of policy outcomes in the mushrooming literature on what might be loosely termed 'policy studies'. Research has focused primarily on a comparative evaluation of the implementation of specific, and often controversial or novel, regulatory programmes. The aim has been to identify dominant national styles of regulation, distinguishing in particular the American from the European style of policy, as, for example, in Vogel's study on environmental policy in the USA and the UK and, to a lesser extent, in Kelman's study of health and safety policy in Sweden and the USA.[17] Studies comparing American regulations with a larger number of European programmes have also been undertaken by Bardacco,[18] who examined the implementation of regulation to protect workers from the hazardous effects of PVC. Brickman *et al.* have compared the design and implementation of regulation on chemical-related hazards in France, Germany, Sweden, the UK, and the USA.[19]

While shedding important light on the diverse cultural settings of regulation, as well as highlighting important divergences in national styles of policy and regulatory techniques, these studies nevertheless share a number of major limitations which restrict their usefulness to the present study.

Once again it would appear that these predominantly American writers have taken, perhaps understandably, the American approach to regulation as both their model and point of departure. This has two major consequences for their findings. First, the adversarial and even judicial style of regulatory rule-making which characterizes the procedures adopted by American regulatory agencies is taken to be the norm. Contrasts are drawn between this and the more consensual approach to the formulation and implementation of similar policies in Europe, above all in the UK.

The European countries are almost uniformly taken to exhibit a much less legalistic, or more discretionary approach to the enforcement of regulatory standards. Industry's compliance is in fact frequently 'bargained' or 'negotiated'. The explanation for this phenomenon is thought to reside in two factors: a preference for loosely drafted legislation, which allows for flexible adjustment to concrete situations, combined with a far greater delegation of discretionary powers to enforcement officers. The latter thus make little use of their formal legal powers, and consequently—again in contrast to the American experience—the courts have a very limited role to play in the regulatory process. The dichotomy which is presented is therefore one of legal versus non-legal forms of bargaining: there is, unfortunately, little attempt to identify, compare, or analyse the divergent techniques of regulation adopted in the different European countries.

Secondly, these writers, in common with the capture theorists discussed above, make a number of implicit assumptions about the function of regulation, again largely derived from the American model. Regulation is assumed to be a *proactive* or anticipatory activity, with governmental agencies unilaterally imposing certain standards on an unwilling, uncooperative industry and strictly enforcing compliance. Furthermore, the sorts of policies analysed are usually concerned with the implementation of a particular type of regulation—such as that relating to health and safety or the environment—which seeks to enforce highly specific technical or scientific standards. Such rules, which are more common in the USA, have been used to force higher standards on firms. In other words, this form of regulation has an important innovative function: it has been used as a positive incentive to shape behaviour rather than simply constrain it.[20] Whether regulation in general has traditionally performed a similar *instrumental* role, and whether it has traditionally been enforced with similar intensity in European countries are questions which are neither raised nor considered.

Unfortunately, a similar perspective on regulation dominates the work of a number of European policy-analysts who have compared the implementation of regulatory programmes within and between

European countries. On the one hand, their focus has been restricted, predominantly, to newer, more controversial regulatory programmes. Environmental policy and the regulation of health and safety at work are again popular themes. On the other hand, in seeking to offer explanations for the relative success or failure of policy programmes, these authors have characterized legal variables in a broadly similar manner to the American analysts. The formal legalistic approach of, for example, West German regulatory bodies, many of which are staffed by civil servants who have had legal training, is compared to the *ad hoc* pragmatism of their British counterparts. This pragmatism is perceived as a function of the considerable discretion granted to British governmental officials in order to secure regulatory compliance. Hence the latter are viewed as being able to adopt a more flexible approach, which often yields more successful results.[21]

The present study will seek to demonstrate that regulation can in fact fulfil a number of quite different objectives, which are not necessarily related to the pursuit of innovatory goals or to the provision of incentives to incorporate more exacting technical standards. Obviously, traditional economic regulation, such as administered control of prices or costs, does not readily conform to this particular vision of regulation; its function has been to constrain rather than to promote. But even the more technically oriented forms of regulation, including regulation of product safety, may serve other ends. For example, in Chapters 3 and 4 I examine the way in which regulation both of product safety and of price have served broader protectionist or mercantalist ends in France. Furthermore, as Chapter 4 illustrates, even the goals of modern product-safety regulation have not been unilaterally imposed by governments on an unwilling industry. The standards incorporated into French and British legislation are often the result of a long period of concertation between the regulatory authorities and the industry. The 'pre-regulatory' period—that is, the period immediately prior to the adoption of formal regulatory standards—may be of considerable importance to understanding why regulation assumes a particular legal form, and is therefore a key to understanding the subsequent development of relations between regulator and regulated.

A more fundamental criticism that can be levelled at the 'policy studies school', which, I have suggested, seeks primarily to identify the cultural variants in national styles of policy, is precisely that it does no more than that. Thus, even when it captures real divergence, this type of 'cultural analysis' often leaves its causes unexplained. As Hall has argued: 'Culture is not inherited but learned ... There must be vehicles for the creation and trans- mission of ... culture; and cultural analysis must say more about those vehicles.'[22]

An alternative approach: Regulation as a dynamic process

This apparent failure to analyse the process of 'cultural trans- mission' is perhaps to be explained by the somewhat static perspec- tive on regulation which the literature on policy studies has implicitly adopted. That literature has been primarily concerned with the specificities of particular regulatory schemata, and not with the impact of their form and design through time, or across the broader dimension of government–industry relations. In order to understand the processes by which regulation can function as a vehicle for the transmission of certain values, the focus of study must be shifted in a number of ways. Some of the shortcomings of the various approaches to regulation discussed above may then be overcome, while some of their positive features can be maintained.

Firstly, by focusing on three interrelated themes, namely the impact of regulation on competitive processes and the tensions it produces, the potential diversity of mechanisms used by national regulators and their regulated firms to reconcile their conflicting aims and objectives, and finally the processes by which inter- dependent relations become institutionalized in this ongoing pro- cess of bargaining and negotiation, this book embarks on an analysis of regulation above all as a *dynamic* process. The relation- ship between regulation and the market is perceived as being in a state of change. If, as subsequent chapters contend, the changing structure of the pharmaceutical industry generates new competitive pressures or forces, it is highly probable that regulatory goals and means will require compensatory adjustment to reflect these changes. Regulatory change, however, is not easily accomplished, especially where the interests of powerful economic actors such as the multinational pharmaceutical firms are at issue. The process of adjustment may itself lead to renewed tensions between regulator and regulated and may generate further structural change within the pharmaceutical market, thus stimulating demand for compensatory regulatory adjustment.

It is the dynamic nature of regulation which sets processes of interest intermediation in motion and which contributes, in the language of interest-group theory, to the production or specification of resources with which industry and government can bargain to establish their respective spheres of influence. Legal factors are important here, because legal resources may be necessary to defend existing privileged positions or, in the case of new market-entrants, to challenge pre-existing patterns of bargaining and negotiation. Legal authority is not, as interest-intermediation theorists have implied, necessarily the monopoly of governments; resources previously monopolized by government can be turned by industry to their own advantage. Chapter 6 offers an example of such a development in the context of British legislation on product safety; the research-based firms have attempted to secure a stricter enforcement of rules on product safety, in order to frustrate potential competition from rival generic manufacturers.

From this perspective, another, equally important dynamic of the regulatory process must be emphasized. As we shall see in later chapters, it is inevitable that in the process of regulating the affairs of an industry over a prolonged period of time, governmental authorities will acquire a greater knowledge of the industry, and might therefore be expected to exhibit a greater expertise in their dealings with it. Contrary to what conventional capture-analysis would appear to assume, the French and British pharmaceutical industries have in practice been confronted with the prospect of more rather than less government infringement of their commercial freedom, and they are constrained to react accordingly. Given the complexity of regulation, neither government nor the industry could be said to enjoy a position of continual domination in the way that conventional capture-theory might suggest. A more accurate picture of the relations between the two sides can be gained if we focus on the methods used to establish or maintain an influence, whether dominant or otherwise, on that process.

Secondly, if regulation is approached from a dynamic perspective, this in turn implies that analysis cannot be confined to a study of the bargained enforcement of specific national regulatory programmes—the traditional approach taken in the literature of policy studies. The process of negotiation and bargaining must be situated in a wider context. This book will examine the linkages between regulatory programmes and their combined impact on market structures and competitive processes, and their consequences for government—industry relations. Moreover, because its subject-matter is the recurrent nature of the tensions created by government intervention in the competitive process, it raises the question of whether the form which that bargaining process assumes, be it legal or non-legal, can function as a precedent for the resolution of future problems. Precisely because these various regulatory regimes have a cumulative impact on the structure of the pharmaceuticals market, adjustments to the overall regulatory framework, and not just the formulation, implementation, and enforcement of individual regulations, may become a matter for bargaining between industry and government.

Thirdly, a dynamic perspective on regulation moves the focus of analysis to a comparison of the regulatory instruments in operation in each country and the linkages which they may produce between government and industry in different legal environments or cultures. In the process of regulation, culturally formed assumptions about the purpose and role of law are of particular significance. I have argued that interest-intermediation theorists have tended to concentrate on sectorally specific, personal linkages between government agencies and regulated firms, at the expense of exploring the importance of broader 'externalities'. Yet, as Hayward has remarked, 'the operation of culturally based dominant values ... inhibits or precludes some kinds of arrangements, but favours others'.[23] The second section of this chapter discusses, at a general level, some of the principal differences in such arrangements in France and the UK.

However, there is some argument, indeed scepticism, about the independent explanatory power of cultural variables, especially when applied to the analysis of particular industrial sectors: the very terms 'legal culture' or 'political culture' defy precise definition and are thus assumed to be of limited value as conceptual tools. As essentially 'catch-all' terms, they refer to a loose set of variables which include customs, attitudes, values, and norms. Law is, of course, essentially normative, and this ought, prima facie, to make the operationalization of the concept more feasible than that of the related notion of political culture.[24] The variables grouped under the broad umbrella of 'legal culture' are, however, equally diffuse.

They have been summarized by Friedman as 'the values and attitudes which bind the system together and determine the place of the legal system in the culture of society as a whole'.[25] A straightforward comparative analysis of the regulation of competition in the pharmaceutical industry in the UK and France would undoubtedly reveal significant, if static, variations in approach, but it would not explain why such differences arise. The broader notion of legal culture, with all its definitional difficulties, is needed to explore the dynamics of the regulation of competition. In the following chapters the concept is used, rather than defined, as encompassing the various nationally distinctive features which mediate the regulatory process, which determine the way in which different rules interact to create negotiating frameworks, and which contribute to the specification of bargaining resources.

The notion of institutionalization of linkages or interdependent relationships is used as a key concept here to understand the processes by which 'cultural' factors interact with regulatory structures to produce, in the first instance, distinctive patterns of policy implementation in each country and, in the second instance, divergent approaches to subsequent issues of regulatory adjustment. There is in fact a growing body of literature on what is termed by its proponents 'the new institutionalism'.[26] In this study, institutions are not treated as synonymous with organizations,[27] but the process of institutionalization of linkages is taken to mean the development of routine relationships between separate organizational spheres, both through time and across specific issues in regulation. Although such routinized practices may eventually approximate to 'enduring systems of social beliefs and socially organised practices',[28] which become widely diffused, the scope of this particular study is too restricted to form a basis from which to draw wider conclusions about the role of legal culture in government–industry relations in general. Acknowledging Wilks's exhortation that 'more specific and applied studies are essential to refine intra-institutional cultural dynamics',[29] it is hoped that this comparative case-study of the dynamics of regulation in a key industrial sector will contribute to that process.

The remaining chapters of this book are therefore concerned with a comparison of the role which law plays on the one hand in the process of regulatory adjustment, and on the other in providing a framework for the development, and subsequent institutionalization of negotiating processes through which adjustment might be accommodated or accomplished. Before turning to the subject-matter of the individual chapters, however, it is necessary to examine the reasons for selecting the regulation of the British and French pharmaceutical industry as a basis for comparative study.

Comparing Government–Industry Relations in the UK and France

The French and British traditions of economic intervention

In terms of their economic development, their political institutions, and their legal system, the two countries under study here are perceived as differing profoundly in their approach to, and practice of, economic intervention. As Andrew Shonfield has remarked, 'In the history of capitalism Britain and France supply the convenience of sustained polarity.'[30] The contrasts between France and the UK are argued to be at their starkest in the areas of economic and industrial policy and, at a general level, to endow each government's relations with its industry with its own special character-istics. French government–industry relations 'operate within the context of a historical background that takes for granted a close relationship between government and industry, that accepts that the state should articulate historical priorities and expects that such priorities will continue to maintain an almost 'mercantalist' con-cern with French economic interests'.[31] Relations between British business and government, on the other hand, are often described as contradictory: the relationship is 'typified by industry's suspicion of "intervention" on the one hand, and a curiously paradoxical recog-nition that government has a responsibility towards industry on the other'.[32] At a general level, the contrasts between the British and French 'style' of government–industry relations are attributed to three sets of divergent factors, each of which are of considerable relevance to the concerns of the present study: the traditions of public authority and its legal articulation; the organization of its bureaucracy; and the role of interest-groups in the policy process. As the first two factors are related, they will be dealt with together.

Traditions of public authority and bureaucratic organization

Traditions of public authority and attitudes to the legitimate exercise of public power vary considerably between the two countries. This difference is reflected firstly in the organization of government bureaucracy, secondly in the nature of legal power accorded that bureaucracy, and thirdly in the instruments of control available to ensure the legitimate exercise of that power.

In a major comparative study of government–industry relations in which he outlines three models of industrial adjustment, Zysman characterizes France as approximating most closely to his state-led, as opposed to the market-led or tripartite-negotiated, model.[33] Bureaucratic autonomy and a coherent, codified, rational legal system facilitate state intervention in the economy and are essential features of state-led industrial policy:

State-led strategies of adjustment require state structures that permit bureaucrats partial autonomy from parliament and from interest groups that attempt to influence them. They also require that bureaucrats have both the legal discretion to discriminate between firms when implementing policy and the administration and financial instruments to exert their will.[34]

In a similar vein, Hall has contended that policy innovation is easier when officials holding a preponderant share of power are relatively free of vested interests.[35] The UK, however, is seen to fit less easily into any of Zysman's three categories and is conventionally seen as occupying an intermediate position between the market-led and tripartite-negotiated models.[36] In addition, one must also recognize the 'long tradition of conservative empiricism' in British constitutional theory and practice, in which attempts 'to found the political order on rational principles has been rejected in favour of the authority of experience and the continuity of practice'.[37]

Although the empirical relevance and explanatory value of such general theories of 'state-led versus market-led' adjustment, or of theories of 'strong versus weak' states,[38] are a matter of some debate,[39] these theories do serve to acknowledge important differences in the nature of public authority and in the relationship between public authority and private enterprise in each country — contrasts which are of particular relevance to this study.

For example, in contrast to France, the UK has never embraced the notion of the independent bureaucrat, invested with a considerable battery of autonomous powers to be wielded 'in the public interest'. Instead, the myth of ministerial responsibility has perpetuated the idea that the bureaucrat is the anonymous servant of a Minister of the Crown, who, in turn, must account to Parliament for the exercise of his or her executive powers. In Fifth Republic France, the functions of Parliament are more limited. The areas in which Parliament may legislate are specifically defined by the Constitution.[40] Most of the instruments of industrial policy are formulated, as well as implemented, by regulatory powers which require no explicit legislative backing.

Two further features distinguish French bureaucracy from its British counterpart: its hierarchical nature and its fragmentation. Again, legal factors contribute to the creation of divisional autonomy within ministries and to the emergence of a 'pecking order' within the bureaucracy. Divisions of ministries invariably have their powers and duties spelled out in detail in legal instruments such as the *arrêté*. However, as Suleiman has remarked of this allocation of powers, 'power and responsibility are widely distributed without the least concession to rationality'.[41] Divisional responsibilities are jealously guarded and *batailles des compétences* frequently emerge where civil servants are reluctant to surrender their powers to a rival division.[42]

The structure of the French ministries contributes further to the autonomy of the civil servant. There is no equivalent in France to the British Permanent Secretary, whose ostensible role is to co-ordinate departmental policy: 'French ministries are in effect confederations of divisions.'[43]

The fragmentation and rigid structure of the French Civil Service is reinforced by another aspect of the statist tradition in France, the dominance of the *grands corps*. These group together officials who have been recruited through the various *grandes écoles* and who allegedly maintain a tight grip on strategic positions within the administration.[44] The training of these élite groups, whose expertise allegedly prevails in the sectors for which they have responsibility, stand out in marked contrast to the traditional cult of the generalists in the British Civil Service, where social class and education are of continued significance in recruitment to senior posts. This is yet another feature of the conventional world of British government; indeed, Gladstone once suggested that the public schools were part of the British Constitution.[45]

These different perceptions of the proper role of public authority have had two important consequences for the development of public law in each country. On the one hand, there is the well-known suspicion, in the UK, of administrative law and of the judges who enforce it; the comparative absence of a distinctive body of jurisprudence in this area, administered by separate administrative courts, was, at least until recently, a notable feature of the British legal system.[46] On the other hand, another feature of British public law which has passed relatively unnoticed is the absence of anything equivalent to the concept of 'public service' which characterizes French administrative law and which legitimates state intervention in society.[47] This instrumental view of administrative law has developed side by side with modern bureaucracy in France.[48] In the UK, in contrast, administrative law has developed largely as a body of procedural guarantees rather than of substantive principles. Whereas the concepts of British administrative law have been evolved primarily to curb and control state intervention in society, in France administrative law is seen as the 'vecteur privilégié de l'action administrative'.[49]

Throughout this study I shall assess the implications of these different traditions for the nature and direction of state intervention in the pharmaceutical industry—in the context of the formulation and implementation of the various regulatory programmes on prices, product safety, advertising and promotion—and for the development of competition policy and legislation.

Private interest-groups in the UK and France

At a general level, the role of business associations—especially so-called peak associations of employers—in the formulation and implementation of economic policy in both the UK and France is a matter of some debate. In France the major economic interest-groups, including the umbrella association of employers, have allegedly 'achieved only a limited degree of recruitment and cohesion'[50] and have enjoyed at best a marginal influence on the policy process.[51] Corporatist practices—that is, the institutionalized co-option of business and labour associations into the process of policy making[52]—are regarded as rare in France: 'in nearly everyone's ranking of societies on a scale of liberalism v. corporatism, France is . . . unequivocally the least corporatist state within

Western Europe'.[53] In the UK the influence of the Confederation of British Industry (CBI) on the direction of industrial policy, while perceived as somewhat greater under Labour than Conservative governments, has also remained marginal.[54] Efforts in the direction of corporatist practices in the UK have been 'sporadic, hesitant and ineffective'.[55]

The greater incorporation of certain sector-specific associations in those aspects of the formation of industrial policy which are of direct concern to their members' interests has led some theorists to identify the emergence of what has been defined as 'sectoral corporatism', a trend which has allegedly become more important in the UK in the 1980s.[56] Interestingly, this process of incorporation may be a product of, or can be strengthened by, legal mechanisms—or more accurately their absence. In particular, the practice of what Boddewyn terms 'mandated self-regulation', where the association representing a specific industry is 'ordered or designated by government to develop, use and enforce norms' to regulate the behaviour of its members, is seen as increasingly common in the UK.[57] As we will see in Chapter 8 of this book, this form of self-regulation has been a dominant feature of the control of pharmaceutical advertising and promotion in the UK, where the industry association, the ABPI, is charged with the dual tasks of formulating and enforcing a code of practice on advertising standards.

The prevalence of sectoral or meso-level corporatism[58] in France is a matter of some contention. Keeler, for example, has attempted to justify the applicability of the corporatist model to the agricultural sector in France and its powerful farmers' associations, and on this basis has argued that institutionalized links between government and industry have been developed by distinctive mechanisms in France. In particular he argues that extensive participation by industry in government advisory committees can act as an alternative mechanism of interest intermediation, which functions as a surrogate for straightforward consultation and participation in the policy process.[59]

Despite the obvious divergences in the French and British traditions of public authority, and in their legal articulation, no attempt has been made to link these variations with the observed differences in the patterns of participation of private-interest groups in the process of government intervention or the regulation of industry in each country. Yet it is surely insufficient merely to identify partici-

pation or incorporation of industry in policy processes. This is an
end-state, expressed in a particular structural form. One should,
instead, examine closely the nature of participation, how it is
accomplished and on what terms, and the ends which it serves.
Divergent legal traditions or cultures are obviously a key factor
here, as I shall argue in the following chapters. It is necessary to
compare how different traditions of public authority are expressed
in divergent legal mechanisms, which in turn provide, to a greater
or lesser degree, for the participation of industry in the formulation
and implementation of policy. Furthermore, it is important to
determine the consequences for industry, as well as for government,
of incorporation or participation in the process of regulatory
adjustment. In the case of the pharmaceutical sector, where a complex web of regulatory rules governs the activities of industry, the
value of participation in one regulatory arena, in terms of bargaining power and subsequent capacity to influence related aspects of
government–industry relations, must be established. In other
words, the participation of industry in self-regulatory schemes to
control advertising promotion can tell us little about its overall
relationship with government. One must understand, for example,
the function of advertising regulation in the context of its relationship to other regulatory regimes. This is why a dynamic perspective
on regulation, which focuses on the institutionalization of interdependence, is so important. In this way we can forge a link
between the divergent nature of legal cultures and the institutionalization of bargaining processes.

In seeking to compare the various legal mechanisms used in the
regulation of the pharmaceutical industry in the UK and France,
and in attempting to investigate the way in which different techniques of regulation contribute to the institutionalization of interdependent relations or linkages between regulator and regulated,
this study will, I hope, go some way towards bridging a major gap
in the existing literature on comparative government–industry
relations.

The Structure of the Study

The sequence in which the following nine chapters of the book are
presented, as well as their individual content, is designed to develop
the three major themes discussed here: the impact of regulation on

competitive processes; the nature of the legal mechanisms and legal techniques embodied in regulatory programmes; and finally the role which law can play in constructing and institutionalizing relationships of interdependence between government and industry in the UK and France. The various regulatory schemes governing the control of prices and profits, product safety, cost-containment policies, advertising promotion, competition, and patent law, are analysed, with a view to understanding the role which law plays in the dynamics of regulation and the institutionalization of particular patterns of government–industry relations. Chapters 3, 4, 5, 6, 7, and 8 therefore investigate how bargaining frameworks can emerge, and attempt to identify the processes which allow them to become stable forums in which to negotiate about changing sets of issues and conflicts. As I have already stressed, this book does not aim to provide a comprehensive account of every aspect of pharmaceutical regulation. That said, however, in order to understand the distinctive contribution of law to government–industry relations in this complex sector, it is necessary to go into some detail regarding the legal technicalities of the various regimes under discussion.

Chapter 2 develops the first of this study's themes: the impact of regulation on competitive processes. It highlights the recurrent nature of regulatory tensions and conflicts. The structure of the British and French pharmaceutical industries, their recent performance, and the comparatively weaker position of the French-based industry on international markets are discussed. The chapter goes on to review the major practical problems involved in the regulation of an oligopolistic market, with particular attention being given to the legal nature of the barriers to entry to the pharmaceutical market.

The six subsequent chapters are devoted to a detailed analysis of the different aspects of pharmaceutical regulation and to a comparison of different regulatory techniques. The socialization of health care and the public provision of pharmaceutical products forced issues of cost on to the regulatory agenda in the early 1950s. The initial efforts of each government in this direction are evaluated in Chapter 3. This chapter will compare and evaluate the development of price control and profit control in each country, and will examine the relative merits and shortcomings of the two very different approaches to controlling pharmaceutical prices in the period up to the 'second oil shock' of 1979, when French and

British governments alike were forced to deal with the adverse effects of major inflationary pressures. In this context, the very different patterns of relations between regulator and regulated which emerged in this early period are assessed. As I have mentioned above, the interests of pharmaceutical firms have traditionally been represented by powerful, well-organized associations, the ABPI in Britain and the SNIP in France. As Chapter 3 will illustrate, these associations were formed before the emergence of much of the modern regulations discussed in this book, and they have exercised an important influence upon the course of its development. There are substantial variations, however, in the degree of success which each association has achieved in influencing the regulatory process.

Control of product safety, which featured as a major issue on the regulatory agenda in the subsequent decade, is examined in Chapter 4. The introduction of controls on product safety has had important consequences for competition within this sector. Their implementation has produced new conflicts and new tensions: firstly because safety regulation is perceived as hindering the process of innovation, which is traditionally regarded as the motor of product competition; and secondly because, as Chapter 4 will establish in greater detail, there is always the possibility that safety regulation might be implemented in a way that would compensate for the deficiencies in the existing schemes of profit control and price control. In effect, if regulators chose to license new products on the basis of criteria which provide for the comparative evaluation of a new product's therapeutic advantages as against those of a product which was already on the market, this would represent a considerable infringement of the industry's commercial freedom. In Chapter 4 I examine the way in which the pharmaceutical industry in each country has averted this development. This chapter also raises the question of whether the introduction of a new regulatory regime altered the pre-existing patterns of interdependence with government, formed in the process of regulating prices and profits.

Chapter 5 analyses the impact of European Community law and policy on pharmaceuticals, not only on the formation and implementation of policy at the national level but also on the structure of the market itself. This chapter critically assesses the European Commission's harmonization programme for product-safety licensing, a programme begun in 1962 but still incomplete. It also examines the case-law of the European Court of Justice on the free movement of goods. The chapter then goes on to examine the Commission's more recent attempts to tackle the problem of substantial divergence in national pharmaceutical pricing policies, as well as that of reimbursement restrictions. It concludes with the suggestion that although the goal of free circulation of pharmaceutical products has not yet been realized, the Community's initiatives have had an important impact on the structure of the market for drugs in Europe, and in particular they have fuelled the emergence of what will be termed a 'two-tiered' market for pharmaceuticals.

The gradual emergence of this 'two-tiered' market, and the new forms of competitive forces which it has facilitated, including the growth of competition from generic or non-branded products, has created tensions which national regulators must resolve. On the one hand, new actors are emerging to challenge established patterns of relations at the national level, and, significantly, they are relying on certain rights in European law to do so. On the other hand, governments are now restricted by Community law in the choice of instruments which they can legitimately adopt, in particular to contain the growth of national pharmaceutical expenditure.

These latter themes are further developed in Chapters 6 and 7, which examine, respectively, the formulation and implementation of recent British and French pricing policies against the background of this changing market structure. Since the late 1970s each government has embarked on various programmes to curb health-care costs. These initiatives, usually referred to as 'cost-containment measures', are explored in Chapter 6, which examines the recent evolution of the British system of pharmaceutical profit control, and in particular the introduction of the so-called Limited List in 1985. In Chapter 7 the efforts of successive French governments to reform and modernize their system of pharmaceutical price control are critically appraised. In both chapters the extent to which the earlier systems of regulation, discussed in Chapters 3 and 4, have acted as a constraint on the realization of each government's reformist goals is considered, and I examine whether the established patterns of government–industry relations have been displaced—by the attempt to introduce new and stricter forms of control on the one hand, or by the emergence of new forms of competition on the other. In both chapters the role of legal factors in structuring processes of change and adjustment is considered.

Chapter 8 is devoted to an issue closely related to the topic of price control but so crucial to the process of product competition in this sector—product differentiation through pharmaceutical promotion and advertising—that it merits separate treatment. The chapter compares the approaches adopted in the UK and France to the regulation of the quality and content of promotional material on the one hand, and to the control of the amount of expenditure devoted to advertising on the other, and provides further evidence of divergence in legal traditions, both in the nature of regulation techniques in operation and in the bargaining over what are conceived to be legitimate objectives of regulation in each country.

Chapter 9 deals with the general regulation of competition in each country. It aims to fulfil several objectives. In the first place, it considers whether the mechanisms of general competition and patent law might offer an alternative, more effective method of price control. It examines some of the difficulties faced by the relevant national, as well as European, authorities in applying competition law to an oligopolistic market, especially a market in which patent protection is all-important. In the second place, it compares techniques of competition and patent law in the UK and France, contrasting each with European law. This will provide further evidence of the operation of divergent legal traditions. In the third place, it assesses the supplementary role which competition and patent law has played in strengthening the more specific price-control regimes in each country. The interaction of these different forms of regulation can once more provide useful illustrations of the impact of divergent legal techniques and regulatory philosophies in each country.

Chapter 10 returns to the three themes outlined in this introductory chapter, and on the basis of the detailed study of the regulation of this particular sector it offers some conclusions about the impact of law on the nature of relations between government and industry. It is acknowledged that, given certain distinctive features of the pharmaceuticals market, and the particular nature of the relationship between regulator and regulated as buyer and seller respectively of pharmaceutical products, pharmaceutical regulation might be deemed something of a special case. It is nevertheless contended that, in the context of the current attempts to extend formal regulation to a number of other manufacturing and service sectors, and in particular with the recent privatization of publicly owned industries exhibiting structural problems similar to those of the pharmaceutical sector, prospective regulators, as well as students of regulation, may draw useful lessons from a detailed analysis of 40 years of sustained effort on the part of successive British and French governments to regulate and simultaneously promote effective competition in their respective pharmaceutical industries.

Notes

1. G. Kolko, *The Triumph of Conservatism* (New York: Free Press, 1965); G. Stigler 'The Theory of Economic Regulation', *Bell Journal of Economics and Managerial Science*, 2 (1971), 21–45.
2. See R. Cranston, 'Regulation and Deregulation: General Issues', *University of New South Wales Law Journal*, 5 (1982), 1–21.
3. R. Baldwin and C. McCrudden, 'Regulatory Agencies', in Baldwin and McCrudden (eds.), *Regulation and Public Law*, (London: Weidenfeld and Nicolson, 1987), 11.
4. T. Lowi, *The End of Liberalism: The Second Republic of the United States*, (New York. Norton, 1979).
5. P. Dunleavy, 'Some Political Implications of Sectoral Cleavages', *Political Studies*, 28 (1980), 364–83.
6. S. Wilks and M. Wright, 'States, Sectors, and Networks', in Wilks and Wright (eds.), *Comparative Government–Industry Relations* (Oxford: OUP, 1987) 279–91.
7. C. Lindblom, *Politics and Markets: The World's Political-Economic Systems* (New York: Basic Books, 1977), 175.
8. G. Poggi, *Law in the Modern State* (London: Macmillan, 1978).
9. J. Habermas, *Communication and the Evolution of Society* (Oxford: Blackwells, 1979).
10. G. Teubner, 'Reflexive Law', *Law and Society Review*, 17 (1983), 240–95.
11. J. Winkler, 'Law, State and the Economy', *British Journal of Law and Society*, 2 (1975), 103–19.
12. M. M. Atkinson and W. D. Coleman, 'Corporatism and Industrial Policy', in A. Cawson (ed.), *Organised Interests and the State: Studies in Meso-Corporatism* (London: Sage Publications, 1985), 21–33.
13. M. M. Atkinson and W. D. Coleman, 'Strong States and Weak States: Sectoral Policy Networks in Advanced Capitalist Economies', *British Journal of Political Science*, 18 (1988), 47–67.
14. R. A. W. Rhodes, 'Power-Dependence, Policy Communities and Inter-Governmental Networks', *Public Administration Bulletin*, 49 (1985), 18–31.

15. Wilks and Wright, 'States, Sectors and Networks'.
16. See, however, Atkinson and Coleman, 'Strong States and Weak States', who attempt to elaborate an 'organizational logic' with which to appraise policy networks.
17. D. Vogel, *National Styles of Regulation: Environmental Policy in Great Britain and the United States* (Cornell: Cornell University Press, 1986); S. Kelman, *Regulating America; Regulating Sweden* (Cambridge, Mass.: MIT Press, 1981).
18. J. Bardacco, *Loading the Dice* (Boston, 1984).
19. B. Brickman and S. Jasanoff, *Regulating Chemical Hazards* (Ithaca: Cornell University Press, 1985).
20. Hans Jarass points to the distinction drawn in German public economic law between *Wirtschaftsaufsicht* and *Wirtschaftslenkung*, in 'Regulation as an Instrument of Economic Policy', in T. C. Daintith (ed.), *Law as an Instrument of Economic Policy* (Berlin: De Gruyter, 1988), 89.
21. A. Peacock *et al.*, *The Regulation Game* (London: Anglo-German Foundation, 1984).
22. P. Hall, *Governing the Economy: The Politics of State Intervention in Britain and France* (Oxford: Blackwell, 1986), 9.
23. J. E. S. Hayward, 'Institutional Inertia and Political Impetus in France and Britain', *European Journal of Political Research*, 4 (1976), 341–59.
24. For a discussion of the possible usages of this concept, see R. Inglehart, 'The Renaissance of Political Culture', *American Political Science Review*, 82 (4) (1988), 12203–30.
25. L. Friedman, 'Legal Culture and Social Development', *Law and Society Review*, 6 (1969), 19.
26. J. March and J. Olson, 'The New Institutionalism: Organisational Factors in Political Life', *American Political Science Review*, 78 (1984), 734–49; R. Scott, 'The Adolescence of Institutional Theory', *Administrative Science Quarterly*, 32 (1987), 494–531.
27. Cf. Hall, *Governing the Economy*, p. 19.
28. Scott, 'The Adolescence of Institutional Theory', p. 499.
29. S. Wilks, 'Institutions and Cultures in the Comparative Analysis of Political Economy', unpublished paper (Liverpool, 1989).
30. A. Shonfield, *Modern Capitalism* (London: Royal Institute of International Affairs/OUP, 1965), 71.
31. A. Cawson, P. Holmes, and A. Stevens, 'The Interaction between Firms and the State in France: The Telecommunications and Consumer Electronics Sectors', in Wilks and Wright, *Comparative Government–Industry Relations*, p. 10.
32. K. Corfield, 'An Industrialist's View: The Private Sector', in D. Englefield (ed.), *Today's Civil Service* (Harlow: Longman, 1985).

33. J. Zysman, *Governments, Markets and Growth* (Ithaca: Cornell University Press, 1983).

34. Ibid. 300.

35. P. A. Hall, 'Policy Innovation and the Structure of the State: The Politics-Administration Nexus in France and Britain', *The Annals*, 466 (1983), 46.

36. W. Grant, *Business and Politics in Britain* (London: Macmillan, 1987).

37. M. Loughlin, 'Tinkering with the Constitution', *Modern Law Review*, 51 (1988), 536.

38. P. J. Katzenstein, *Between Power and Plenty: Foreign Economic Policies of Advanced Industrial States* (Cambridge, Mass.: Harvard University Press, 1978).

39. Wilks and Wright, 'States, Sectors and Networks', p. 283.

40. Arts. 34 and 37 of the Constitution of the Fifth Republic. For an English translation of these see S. E. Finer, *Five Constitutions* (Sussex: Harvester, 1979), 279.

41. E. Sulieman, *Power, Politics and Bureaucracy* (Princeton, NJ: Princeton University Press, 1974), 213.

42. F. Baecque and J.-L. Quermonne, *Administration et politique sous la République* (Paris: Presse de la Fondation nationale des sciences politiques, 1985), 108.

43. P. Holmes and A. Stevens, 'The Framework of Industrial Policy Making in France', *University of Sussex Working Paper on Government–Industry Relations*, (1986), 12.

44. J.-C. Thoenig, *L'Ère des technocrates* (Paris: Éditions d'organisation, 1973); E. Sulieman, *Elites in French Society* (Princeton, NJ: Princeton University Press, 1978).

45. Quoted in C. Turpin, *British Government and the Constitution* (London: Weidenfeld and Nicolson, 1985), 16.

46. C. Harlow and R. Rawlings, *Law and Administration* (London: Weidenfeld and Nicolson, 1984), chaps. 1–3.

47. J. Chevallier, 'L'intérêt général dans l'administration française', *Revue internationale des sciences administratives*, 41 (1975), 325. For a discussion of the absence of this concept in British public administration see B. Chapman, *British Government Observed* (London: Allen and Unwin, 1963).

48. P. Legendre, 'La bureaucratie et le droit', *Revue historique du droit français et étranger*, (Paris: Sirey, 1974).

49. P. Allies, J. Gatti-Montain, J. J. Gleizal, A. Heymann-Doat, D. Lochak, and M. Miaille, *L'Administration dans son droit*. (Paris: Publisud, 1985), 137.

50. J. E. S. Hayward, *Governing France: The One and Indivisible French Republic*, (London: Weidenfeld and Nicolson, 1983), 66.

51. V. Wright. *The Government and Politics of France* (London: Hutchinson, 1983), 238; F. L. Wilson 'Alternative Models of Interest Intermediation. The Case of France', *British Journal of Political Science*, 12 (1982), 173; F. L. Wilson, 'Interest Groups and Politics in Western Europe: The Neo-Corporatist Approach' *Comparative Politics*, 16 (1983).

52. Katzenstein describes democratic corporatism as having three distinguishing traits: an ideology of social partnership; a relatively centralized and concentrated system of interest groups, and the coordination of conflicting objectives through continuous political bargaining. See further P. J. Katzenstein, *Small States in Word Markets* (Ithaca: Cornell University Press, 1985), 32.

53. C. Crouch, 'Sharing Public Space', in J. Hall (ed.), *The State in History* (Oxford: Blackwells, 1986), 210.

54. W. Grant and D. Marsh, *The CBI*, (London: Hodder and Stoughton, 1977); Grant, *Business and Politics in Britain*.

55. Grant, *Business and Politics in Britain*, p. 252.

56. G. Lembruch, 'Concertation and the Structure of Corporatist Networks', in J. H. Goldthorpe (ed.), *Order and Conflict in Contemporary Capitalism* (Oxford: OUP, 1984), 60–81.

57. J. J. Boddewyn, 'Advertising Self-Regulation: Organisation Structures in Belgium, Canada, France and the United Kingdom', in W. Streeck and P. Schmitter (eds.), *Private Interest Government: Beyond Market and State* (London: Sage, 1984), 34.

58. Cawson, *Organised Interests and the State*, p. 11.

59. J. T. S. Keeler, 'Situating France on the Pluralism-Corporatism Continuum', *Comparative Politics*, 17 (1985), 229–49.

2

The Economics of the Pharmaceutical Industry

The primary aim of this chapter is to describe the economic context in which regulation of the drug industry occurs and to explore the interaction between law and market structure. It will set the scene for the exploration of one of the main themes of this book—the tension between regulation and competition. While commentators on the modern pharmaceutical industry are often at variance over the nature of its social and economic contribution to health, and over the true role of its products in improving the standard of health, they are united in the observation that as an industrial sector and a product market it is *sui generis*. The patterns of ownership and organization and the processes of competition within the sector, as well as the distinctive structure of the demand for its products, set it apart from other manufacturing sectors and present regulatory bodies with a very particular set of problems.[1]

The first section of the chapter is essentially concerned with the structure and organization of the sector. It includes a short account of the industry's development since the early commercialization of synthetic chemicals, concentrating mainly on changes in market structure in the UK and France in the last two decades, and in particular on the trends towards globalization in the industry. In this context, the relevance of national regulatory efforts for a globally organized industry is considered.

The second section reviews the major obstacles encountered in the regulation of an oligopolistically organized sector. The approach taken here focuses on issues of market structure and the conduct and performance of the industry and is derived from the conventional 'industrial organizational' approach to oligopoly which has traditionally dominated economic analysis of the sector.[2] Market structure determines the conduct of firms in the industry, and that conduct in turn determines the quality of the industry's performance. Many of the important barriers to entry which are a feature of the market for pharmaceuticals are attributable to legal and regulatory factors. Interventionist measures such as the regulation of prices and safety, as well as the provisions of private law— the law on intellectual property, for example—have an equally important impact on market structure, an impact often unforeseen or unintended by regulators.

An appreciation of the legal aspects of market structure is of particular relevance to an understanding of the role of law in structuring the dynamics of government–industry relations in this complex sector. In the first place, regulators have been forced to address a succession of policy problems in the pharmaceutical sector. The 'socialization' of health care and the public provision of pharmaceutical products forced issues of cost control and containment of demand on to the policy agenda in the early 1950s. Control of product safety emerged as a major issue in the following decade, and since the late 1970s governments have been attempting to impose further constraints on health-care spending while preserving the international competitiveness of their domestic industry. Although distinctive regulatory frameworks have been erected to serve these separate objectives, they are nevertheless interrelated in terms of their economic effect. As the second section demonstrates, where regulation operates as a barrier to entry, this may lead, albeit indirectly, to increased concentration within the sector, less competition, higher prices, and therefore a greater charge on public funds. Consequently, regulators may seek, usually at the behest of the industry, to make compensatory adjustments elsewhere in the regulatory framework. If, for example, there is concern over the possible anticompetitive effects of more severe regulations on product safety, subsequent changes to other sets of rules affecting the innovation process, such as patent protection, may be made. In other words, considerable potential for bargaining between government and the industry is to be found in the way in which regulations structure the market.

In the second place, if, as industrial organizational theory suggests, structure determines conduct, and that conduct in turn influences the performance of the sector, regulators who attempt to influence or modify industry performance have, at least in theory, a choice of level as well as instrument when they intervene in the operation of drug markets. They can seek to effect structural change, eliminating or lowering barriers to entry, or they may rest content with largely palliative measures restricted to regulating certain forms of conduct. The eventual nature and course of intervention will, of course, be dictated by a variety of complex political and legal or institutional factors as much as by economic logic. It is with the role of such legal and institutional factors that the remaining chapters of this book are concerned.

Market structures are never static. As the pharmaceutical sector matures and existing structures disintegrate, new competitive forces are emerging, posing new challenges both for regulators and for the industry. The possible emergence of price competition to replace the product-based form of competition which has dominated the sector is examined in the third section of this chapter.

The Organizational Structure of the Pharmaceutical Market and the Role of National Regulation

Globalization and competition

A perennial problem attending any analysis of relations between governments and the pharmaceutical industry is to determine the true relevance of national markets and national regulatory structures. The international structure of ownership of the firms supplying the British and French markets and the globalization of their activities make it difficult to conceive of regulatory issues in purely national terms. This process of globalization, which is examined below, has had two main effects on market structure. In the first place, because of the combined impact of controls on prices and safety, direct imports of finished drug products, i.e. drugs in prescribable form, have traditionally remained low in both countries. In the United Kingdom British firms or British-based affiliates of foreign multinationals provide over 80 per cent of the medicines purchased by the NHS.[3] In France some 90 per cent of the products reimbursed by the national social-security institutions are supplied directly by firms operating within the national territory[4]. In 1987 there were respectively 212 and 326 firms operating in the UK and France, but only a few were of real importance in terms of overall size and share of the national market, and even fewer were nationally owned and operated. Foreign-owned companies account for some 40 per cent of total British production, some 43 per cent of net asset value, and almost two-thirds of all sales of prescription medicines to the NHS.[5] In France foreign-owned firms now account for at least 40 per cent of production and 47 per cent of reimbursable sales.[6]

In the second place, many firms which are nationally owned, in the sense that their head office is located in one country, are organized on a global scale. In its evidence to the House of Lords Select Committee on Overseas Trade and Industry, Glaxo, one of the largest and most successful of the British pharmaceutical houses, claimed to be located in over forty countries.[7] Over 78 per cent of its total sales in 1984 were made overseas. Sanofi, the second largest French firm, derives over two-thirds of its total income from its activities outside France.[8]

This latter aspect of globalization presents national or home governments with a dilemma. Growth rates in world consumption of pharmaceuticals are thought to be slowing down as the markets of some of the 'developed countries' 'mature' more quickly than others.[9] Japan is the singular exception to this trend, and European and American transnational corporations (TNCs) are scrambling for their share of an intensely lucrative but highly protectionist market. Business analysts argue that it is now necessary to have research facilities in more than one country, in order to sustain the pace of innovation necessary to compete on international markets. To date, the American TNCs have enjoyed greater success in locating facilities in Japan than their European rivals, a development which has caused concern both at national level, particularly in France, and at the European Commission. It is only in recent years that the European TNCs have begun to establish a significant presence in the American market. A combination of the disruption of European markets in the Second World War, strict national restrictions imposed on currency and capital movements, followed by the impact of restrictive licensing-agreements negotiated between American companies and their smaller European rivals, forced British and French TNCs to concentrate their export activities on former colonial markets.[10] Although rates of consumption continue to grow in these markets, local restraints on expenditure make them increasingly less lucrative.

In 1985 the world's leading 100 companies accounted for 80 per cent of total world-wide sales (excluding sales by and in command economies). Burstall has shown the extent to which these companies operate on a world-wide basis. Only the Japanese firms concentrate primarily on the domestic market. Whereas five British multinationals rank among the top twenty-five companies and Glaxo is now the world's second largest pharmaceutical company, French firms have not internationalized their activities with the same degree of success. Only three French firms, one of which, Roussel-Uclaf, is in fact partially owned by the German company Hoechst, make it into the top fifty, and by 1987 there were no French companies among the world's top twenty-five.[11] Sanofi is actively seeking to strengthen its position in the American market, as indicated by its unsuccessful take-over bid for A. H. Robbins in early 1988. French firms rely on a significantly higher share of their domestic market than do their other European and American rivals. Their best-selling products have failed to penetrate foreign markets to the same extent.[12] This relative failure to compete fully at international level alongside its traditional rivals—that is, the UK, Germany, Switzerland, and the USA—has remained a national preoccupation, which has not been without influence on many aspects of French regulatory policy. I will return to this issue in Chapters 4 and 7.

Ownership and organization

It might also be added that the pharmaceutical sector has traditionally been dominated by privately owned companies. Although in the UK partial public ownership or nationalization of private assets has been retained as a commitment in the Labour Party's manifesto for over 15 years, there has been little enthusiasm for such a policy when the party has been in office. The French state acquired an indirect interest in the pharmaceutical industry in 1976, when the national oil company, Elf-Erap, rationalized and extended its holdings in the sector, with the creation of Sanofi. Nationalization of the drug industry was a key issue in the joint programme of the French Communist and Socialist parties in 1978, and when the Socialists gained power in March 1981, 25 per cent of the industry's total assets were taken directly into public ownership; this included the complete nationalization of Rhone-Poulenc the acquisition by the state of a 34 per cent shareholding in Roussel-Uclaf, both concerns numbering amongst France's largest companies. The question of whether a change in ownership implied a change in policy, or precipitated a change in managerial goals and style will be explored at length in Chapter 7.

The high penetration of foreign capital into national markets is in turn intimately related to the organizational structure of the sector and to the extent of product and geographical diversification within it.

Product and geographical diversity

Most of today's major drug-companies conform to one of two patterns as far as the diversification and development of products is concerned. The American TNCs started out as pharmaceutical supply houses, selling cures and tonics. Pharmaceuticals are still their main products, although many have since diversified into health-care products, animal health, cosmetics, and fine chemicals—areas technologically related to pharmaceuticals. In Europe companies such as the British ICI or the German IG Farbenindustrie followed a different path, diversifying out of dyestuffs and organic chemicals into pharmaceuticals. It was Paul Ehrlich's search for the 'magic bullet', involving work on coal-tar derivatives, which produced the antisyphilitic substance Salvaresan. The discovery of sulpha drugs was also derived from work on the supposed antibacterial properties of dyestuffs.[13] These successes attracted other big chemical groups into the industry, once it became clear that the active ingredients of drugs would be manufactured from synthetic substances and not from vegetable and animal extracts. The diversity in the product profiles of many European firms reflects these origins, and most manufacture and sell a wide range of intermediate products which have further use in industry. A number of British firms originally diversified out of foodstuffs (Glaxo) or toiletries (Boots), but, as a 1972 NEDO report commented, there had been 'few cases of outward diversification by pharmaceutical companies' in the UK.[14] A 1980 OECD report, commenting on the general world-wide trend towards greater product diversification, noted that a comparatively high proportion of the turnover of UK-based firms was derived from the production of 'pure' pharmaceuticals.[15] Nevertheless, these firms are involved in a large number of related activities, including the manufacture of intermediate chemicals, cosmetics, and animal products. Several of the larger firms have, or have had, a substantial interest in generic as well as branded products. The growing importance of the market for non-prescription or 'over-the-counter' medicines to traditional pharmaceutical companies is illustrated by the recent joint venture of Proctor & Gamble, Syntex, Johnson and Johnson, and Merck, the world's largest drug company.

The development of the French industry conforms neither to the American nor to the Anglo-German pattern. Legal restrictions on the sales of 'secret remedies' and on ownership of firms by non-pharmacists, explored in detail in Chapter 4, proved a considerable obstacle to chemical firms trying to diversify into medicines. Until the 1940s the French pharmaceutical sector was dominated by several thousand small family-owned *pharmacies d'officines* (dispensaries) and a few larger family-owned concerns such as Roussel. Following the discovery of, and ensuing European demand for, penicillin and antibiotics in the 1940s, chemical firms with experience in fermentation techniques became involved in pharmaceuticals, as this microbiological technique was found to be the most efficient for large-scale production. Legislative reform was eventually introduced in France to allow firms to adapt their structure to changing forms of production, but many very small firms have either continued to exist alongside the growing number of large ones or pooled their expertise in various forms of joint venture. Even by the late 1980s, after several decades of mergers and rationalization, pharmacists and chemists retain prominent positions on the boards of the bigger French firms, and a considerable number of small firms with narrow product-ranges have survived. Larger companies such as Rhone-Poulenc, which have become more closely involved with the production of chemicals and more intimately connected with the problems of the French basic chemical sector in the last decade, have tended to seek economic salvation at first through diversification and, more recently, through the pursuit of vigorous foreign take-over policies. Consequently, the leading French companies are now involved in a wider range of activities than many of their European counterparts.[16]

The organization of pharmaceutical research, production, and marketing on multinational lines is of primary importance to sustained profitability. This process was initiated at a comparatively early stage of the growth in the industrial manufacture of chemicals and has continued to develop in an unproblematic fashion. A number of recent business histories trace the process of multinationalization—that is, the setting-up, by companies such as Glaxo, May and Baker, and ICI, of national subsidiaries which carried out research as well as manufacturing and selling products—in the period up to the Second World War.[17] In his recent study of the organizational evolution of American multinationals, Bartlett concluded that pharmaceutical companies

spend more time modifying the 'physiological' and even the 'psychological' characteristics of their organisations. They seemed to view the required change from unidimensional to multidimensional organisation as an adaptive evolutionary process rather than as a series of . . . traumatic reorganisations. In contrast to companies . . . which followed the 'strategic crisis-structural' reorganization route, these companies developed, adjusted and integrated the required new skills, structures and processes gradually but continuously.[18]

The trend towards precocious globalization is attributable in part to the characteristics of the product itself and in part to the operation of national regulatory frameworks. In many industrial sectors, marketing alone is the key to success; the marketing, research, and manufacturing of pharmaceuticals can all be of equal importance, and the high potential rewards for success, or large penalties for failure, have combined to produce a highly volatile operating environment. Innovative companies tend to spread their risk across national markets, especially when their product has a low price elasticity. Once established, local subsidiaries tend to expand, a development which was encouraged by the imposition of tariffs and quotas on pharmaceutical imports in developed and under-developed countries alike in the 1950s. As protectionism gave way to controls on product safety in the 1960s and to cost containment in the 1970s, the desirability of creating local subsidiaries serving national markets has, if anything, been reinforced.

The pharmaceutical manufacturing process

The distinctive nature of research, manufacture, and marketing in the pharmaceutical sector readily lends itself to 'multiple organizational levels' within companies, and the division and delegation of levels along national lines is technically relatively straightforward.

The pharmaceutical production process is divided into two distinct phases. The primary phase is the bulk manufacture of active or pharmaceutical ingredients, traditionally by fermentation techniques, by the production of synthetic organic chemicals, or from naturally occurring animal and vegetable sources. In fact production systems based on this latter process have declined dramatically, and for the most part pharmaceutical compounds are manufactured by batch-processing techniques.

A combination of economic considerations and criteria relating to quality control have led to centralized primary production, a trend reinforced by the development of new products such as synthetic hormones, which has led to the development of specialized plant and equipment requiring large amounts of capital and specialist technical staff.[19] But, as the volumes involved are small and transport costs are comparatively low, the final location of centralized facilities for primary production may be influenced by the nature of the regulatory environment. The development of modern production processes associated with biochemical and gene-technological methods will have some further impact on techniques of primary production and the location of plant. Increased capital intensiveness, requirements in regard to space, and the need for close and continual monitoring of quality, especially in the application of biotechnology to fermentation processes, could bring more rather than less centralization in the future.[20] In consequence, national governments are actively seeking to attract biotechnological research.

Subcontracting production of new chemicals in foreign markets is comparatively rare. The production of certain key organic chemicals is often restricted to one or two major companies. Within the companies themselves, a single product or product group is produced in a single plant, which supplies the world drug-market on the basis of a 'world product mandating system'. For example, ascorbic acid (Vitamin C) in dosage form is offered by over 100 companies, but the entire output of the vitamin itself is controlled by three companies: Merck, Pfizer, and Hoffmann-La Roche.[21]

In the secondary or 'downstream' production phase, the active ingredients, now in 'intermediate form', are put through processes of compounding, granulating, tableting, and packaging. This is a simpler and technically less demanding process, which is cheaper in terms of capital and skilled labour and is invariably carried out in the country of marketing.

Research and development has traditionally followed a similar pattern: serious innovative research is traditionally carried out in the country of origin, but product development, and clinical trials in particular, are usually undertaken in a number of potential national markets. However, there are indications that in the past decade the extent to which R. & D. is being internationalized is increasing. The proportion of the research budget spent abroad by major American drug-firms almost tripled between 1970 and 1980. In the 1980s there has been a considerable growth in the number of cross-border agreements on collaborative research concluded between TNCs, particularly in biotechnology.[22]

Locational strategy and national regulation

Given the high level of globalization within the industry, it is almost meaningless to talk of 'national' firms; the terms 'foreign-based' and 'home-based' are more appropriate. The latter refers to companies whose central management and head office is located in the country under study but whose subsidiaries are located elsewhere, while the former refers to subsidiaries of parent companies whose head office is located abroad.

It does not necessarily follow from this process of globilization that national regulatory frameworks are irrelevant to company strategy. If one takes, for example, home-based firms whose headquarters are located in countries with a colonial past, the home market may constitute an important point of reference for regulators elsewhere, invoking caution on the part of public policymakers in the reference market.

For foreign-based firms it would seem that 'there are considerable and systematic variations in the extent to which particular activities are centralised and decentralised.'[23] The degree of autonomy granted to a local subsidiary and the selection of particular tasks allocated to it is not totally independent of national regulatory considerations. In his study of the activities of foreign firms located in the European Community, Burstall argues that the recent development of a fuller range of facilities is in part a response to pressure on industry from national governments to contribute to employment, investment, and the balance of payments.[24]

Locational decisions depend upon a complex interplay of regulatory 'externalities' and internal company strategy. For example, the countries of the European Community have become an increasingly favoured location for research and development by US-based companies seeking to evade the stricter regulatory requirements of the Food and Drug Administration (FDA) on the clinical and developmental stages of a new product.[25] Legal restrictions on the use of healthy volunteers in clinical trials in France have made that country less attractive as a location for innovative research by foreign multinationals, while a combination of protectionist controls and price restrictions on finished drug products conspired to make the trading of bulk pharmaceuticals between foreign-based parent and local companies more attractive.

Conversely, in the UK a variety of circumstances, ranging from the early availability of patent protection for chemical substances and medicinal products[26] to the availability of skilled, relatively cheap personnel, favourable exchange-rates, a shared language, and geographical proximity to continental European markets, has meant that in practice the UK has been a favoured location for satellite research-centres. More recently, as we will see in Chapters 3 and 6, the British system of profit control — the Pharmaceutical Price Regulation Scheme (PPRS) — has rewarded capital investment in the UK, so that a number of local subsidiaries are engaged in the manufacture of active ingredients, usually under licence to the parent company.

Table 1 gives some idea of the nature of activities carried out by local subsidiaries. It is clear that EC-based and non-EC-based multinationals have followed a slightly different pattern of policy on location. It has been suggested that the American and Swiss companies, which are in general 'first generation' TNCs, have paid the price of precociousness and succumbed to national pressures to localize their production. The geographical proximity of European markets for EC-based TNCs, as well as increased harmonization of national regulation, could also account for these divergences.

Table 1 also suggests that many local subsidiaries are engaged in research and primary manufacture, as well as in the more traditional secondary manufacture. It would be necessary to gain some idea of the intensity of that activity in relation to the firm's global output, research funding, and so on before reaching any firm conclusions about the impact of national regulation. Multinational firms, by definition, exploit the territorial limitations of national controls. Closer examination of trade in intermediate substances, and of the 'invisible and capital account', i.e. international receipts

Table 1. Activities of Local Subsidiaries

Company	Output category	Location of facilities		
		France	Ireland	United Kingdom
US-based				
Abbott	A	z		
American Cyanamid	B	yz		xyz
Am. Home Products	C			z
Bristol Meyers	B			
Johnson and Johnson	C			z
Lilly	B	z		xyz
Merck and Co.	C	xyz	y	xyz
Pfizer	C	xz	y	xyz
Schering-Plough	A	xyz		
Searle	B	xyz		xyz
Smith Kline	C	z	y	xyz
Squibb	B	yz	y	y
Upjohn	A	xyz		yz
Warner	C			yz
Swiss				
Ciba-Geigy	C		z	xyz
Hoffman-La Roche	C	z		xyz
Sandoz	C			z
Swedish				
Astra	A	xyz		z
German				
Bayer	C	xyz		
Boehringer-Ingelheim	C	xyz	y	
Boehringer Mannheim	C			
Hoechst	A	x	z	xyz
Merck AG	B	x	z	

Location code: x=R. & D.; y=active-ingredient production; z=dosage assembly.
Output category: A=less than $100 m.; B=$100–200 m.; C=greater than $200 m. within the Community.
Source: M. L. Burstall, *The Community's Pharmaceutical Industry* (Luxembourg: Commission of the European Communities, 1985).

and payments of profits, new investment, royalties and service fees, dividend and interest remittances,[27] suggests that the multinational organization of the industry leaves considerable scope for the manipulation of trading returns and profit figures submitted to national authorities. The control of such activities remains a major problem for regulators world-wide.

Globalization and national regulation

It can be argued that as a result of the process of globalization national regulatory policies have become more relevant as a focus of study. Although the British and French markets are tiny, each accounting for only 4 per cent of total world consumption, the two countries are among the world's 'top seven' in terms of the production, innovation, and sales of their home-based companies, even if the position of France in this league is regarded as precarious.[28] It is largely because of the desire of the regulators and regulated to maintain this level of international competitiveness, and the benefits it brings to the national economy, that the operation of national regulatory policies remain a valid topic for study. These policies cannot be divorced from macro-economic considerations. In both countries the continued economic health of the pharmaceutical sector is viewed as vital to that of the nation. Although the industry is largely capital intensive rather than labour intensive, it has accounted for a stable level of some 65,000 jobs over the last decade in each country, one-third of these being for 'skilled' personnel. It has been estimated that in the UK the drug industry is responsible 'indirectly' for a further 140,000 jobs in related manufacturing sectors.[29]

A major economic contribution of both the British- and the French-based firms has undoubtedly been to the balance of trade, and therefore to foreign-currency earnings.[30] Moreover, this strong economic performance must be seen in the context of a general worsening in the trade deficit in both countries. The economic importance of the pharmaceutical industry—which now includes itself among the 'sunrise' industries—becomes even more compelling when one considers the pessimistic forecasts for the rest of the decade. In the UK the trade surplus earned by oil exports has declined rapidly. In both countries sectors—such as textiles and commercial electronics—which once enjoyed relative strength in overseas markets have moved into heavy deficit. Related sectors, particularly basic chemicals, have only recently emerged from a period of stagnation, with rather major losses in international competitiveness. This has had adverse effects on the overall profitability of the large, vertically integrated companies such as ICI or Rhone-Poulenc.

National governments are also constrained to assume health and welfare functions of increasing cost and complexity. Consequently, there is greater intervention in the activities of the industry. Recent developments in regulatory policy in the UK and France conform to this pattern.

If the continued relevance of national measures cannot be disputed, the dangers of measuring the performance of the industry solely on the basis of regulatory change at the national level must be avoided. A number of American Studies, for example, have sought to link the alleged decline in the competitive strength of the American drug-industry with the introduction of onerous safety regulations: the USA's share of world spending on pharmaceutical research has allegedly dropped in the past 20 years, its share in world trade has fallen, and the number of new chemical entities (NCEs) discovered by American companies has declined.[31] Yet many of these studies either ignore or underestimate the extent of the operations of American companies outside the USA. While it is readily admitted that the economic effects of national regulation on a multinationally organized sector are hard to predict or measure with any real accuracy, this does not make the study of the processes of regulatory decision-making otiose; it merely adds to its complexity.

The pharmaceutical companies themselves recognize the importance of national demands and constraints and respond to them, while seeking to maintain global profitability. Thus according to their supporters the industry is 'faced with the challenge of being simultaneously responsive at the national level while maintaining the competitive efficiency that comes from global coordination'.[32] The detractors view the situation differently:

international uneven development is both created by, and facilitates the domination of, giant finance-capitalist firms. Hence transnationally organized capital ... circumvents and takes advantage of differences in national regulation; while it may desire their coordination, it by no means requires their elimination.[33]

Viewed from either perspective, the central importance of national regulatory regimes on the past and future development of the industry cannot be denied.

The European dimension: A changing market or a changing regulatory framework?

Preoccupations with the continued prosperity and competitivity of the European-based industry are not restricted to national policy-makers and regulators. The institutions of the European Community, particularly the Commission, take an active interest in the sector. Post-war economic recovery and the gradual, if incomplete, elimination of barriers to trade within the EC in the 1960s have made that market more attractive. The combined ethical-drug market of the twelve EC member states (estimated in 1985 at 25 per cent of world consumption) is now larger than that of the USA (23 per cent) or Japan (16 per cent), but it is by no means a unified market. Considerable non-tariff barriers to trade remain, including divergent national regimes in relation to product safety and pricing, as well as the market-compartmentalizing strategies of many TNCs. Their eventual elimination, on the completion of the internal market in 1992, is seen by the Commission as a matter of high priority if the European-based drugs-industry is to attain a competitive lead over American and Japanese rivals, particularly in high-technology and biotechnology-based medicines.

Although the Commission has yet to articulate a coherent common industrial policy, or indeed a common health-policy, a series of Community directives harmonizing product-licensing and, more recently, dealing with pricing, have a direct impact at national level. These directives, and the Treaty's provisions on free movement of goods and competition, as interpreted by the Court of Justice and applied by national courts, not only have implications for the changing structure of the industry's market but add an important new dimension to national government–industry relations in this sector, creating novel problems which must be resolved at the national level. And yet national responses will be constrained by Community law. Given, for example, the existing high penetration of American and Swiss firms in the EC, the advantages of an integrated market will be available to these firms, and indeed to other potential entrants—such as Japanese pharmaceutical com-

panies—who might locate facilities in Europe. National governments may wish to promote or protect the interests of their
domestic or home-based firms in the future, perhaps through
financial incentives for research and development facilities.[34] Their
ability to provide such incentives will, of course, be subject to the
provisions of EC law.

National Regulation, Oligopolistic Competition, and Industrial Strategy

A significant feature of the pharmaceutical sector is the level of
concentration within it, a factor not, of course, unrelated to the
dominance of TNCs. Furthermore, the nature of the competitive
process within it is distinct. In terms of the standard measure of
concentration—the five-firm sales-concentration ratio—the industry
as a whole appears less concentrated than other sectors. Whereas
the weighted average for all recorded industries was 70 per cent
in 1979, that of the pharmaceutical preparations sector was only
39.3 per cent.[35] Furthermore, as associations such as the SNIP or
the ABPI are quick to point out, no single British or French, or
indeed European firm has as much as 8 per cent of the domestic
market. Similarly, no single drug accounts for more than a small

Table 2. Concentration of Market Shares on an Ownership Basis in 1982.
(Figures for concentration of market shares by product in 1982 are given in
brackets.)

Share held by top companies 1	5	10	15	20	25	50	% Total Market
France	9	29	41	50	57	63	81
	(1.3)	(5.6)	(9.4)	(27.1)	(38.9)	(59.1)	(76.6)
Germany	6	24	37	46	53	59	75
	(1.7)	(5.6)	(8.3)	(21.9)	(31.6)	(49.6)	(65.6)
UK	7	27	43	53	61	67	88
	(2.6)	(10.7)	(17.9)	(43.0)	(57.5)	(77.5)	(90.3)
Total EC	3	15	27	43	53	61	67
USA	8	30	50	63	71	77	90
Japan	5	24	36	47	55	60	81

Source: Burstall *et al*, *The Community's Pharmaceutical Market*, p. 87–8: (Affiliates
are treated as part of parent companies).

share of total national consumption. However, a closer look at products and market shares suggests a certain degree of market dominance.

As Table 2 illustrates, not only are the British and French industries fairly concentrated by EC standards, but the top ten companies in both countries do in fact control over 40 per cent of total sales, and the top twenty nearly 60 per cent. This pattern has remained constant in the UK over the last decade at least,[36] but concentration levels have undoubtedly increased in France, where governments have actively promoted rationalization.[37]

A more accurate picture of concentration can be obtained by subdividing the pharmaceutical market: firstly into the market for ethical drugs sold on prescription, proprietary products which can be bought directly through retail outlets, and the animal-health market; and secondly by further dividing prescription drugs into therapeutic submarkets, on the basis of similar prophylactic qualities. The British Pharmaceutical Index divides the ethical market into ninety-two therapeutic submarkets. Specialized drug products have a very low level of substitutability within these submarkets.

Product competition versus price competition

As a result of this low level of substitutability, competition within therapeutic submarkets is centred primarily on product and promotion rather than on price. This process is reinforced by the unique nature of consumer demand, a feature which reinforces product-based competition. Although the British NHS or the French Caisse nationale de l'assurance maladie des travailleurs salariés (CNAMTS) are major purchasers, who should, in theory, enjoy almost monopsonistic positions on the market for prescription drugs, their potential bargaining power is diluted by their traditional inability to exercise much influence over the choice of goods they buy. Product selection is largely the individual doctor's privilege, and in both countries, by convention, the doctor's freedom of choice in prescribing the most appropriate drug is almost total. Usually, the doctor will have only a vague notion about a product's cost, and he or she is relatively isolated from the source of payment for this selection.[38] Prescription drugs can only be obtained from a registered pharmacist, whose terms of service and professional code of conduct oblige him or her to fill the prescription exactly as it is written: substitution is not permitted in either country.[39] Hence the patient and the doctor remain relatively insensitive to price differences between drugs. The choice of product is determined by its qualities, not by its cost.

How competitive are oligopolistic markets?

The question of the nature and degree of competition within the pharmaceutical market is a controversial one. In seeking to reassure public policy-makers that the pharmaceutical sector is not immune from 'normal' market forces, several economic analysts emphasize its dynamism—that is, the high level of company movement in and out of therapeutic submarkets—as an indication of the overall competitiveness of the sector. Innovation secures competition, which in turn ensures reasonable prices in the long term. When companies introduce new patented drugs, they move to the top of the league in the relevant submarket, but their stay there is relatively short, as rivals develop similar but improved products, or indeed introduce substantially new ones. An extreme case is Tagamet, whose manufacturer, Smith, Kline & French (SK&F), enjoyed a virtual monopoly of the European market for anti-ulcer treatments from 1976 until 1981, when Glaxo's Zantac and Randil were launched. Sales of Tagamet dropped by over 35 per cent in some markets.[40] The key to successful product-differentiation is therefore innovative capacity as well as financial strength. On this analysis, such dynamism arguably renders price control redundant, at least in the long term. Moreover, regulators can hinder the process of innovation, which is the engine of competition, not only by imposing low prices but also by introducing overly stringent safety-requirements, which hinder the innovation process.[41]

The essentially non-interventionist philosophy which underpins this analysis of oligopolistic competition has several shortcomings. Firstly, it ignores the possible social costs of product-based competition, and secondly, it overlooks the consequences of existing levels of concentration within the sector, as well as the operation of barriers hindering entry to it. The major social costs of product competition can be attributed to the adverse impact it has on price competition. Manufacturers devote excessive resources to promoting product characteristics. Differences between products within the same therapeutic subclass may be only minor, and the waste of scarce scientific and other resources on trivial product-changes, so-called molecular manipulation, which is designed to circumvent patents protecting major new discoveries, is considerable. Much of the industry's research budget is allegedly devoted to searching for products which are easy to imitate. In 1972, for example—during the heyday of the industry's innovatory period—1,500 products were patented in the UK; of these, forty-five were genuinely new, 150 were 'major innovations', and the rest were 'me-too' products—i.e. molecularly distinct but therapeutically identical. A former medical director of the American firm Squibb testified before a Senate subcommittee that during his tenure at the company an estimated 25 per cent of research funds were devoted to 'worthwhile' projects and the remaining 75 per cent to the development of copies and combinations.[42] The patent system, examined below, can exacerbate these problems by sheltering socially worthless but privately profitable research.[43]

As far as levels of concentration are concerned, these are in themselves a cause and a consequence of the product-based nature of competition in this sector. The relative ease with which companies allegedly move in and out of submarkets should not be allowed to obscure the fact that entry barriers to the industry as a whole are high. One observer has compared the process of movement to a game of musical chairs, 'where most entrants merely come from another league where the rules of the game are exactly the same'.[44] New entrants are rare, and those who do succeed in breaking into a national market are either foreign drug-firms or firms engaged in related business diversifying into the industry. The typical therapeutic market is therefore a more or less stable oligopoly, where manufacturers have a wide discretion in setting price levels.

Product competition and barriers to entry

Few governments have in practice been content to leave matters of drug pricing entirely to the market, and even in countries which do not impose direct price-control, vigilant enforcement of competition law has been relied upon to prevent firms abusing their dominant positions within therapeutic submarkets—in the USA and West Germany, for example. Those which do impose price controls usually subscribe, to a greater or lesser degree, to the orthodoxy of product competition, and this is reflected in the way in which controls are conceived and applied. France and the UK are no exception, as later chapters will reveal. If product competition is assumed to be either the most desirable or the only possible form of competition, however, the adverse effects of barriers to entry into therapeutic submarkets must be either eliminated or contained, and governments therefore seek to ensure that product competition is *effective*. In the remainder of this section it will be argued that it is in this latter process that the central tensions between regulation and competition are located. Regulation can hinder competition by increasing barriers to entry; but without intervention of some form, those same barriers can also retard competitive processes.

Industrial-organization theory identifies three main barriers to entry: economies of scale and advantages in regard to absolute cost; product differentiation; and compliance with regulatory standards. All three are intimately connected with the process of pharmaceutical regulation.

Economies of scale

Barriers relating to economies of scale arise when firms must grow to a large size in order to achieve low production-costs. It is commonly argued that there are no really significant economies of scale at either of the two major stages of drug manufacture, although sophisticated technological quality controls on the manufacture of active ingredients may be efficient only if used on a large scale. Large, vertically integrated operations may also enjoy preferential access to raw materials. The 'problematic' barriers relating to economics of scale arise from the product-based nature of competition within the sector. They occur at the promotion and marketing stages, and at the R. & D. stage. Because the industry is knowledge intensive and marketing intensive, the high absolute cost of promotion, plus its spill-over effect via the trade-mark and brand-names system, create economies of scale which effectively block the entry of small firms. The introduction of new drugs tends to be confined to the major companies because of the large cost of, and the economies of scale in, R. & D. stricter regulatory requirements, and the technical demands for new breakthroughs, all of which require the resources of a large firm. Grabowksi and Vernon have demonstrated for the US market that while the share of drugs sales of the four largest companies remained fairly constant between 1957 and 1971, the same four firms which had accounted for 24 per cent of NCEs in 1957 now produce 49 per cent.[45] In a later study, Reekie and Weber put forward considerable evidence to suggest that R. & D. now increases in proportion to firm size.[46] In 1985 it was estimated that the cost of developing a successful major new drug was around $50 million or more; if the wasted expenditure on abandoned products is included, the figure rises to $90 million.[47] Smaller firms which have discovered a new active ingredient are thus often compelled to enter into licensing agreements with one of the larger companies to ensure its commercialization.

Product differentiation

i. Patents

Product differentiation constitutes the most formidable and, from a legal point of view, the most complex of barriers to entry into the pharmaceutical sector. The process of product differentiation is intimately connected with the protection of patents and trade marks, the latter operating as a 'critical complement' to the former. Under current French and British law, patent protection effectively confers a qualified monopoly on the manufacturer by preventing rivals marketing a similar product for a period of up to 20 years. As Lall has observed, 'the problem of drug patents has been a vexed one, and much has been written on both sides of the debate, without a clear answer emerging on the optimal form of legal protection to be granted to private innovators'.[48] Although new active ingredients may take a number of years to develop and perfect, they can be copied with relative ease, so that patent protection is of particular significance in this sector The twenty-year period of protection is justified on the grounds that the recipients of the privilege are given a monopolistic position which enables them to charge higher prices than they otherwise could, but the short-term loss of welfare due to these higher prices is supposedly offset in the long run by a higher rate of innovative output and a decline in the price of the protected product, after the recoupment of a 'fair' return on the R. & D. investment.

From the regulatory point of view, perhaps the most worrying aspect of patent-protected monopoly is that it can permit 'excess-ive' profits to be earned by pharmaceutical firms. Although it is often argued that prices tend to be lowered on, or shortly before, patent expiry, a number of studies of the American market, where prices are unregulated, have not been very optimistic about the impact of patent expiry on market share or price levels. In his study of twelve products, Statman[49] reported that 'success of the original brands in maintaining their market shares was not the result of price reductions', but rather doctors had come to identify the drug with a specific brand name, so that the original seller by and large maintained his prior position on the market. Only four of his sam-ple showed any substantial decline in price. Bond and Lean examined sales and prices in two therapeutic areas and found generally that the first company to sell the drug in the market maintained its market position without any substantial decline in price. In the case of the American TNC Merck, whose dominance of the market for antidiuretics persisted in the face of competition from cheap and highly promoted substitutes, the authors concluded that 'the product differentiation advantage of being first with a "breakthrough" product is very substantial indeed'.[50] A recent study by the British generic manufacturer Thomas Kerfoot con-tended that generic substitution of some 200 drugs commonly pres-cribed under the NHS would save approximately £200 million.[51] The large research-based firms argue that their patent-protected profits are far from being excessive, and are necessary to finance the very innovation which improves health care and fuels competition in the long run. There are no easy solutions to these regulatory conundrums. Obviously, patent protection is not absolute: most legal systems, including the French and British, have mechanisms to counter abuses. Chapter 9 will seek to demonstrate that the pre-ferred approach has been to negotiate compromise solutions in regard to different forms of legal protection for product innovation. Chapter 9 will also deal with the controversy over the 'effective length' of patent protection. The industry contends that a combina-tion of onerous legislation on product safety and long lead-times for drug development prevents commercialization of a product until some 9 to 12 years after its discovery and first patent registra-tion, reducing the period of effective monopoly.

ii. Brand names

In addition to patents, other forms of perpetual rights in regard to intellectual property, in particular trade-mark rights in brand names, can be used to extend a product's monopoly by building up brand loyalty. Reekie has argued that product 'branding' is the most effective barrier to entry.[52] As Chapters 5 and 6 will illustrate, assertion of property rights in data submitted in support of licensing applications has also become a potentially effective way of suppressing generic competition.

The salience of brand loyalty, and the massive expenditure devoted to its promotion and perpetuation, is of sufficient magnitude to be considered a separate barrier to entry to the industry. The larger the firm and its turnover, the larger its promotional budget.[53] A recent study suggested that product differentiation poses a very specific set of regulatory problems:

Whereas most elements of industry structure are relatively independent of the competitive behaviour of firms, product differentiation is both a result and a determinant of that behaviour. Unlike patent grants and regulatory requirements, which come from government, or certain scale economies, which may be technologically imposed, product differentiation originates as a set of policies which firms themselves decide to embark on; once carried out, these constitute a structural barrier.[54]

If competition is treated as primarily product-based, national regulators are faced with a dilemma. Where, in the interests of a better allocation of public resources, restraints are imposed on promotional expenditure, companies must still be able to promote new products to doctors in order to break into new markets. The problem here is one of demarcation: at what point does promotional literature cease to be informative and at what level does promotional expenditure perpetuate and strengthen rather than weaken market concentration? These complex issues will be considered in Chapter 8, which deals with the regulation of advertising.

Formal regulation as a barrier to entry

The introduction and development of costly national—and now European—requirements in regard to product safety are often viewed as an additional barrier to entry, especially in the innovative sector. Controls on product safety now extend beyond the developmental stages to manufacturing, marketing, and, more recently, post-marketing surveillance. A pharmaceutical firm needs considerable resources to satisfy the increasing number of onerous requirements imposed by national governments in the interests of consumer protection. In addition, as the development time for a new drug is prolonged, a firm will have to be prepared to tie up substantial capital for a number of years. Again, this may be easier for larger firms who have larger reserves or who can obtain more preferential treatment on finance markets. Safety controls may have an indirect impact on product competition if innovation slows down and fewer new products are released on to the market. The impact of regulation on innovation is a matter of some controversy among economists and social theorists. The introduction of strict regulatory controls on product safety, first in the USA and latterly in Europe, has coincided with a fall-off in the rate of innovation.[55] The alleged link between the proliferation of regulatory requirements and a drop in the rate of innovation is further explored in Chapter 4. Controls on prices and profits may also adversely affect the rate of innovation and consequently impair product competition, if firms earn insufficient returns to plough back into research and development.

It cannot be assumed that every aspect of pharmaceutical regulation can be explained in terms of a continuous search for economic efficiency: governments pursue wider goals in the public interest. Nevertheless, the effects of regulation are most often assessed in economic terms. As long as the pharmaceutical sector is viewed as a research-intensive sector, in which growth and efficiency is sustained by innovation, there will be an obvious reluctance to impair the process of product competition.

The Changing Competitive Environment and the Emergence of Price Competition

The changing competitive environment of the European pharmaceutical industry has been the subject of recent academic debate.[56] Certain changes in the structure of the market, as well as budgetary constraints, have prompted a reassessment of the product-based perspective on competition. Four separate developments, adumbrating the possible development of price competition, can be identified.

Parallel imports

In the first place, product competition is primarily a feature of markets which are divided along national lines. Within the EC, government controls on prices and profits or company marketing strategies have produced considerable variations in prices for identical products in different countries. At the same time, some, but by no means all, barriers to trade in drugs have been removed. The practice of parallel importing—that is, the importation of identical branded and patented drugs marketed in low-price countries such as Italy, Spain, Portugal, or France, into high cost countries, including West Germany, the Netherlands, and, after 1982, the UK has increased in recent years. An estimated 10 per cent of UK drug sales, worth approximately £180 million in 1989, are parallel imports. Table 3 gives an indication of the size of price differentials in the EC in 1989.

The phenomenon of parallel importing has had a pronounced impact on the pricing strategies pursued by companies and has generated a complex response from regulatory authorities, who find their combined roles as sponsors and paymasters of the industry brought into potential conflict. This is examined in detail in Chapters 5, 6, and 7.

Generic competition

The growth of the generic sector constitutes a second structural change leading to increased price competition. The overall number of drugs still in patent has declined dramatically. In the UK in 1973, for example, about 70 per cent of the sales revenues generated by the top 100 medicines were protected under current patents. A decade later, and despite the extension of the patent term from 16 to 20 years in 1978,[57] the proportion had been halved. The trend is the same in France, but an important structural difference between the British and French drug-markets should be noted.

On the expiry of a product patent, rival manufacturers usually market similar products containing the same active ingredients. These copies may be marketed under a competing brand name or

Table 3. Price differentials in Europe

Drug	Manufacturer	United Kingdom		West Germany		Italy		France	Belgium
		Price Index	Sales ($m)	Price Index	Sales ($m)	Price Index	Sales ($m)	Price Index	Price Index
Ventolin	Glaxo	1.00	95	2.09	16	0.52	–	–	0.81
Zantac	Glaxo	1.00	175	1.44	130	1.12	230	0.79	1.00
Tenormin	ICI	1.00	60	1.39	25	0.85	12	0.39	0.52
Voltarol	Ciba-Geigy	1.00	80	0.74	50	n/a	50	0.46	0.56
Adalat	Bayer	1.00	120	1.17	80	0.81	80	0.52	0.78
Zovirax	Wellcome	1.00	20	0.98	20	0.66	14	0.80	0.67

Source: Financial Times, 6 Nov. 1989.

merely under the product's generic name, i.e. the officially approved chemical name for the active ingredient. The UK is unusual among European countries in having a substantial market for the latter form of copy—the pure generic. It is the only major European country where pure generics feature in the top twenty prescriptions written by doctors.[58] About 39 per cent of their prescriptions are already written in generic form. In France, however, so-called generic competition is, in effect, competition between the original brand and alternative branded generics containing the same active ingredients. Pure generics only account for some 2 per cent of the market, a state of affairs often attributed to French doctors' dislike of generic products, as well as to the adverse consequences of strict price-control.[59]

In these changed market conditions it has been estimated that a drug may lose half its sales within 2 years of the expiry of its patent, especially in jurisdictions which actively promote generic competition. When the patent on Aldomet, a heart drug owned by the world's leading pharmaceutical company, Merck, expired in 1984, the drug dropped from fifth to seventy-second place in the league-table of best-selling pharmaceuticals in America.[60]

The over-the-counter market

A third structural change is the recent growth of the OTC (over-the-counter) market, which stimulates competition among distributors as well as producers. Cost-conscious governments are actively promoting policies of self-medication, encouraging the public not to seek medical advice unless necessary. A number of products which had only been available on prescription for a number of years have recently been granted a change of legal status. As these products are usually out of patent, it is assumed that price competition will flourish. Indeed, the prices of OTC medicines are currently not subject to any form of regulatory control in either the UK or France.

Competition at the wholesale and retail stage is also stimulated, as pharmacies and other forms of retail outlets compete for a share of an increasingly lucrative market. Again, however, there are important differences between the two countries. In France the categories of product admitted for reimbursement are wide, and the pharmacist's legal monopoly over the sale of medical products, a term which is also broadly defined, is extensive. The French OTC market has until recently remained among the smallest in Europe.[61]

Techniques of cost containment

A fourth change emanates from the demand side of the market but has implications for the structure of the supply side, as well as for the competitive process. Policies of cost containment, which will be analysed in detail in Chapters 3, 6, and 7, may indirectly promote price- or product-based competition. On the one hand, the adoption of 'negative' and 'positive' lists, or market-entry lists, admitting or excluding prescription products from public reimbursement, have become a favoured method of reducing health expenditure and now operate in both the UK and France. These lists tend to be compiled on the basis of price and upon assumptions of homogeneous competition between generally well-established or older products.[62] On the other hand, new products for which competition is heterogeneous—that is, from different medicines prescribed for the same indication—are increasingly the subject of *transparency lists*. These lists represent an official estimate of the cost-effectiveness of a product and are designed to increase the therapeutic and economic transparency of the drugs market, thereby indirectly promoting price-based competition. Economic analysts predict that if considerations of comparative cost remain at the forefront of government concerns, price competition may eventually emerge even between newly patented therapeutic alternatives.[63]

The emergence of a two-tiered market?

In the immediate future it is more likely that a two-tiered market-structure will emerge, reflecting the dichotomy between the strategies pursued by globally organized, research-based companies, who seek to promote their innovative products world-wide, and those firms, including small independents and generic firms, selling mainly to more restricted national markets. The eventual completion of the internal European market is of significance for both strategies. On the one hand, harmonization of intellectual property laws is in the interests of generic manufacturers, as the originators of the drug will no longer be able to use their rights to partition markets. On the other hand, the harmonization of regulations on product safety is potentially in the interests of research-intensive firms, who will be able to introduce their new products on to a larger market without having to comply with up to twelve separate sets of national laws. A parallel danger of harmonization, at least from the perspective of the research-based industry, is, of course, that it can facilitate the marketing of generics or rivals across national boundaries.

These structural changes might present governments with new opportunities to promote effective product competition. They might also yield new obstacles to their dealings with the industry. On the one hand, the potential emergence of price competition in the 'generic' tier of the market may offer scope for closer, more effective control over health-care costs. It could bring sufficient information and transparency into the market to allow for more effective governmental control over product competition in the second, 'research intensive tier'. This is self-evidently not in the interests of firms which are increasingly exposed to international competition. On the other hand, the development of the EC's internal market could also lead to cross-boundary mergers, as well as to take-over moves by non-EC firms seeking a foothold within the EC.[64] National governments and the European Commission are therefore likely in future to be confronted with the task of dealing with an increasingly economically important and powerful sector. It is very likely that in the 1990s a different set of tensions between regulation and competition will emerge between national governments and their home-based firms.

Conclusion

In this chapter I have examined a number of the distinctive features of the pharmaceutical sector: the globalization of its activities, its predominantly oligopolistic structure, and the predominance of product-based competition within it. I have argued that despite the international nature of the industry, national regulation remains a valid topic for study. I have also attempted to demonstrate some of the obstacles facing governments when they seek to regulate this complex sector. On the one hand, they strive to maintain the international competitiveness of their home-based firms; on the other hand, they wish to guarantee a safe supply of reasonably priced pharmaceutical products. The limited, product-based nature of competition which has characterized the sector since the Second World War generates a particular set of problems for governments concerned to ensure that they are paying a reasonable price for drugs. The high barriers to entry to the market restrict competition still further, and the line between wasteful and effective competition is a particularly hard one to draw. Given these complexities, it is perhaps inevitable that bargained solutions will emerge in the regulation of the pharmaceutical market.

As this chapter has argued, competitive forces are undoubtedly changing, as are the goals of regulation. It is important to ascertain and compare the nature and speed of change in each country, and it is equally important to determine who can control the direction and pace of this change, and by what mechanisms. It is precisely here that law plays an important role. In terms of the analysis suggested in Chapter 1, existing regulatory frameworks, and the bargaining structures to which they contribute, may act as constraints upon the strategies adopted both by governments and by firms. They may also offer important 'resources' enabling each party to pursue their respective objectives under changed or changing market conditions.

In order fully to understand the dynamics of this process of bargaining and negotiation, it is necessary to examine the origins and development of the various forms of regulation which influence competition in the pharmaceutical market. The dynamics of change are best approached through a chronological analysis of the relevant regimes. In this way we can also begin to understand how interdependent relationships between regulator and regulated emerge and become institutionalized across regulatory programmes.

Notes

1. One can, of course, argue that each and every manufacturing sector presents its own particular set of problems. The most important distinguishing feature of the pharmaceutical sector is undoubtedly the fact that its products are not subject to the normal operation of the laws of supply and demand.
2. F. Scherer, *Industrial Market Structure and Economic Performance*, 2nd edn. (Cambridge, Mass.: Harvard University Press, 1980), esp. chaps. 5–8.

3. National Economic Development Office, *Focus on Pharmaceuticals*, (London: NEDO, 1986).
4. Conseil Économique et Social, *L'Industrie pharmaceutique*, report by Bernard Maurize, JO, Avis et Rapports, no. 1, 28 Jan. 1986. Hereafter CES Report, *L'Industrie pharmaceutique*.
5. NEDO, *Focus on Pharmaceuticals* (1986).
6. CES Report, *L'Industrie pharmaceutique*, p. 6; SNIP, *L'Industrie pharmaceutique en France: ses réalités* (Paris: SNIP, 1987).
7. Select Committee on Overseas Trade, House of Lords Papers, 238, (1985) III, 251 (London: HMSO, 1985).
8. Sanofi, *Annual Report* (Paris: 1986).
9. M. L. Burstall, *The Community's Pharmaceutical Industry* (Luxembourg: Commission of the EC, 1985), 60
10. R. P. T. Davenport-Hines, 'Glaxo as a Multinational before 1963', in G. Jones (ed.), *British Multinationals* (Aldershot: Gower, 1986), 137–61. See also J. A. Slinn, *A History of May and Baker, 1934–84* (Cambridge: Cambridge University Press, 1984) and J. M. Liebenau, 'Marketing High Technology: Educating Physicians to Innovative Medicines', in Davenport-Hines (ed.), *Markets and Bagmen*, (Aldershot: Gower, 1986), 118–40.
11. Burstall, *The Community's Pharmaceutical Industry*, p. 20, Table 3.3; *Le Monde* 15 Apr. 1989.
12. Ibid. 65.
13. United Nations, *Transnational Corporations and the Pharmaceutical Industry* (New York: United Nations, 1979), 23.
14. NEDO, *Focus on Pharmaceuticals*, (London: NEDO, 1972), 18.
15. B. Teso, *The Pharmaceutical Industry* (Paris: OECD, 1979), 22.
16. Burstall, *The Community's Pharmaceutical Industry*, p. 20, Table 3.3.
17. Slinn, *A History of May and Baker*.
18. C. A. Bartlett, 'How Multinational Organisations Evolve', *Journal of Business Strategy*, 3 (1982), 24.
19. NEDO, *Focus on Pharmaceuticals* (1972).
20. J. Howells, 'Spatial Location and Decision-Making in the Pharmaceutical Industry', Ph.D. thesis (Cambridge, 1984).
21. United Nations, *Transnational Corporations*, p. 38.
22. J. H. Dunning, 'International Direct Investment in Innovation: The Pharmaceutical Industry', in Dunning, *Multinationals, Technology and Competitiveness* (London: Unwin Hyman, 1988), 122–43. See also *Financial Times*, 'Survey on Pharmaceuticals', 6 Nov. 1989, 27.
23. M. L. Burstall, J. H. Dunning, and A. Lake, *Multinational Enterprises, Governments and Technology: The Pharmaceutical Industry* (Paris: OECD, 1981).

24. Burstall, *The Community's Pharmaceutical Industry*, p. 63.
25. W. E. Comanor, *The Political Economy of the Pharmaceutical Industry*, University of California Department of Economics Working Paper (Santa Barbara, 1984), 98.
26. L. F. Haber, *The Chemical Industry, 1900–1930* (Oxford: Clarendon Press, 1981).
27. NEDO, *Focus on Pharmaceuticals* (1972).
28. R. Chew, T. Smith, and N. Wells, *Pharmaceuticals in Seven Nations* (London: Office of Health Economics, 1985), 29.
29. ABPI, *Annual Report 1985–86* (London: ABPI, 1986).
30. House of Lords Papers, 238 (1985) III, p. 44.
31. National Academy of Engineering/National Research Council, *The Competitive Status of the US Pharmaceutical Industry* (Washington: National Academy Press, 1983).
32. Bartlett, 'How Multinational Organisations Evolve', p. 25.
33. S. Picciotto, 'Slicing a Shadow', in L. Hancher and M. Moran (eds.) *Capitalism, Culture, and Economic Regulation* Oxford: OUP, 1989), 11–48.
34. P. de Wolf, 'The Pharmaceutical Industry: Structure, Intervention and Competitive Strength', in H. W. de Jong (ed.) *The Structure of European Industry*, 2nd ed. (The Hague: Kluwer, 1988), 211–44.
35. British Statistical Office (1979), quoted in J. Howells, 'Spatial Location'.
36. NEDO, *Focus on Pharmaceuticals* (1972, 1986).
37. B. Chesnais, 'L'industrie pharmaceutique en France', *Revue d'économie industrielle*, 31 (1981), 21–38.
38. W. D. Reekie, *The Economics of the Pharmaceutical Industry* (London: Macmillan, 1975), 36.
39. The 'Terms of Service' for British doctors and pharmacists are prescribed by regulations made under various NHS Acts. Para. 2(1) of the 'Terms of Service for Chemists' in pt. 1 of sched. 4 to the National Health Service (General Medical and Pharmaceutical Services) Regulations 1974, S. I. 1974, no. 160, as amended by S. I. 1985, no. 290, in conjunction with disciplinary powers exercised by the Pharmaceutical Society currently regulate prescribing in the UK.
40. *The Economist*, 2 Feb. 1987, 53.
41. W. D. Reekie and G. Teeling-Smith are the main British proponents of this approach. See, for example, W. D. Reekie, 'Price and Quality Competition in the US Drug Industry', *Journal of Industrial Economics*, 26 (1978), 223–37.
42. M. Silverston and P. Lee, *Pills, Profits and Politics* (Berkeley: University of California Press, 1974), 40.
43. *The Economist*, 16 Feb. 1974, 88.

44. Reekie, *The Economics of the Pharmaceutical Industry*, p. 45.
45. H. Grabowski and R. Vernon, 'New Studies of Market Definition', in R. I. Chien (ed.), *Issues in Pharmaceutical Economics* (Lexington, Mass.: Lexington Books, 1979).
46. W. D. Reekie and M. Weber, *Politics, Profits and Drugs* (London: Macmillan, 1979), 146–51.
47. R. Chew *et al.*, *Pharmaceuticals in Seven Nations*, p. 29.
48. S. Lall, 'Price Competition and the International Pharmaceutical Industry', *Oxford Bulletin of Economics and Statistics*, 40 (1978), 9–21.
49. M. Statman, 'The Effect of Patent Expiration on the Market Position of Drugs', in R. B. Helms (ed.), *Drugs and Health* (Washington: AEI, 1981), 140–50.
50. R. S. Bond and D. F. Lean, *Sales Promotion and Product Differenti ation in Two Prescription Drug Markets*, Staff Report to the Federal Trade Commission (Washington, 1977).
51. *Pharmaceutical Journal*, 23 Apr. 1988, 528. These differences were also highlighted in earlier studies. Prices of drugs in countries not observing patents were invariably lower. A survey carried out in 1974 comparing prices of leading drugs in the UK with those obtainable from Italy or Denmark found, for instance, that Eaton (US) were charging the NHS 102 times the alternative price for nitrofurnaton; ICI (UK) were charging sixty times the price for propanolol; and Smith Kline (US) were charging 145 times the price for trifluoroperazine. A comparison of the cost of four leading drugs in the UK to the NHS showed that those drugs could have been obtained at about 25 per cent of actual cost (*Sunday Times*, 27 May 1973).
52. W. D. Reekie, *Monopoly and Competition in the Pharmaceutical Industry* (London: Macmillan, 1969), 5.
53. Monopolies and Mergers Commission, *Chlordiazepoxide and Diazepam* (London: HMSO, 1973), 40.
54. United Nations, *Transnational Corporations*, p. 34.
55. S. Peltzman, 'An Evaluation of Consumer Legislation', *Journal of Political Economy*, 81 (1973), 1046–91; J. E. S. Parker, 'Regulating Pharmaceutical Innovation', *Food, Drug and Cosmetic Law Journal*, (1977), 163–79.
56. Chew *et al.*, *Pharmaceuticals in Seven Nations*, p. 8.
57. Patents Act 1977, sect. 1.
58. B. O'Brien, *Prescribing Patterns in Europe* (London: Office of Health Economics, 1984), 2.
59. M. Deletraz-Delporte, 'Les Produits génériques: droit comparé et analyse du droit français', thesis (Université Paris Sud, 1983).

60. *The Economist*, 4 Feb. 1989, 64.
61. CES Report, *L'Industrie pharmaceutique*, p. 82. See also *Financial Times*, 'Survey on Pharmaceuticals', 6 Nov. 1989, 30.
62. K. Von Grebner, 'Pricing Medicines', in G. Teeling Smith (ed.), *Health Economics* (London: Croom Helm, 1987), 229–49.
63. Thi Dao, 'Pharmaceutical Competition', in Teeling Smith, *Health Economics*, p. 259.
64. For further details see *Financial Times*, 'Survey on Pharmaceuticals', p. 27–31.

3

Post-War Price Control: Evolving Patterns of Institutionalization

This chapter, as its title suggests, examines the early attempts at pharmaceutical price control in the UK and France. Its purpose is to map out the organizational and legal factors which produced, first, divergent approaches to the assessment of the industry's competitive behaviour and, secondly, different techniques of securing cost control. Chapter 2 suggested that the special conditions of demand for prescription drugs are an important structural determinant of the market for pharmaceutical products. Under the common banner of equal access to health care, the post-war British and French welfare states operate two very different systems of health care. The main differences between them can be subsumed under three headings: methods of finance and payment, organization and administration, and finally the mix between public provision and private care. The first section of this chapter is concerned with the impact of these various differences on the provision of, and payment for, pharmaceutical products. As demand for drug products is mediated through different institutional structures in the two countries, each produces its own peculiar set of problems and priorities, each also offers the possibility for different techniques of government intervention and for the design of a variety of legal tools to keep publicly funded pharmaceutical expenditure under control.

The second section traces the origin and development of the French and British systems of pharmaceutical cost control, both set up at a time when the market for branded medicines was expanding rapidly. It was in this period that the dominant patterns of product competition emerged. Each government began seeking ways of ensuring that this competition was efficient, and set about designing suitable instruments for achieving this end. The third section assesses the operation of the resultant controls in the period up to the 'second oil shock' in 1979, which prompted a reappraisal of levels of public expenditure in both countries.

Pharmaceutical Demand and the Organization and Delivery of Health Care

The socialization of health care

One of the most important variables distinguishing the market for drugs in France and the UK is obviously the latter's National Health Service and the very different route to the socialization of medical care represented by its creation in 1946. In France the general principle is that the patient should pay directly for health care, while, at least in theory, British health care is free. Compulsory-insurance schemes for specific categories of workers formed the basis of health protection in the inter-war period in both countries, but whereas the universalized system of health care, funded primarily from general taxation, was introduced in one sweeping Act in the UK, universal provision was established more gradually in France, beginning with the ordinances of October 1945 and culminating in the law of 1967.[1] Strategies of expenditure control differ profoundly when one system retains the insurance-based approach and the other struggles to maintain the principle of universal provision. In France many of the techniques for controlling demand operated by the pre-war semi-public insurance funds were in fact carried over into the post-war system, whereas the British NHS was compelled to find an entirely new set of solutions.

Control on drug demand and expenditure is also influenced by two further aspects of health-care delivery: its organization and the role of private provision. Organizational factors create pressures and priorities for health spending which are specific to each country, while private health care can act as a safety valve or stopgap for a government which is politically constrained to avoid cutting public expenditure.

Health-care provision in the UK is currently subject to a good deal of central control from a large umbrella-ministry,[2] whereas in France more limited interventionist powers are distributed between the Ministry of Health and Social Security and regional and local authorities. The latter are especially involved in the provision of hospital services. Such factors have indirect implications on strategies for keeping down pharmaceutical expenditure. Some form of control, for example, over the number of doctors who issue prescriptions is seen by health economists as fundamental to controlling the cost of a service, the demand for which is potentially infinite.[3] In the UK, the Department of Health can exercise control over the number of doctors, who are in effect its employees,[4] and over their revenue. Doctors are currently paid on a per capita basis, with certain additional capital allowances at centrally determined rates. They may supplement this income with earnings from private practice. In France the governmental authorities can only control the rising number of doctors by indirect means, for example by restricting the numbers entering medical school. The health insurance funds pay for the doctors' services on a 'fee for service' basis—which actually acts as an incentive to prescribing—but have no legal means of controlling either the number of doctors in practice or their prescribing behaviour.[5] General practitioners compete fiercely for custom and are prone to handing out unnecessary prescriptions to dissuade patients from consulting a rival doctor.

While the role of private medicine in the British system has yet to be fully resolved, the provision of health care in France has always rested on 'a co-existence of a public and a private sector and for-profit and not-for-profit providers of both ambulatory care and hospital services'.[6] The private sector also operates as an important means of containing public costs, even if it makes control of overall-health consumption more complex. Two-thirds of all French physicians are in private practice, providing 90 per cent of the services for ambulatory patients but less than 50 per cent for those in hospital care. Their fees and their legal relationship with the state, the health insurance funds, and their patients were regulated by the Charte Médicale of 1927 and by a series of subsequent agreements or 'conventions' negotiated with the health insurance funds and ratified by the Minister of Health. A basic principle of these successive agreements has been to give physicians in private practice certain privileges in return for surrendering their freedom to set fees.[7] A rapid increase in doctors in the 1970s weakened the bargaining power of the medical unions and strengthened the hand of the funds.[8] It is estimated that there are presently twenty-four doctors per 10,000 of the population in France, as against fourteen per 100,000 in the UK.[9]

Managing pharmaceutical provision

The French post-war legislation on social insurance perpetuated the administrative fragmentation which had characterized the former quasi-public system. Specialist local health-funds, administering health-care insurance at local level for particular groups of workers, subsisted alongside a *régime général* for industrial and factory workers.[10] The 1945 ordinances extending social protection envisaged that these special regimes would eventually be absorbed into the general regime, but the former guarded their autonomy jealously and continue today to provide cover for certain risks, including medical expenditure and drug reimbursement (*prestations en espèce*). Although insurance coverage is now almost complete, the structure of social-security provision in modern France remains byzantine: the administrative costs of running a multitude of separate schemes and the waste of resources caused by duplication and overlap have been the target of continued criticism but of few concrete reforms. It is estimated that some 250,000 persons are currently employed in the administration of French health-care expenditure, at a cost equivalent to 8 per cent of total health spending.[11]

As far as the *régime général* itself is concerned—which now covers some 80 per cent of the population and assumes 78 per cent of the total cost of health care and 75 per cent of the cost of drugs[12]—its functions in regard to health insurance are administered through a tripartite structure. At its apex is the Caisse nationale de l'assurance maladie des travailleurs salariés (CNAMTS), which is a public law corporation (*établissement public à caractère administratif*) with financial autonomy. It is in the joint *tutelle* of the Ministry of Health and Social Security and the Ministry of Finance, who subsidize schemes in deficit. Since the reforms of 1967, the CNAMTS has legal responsibility for the financial solvency of, *inter alia*, insurance for sickness, maternity, and invalidity. Although rates of contribution and compensation are determined by the ministries, the CNAMTS plays an important consultative role in all legislative and regulatory proposals affecting the provision of health care in general.[13] In addition to the various schemes for compulsory health-insurance, private associations—the mutual societies or *mutuelles*)—provide supplementary health-insurance against risks which are not covered, or only partially covered, by the state

system. This is another example of the importance of the complementary functions of the private sector in France. It is estimated
that approximately 70 per cent of compulsory members are also
registered with one of the numerous private schemes.[14]

In the UK, spending on health care is financed almost entirely
through general taxation and national-insurance contributions,
although patients are increasingly expected to contribute directly to
the costs of treatment.[15] By rejecting the insurance principle, under
which revenue would have come from earmarked contributions,
the founders of the NHS inadvertently ensured that it would always
have to compete with other government departments for general
tax revenue. The organizational arrangements for, and funding of,
Family Practitioners Services (FPS) have, however, followed a different path from other aspects of health care. Family Practitioner
Committees (FPCs) were created in 1974 to administer the contracts of general practitioners. FPCs are administered directly by
the Department of Health and not through the decentralized
regional authorities which have responsibility for hospital and community services. Budgets are centrally negotiated, but expenditure
on care provided by family doctors is 'demand determined' and, in
contrast to expenditure on hospital services, which is 'cash limited',
has always been met in full.[16]

In both countries prescription drugs are dispensed by registered
pharmacies. In the UK 'prescription-only medicines' (POM) and
'pharmacy-only' (P) products must be obtained from a pharmacy,
while products on the General Sales List may be sold, subject to
certain conditions, in most retail establishments.[17] Chemists are
remunerated for their work on the basis of professional fees and
allowances, their drugs costs being reimbursed on the basis of a
drugs tariff compiled by the Department of Health.

A distinguishing feature of the French system of distribution is
the extensive monopoly enjoyed by retail pharmacists over the sale
of all medicines. Article 511 of the Code de la santé publique (CSP)
defines a medicine as any substance or formula presented as having
curative, preventive, or diagnostic properties, or as modifying, cor-
recting, or restoring organic functions. Article 512 states that only
pharmacists may sell such products. There is no equivalent in
France to the General Sales List; sales outside pharmacies of any
product which is presented as a medicine are illegal. Only 7 per cent

of all medicines sold in France are bought without a prescription, compared to around 20 per cent in the UK.[18]

Controlling drug consumption in the post-war period

Attempts to control the share of pharmaceuticals in the French health-care budget date back to the introduction, in 1928, of what have proved to be the two cornerstones of post-war French control on pharmaceutical expenditure: the principle of approved lists of reimbursable products and that of the *ticket modérateur*. By providing that the patients should bear a certain proportion of health costs directly, the latter acts as a disincentive to consumption and should sensitize the consumer to price differentials. In addition, a patient is only reimbursed the cost of his or her drug if the product is included on an official list of approved products. A decree law of 28 October 1935 attempted to divide products into four categories, fixing different rates of reimbursement on the basis of a product's value and its price in relation to standard formulae, i.e. generic preparations. This precocious attempt to discourage the growth of unnecessarily costly branded products appears to have floundered for reasons of administrative complexity, and no attempt to revive it was made when the social-security coverage was considerably extended and the legislation revised in 1945. Instead, a single rate of reimbursement (80 per cent) for all categories of insured persons was fixed for products included on an approved list. This system was the object of considerable adverse criticism, both from doctors, who saw it as an intrusion on their freedom to prescribe, and from the beneficiaries, who had been insured under the terms of the earlier legislation and who consequently felt that their level of protection had been reduced. A later law of 1948[19] attempted to resolve matters by extending the list of reimbursable products, to be updated by a special commission on the basis of quality, economy, and price. Prima facie, the price of any product included on the list had to be less than 120 per cent of the equivalent magistral preparation. These two sets of controls, the selective list and the *ticket*, in conjunction with controls on the prices paid for drugs by the insurance funds, have provided an important basis for later attempts at fine-tuning pharmaceutical expenditure.

The cost of universal and comprehensive health care under the NHS, and the cost of medicines as a charge on the state, have proved a constant concern to successive UK governments, but in the crucial early years of the NHS a coherent strategy of general control was totally absent. Three aspects of early health policy combine to offer some explanation for this striking lacuna: the lack of consideration given to the financial implications of the setting-up of the entire system, the traditionalism of the politicians, and, more particularly, the British Civil Service and the power of the medical profession.

In the first place, the cost of setting up the NHS was calculated largely on the basis of pre-war expenditure on health care. It was assumed that demands of the system would be finite; as the population grew healthier, the cost of care would decline. As Klein suggests, no thought appears to have been given to the possibility that a national health service would have a financial and political dynamic of its own.[20] As for traditionalism, the Ministry of Health was regarded as a repository of regulatory rather than executive functions. Thus it was reluctant to take on direct administrative responsibilities for a complex service.[21]

The 1944 White Paper setting out the plans for a national health service, and the 1946 Act which implemented these were both vague on issues of cost. The former contained a series of compromises on the institutional framework for universalizing medical care, while the latter turned these compromises into a series of contradictions, which remain at the heart of the system even today.[22] These included important compromises on the role of private medicine and on the status of the medical profession, which fought to maintain its professional autonomy. The detailed working-out of these problems over the last 40 years need not detain us here, but together they embody a fundamental irony of the NHS as set up in 1948 and as perpetuated since then, namely 'that it could exercise least control over the gatekeepers to the system as a whole: the general practitioners'.[23] Although the NHS is a nationally funded organization, it continues, despite several major structural reorganizations to provide primarily local services. In contrast to the French post-war legislation, the 1946 Act made no specific provision for control over demand for medical supplies. In a system financed from general taxation as opposed to earmarked funds, global expenditure-limits were the preferred method of control.

Pharmaceutical Price Controls

Pricing policy after the end of the Second World War

These organizational divergences have undoubtedly shaped the subsequent evolution of official policy on the prices at which drugs are bought for the respective systems of health care. In order to understand this process, it is necessary to examine the legal context of price control. This section compares and assesses the introduction of the post-war controls in each country.

Voluntary controls in the UK

As in many other areas of social policy, the emergency arrangements of the war years, while providing a blueprint for detailed administrative control, also established a useful basis for concertation during the reconstruction years.[24] It is to the industry's credit that it succeeded in eradicating the threat of the former while building on the latter. In terms of their economic strength and importance at the end of the war, French- and British-based industries were broadly equivalent.[25] Yet the organizational strength of the latter in the immediate post-war period stands out in comparison, and its peculiar contribution to the British post-war settlement on price control should not be underestimated. A permanent representative organization—the Wholesale Drug Trades Association (WDTA)—had been formed in 1930, changing its name to the Association of the British Pharmaceutical Industry in 1948, to reflect the changing nature of the industry. The WDTA co-operated actively with the Ministry of Supply's special Central Pharmaceutical War Committee and ensured the compliance of its members with the various wartime emergency measures, including price control. Cartels and joint agreements, officially endorsed as the most effective means to counter wartime shortages, continued to flourish in the post-war period.[26]

Industry's greatest fear was that the creation of a nationalized health service with monopsonistic purchasing-powers could spell the premature death of brand-name products. At the time of the creation of the NHS there was already a precedent for comparative lists which could easily have provided the basis for a pro-generics policy. In 1941 a National War Formulary, listing drugs considered either useful or essential, had been set up by the Ministry of Health for all drugs dispensed under the National Health Insurance System, and in 1945, despite protests from industry, the Ministry published a comparative list of products for inclusion in the formulary. Powers to compile such lists were not subsequently incorporated into the National Health Service Act 1946, a concession which the industry secured on the basis of its economic position and the strength of its organizational links. Its vital role in rebuilding the British export trade and in redressing the balance of payments allowed the Association to win concessions from the Minister of Health and thus allay its members' fears that the creation of the NHS would mean the end of prescribing by brand name. In its report for the year 1948–9, the year in which the NHS came into operation, the ABPI noted confidently that:

the authorities have shown due appreciation both for the need for liberty of individual judgement on the part of the prescriber and the role which the protection afforded by a proprietary right may play as an incentive to progress on the part of the manufacturer. The Association ... has contested wherever it has arisen any empirical and undiscriminating assessment of branded preparations as a class. It has been recognized that the coexistence of a sufficiently protected field of endeavour for the genuine pioneer on the one hand with the field of open competition on the other, is probably the best guarantee of improved pharmaceutical presentation consistent with economy.[27]

The emergence of statutory controls in France

French drug-manufacturers also enjoyed a tradition of effective organization, and indeed of self-regulation, in the inter-war period. (This will be discussed further in Chapter 4.) Until the outbreak of the Second World War, drug prices were unregulated: the retail pharmacist determined the selling price of all medicinal products. Fierce competition prevailed at the wholesale level, and in order to counteract the growing phenomenon of discounting, the powerful manufacturers' and wholesalers' associations in 1908 formed the *Confédération interpharmaceutique de réglementation*, which later became the *Comité intersyndical de réglementation*, to impose a system of resale price maintenance on its members. The benign disposition of the courts and administrative authorities to these price cartels is perhaps illustrated by an early judgement of the Cour de Cassation, which found that all wholesalers should respect the price fixed by the manufacturer, irrespective of whether they were members of the cartel.[28]

As was the case for most essential goods, a prize freeze had been imposed for the duration of the war on manufacturers' prices for all medicinal supplies. Occasional increases were authorized by ministerial order. Although various forms of administered prices were imposed on industrial goods and services after the war, the prices of medical products, along with other strategic goods such as petroleum, remained frozen. Further increases were made subject to particularly stringent controls, imposed under the sweeping regulatory powers granted to the Ministry of Finance under ordinance 45-1483 of 1945. This legislation, which was passed primarily to deal with post-war shortages, remained the corner-stone of administered price controls in France until 1986. It endo-wed the Minister of Finance with extensive discretionary powers to calculate and set prices throughout the economy by whatever means he or she deemed appropriate in the furtherance of a wide range of objectives.[29] Article 19 of the ordinance provided that drug prices were to remain frozen at 1939 levels, but an *arrêté* of 1948 introduced a special system of pharmaceutical price control, the *régime de cadre de prix* or price framework.[30] It provided that manufacturing prices were to be calculated by adding a fixed rate of return or profit, determined by the Ministry of Finance, to the manufacturer's own estimate of basic costs. This rate was deemed to cover overheads, publicity, research, capital investment, as well as profits.

The imposition and subsequent retention of price control on pharmaceutical products thus marked a significant departure from the earlier, non-interventionist approach in France. A number of reasons may be advanced to explain the divergence from British post-war experience. In the first place, France had not only been occupied but had sustained a far greater level of economic disruption and dislocation, factors which justified the retention of a general regime of administered price controls for some years after the war. Secondly, and more specifically, the demand for drugs outstripped national manufacturing capacity. In the immediate post-war period French birth-rates were the highest in Europe, while the numbers of war-wounded requiring medical treatment imposed further strains on the system. Thirdly, the imposition of stringent import controls on basic drugs and active ingredients, including antibiotics and penicillin, while protecting home-based firms, made the development of a substantial black market a very real threat. Fourthly, although the manufacturers' trade association enjoyed considerable power in the inter-war years, it did not enjoy the same continuity of influence as the ABPI. It had been dissolved in 1940, only to be reconstituted in 1944 and endowed with substantial corporatist-style regulatory powers over its membership by the subsequently discredited Vichy regime. The *Chambre syndicale* could not boast the equivalent of its British counterpart's track record on wartime co-operation on prices and supplies, nor was there much overt support for a return to cartel-like practices or corporatist governance structures in Fourth Republic France.[31]

Institutionalized divergence: Formalism versus self-regulation

The subsequent persistence of this regulatory divergence can be attributed, at least in part, to the very different legal context in which price control developed. Issues of cost control and the search for value for money in public expenditure continued to plague British firms. Within one year of the inception of the NHS, the number of prescriptions issued was almost twice the original number forecast, and estimates of government spending were rapidly revised.[32] The Labour government of the time was forced to enact powers to impose charges for prescription medicines. It also began investigating the true cost of the goods it purchased. A paper submitted to the Committee of Public Accounts (CPA) of the House of Commons in July 1952 made it clear that the rise in the total drugs bill was directly attributable to the increase in proprietary or brand-name prescriptions. In 1947, the year prior to the launch of the NHS, branded products accounted for 7 per cent of total prescriptions. By 1951 this had increased to 23 per cent. Per capita consumption had risen much more slowly.[33]

If branded drugs were at the root of expenditure problems, then some means for controlling their use had to be found. In 1949 the Joint Committee on Prescribing (the Cohen Committee), a government advisory committee whose membership included medical experts, had recommended that all NHS doctors should be discouraged from prescribing expensive brand-named products which did not offer sufficient advantage over their generic equivalents.[34] To this end, it introduced a six-tier classification-scheme for all drug products, based on therapeutic value, and suggested that those medical products which fell within certain categories—in effect branded products which had an official therapeutic equivalent—'should be prescribable only provided ... when satisfactory arrangements for price are made between the Health Departments and the manufacturers'.[35]

The Cohen Committee's recommendation of some sort of negotiated agreement between the Ministry and the manufacturers struck the right chord of traditionalism with the former and provided the latter with an opportunity to protect profits on the sale of their branded products. Industry had already established a solid organizational base on which to negotiate, but it had the further advantage of a benign legal environment. Any desire to impose formal restrictions at a time when the incoming Conservative government had issued a general promise to make a bonfire of wartime controls was notably absent from official policy.[36]

The ABPI not only reacted to government proposals; it often pre-empted them with its own recommendations. Its membership was reorganized into special divisions, dominated by the British companies which manufactured branded products, and these in turn formed negotiating committees and spawned special working parties.[37] The Ministry of Health on the other hand, approached matters in a highly pragmatic and often tentative way. As the government-appointed Hinchcliffe Committee on Effective Prescribing later revealed in its interim report in 1957, the Ministry lacked basic statistical information on levels of drug consumption and on the use of more expensive, branded products. An earlier report, prepared by the Guillebaud Committee, a small committee appointed by the Minister of Health in 1953 to investigate rising costs in the NHS, had also concluded that the lack of statistical information made it difficult to make any firm recommendations on what it considered to be a general drift towards new, expensive, branded products. The Committee stressed that it had been unwilling to undertake detailed statistical investigations of drug costs while the Ministry was engaged in sensitive negotiations with the ABPI. A useful opportunity for an independent body to gather wider knowledge of the industry was consequently lost.

Products were priced for reimbursement purposes on the basis of a tariff calculated as an average of manufacturers' costs. The actual cost of individual products was often unknown. Nor were the civil servants particularly anxious to use their existing legal powers under the Defence Regulations[38] to obtain information about manufacturers' costs, claiming that there was no point in using these supplementary powers as long as there was no system of price control.[39] A vicious circle had therefore emerged: formal investigatory powers made sense only in the context of formal price controls, but without the necessary information which the use of the former set of powers might have yielded, the latter were impractical.

Even if government was reluctant to impose a statutory framework of price control, informal or non-legal methods of control were potentially available. Firstly, as the Treasury was ultimately the major purchaser in the home market, drug companies might have been placed on a similar footing to general contractors to government, who at that time received a standard rate of return on sales to government of between 7 and 15 per cent on investment.[40] Alternatively, the number or type of products qualifying for reimbursement might have been restricted. The logic of the Cohen Committee's suggested system of classification was to revive the National War Formulary, suppressing expensive, branded products which were not of higher therapeutic value than a generic equivalent. The availability of surgical appliances on prescription was already regulated in this way.[41] However, the Ministry was reluctant to risk the ire of the doctors, who resisted interference with their freedom to prescribe the drug of their choice.[42] At an early stage in the battle for cost control, the ABPI, following a complaint about the Department's failure to consult prior to the distribution to doctors of information on prescribing, secured a promise that consultation would precede any further action on the Minister's part.[43]

The potential abuses of brand names and the problems of controlling a multinationally organized industry were, however, becoming readily apparent. The Treasury was actively seeking to control spending on health, and the Committee of Public Accounts (CPA) kept up pressure on the Ministry to establish mechanisms for determining the true price of drugs and to ensure effective competition within the industry, insisting that the Minister should use the available legal powers under the Defence Regulations to obtain detailed information on individual firms' costs.[44] In its 1951–2 report the Committee found that:

The Department have made no investigation of manufacturer's costs; they believe that competition within the industry has been sufficient to ensure that the list prices are fair ... The Committee do not know on what evidence this belief is based; they observe, moreover, that the Ministry have not tested by cost investigation the prices paid for proprietary products, which are clearly not determined by competition.[45]

The Committee was of the view that the obvious way to proceed to an investigation of costs and value for money was to compare new, branded products with readily available standard equivalents,[46] but the Minister remained reluctant to base a comprehensive pricing policy on comparative classification, preferring a series of pragmatic inquiries and bilateral investigations with individual firms into the costs of a limited range of products in different therapeutic categories.[47] The role of the Cohen classification scheme was reduced to that of informing doctors about the costs of prescribing. The results of these negotiations, it was later confessed to the CPA, were mixed.[48] The foreign multinationals, and especially those who enjoyed a monopoly of supply, refused to bargain, and negotiations in general proceeded slowly. The *ad hoc* investigations, revealed, however, that prices for branded products were indeed too high, while a further inquiry into generics had exonerated their manufacturers from any charge of excess profits.[49]

The Minister reacted by threatening to blacklist a number of branded products. It should be pointed out that in reality 'the power of blacklisting was one of moral suasion on the doctor'.[50] Lacking mandatory powers to prohibit the prescription of a particular drug, exhortation, backed by the threat of a local enquiry into an individual doctor's prescribing patterns, was the only weapon. In the hands of the major customer for branded products, this weapon had considerable potential.

As a consequence of this lack of progress, the Minister announced, in May 1954, that the *ad hoc* inquiries and negotiations would be abandoned. All future price-negotiations would proceed on a new basis, namely, that the industry's profits should be aligned with those earned by other government contractors. These target rates of return were to be applied to profits on sales of branded proprietaries—now approximately 90 per cent of total NHS expenditure. The ABPI immediately petitioned the Ministry, urging that profit margins of the order held to be appropriate to Government contracts were inadequate for their entire business, including private and export trade ... and compared unfavourably with earnings in private industry generally; that in any event proprietaries needed relatively high margins to balance lower returns on other pharmaceutical business, particularly standard drugs; that the contracts basis was inapplicable since there was no question of Government contracts for particular quantities of any proprietary and NHS trade was through normal channels, exposed to all ordinary market risks, and lacking most of the advantages of contractual selling; and also that freezing profits in relation to capital employed would in their view kill incentives to efficiency.[51]

The ABPI also informed the Minister that its members were willing to co-operate in formulating 'alternative proposals for arriving at mutually satisfactory prices' for branded products.[52] The lasting implications of the ABPI's success in finally imposing its own scheme on the Ministry cannot be underestimated. Internally, its membership was divided on the need for control but united in its fear that the Minister would legislate in the absence of co-operation. Public concern about prices was mounting, and the Ministry was threatening a tougher line in negotiations.[53] An alleged import-cartel between suppliers of insulin was referred to the newly formed Monopolies and Restrictive Practices Commission.[54] Even within the Association, certain firms were prepared to accept that excesses did exist.[55]

Considerable disagreement on the government side as to the scale of the problem of excessive profits, and the solution to it, complicated matters further. The Treasury was cautious, stressing the fundamental problem confronting the Ministry:

It is necessary to reconcile the particular interest of the Health Service in obtaining economical supplies of drugs to the wider public interest in the continuance of a developing pharmaceutical industry.[56]

The subsequent negotiations between the Ministry and the ABPI on alternative policy for controlling the price of branded products stretched over a three-year period. There appears to have been some Treasury involvement, but this was only indirect.[57] Although modified in the course of negotiations, the essential features of the ABPI's proposal were retained in the final version of the Voluntary Price Regulation Scheme (VPRS), as accepted by the Ministry in 1957.[58]

This scheme, which was to run for an initial five-year period, aimed to secure 'fair and reasonable' prices for some 90 per cent of branded drugs available on the NHS. Manufacturers seeking prices for new products, or price rises for existing drugs, were to deliver certain details of their product costs. The reasonableness of the requested price was to be established by the use of comparative formulas. Significantly, the latter, devised and subsequently applied by the industry, bore no resemblance to the official Cohen system of classification. Three alternative general formulas for determining maximum prices were envisaged: the 'export criterion', which was to be applied where more than 20 per cent of the output of a given medicine was exported; the 'standard equivalent' test, which related price to that of the generic equivalent; and the 'trade-price formula', relating prices to the cost of basic ingredients, with added allowances for R. &. D. costs, processing, and packaging. In addition, the scheme envisaged direct negotiations between a manufacturer and the Minister, but only if the former so desired. The scheme also allowed for a so-called 'three-year freedom period' or exemption period for new drugs, to allow for research costs to be recovered.[59]

From a regulatory perspective, certain features of this voluntary scheme appear remarkable and deserve further analysis. Firstly, it gave the Minister little concrete information on costs. The trade-price formula could provide this—but this was very much a fall-back test. Secondly, the export criterion—which was based on a weighted average of export prices—was given priority over the other two categories, in the belief that export prices were competitive. Such a belief is, of course, hard to sustain in a product market protected by world-wide patents, but the Ministry's espousal of it was particularly remarkable in view of the fact that an earlier trial run of the scheme on 200 products actually resulted in higher average prices.[60] To allay any fears, the ABPI gave a written undertaking on behalf of its members that where formula prices proved higher than current prices, these would not be increased, except when an increase was justified by costs.

This particular undertaking is the key to the third feature of the scheme: its *entirely voluntary* and *informal* basis. The undertaking itself, and indeed the VPRS, was legally unenforceable, either by the Minister against the ABPI or by the latter against its membership. Although the Association introduced certain changes to its constitution and rules,[61] strengthening the position of the manufacturers of branded drugs, adherence to the provisions of the VPRS was never made a condition of membership. Fourthly and finally, the scheme completely passed over two fundamental problems: firstly, the thorny issue of transfer pricing—that is, the value of transactions between foreign parent and local subsidiary—and secondly, the control of the allegedly excessive expenditure on advertising and promotion. Prices for raw materials and intermediate products were supplied by the individual firm, the Ministry having no powers to request access to the books of parent companies or foreign suppliers. Nor were special provisions requiring details of advertising expenditure included in the first VPRS. Indeed, the 'freedom period' encouraged firms to concentrate a large volume of promotional expenditure in the first 3 years.

Despite the prolonged controversy surrounding pharmaceuticals prices, and despite the lack-lustre experience of the first decade of attempted control over pharmaceutical demand, the VPRS amounted to little more than a loosely worded declaration of intent. Each side promised 'reasonable' behaviour, but a combination of the 'freedom period', the world-wide patent system, and the absence of formal powers to investigate costs conspired to ensure that the industry was at best only 'honour bound' to deliver its side of the bargain. Admittedly the price of dishonesty could be high—an unofficial blacklisting of products among doctors in the short term, and perhaps the introduction of formal, more far-reaching powers in the longer term—but the Ministry was ill equipped to contest each firm's calculation of its costs and profits. In a subsequent report the CPA concluded that:

the Ministry have little or no information about costs or profits relating to proprietaries . . . and the only information available about trading results is such as is afforded by the published accounts of firms engaged in pharmaceutical manufacturing . . . This information while indicating high profits is inconclusive.[62]

The Subsequent Performance of the Two Systems of Control

Comparing legal style and technique

In terms of legal style and technique, the contrast between the goals and instruments of the French and British systems of price control could not be more striking. On the one hand, with the price-framework system, France had opted for strict formal control over individual drug prices based on fixed formulas. On the other hand, the UK had adopted a voluntary system of control over the profits of individual companies; nor was the adoption of a fixed-profit formula considered. Both systems were put into practice at a time when the pharmaceutical market was undergoing profound changes. The market share of branded proprietaries was expanding, methods of production were changing, and the industry itself was becoming increasing multinational.

Can one form of control be deemed more successful than the other in terms of their respective regulatory goals? Obviously there are different standards by which to measure success. Nevertheless, on the basis of various official statements issued at intermittent intervals throughout the period up to 1978, we may assume the common goals espoused by each system to include the continued provision of a range of useful medicines at reasonable prices which would also provide sufficient reward and incentive to a research-based industry. The pursuit of this objective offers a common standard against which performance may be assessed. In essence, each government had chosen to exercise some control or influence over the process of product competition, but had they equipped themselves with the necessary instruments to do so effectively?

The performance of the VPRS

The British VPRS in fact precluded the Ministry of Health's dealing closely with individual products; indeed, its aim was the avoidance of investigation into actual costs and profits. Certainly firms negotiated prices for individual products, but the agreed level reflected an assumption that a company's *overall* profits on its NHS sales were reasonable. It is evident that the non-legal and highly discretionary nature of the scheme accommodated bargaining which was perceived as necessary for adjustment to the changing market conditions.[63] Under the first VPRS (1957–61), prices were negotiable at the company's option only. Products which promised to be good export-earners could be sold at a considerable profit if a firm convinced the Ministry that the British price would be taken as a reference price in important markets. The Ministry had to rely on information about pricing and cost supplied by firms, and, as it had no powers to backdate price settlements, the firm had every incentive to drag out negotiations. This was a favourite tactic of the Swiss firms, who even postponed entry into the VPRS until 1960.[64] The overall savings attributed to the scheme were small, and, in official circles at least, it was not considered to be a success.[65]

The Ministry acknowledged that the major test used in the VPRS, the export criterion, actually 'enabled a drug manufacturer to charge for a proprietary preparation a price three times higher than that of the unbranded equivalent'.[66] Yet in the second and third renegotiations of the VPRS, in 1961 and 1964 respectively, the Ministry ignored the CPA demands that the export-criterion test should be replaced with one which compared the price of generic products, or that industry should pay back excess profits. Both were resisted on the ground that they would be too costly to administer.[67] Indeed, the second and third versions of the scheme (1961–4 and 1964–8) provided for more rather than less negotiation as the importance of the various 'tests' appears to have gradually declined. Under the third VPRS, the 'freedom period' was modified so that genuinely innovative products were free from control for 4 years while freedom for other products was restricted to 2 years, with the proviso that in both cases the Ministry might grant extensions in special circumstances. By 1964 over 50 per cent by value of NHS drugs were subject to direct negotiation.

The Ministry's preference for flexibility was undoubtedly a reflection of its dual role of sponsor and regulator,[68] but two further aspects of this silent but unmistakable drift towards greater bargaining are worthy of note. Firstly, there was little public debate on the VPRS or its renegotiations, despite the growing size of the drugs bill. Nor was evidence of abusive pricing practices lacking. The CPA remained a vociferous critic of the industry and the VPRS, but its recommendations, like those of most parliamentary select committees, received comparatively little attention in the House. Renegotiations were conducted in secret between the Ministry and the ABPI, and, with the exception of the CPA's intermittent scrutiny, there was little real external control on the implementation of the scheme.

This approach in itself is perhaps a reflection of certain peculiarities of British constitutional practice and legal tradition. The commitment to the principle of ministerial accountability for executive acts, although a legacy from less interventionist times, was deliberately retained in the post-war period, despite the much more extensive nature of government involvement in the economy.[69] Yet this principle operates as an executive shield from detailed scrutiny and not as a parliamentary sword. As far as the administration of the VPRS was concerned, it is clear that the Minister considered himself accountable to Parliament on questions of the *average* rates of profits earned on NHS sales but not in regard to individual firms' profits or prices. Commercial confidentiality might have precluded the release of concrete information on the operation of the VPRS, but when the Labour government referred the whole matter of the relationship between the industry and the NHS to an *ad hoc* inquiry in 1965, the Ministry refused to allow its own evidence to be made public.[70]

A second and related feature is the commitment to informal rules in the design of the scheme and the attendant informal or supplementary nature of the powers which have characterized its enforcement. The silent drift to direct bargaining was accomplished without any formal debate precisely because there were no formal rules to amend. Two sets of supplementary powers were theoretically at the Ministry's disposal: firstly, the powers to impose by order maximum prices for medical supplies and to require their suppliers to provide information on costs;[71] and secondly, the powers granted by the Patent Act 1949. Section 46 of this Act, the provision on compulsory licences, which is examined in more detail in Chapter 9, provided that any government department may make use of and exercise any patented invention for the service of the Crown.[72] Yet both were used with restraint. It was argued by civil servants that

the exercise of these powers ... would be at variance with the general voluntary basis on which arrangements with the industry ... have been founded, and would jeopardise the prospects of continuance of any such voluntary arrangements.[73]

The continued refusal of the major Swiss companies to supply information on prices prompted the Ministry to use its statutory powers. This followed the total breakdown, by 1960, of negotiations which had dragged on for more than 3 years. Section 46 of the Patents Act, however, was used on only one occasion — in May 1961, when price negotiations with the predominantly American suppliers of the tetracycline group of drugs reached a stalemate. Substantial differences in world prices had come to light in the course of patent litigation in the USA and were used by the Labour opposition as ammunition to mount a rare public attack on the VPRS.[74] The Minister, taking advantage of his monopsonistic purchasing power invited central tenders for widely used hospital medicines. Although Section 46 restricted compulsory licences to Crown use, which did not include the Family Practitioner Services, and therefore some 80 per cent of consumption, significant savings were nevertheless obtained due to the substantial differences in price between the original patentee's price and that of the Section 46 supplier.[75]

And yet in the subsequent renegotiations on the fourth VPRS formal powers of enforcement were to remain supplementary. The ABPI, however, was requested to supply the Ministry with more information on price formation in the industry and to bring the recalcitrant foreign companies into line. Paradoxically, the VPRS's evident failings led to more rather than less interdependence between industry and government.

This informal, non-interventionist approach was continued under the Wilson and Callaghan Labour governments; however, the substantive provisions of the voluntary scheme were eventually made more onerous. The majority of these changes, which related to control of advertising expenditure, are discussed in Chapter 8. Despite a manifesto commitment to nationalize the industry, the Wilson administration proved markedly lukewarm to the recommendations of the Sainsbury Committee, which it had appointed to conduct a thorough investigation of the industry in 1965.

On the basis of reports from independent accountants, Sainsbury had concluded that the VPRS had manifestly not guaranteed that all prices were reasonable. It considered that an examination of the reasonableness of overall profits without a detailed examination of the prices of individual medicines was inadequate because it failed to identify the specific products that were largely responsible for a firm's profits. The technical staff and organization of the Ministry were insufficient to enable them to conduct effective negotiations. The Ministry employed neither accountants nor chemical engineers familiar with pharmaceutical manufacture. Finally, the officials lacked clear policy guidance on which to base their judgement of what was 'fair and reasonable'.[76]

Sainsbury concluded that a comprehensive system of cost reporting was needed to strengthen the Ministry's negotiating hand.

Under the proposed system, firms would submit firstly a standard cost return (SCR), showing direct costs of labour and materials as well as indirect costs apportioned to the product, and projecting anticipated sales and expected profit-margins, and secondly an annual financial return (AFR), showing the results of its NHS business. The Ministry would then compare its own estimates of cost with those shown in the SCRs and negotiate the prices of medicines on this basis and in the light of the AFRs. The latter, but not the SCRs, were incorporated into the fourth VPRS in 1969. Hence the system remained essentially one of aggregate profit-control.

In strictly legal terms, the VPRS retained its voluntary character, even after the negotiation of its sixth version in 1978, when its nomenclature was changed to the Pharmaceutical Price Regulation Scheme (PPRS). The new name reflected the industry's subjective interpretation of its commitment to it rather than any significant accrual of new legal powers to the Minister. The old emergency powers to impose prices by order and to obtain information were now incorporated in the National Health Act 1977, and the power to work compulsory licences in the service of the Crown was extended, in 1968, to include the Family Practitioner Services.[77] These powers have remained, at least in the eyes of the civil servants, very much reserve powers.[78] The PPRS, which came into operation in 1978, will be considered in fuller detail in Chapter 6.

The failure of French price controls

On the face of it, one might assume that the French system of statutory pricing, in conjunction with the controls over the selection of reimbursable products, offered greater scope for the realization of regulatory goals. Although prices remained relatively low, the volume of consumption grew steadily at about 11 per cent per annum throughout the 1960s, so that net expenditure on pharmaceuticals continued to rise at an alarming rate.[79] It will be recalled that controls on reimbursement by the health insurance funds were operated independently of those on price control, the former under the auspices of the Minister of Health and the latter by the Minister of Finance. In theory, their potential co-ordination would have allowed the authorities to fashion a powerful means to stimulate as well as monitor product competition. In fact such co-ordination was never achieved, and in practice the reimbursement system operated to compensate for the adverse effects of price control on industry. Some 18,000 products were listed as officially reimbursable in France in 1953, compared to an average 9,000 available on the British or German markets. The special commission set up under the 1948 law had very limited powers to exclude a product from the reimbursement lists: it could only refuse inscription to products which were of no therapeutic value whatsoever, products which had been advertised to the public, or products which were solely for dietary purposes.

The legal form as well as the administration of the pharmaceutical price framework—the *cadre de prix*—was ill conceived and ill suited to the needs of an increasingly modern, transnationally organized industry. A distinctive feature of the regime, it will be recalled, was that prices for every new product were calculated by adding a fixed rate of return, determined by the Minister of Finance, to the basic manufacturing costs. As manufacturer's actual costs were ignored, the system operated as an incentive to increase rather than minimize other costs. Research costs, for example, were fixed at 7 per cent of the final price, with the result that non-innovative companies were over-compensated, while innovative firms were discouraged. Transfer pricing was widely practised. Unlike the British Ministry of Health, the Direction des prix at the Ministry was staffed by civil servants with some accountancy expertise, but it too had insufficient administrative resources to enforce its statutory powers to require detailed information on the costs of raw materials and had been unable to devise an adequate method of assessing costs within the industry.[80] Furthermore, it was becoming increasingly difficult to calculate and accurately apportion costs on a product-by-product basis. Production no longer took place primarily in small dispensaries but in large, often multinational firms. The larger companies could obtain high prices by importing the basic ingredients or a semi-finished product from a foreign subsidiary at vastly inflated prices.

The influential Rueff-Armand Report, which reviewed the operation of the regulation of pharmaceutical prices and safety, pointed to the inefficiencies which this regulation nurtured. Restrictions limiting share-ownership in pharmaceutical firms to qualified pharmacists had starved companies of capital and management and had either operated as an important brake on economic growth or left small firms susceptible to take-over by foreign firms, who were denied an alternative route into the French market. Only a few home-based family firms, such as Roussel-Uclaf or Pharmuka, had expanded sufficiently to engage in the expensive long-term research and development which was increasingly necessary for innovation. As a result of the irrationalities of the price-control system, foreign firms devoted few resources to research and development on French territory, preferring instead to import intermediate substances from parent companies established abroad.[81] Limited reforms were introduced in 1959. The rules on capital contributions from non-pharmacists were liberalized, although pharmacists were still required by law to constitute a majority on the board of directors and to hold key managerial positions. Price controls were also amended; fixed rates for overheads and other costs were replaced by calculations based on the manufacturer's true costs, but the principle of the fixed rate of profit was essentially retained. For genuinely 'new' products, profit rates were higher during the first 2 years of marketing. As no satisfactory method of distinguishing 'newness' could be determined, the system did not really act as an incentive to efficiency.[82]

A further flaw in the price-framework system was that prices of products already on the market were neither systematically reviewed nor varied to reflect increases or decreases in basic costs. To obtain higher prices, firms would abandon commercialization of existing products and reintroduce them under a different name or in a slightly different formulation; hence the large number of products, especially combination or 'me-too' drugs, on the French market. If anything, the excessive rigidity of the periodic price freezes produced the opposite of the intended result. Many cheaper, therapeutically useful products disappeared from the market, while the administrative resources of the reimbursement and safety authorities were severely stretched as they struggled to process the stream of costly 'pseudo-novelties' which flooded on to the market.[83]

To counter the upward drift in prices, the Minister of Finance used his extensive discretionary powers under the 1945 ordinance[84] to impose a series of special price freezes between 1950 and 1967,[85] as well as compulsory price reductions or *baisse autoritaire* of up to 5 per cent.[86] This merely encouraged firms to abandon old products in favour of pseudo-novelties.

The very formalism and fragmentation of legal powers made it difficult to reform this increasingly irrational and anachronistic system. On the one hand, the price-framework system, and indeed the reimbursement system, were based on formal legal rules which had to be amended by formal processes. While it is technically within the executive powers of a minister to alter *arrêté*-type measures without parliamentary consultation, the political difficulties involved in replacing one set of rules with another were enormous. Reform was conditional on securing agreement between the various ministries involved in the tutelage of the industry as to what might replace the price-framework statute. On the other hand, as long as the Minister of Finance retained extensive discretionary powers, the firms were unwilling to provide the detailed financial information which was seen by the former as a prerequisite to more flexibility. The Ministry of Finance has traditionally been seen as one of the government departments least amenable to any form of influence from industry.[87]

It would be misleading to equate this proliferation of formal rules to an active or constructive policy on pharmaceutical prices; rather, their systematic distortion was passively tolerated, and any incentive to compete internally became redundant. Strict import controls on finished products, the lax system of reimbursement, and the scope for transfer pricing conspired to stifle competition from foreign products, so that French industry was not only able to tolerate the ostensibly rigid system of control but actually flourished.[88]

This happy state of affairs was by no means permanent, however. In the first place, the prospective completion of the first phase of the Common Market in 1964 and the anticipated liberalization of controls on imported products threatened to disrupt the protected isolationism of the French market, exposing the industry's weaknesses as far as competition was concerned. The reports prepared in the context of the Fifth Plan highlighted the long-term anticompetitive effects of a pricing system which, in an increasingly internationalized environment, encouraged neither exports nor research. Smaller firms were now especially vulnerable to take-over by foreign firms anxious to break into the protectionist French market. Some 20 per cent of the industry was already in foreign hands, and this would increase in subsequent years. Compliance with the new European requirements on the testing of drug safety would make it necessary for French companies to engage in clinical trials and product research for which they were ill equipped.[89] The industry had also become more concentrated: the number of firms had shrunk from 1,000 in 1945 to 400 in 1966, while the twenty-five largest firms were by then responsible for 42 per cent of national production. It was hoped, somewhat piously, that, if nothing else, increased concentration might lead to lower prices through the realization of economies of scale and the development of fewer and more sophisticated products.[90] The Fifth Plan also forecast that, following the extension of social-security coverage by the reforms of 1968,[91] pharmaceutical expenditure would increase dramatically to between 22 and 23 per cent of the total expenditure on social assistance under the *régime général*.[92] Stricter controls on consumption had to be imposed.

The search for rationality

If the dual objectives of holding down public expenditure while promoting an industry capable of competing on European markets were to be realized, the two separate systems of price-control and reimbursement had to be properly integrated and a constructive policy pursued on product selection. In 1968, following protracted interministerial negotiations, the price framework was replaced by a new system of controls—the *grille de prix* or price scale.[93] As with the former system, it was the prices of individual products rather than profits which were controlled, but with the crucial difference that the manufacturer's true costs would be fully reflected in the sanctioned price. It was now up to the manufacturers to propose a selling price and to justify it on the basis of financial and accounting information relating both to the product in question and to the firm's overall economic position. (In certain respects this system was not dissimilar to that recommended by the Sainsbury Committee in the UK, although calculations were based on past profits rather than forward projections.) This supporting documentation was then separately considered by both the *Direction générale de la concurrence et de la consommation (DGCC)* at the Ministry of Finance, which had 15 days in which to notify the applicant of its opposition, and by the *Direction des industries chimiques, textiles et divers (DICTD)* at the Ministry of Industry. The role of the latter was merely advisory.

In practice the real locus of price control was to be transferred to the reimbursement machinery. A new *Commission de reim-*

boursment de la sécurité sociale (the Coudrier Commission) was created in 1967.[94] It was entrusted with two roles. Firstly, it had to evaluate a new product for reimbursement purposes, and secondly, it had to recommend a reimbursement price. In practice these tasks were interconnected. Each product had to be evaluated in accordance with two positive criteria: its contribution to an improvement in the standard of health care; its contribution to economy in the cost of health care. If two rival products were of equal therapeutic value, preference was to be given to the one which resulted from the greatest research effort or to the one whose price was lower (Article 3). The Commission could also recommend the removal of certain products from the list, such as products which would lead to increased consumption or unjustified expenditure (Article 4). Application of the positive criteria implied a comparative approach: a new product should be better than anything on the market, while older, less effective products would, in theory, be removed from the list as more modern therapies came on to the market.

The Commission itself was given limited investigative powers (Article 14), and the Secretariat at the *Direction de la pharmacie* was reorganized and strengthened to provide fuller support (Article 7). The Minister of Health was legally obliged to consult the Commission prior to inscribing a product on the list (Article 8). The health insurance funds were legally prohibited from reimbursing products not included on the list.[95] A failure on the part of a firm to co-operate could lead to the *radiation* or exclusion of one of their existing listed products. In keeping with the distinction drawn in the decree, the Coudrier Commission divided its functions between two subgroups: one to deal with the 'technical dossier', which contained the relevant medical and prescribing information, and the other to examine the 'economic dossier', which was intended to justify the price requested by the manufacturer for the product. Representation on the subcommittees reflected this division of labour. The technical subcommittee comprised external, as opposed to in-house, medical and scientific expertise, while the economic subcommittee was constituted by three representatives from the major health insurance funds, from the Ministries of Health, Economy, and Finance, as well as an economic expert. Two industry representatives were added in 1972.

This system offered far greater scope for official intervention at the level of prices and product selection than did the loosely framed British VPRS. Whereas the British drug-industry had been closely involved in drawing up a scheme which offered little scope for any real administrative control, the involvement of the French firms was confined to a limited participation in the application of the new system. Significantly, the proposed new advisory committee on prices, composed of representatives of the health insurance funds and the SNIP, the industry association, never actually met.[96]

As the Vernejoul Report had indicated in 1968, the true test of the new approach would lie in the method of its implementation rather than in its formal design.[97] It was hoped that the new price-scale system would operate as a general framework within which realistic prices could be negotiated rather than as a rigid set of rules. In practice the new system contained too many elements of the old regime to allow this goal of increased rationality to become a reality. The incentive artificially to inflate the costs of raw materials in the calculation of the first stage of the selling price—the *prix de revient industriel*, which included the cost of ingredients, manufacture, labour, and quality control—remained high as long as this provided the basis for the calculation of allowable profit rates.[98]

Obviously this system exacerbated rather than prevented transfer pricing, both between foreign parent-companies and their subsidiaries and between French-based companies. These latter, although members of the same group, were treated as juridically distinct for tax purposes. In order to take advantage of this loophole, several of the larger French companies such as Delagrange relocated facilities for the manufacture of intermediate products outside France.[99]

An indication of the difficulties faced by the French customs authorities in establishing 'arm's length' or uncontrolled prices came to light in the criminal prosecutions brought against the Swiss manufacturer Sandoz for breach of the French Customs Code.[100] Sandoz-Switzerland sold two active ingredients, ergotamine tartrate and dihydroergotamine methane sulphonate, by way of exclusive licence to its French subsidiary, Sandoz-France. Sandoz were charging 67 Swiss francs per gram for the first product and about 90 Swiss francs for the second, prices which the French customs alleged to be at least twice as high as those charged by rival manufacturers. Litigation commenced in 1958 and eventually reached the European Court of Justice in 1979.[101]

As the price of fine chemicals was no longer subject to control, neither the *Direction de la Concurrence* nor the Coudrier Commission could fully investigate the prices submitted by individual firms. Between 1966 and 1969 national production of intermediate products had grown by 18.4 per cent, while imports had increased by 79 per cent in the same period.[102] A study commissioned by the Ministry of Industry on the basis of company declarations submitted in accordance with decree 70-441[103] revealed a net deficit in technical exchange—that is, patent and licensing fees and technical assistance and know-how—valued at some 28.5 million francs.[104] The balance of trade in fine chemicals continued to worsen throughout the next decade. If the goal of the new system had been to promote a stronger research base in France, then perhaps this was the most telling indictment of all.

If the Coudrier Commission had chosen to interpret and implement its powers strictly, and had obtained sufficient economic and technical information about each product to perform a truly comparative evaluation of one product's efficacy as against that of another, it might have produced a truly selective list of medicines which would have stimulated product competition. In fact the Commission lacked the necessary administrative and technical resources[105] to form anything more than an impressionistic view of the therapeutic value or research effort involved in each of the 1,000 dossiers which it considered annually;[106] instead it devised an arbitrary and rigid method of quantifying in monetary terms the supposed additional therapeutic value offered by new products. Products were graded on a scale of 0 to 10 in terms of their relative

Table 4. French Commercial Trade Balance for Intermediate Chemical Products (million Fr. francs)

Year	Imports	Exports	Net balance
1970	1,132	433	− 709
1976	2,043	732	−1,311
1977	2,263	928	−1,335
1978	2,175	1,173	−1,002
1979	2,859	1,085	−1,774

Source: SNIP, *L'Industrie pharmaceutique: ses réalités* (Paris, 1981)

innovative value compared with those already on the market. A major innovative product would be rated at above 7, but the vast majority of products were evaluated at between 0.5 and 5 by the technical committee. The economic committee automatically fixed prices of products which had been awarded less than 3 points at 10 per cent lower than those already on the market and paid no attention to the economic situation of the individual company. The price scale was not used as a point of departure for negotiation, as had originally been intended, but rather as a rigid set of constraints applied without any real attempt to distinguish between different companies or products. Few new applications were excluded from reimbursement, nor were older products which had been superseded by technically superior medicines.[107]

This is not to say that the new system worked entirely in industry's interests. Annual price increases granted under the price-scale system averaged about 2 per cent per annum.[108] The Ministry of Finance, although now relegated to a secondary role in determining the price of individual products, retained its general powers to impose price reductions for products already on the market. Whereas the Coudrier Commission had been prepared to allow industry to recover the increased costs of raw materials generated by the inflationary pressures of the mid-1970s, between 1975 and 1977 the Minister effectively reversed this policy by imposing a compulsory reduction of between 2 and 5 per cent on over 400 drugs, in the interests of general anti-inflation policy.

Pharmaceutical price controls and general price control

These special regimes for controlling profits and prices, once established, appear to have been isolated from developments taking place in general price-control regimes governing the economy as a whole. While this was to the advantage of UK-based firms, this was not so in the case of their French counterparts. In the UK, where general, formal price controls were reintroduced in 1966[109] and maintained in various forms until 1980,[110] exemption from the application of a potentially more rigorous regime to the price of individual products undoubtedly worked in the industry's favour.

The French pharmaceutical industry was not so fortunate. In 1966 a general relaxation of administered price controls[111] on a wide range of products was prompted by an EEC Council recommendation on short-term economic policy measures.[112] As we have seen, pharmaceutical prices were only partially liberalized 2 years later. There was little scope for industry to challenge its exclusion from the 1966 measures on legal grounds. The only constraints on the exercise by the Minister of Finance of his or her powers under the 1945 ordinances, on which price controls were based, were the constitutional principles of equality of treatment and non-retroactivity.[113] The French administrative courts have been reluctant to utilize the former principle to overturn decisions relating to matters of economic policy, and have recognized the Minister's discretionary powers to distinguish between different economic sectors in the imposition of price controls.[114]

Conclusion

To conclude this evaluation of the initial attempts at price control in the UK and France, it is perhaps best to return to the question of whether either of these regimes can be judged to be more efficient than the other in securing effective competition. It will be recalled that both systems were introduced at the crucial period when branded products were first making their impact on the pharmaceutical market. Despite their considerable differences in approach, neither system effectively prevented the industry from passing on the costs of unnecessary or wasteful competition to the public authorites. The goals of the French system were arguably more ambitious in that it sought to control the volume of products on the market as well as their price, but the rigidity of the latter controls only exacerbated the problems of volume. The overriding objective of the French system was in fact the maintenance of low prices rather than the promotion of effective competition between products, despite the availability of a range of legal instruments with which to accomplish this goal. Although efforts were made to distinguish genuinely 'new' products, the administrative bodies entrusted with the task were never equipped with the powers or resources to carry out their duties effectively. Paradoxically, despite the panoply of formal controls, direct interference in the industry's commercial strategies was minimal. As long as the French market for finished products remained a relatively insulated one, the promotion of effective, research-based competition between products remained a secondary consideration for government and industry alike.

It is important to stress that, despite their failings, each pricing regime contributed to the creation of a very different pattern of government–industry relations in the two countries. Furthermore, these differences were underscored by the legal character of the regime and the climate in which they were implemented. Two distinct approaches characterized the initial formation and subsequent implementation of price-control strategies in the UK and France. Firstly, the French system of controlling drug prices was, from the creation of a socialized system of health care, encapsulated within a formalistic legal framework based on extensive executive powers. In the UK, on the other hand, a system of profit control has evolved within an almost entirely non-statutory, voluntaristic framework, albeit underpinned by the monopsonistic purchasing power of the NHS. Secondly, whereas British-based industry could bargain and negotiate with a single, unified health department, which was at once its sponsor, regulator, and major customer, the French pharmaceutical industry was confronted with a fragmented administration, where formal legal powers over pricing and reimbursement were unevenly distributed between several ministries, none of which played the role of sponsor. A combination of informal controls and a single negotiating partner allowed the British-based companies to foster and develop a benign, flexible framework within which to bargain extensively over mutually acceptable rates of profit. Their French partners were unable and unwilling to achieve a similar relationship with their regulatory masters. As long as the Minister of the Economy continued to wield extensive powers over its prices and profits, and the Coudrier Commission interpreted its own mandate inflexibly, the industry had no incentive to enter into a similar dialogue with the Ministry of Health; and as long as reimbursement controls remained ineffective, it could realize increases in its profits by alternative means, though these increases were limited. In this light, its boycott of the special advisory committee set up under the 1968 legislation is understandable.

If formal but fragmented powers were the dominant feature of the French system throughout the period surveyed here, self-regulation and interdependence were the two major hallmarks of the

British system. The adoption of the first VPRS in 1957 was indeed a dual victory for the industry: it not only diverted the assumption of intrusive formal legal power but also removed a more immediate threat. As the largest single customer for prescription products in the UK, the government had immense economic power or *dominium* to compensate for the absence of formal regulatory powers. While it might be argued that this potential economic might was what made the system of self-regulation a feasible one from government's point of view, I have tried to demonstrate in this chapter that the successive VPRSs in fact functioned as a very effective block on the mobilization of the government's economic power.[115] Such a mobilization would have alienated industry and destroyed the basis for co-operation over profit control on which government had come to rely. A similar interdependence was totally absent in France. Although representatives of industry sat on the Coudrier Commission, their role in the implementation of individual decisions on pricing was negligible, and industry's role in the formulation of policy was virtually non-existent. Discrete policy shifts towards a more bargained, flexible form of control, accomplished with relative ease in the British system in response to the changing structure of the industry, were not possible in France. The latter's system remained outmoded and ill suited for the regulation of a complex, globally organized industry.

In Chapter 2 I suggested that the patterns of competition in the pharmaceutical sector are gradually changing, and in particular that price competition is emerging. How have the divergent patterns of government–industry relations performed in this changing market context? Have differences persisted, or have the patterns of regulation discussed here broken down? Before answers to these questions can be attempted (see Chapters 6 and 7), it is necessary to consider the impact of two further sets of regulatory developments on the evolution of government–industry relations in the two countries: the introduction of controls on product safety, and the development of European rules on safety and, more recently, on price control. In Chapter 4, which deals with the regulation of product safety, I will examine the extent to which the introduction of these new controls have either altered or merely complicated the overall regulatory picture. Chapter 5 considers the impact of European law and policy, not only on the functioning of these national bargaining arenas but also on the very structure of the market for pharmaceuticals in Europe.

Notes

1. For the history of earlier, 19th-century legislation, see J. Weiss, 'Origins of the French Welfare State: Poor Relief in the Third Republic', *French Historical Studies*, 13 (1983), 47–78. Despite minor reforms in 1983, allowing for contributions from general taxation, health-care provision in France has retained its insurance base.

2. Responsibility for health matters in Scotland and Northern Ireland falls to the Secretaries of State for Scotland and Northern Ireland respectively.

3. B. Abel-Smith and A. Maynard, *The Organization, Financing and Cost of Health Care in the European Community*, Social Policy Series, 36, (Brussels: Commission of the EC, 1979).

4. Health Services Act 1984.

5. A number of health economists have concluded that the 'fee for service' method of payment is an important incentive to higher prescribing. See further B. Abel-Smith and P. Grandjeat, *Pharmaceutical Consumption*, Social Policy Series, 38, (Brussels: Commission of the EC, 1978); B. O'Brien, *Prescribing Patterns in Europe* (London: Office of Health Economics, 1984).

6. S. Sandier, 'Private Medical Practice in France', *Advances in Health Economics and Health Services Research*, 4 (1983), 335–67.

7. See generally C. Prieur, 'L'Évolution historique de l'organisation des relations entre la médecine libérale et les régimes d'assurance maladie 1930–76', *Revue trimestrielle du droit sanitaire et social*, 46 (1984), 301–19.

8. For example, under the 1980 agreement the funds took the risk of creating a double system whereby physicians could choose between charging scheduled fees or setting their fees freely. Faced with developing competition, most doctors charged scheduled fees, so that overall costs were held down. Sandier, *Private Medical Practice in France*.

9. *The Economist*, 16 July 1988.

10. Law of 30 Apr. 1930.

11. *The Economist*, 16 July 1988.

12. CES Report, *L'Industrie pharmaceutique*, chap. 2.

13. Sixteen branches (*caisses régionales*) administer functions which reflect the need for local action such as the negotiation of compensation rates for accidents at work and the fixing of fees for local medical

personnel. The task of registering members and paying out compensation is entrusted to the 129 local offices (*caisses primaires*).

14. Although the number of *mutuelles* fell from 13,000 to almost 10,000 in the 1960s, it has remained at about this level since 1970, despite the Socialist government's efforts to promote the growth of such bodies.

15. At no time in its history have charges contributed more than 6 per cent of the NHS budget. C. Ham, *Health Policy in Britain*, 2nd ed. (London: Macmillan, 1985), 39.

16. See further Ham *Health Policy in Britain*, pp. 48–9, and Office of Health Economics, *Understanding the NHS in the 1980s*, (London: OHE, 1984). For the allocation of hospital funding, see DHSS, *The NHS Planning System*, (London: DHSS, 1976), and DHSS, *Sharing Resources for Health* (London: DHSS, 1976).

17. Section 51 of the Medicines Act 1968 allows the relevant Ministers to specify by order any description or classes of medical product which in their opinion can be sold otherwise than under the supervision of a pharmacist. See Medicines (General Sales List) Order 1977, S. I. 1977, no. 2129, as amended. POM medicines are defined by the Medicines Act sect. 58 and the Medicines (Prescription Only) Order 1977, S. I. 1977, no. 2127, amended by S. I. 1978, nos. 189, 987, S. I. 1979, nos. 36, 1040, S. I. 1980, no. 24. P. medicines are defined by the Medicines Act 1968, sect. 52.

18. CES Report, *L'Industrie pharmaceutique*, p. 49. Medicines containing substances defined as *substances vénéneuses* and classified in one of three tables by *arrêté* of the Minister of Health can only be obtained on prescription (CSP arts. R.5149 and R.5169–R.5211).

19. Loi Solihnac, 18 Aug. 1948.

20. R. Klein, *The Politics of the NHS*, (London: Longman, 1983), 35.

21. Ibid. 9.

22. Ham, *Health Policy in Britain*, p. 40.

23. Klein, *The Politics of the NHS*, p. 37.

24. See generally R. K. Middlemass, *Competition, Power and the State* (London: Macmillan, 1985).

25. L. F. Haber, *The Chemical Industry*, p. 31.

26. See, for example, *The British Insulin Manufacturers' Cartel*, Monopolies and Restrictive Practices Commission, HC 296, para. 32 (London: HMSO, 1951).

27. I. Turner, 'A Review of the History of Relations between the Government and the Pharmaceutical Industry', unpublished paper, available from Henley College of Management, Henley.

28. Cour de Cassation, 3 May 1920. Referred to in M. Tisseyre-Berry et G. Viala, *Législation et déontologie de l'industrie pharmaceutique* (Paris: Masson, 1983), 121.

29. Art. 60 extended the application of the ordinance to prices for all goods and services. For an analysis of the Minister's general powers see J.-M. Auby and R. Ducos-Ader, *Institutions administratives* (Paris: Economica, 1973), 575 ff.

30. *Arrêté* 19659 of 24 Aug. 1948, BOSP, 27 Aug. 1948.

31. J. E. S. Hayward, 'Mobilizing private interests in the service of public ambitions: the salient element in the dual French policy style', in J. Richardson and G. Jordan (eds.), *Policy Styles in Western Europe* (London: Allen & Unwin, 1982), 111–40.

32. Klein, *The Politics of the NHS*, pp. 33–5.

33. Committee of Public Accounts, *Third Report for the Session 1951–52* (London: HMSO, 1952), app. 15.

34. First interim report, quoted in Ministry of Health, *Annual Report for year ending 1950* (London: HMSO, 1951).

35. *Pharmaceutical Journal*, 22 Apr. 1950, 294.

36. See generally Middlemass, *Competition, Power and the State*.

37. J. Sargent, 'The Politics of the PPRS', in W. Streeck and P. Schmitter (eds.), *Private Interest Government: Beyond Market and State* (London: Sage, 1985), 105–27.

38. The Emergency Powers Act 1920 invested the government with wide powers to legislate by Order in Council, after the proclamation of an emergency, for securing the essentials of life to the community.

39. Committee of Public Accounts, *Third Report for the Session 1951–52*, (London: HMSO, 1952), paras. 46, 76, 4903–94.

40. R. Lang, *The Politics of Drugs* (Farnborough: Saxon House, 1974), 145.

41. Committee of Public Accounts, *Fourth Report for the Session 1950–51*, (London: HMSO, 1951), paras. 771–8.

42. Lang, *The Politics of Drugs*, p. 151.

43. ABPI, *Annual Report 1950–51*, (London: APBI, 1952), 12.

44. Emergency Powers Act 1959, sect. 3.

45. Committee of Public Accounts, *Third Report for the Session 1951–52*, paras. 50–1.

46. Committee of Public Accounts, *Third Report for the Session 1952–53*, (London: HMSO, 1953), app. 8.

47. Hansard, 18 May 1953, vol. 515, col. 1726.

48. Ibid. para. 4991.

49. Hansard, 10 Apr. 1954, vol. 527, cols. 887–90.

50. Committee of Public Accounts, *Third Report for the Session 1953–54*, (London: HMSO, 1954), 366, Q.4620–1.

51. Committee of Public Accounts, *Third Report for the Session 1956–57*, (London: HMSO, 1957), app. 2, 568.

52. ABPI, *Annual Report 1954–55* (London: ABPI, 1955), 16.

53. Hansard, 17 June 1955, vol. 348, col. 100.

54. Monopolies and Restrictive Practices Commission, *British Insulin Manufacturers' Cartel*, 21.
55. J. Sargent, 'The Pharmaceutical Price Regulation Scheme', International Institute of Management Working Paper, (Berlin, 1983), 7.
56. Committee of Public Accounts, *Special Report for the Session 1956–57* (London: HMSO, 1957), Treasury Minute.
57. Commenting on the final version of the VPRS, the Treasury made no secret 'that they do not regard this arrangement as one that they would have chosen'.
58. Sargent, 'The Politics of the PPRS', p. 10.
59. This account is taken from Lord Sainsbury, *Report of the Committee of Enquiry into the Relationship of the Pharmaceutical Industry with the NHS*, Cmnd. 3410 (London: HMSO, 1967), 27–8.
60. Lang, *The Politics of Drugs*, p. 148.
61. Sargent, 'The Pharmaceutical Price Regulation Scheme', p. 11.
62. Committee of Public Accounts, *First, Second and Special reports for the Session 1959–60* (London: HMSO, 1960), xviii.
63. Sainsbury Report, Cmnd. 3410, p. 32, para. 97.
64. Lang, *The Politics of Drugs*, p. 168.
65. Ibid. 160–3.
66. Committee of Public Accounts, *Third Report for the Session 1962–63* (London: HMSO, 1963), 152, Q.1557.
67. Lang, *The Politics of Drugs*, p. 170.
68. Sainsbury Report, Cmnd. 3410, pp. 29–31, paras. 88–94.
69. Middlemass, *Competition, Power and the State*, p. 18.
70. Lang, *The Politics of Drugs*, p. 184.
71. Emergency Powers Act 1964, sect. 5.
72. In *Pfizer v. Minister of Health* [1964] A C 414 it was held that the definition of Crown included the Hospital Services but not the General Medical Services.
73. Sainsbury Report, Cmnd. 3410, p. 33, para. 102.
74. Lang, *The Politics of Drugs*, pp. 158–9.
75. Sainsbury Report, Cmnd. 3410, p. 34, para. 111.
76. Ibid. paras. 170–5.
77. Health Services and Public Health Act 1968, sect. 49.
78. Interview with J. Long, Industry Division, DHSS, Apr. 1985; cf. Sargent, 'The Politics of the PPRS'.
79. In its evidence to the Boutet Commission, the CNAMTS estimated that between 1959 and 1968 pharmaceutical consumption was growing at an average of 11 per cent per annum and prices at 5 per cent, so that their expenditure was increasing by 16 per cent per annum—that is, at a rate twice that of the growth in average wages over the same period. J. Boutet, *L'Industrie pharmaceutique* (Paris: La Documentation française, 1975), 128.

80. Ibid. 117.
81. OECD, *Gaps in Technology*, (Paris: OECD, 1969), p. 122.
82. *Arrêté* 22-216 of 12 Sept. 1952, BOSP, 31 Sept. 1952.
83. Report of Carnivet Commission JO, Documents administratifs (1967).
84. Art. 23 gives the Minister wide powers to reduce prices 'lorsque leur niveau est considéré comme trop élevé'.
85. On 1 Mar. 1949; 31 Aug. 1952; 8 Feb. 1954; 15 Apr. 1956; 1 Sept. 1963; 1 Oct. 1967.
86. Sept. 1952; June 1963.
87. E. Friedburg, 'Administration et entreprises', in M. Crozier (ed.), *Où va l'administration française?* (Paris: Éditions oeuvrières, 1974).
88. OECD, *Gaps in Technology*, p. 12.
89. Annexe du Ve Plan, JO 1278 bis (1962), 154–5.
90. See Conseil économique et social, *La Sécurité sociale*, report by R. F. Vernejoul, JO, Avis et Rapports no. 15, 24 Oct. 1968, 773–5 (hereafter, CES Report 1968).
91. Ordinance 67-707 of 22 Aug. 1967 in JO, 24 June 1967.
92. Report of Carnivet Commission, JO, Documents administratifs (1967).
93. *Arrêté* 25-502 of 5 Apr. 1968, BOSP, 9 Apr. 1968.
94. Decree 67-441 of 5 June 1967, JO, 6 June 1967.
95. Art. L266-1 of the Code de la sécurité sociale.
96. Art. 593 CSP; See further Boutet, *L'Industrie pharmaceutique*, p. 118.
97. CES Report 1968, p. 771.
98. The Boutet Report examining the operation of the system in 1970 found that these costs accounted for between 30 and 40 per cent of the average wholesale price. Boutet, *L'Industrie pharmaceutique*, p. 116.
99. See the Commission's reply to European Parliament. Written Question 1793/79, OJ 1979, C131/43.
100. In particular, arts. 35, 414, 426(3), 435, and 459 and decree 68-1021 of 24 Nov. 1968 make it an offence to make a false declaration of customs value on importation, and outlaw illegal transfers of capital abroad through the repatriation of profits which have not been taxed in France.
101. Case 65/69, *Procureur de la République* v. *Chatain* [1980] ECR 1345.
102. L. Velluz, 'La Recherche pharmaceutique: Rapport de la Commission d'étude', in *Pour une politique de la santé*, A, vol. 5 (Paris: La Documentation française, 1975), 141.
103. Decree of 24 May 1970, JO, 26 May 1970.

104. Velluz, *La Recherche pharmaceutique*, p. 142.
105. For a detailed discussion of the organization of the DPHM, see chap. 4.
106. CES Report, *L'Industrie pharmaceutique*, p. 73.
107. J. Dupuy and S. Karsenty, *L'Invasion pharmaceutique* (Paris: Seuil, 1974), 75.
108. CES Report, *L'Industrie pharmaceutique*, p. 73.
109. Prices and Incomes Acts 1966–9.
110. A Pay and Prices Code was operated by the Heath government between 1972 and 1974 (Cmnd. 5205, 1972; Cmnd. 5247, 1973); Counter Inflation (Price and Pay Code) S. I. no. 658, 1973; Counter Inflation (Notification of Increases and Prices and Charges) Order 1973, sched. 2, cl. 17 exempted industries subject to the PPRS.
111. *Arrêté* of 9 Mar. 1966.
112. EEC Council recommendation of 22 Dec. 1966, in OJ, 28 Dec. 1966.
113. R. Pollet et M. Seite, 'Principes de la réglementation des prix', *JCL Droit administratif*, fasc. 90, nos. 220–8.
114. See generally R. Savy, 'Le contrôle juridictionnel de la légalité des décisions économiques de l'administration', AJDA (1972), 6–15.
115. T. C. Daintith, 'Legal Analysis of Economic Policy', *Journal of Law and Society*, 9 (1982), 191–224.

4

Drug Safety and Drug Marketing

In this chapter I examine a second major set of laws which influence the commercial activity of the pharmaceutical industry: the regulation of product safety. Chapter 2 illustrated two distinct ways in which this body of regulation impinges upon competitive processes. First, by making testing requirements more onerous and therefore more expensive, safety regulation may form a barrier to entry for potential rival firms. Second, the implementation of modern regulations on product safety may allow regulators not only to evaluate industry's products on the basis of their intrinsic safety but also to determine their efficacy as methods of treatment in comparison to products already on the market: economic as well as medical criteria may form the basis of such tests of efficacy. In consequence, regulation of product safety, if administered in this way, may pose a considerable threat to industry's commercial freedom. This chapter therefore examines a second source of conflict in the regulatory relationship between government and industry. It investigates the extent to which existing legal and administrative linkages with regulators, discussed in Chapter 3, have influenced the implementation of safety regulation and whether the implementation of these new regulations has necessitated the construction of different frameworks for bargaining. The first section deals with the evolution of the operative criteria on which modern drug-regulation is based. It examines some of the problems inherent in comparing national regimes of product safety and suggests an alternative approach, further developed in the second section. The importance of the 'pre-regulatory' period is discussed here, and the extent to which this period has influenced the administration and organization of modern product-safety licensing in France and the UK is further examined in the third section. This section also takes up some of the issues raised in Chapter 1 in relation to capture theory, and argues for a more nuanced approach to the question of industry's influence over regulatory processes. This theme is developed in the fourth section, where the performances of the two safety-licensing regimes are compared, using detailed case-studies of two key aspects of the licensing process.

Modern Drug-Safety Licensing

Modern systems of drug-safety regulation, dating from the postwar period, are formally based on three principal criteria: efficacy, quality, and safety. Official controls over the quality or purity of medicinal products originated in the seventeenth century, with the publication of quasi-official pharmacopoeias, intended as guides to formulation and quality and to prevent adulteration. By the nineteenth century, embryonic legislation had emerged dealing with the training of pharmacists, the establishment of pharmacies, and the legal role of the pharmaceutical profession in ensuring the quality of the drugs which they prepared. Concepts of safety and efficacy did not feature in the pharmacopoeias, and there were few reasons to incorporate them into law: as long as most medicines in use were derived from herbs, the properties of which were thought to have been sufficiently defined by experience, there was little necessity to do so.[1]

While pharmacists were prepared to accept legal responsibility for the drugs they compounded themselves, they soon questioned the extent of their responsibilities for the new synthetic drugs manufactured on a large scale by the chemical industry. In the interwar period, governments throughout Europe were slow to respond to demands for statutory safety controls. In the UK, beyond the broad provisions of the Food and Drugs Acts,[2] which merely stipulated that drug products were not to be injurious to health, there were few restrictions on the sale of drugs. In France a drug registration system had been introduced in 1941, but it was mainly concerned with quality control and was not particularly scientifically rigorous.

The extension of regulation to embrace the concepts of safety and efficacy is a mid-twentieth-century development which has coincided with the rise of large-scale manufacture and techniques of chemical synthesis, and with the realization that most modern medicines, if sufficiently toxic to be effective, are also potentially dangerous if wrongly used. In most European countries and

elsewhere it was the Thalidomide disaster and the sudden awareness of the scale of injury which such drugs could cause which
provided the impetus for government intervention. Prior to
thalidomide, in the UK and in many other European countries a
product could be marketed without any independent check upon its
safety. As a former chairman of the Committee on the Safety of
Medicines (CSM) observed: 'Lulled into security by the quiet years,
both public and government were unprepared for the therapeutic
explosion of the last 30 years. This complacency was rudely shat-
tered by the Thalidomide tragedy'.[3] The terrible implications of
inadequate or non-existent controls over clinical testing put preventive legislation firmly on the regulatory agenda. Thalidomide
also revealed the weaknesses of the civil tort law in attributing
responsibility for damages to manufacturers, and the difficulties
involved in reforming liability laws added further impetus to the
demand for fuller regulatory controls.[4] Although Thalidomide had
not been marketed in France, the tragedy coincided with another,
purely national, scandal over the failure of existing controls to
prevent the sale of Stalinon, which caused over fifty deaths in
1954.

Meanwhile, the European Commission, recognizing that a common market for medicinal products could only be established if
national laws were harmonized, commenced negotiations on a
common system of drug registration. Its first package of proposals,
presented to the Council in 1962, aimed not to harmonize substantive safety standards but rather to assure the approximation of the
administrative procedures for evaluating product safety. From the
outset, a centralized approach, involving the creation of a European
office to deal with the regulation of product safety, had to be ruled
out as both politically unacceptable to the member states, and
indeed to their industries, and as economically prohibitive. A
compromise solution, based on the *mutual recognition* of national
licences, was therefore preferred.[5] This approach, which should not
be confused with automatic mutual acceptance of different national
licensing criteria, implicitly involved the centralized co-ordination
and eventual harmonization of the administrative procedures for a
decentralized, national evaluation of licensing applications. In
other words, national sovereignty would remain but licensing decisions would be based on progressively standardized scientific and
medical criteria. The eventual goal of the process would be auto-

matic recognition across the Community of a product licence issued in any single member state.

The first EEC Council directive, 65/65, on proprietary medicinal products was essentially a framework measure, which dealt only with the approximation of licensing administration.[6] It set the principles and objectives of a unified common market at their very broadest, namely that no product should be placed on the market without prior authorization. The latter would only be granted if the national authorites were satisfied, on the basis of documentary evidence, of the safety and therapeutic efficacy of the product (Article 5). The UK was not a member of the Community at this time, but the West German government, anxious to protect the interests of its large home-based drug industry took exception to inclusion of the efficacy criteria, as well as to the original intention to include generics within the scope of the directive. In the final event, generics were excluded,[7] and the efficacy test itself was restricted; therapeutic efficacy would only be considered lacking in a medicine which failed to produce pharmacodynamic results (Article 11). These criteria were required to be incorporated into national legislation.

The UK Medicines Act 1968, which came into force in 1971, introduced pre-marketing controls on the testing of new drugs and a comprehensive system of licensing for the manufacture and sale of medicinal products. Section 19 of the Medicines Act 1968, drafted in anticipation of EC membership, provided that a licence would be issued only when safety, quality, and efficacy were demonstrated. Article 601 of the French Code de la santé publique amended in 1968, provides that a marketing authorization will be granted only when the applicant establishes three things: the safety of the product under normal conditions of use, its therapeutic value, and a guarantee of its quality.[8]

Comparative efficacy tests

The implementation of legislation on product safety has to be seen as a dynamic process. The potential power of the administrative bodies responsible for its implementation will increase as they gain experience and expertise in the technical aspects of drug-safety regulation and as scientific knowledge of pharmacological processes improves. This means that industry, while broadly accepting the desirability of uniform standards of safety, must always face the threat that legislation on product safety could be used for wider evaluative purposes, with adverse economic consequences.

Some commentators have argued that where various aspects of drug relation, including price and safety, arc centralized in the hands of a single authority, a *needs* clause, such as that found in Norwegian law, operates in practice.[9] A policy of needs assessment, or the use of rigorous comparative efficacy tests allowing only the most cost-effective treatments to be licensed, would render the development of semi-innovative products, or so-called 'me-toos', less attractive and thus greatly reduce the number of products entering the market. A strict application of efficacy criteria might therefore eliminate wasteful competition or rivalry, offering regulators the opportunity to promote truly innovative competition. In other words, the implementation of safety legislation could be 'subverted' to achieve the ends which control on prices and profits has so far failed to realize. In addition, it could be used to close 'regulatory gaps' in some pricing regimes. In Chapter 3, for example, the ability of French industry to circumvent price controls by bringing new versions of old products on to the market was discussed. A rigorous application of efficacy criteria would defeat such practices.

Comparing national drug-regulations

In this chapter I am essentially concerned with the implementation of drug-safety regulations, their implications for product-based competition, and their impact on marketing strategies. A comparative study of the letter of the law on product safety would only be of limited value in such a highly technical field, where the legislator can only lay down broad guide-lines.[10]

Evaluating and comparing the concrete effects of regulation, whether economic or medical, is notoriously difficult. Distinguishing the effects of regulatory practice from those of medical tradition on the outcome of licensing decisions is, as Quantock has suggested, problematic:

Different countries have their own special problems. Ethnic differences lead to dosage variations. Varying health care standards require different therapeutic approaches, and local therapeutic traditions have developed over the centuries and bring their own complexities.[11]

As most of the data handled by national authorities are highly confidential, it is difficult to compare the treatment of individual applications for licences. Although a few such studies have been undertaken, they are too isolated to provide the basis for general conclusions.[12]

Regulation and innovation: The controversy over drug lag

The economic impact of drug-safety regulation, on the other hand, has been the subject of a substantial number of studies, and indeed of much controversy, particularly in the United States. These studies have sought to establish and analyse the phenomenon of 'drug lag', that is, the adverse impact of increasingly severe controls, contained in the 1962 amendments to the American Food, Drug and Cosmetic Act, on the rate of innovation in the pharmaceutical industry. Because these regulations made experimentation more expensive and time-consuming, new products were either taking longer to reach the American market or, in some cases, were never commercialized at all. Peltzman's original analysis of the problem of drug lag postulated a straightforward statistical correlation between the 1962 amendments and the post-1962 decline in pharmaceutical innovation.[13]

As knowledge and understanding of the effects of modern drugs in humans have developed, regulatory techniques have inevitably grown technically more sophisticated. Regulatory authorities throughout the world require increasingly complex and detailed information about how a substance has performed in a bewildering variety of tests.[14] It is undoubtedly the case that drug companies must comply with far more rigorous standards than 20 years ago. In the UK, for example, the length of time needed to take a newly discovered chemical entity through all the stages of commercial development, from initial discovery and isolation, through the phases of clinical trial, to commercial production, was estimated to have increased from 2.8 years in 1960 to 12 years in 1983.[15] Similar findings have been recorded in French studies.[16]

There are a number of dangers involved in the straightforward transplantation of the debate about drug lag to an analysis of the European situation. In the first place, the methodology adopted in the original studies is dubious. Subsequent analyses of a more sophisticated kind have cast doubt on Peltzman's study and have attributed drug lag to a number of additional causes, including the general international decline in research opportunities.[17] In the 1950s, anti-infective medicines predominated, including antibiotics, antibacterial, and antiviral products. Their use usually involves the administration of a short course of treatment which has as its target the removal of specific disease-bearing organisms from the body; clinical testing was correspondingly straightforward. Since the mid-1960s, however, pharmacological intervention has been increasingly directed at diseases where the goal of therapy, in the present state of knowledge, is the long-term prevention or control of symptoms, cures not yet being available. Inevitably, this shift has been accompanied by a commensurate extension of the period and extent of drug testing. The need to employ more sophisticated research techniques to solve modern medical problems poses a more formidable challenge and has considerably increased both development times and costs.[18] It is generally accepted that increased regulatory requirements are only a part of this process, although the extent of their contribution remains a matter of debate—a debate which will only be resolved on the basis of a disaggregated analysis of different therapeutic classes.[19]

There are even indications that for some types of drugs, regulation may have had a desirable, incentive effect. This is the view of Ashford and Healey who argue that

Regulation may provide the 'hidden foot' which is the impetus for an industry or firm to revise its perception of the strategic alternatives it faces. To the extent that regulation modifies the tacit ground rules within which an industry has operated, it should be a force stimulating rivalry, new entrants, and the search for new technological solutions.[20]

In the second place, it cannot be assumed that the technical standards contained in formal rules are always unilaterally imposed. The perception by business of the need to change its technological course typically precedes the actual promulgation of a regulation. This 'pre-regulation period' can be important for two reasons. Firstly, it allows an industry sufficient time to make technical adjustments, such as developing compliance technologies in anticipation of formal standards. Secondly, industry can capitalize on this previously acquired expertise in order to influence the standards which are subsequently incorporated into formal rules.[21] This has certainly been the pattern in the UK and France, as I shall demonstrate in the next section.

A third and related problem with the transposition of the debate over drug lag is that the constitutional and administrative position, as well as the regulatory practices of European regulatory agencies, are sufficiently different from those of bodies like the FDA as to cast doubts on the relevance of the debate to the British and French experience in the control of drug safety. Regulatory authorities in France and the UK have not generally been forced into the adversarial, juridicized relationship which characterizes the dealings between American firms and the FDA, and which has prolonged the time taken to process applications in the United States.[22] Rather, the relationship is a co-operative or consensual one, which is perceived as being concerned with the resolution of scientific or technical matters to the mutual satisfaction of each side; it is not about the unilateral imposition of a formal set of legal rules on a reluctant group of companies. Indeed, regulatory standards may provide industry with a definite statement of legal requirements, reducing legal uncertainty about the possibility of highly unpredictable liability suits.

I will begin with an analysis of the 'pre-regulatory period', taken as the period up to 1968, when, as I have indicated above, substantial regulatory changes were made to each system. I will also discuss the influence of patterns of government–industry relations, outlined in the previous chapter, on the design of safety regulation.

Pre-regulation and the Origins of Safety Licensing

The origins of the French 'visa' or registration system appeared to owe more to the peculiar structure of the French drug-industry and to the retarded state of French law on patents than to considerations of safety. Chapter 2 discussed the distinctive pattern of development of the French pharmaceutical sector, which, until the Second World War, was dominated by a large number of very small firms, most of which prepared products in the pharmacy dispensary. This structure was itself partly attributable to a prohibition, dating back to 1803, on the sale of 'secret remedies',[23] with the exception of those produced in dispensaries, which were entirely owned and operated by qualified pharmacists.[24] During the inter-war period French exports of fine chemicals and pharmaceuticals grew rapidly, but the country's industrial structure was profoundly unsuited to the commercialization of important new products such as antibiotics, which required large-scale production techniques based on fermentation.[25] The industry association had set up its own registration body to assure buyers of the quality of their products. This was the *Laboratoire nationale de contrôle des médicaments*, which certified products for reimbursement and export purposes on the basis of expert reports. Full protection against cheap imports could only be obtained from government.

The 1941 law which introduced the visa served four broad purposes. Firstly, in order to obtain registration, a product had to be prepared in a French laboratory owned by pharmacists qualified in France. Secondly, although the law recognized industrial pharmacy as a separate professional activity, the corporatist design of the 1941 legislation reinforced the role of the professional associations of pharmacists in the implementation of its provisions.[26] Thirdly, the visa had a 'hybrid character';[27] registration was granted if a product satisfied three conditions—if it was innocuous, of therapeutic interest, and novel. As medicines were not then patentable in France, the inclusion of this last criterion meant that the visa in effect provided the holder with the very protection from imitation that patent law had denied.[28] Fourthly and finally, it aimed to promote safety. The obligation to produce scientific data demonstrating safety could easily be avoided, however, especially if a product comprised a combination of substances whose properties were allegedly known.[29] Complex deliberations on the 'novelty' of products made the registration system slow, cumbersome, and contentious. A number of firms attempted, unsuccessfully, to challenge its legality in the administrative courts.[30] In the meantime, the industry continued to use its own certification system to facilitate exports to the franc zone.

The combined impact of the visa system and the rigorous controls on pharmacy ownership was to ensure that a large number of small domestic firms were shielded from competition from imports. They could also produce a vast number of essentially similar products, this situation being further aggravated by the system of price control, reviewed in Chapter 3, and by subsequent legislative measures on generics. A law of 1946 limited the visa holder's monopoly to 6 years, after which copies could be registered and reimbursed automatically, as long as they were marketed under their generic name plus the name of the maker.[31]

The eventual reform of the visa system in 1959 and the introduction of a special patent for medicines marked an important victory for the French pharmaceutical industry's association, which had campaigned vigorously for a separate system of industrial property protection. The novelty test was suppressed, and the criteria for award of a new visa were limited to safety and therapeutic interest. As a method of product-safety regulation, however, the new visa offered few significant improvements. A ministerial instruction of 1960 offering the official interpretation of the new legislation indicated that applications would be processed as quickly as possible so that the economic interests of the industry would be respected. No provision was made for any form of official/risk benefit analysis or for the elaboration of an official doctrine of therapeutic effect, this task being assigned to the experts. The instruction also indicated that the term 'therapeutic interest' would be interpreted in a manner which would not impede the economic progress of the firm. Although the visa was granted for an indefinite period, no provision was made for post-marketing surveillance of a product's adverse effects.

In reality the new system was simply an official incorporation of industry's own informal system of safety vetting. Its purpose remained primarily protectionist. Having obtained a visa, a firm could only commence manufacture if it also secured an *autorisation de débit* (manufacturing authorization) from the French pharmaceutical inspectorate. Companies not established in France and not therefore amenable to the jurisdiction of the inspectorate could not market their products. Importation of finished products was not a legally recognized activity,[32] and so trade was restricted to active ingredients or intermediate products.[33]

The early safety regulations functioned as a protective façade behind which French industry developed in an uneven and not particularly efficient fashion. As such, they complemented the system of price control. Their implementation was primarily tailored to the industry's short-term economic priorities, including the evasion of the impact of restrictive price-controls discussed in Chapter 3. Firms frequently withdrew products from the market only to remarket a modified version under another name in order to obtain a higher price. Such tactics might well have run aground but for the loophole in the 1945 legislation, which provided for a mere registration system for products comprising known substances.[34]

Self-regulation and product safety in the United Kingdom

The introduction of comprehensive licensing controls in the UK could not be described as necessarily inimical to industry's interests, even if the eventual legal form which the system assumed—that is, a licensing authority with extensive statutory powers—did not conform to the ABPI's initial intentions. As an export-oriented sector, it was already familiar with the safety requirements of other jurisdictions. In 1959 the ABPI had advocated the creation of an independent voluntary trust to vet products,[35] a concept which made some impression on the Joint Standing Committee on Health (chaired by Lord Cohen) to which the government had referred the entire safety issue following the Thalidomide tragedy.

Lord Cohen published an interim report in 1962 and a final report in 1963.[36] Although its members had agreed that it was neither desirable nor practicable to transfer entire responsibility for safety testing to a central authority, they had been divided on the nature of the powers to be attributed to the regulatory body which they proposed should scrutinize data supplied by industry. Some favoured the ABPI's voluntaristic solution, while others contended that public concern could only be alleviated by the creation of a government-appointed body with statutory licensing powers. A compromise was reached in Lord Cohen's final report: an interim system of voluntary control, administered by an *ad hoc* body of scientific experts—the Committee on the Safety of Drugs (CSD)— was brought into operation in 1964 and was to be replaced by a statutory scheme after a trial period of 2 or 3 years. Safety issues also fell within the terms of reference of the Sainsbury inquiry into the relations between government and industry, discussed in Chapter 3.[37]

The voluntary system worked well in practice. The CSD paid repeated tribute to industry's willing co-operation and compliance. Even if the CSD or the Minister lacked the statutory powers to prevent the sale of an unsafe product, the industry could not afford to risk the ire of its largest customer. A ministerial circular warned doctors against prescribing any product marketed without the CSD's approval.[38] For its part, the ABPI undertook to ensure the co-operation of its members and, on receipt of a complaint from the CSD, would bring informal pressure to bear.[39] By its terms of reference, the CSD, or Dunlop Committee as it came to be known, was entrusted with the task of establishing safety, quality, and efficacy, although no particular meaning had been ascribed to the latter term. The Committee consequently divided its work between three subcommittees corresponding to the stages in the testing of a new drug: toxicity in animal studies, clinical trials and efficacy, adverse reactions from marketed products. The first two committees demanded fairly extensive documentation, summarizing a series of elaborate tests. They met monthly and were staffed by external experts. Administrative back-up was provided by a small secretariat at the Ministry of Health. With an average of over 600 applications to process each year, considerable trust had to be placed in the reliability of the data compiled by industry.

This high level of co-operation undoubtedly played an important role, firstly in the formulation of technical standards, and secondly in their method of implementation. The British authorities depended on industry, via the ABPI, to play an active role in the setting of safety standards. After all, no one had much experience to call on and, as one member of the CSD observed '[we] felt we were running a research unit rather than a quango'.[40]

On its own initiative, the ABPI had set up its own study group on clinical trials in 1962. The incumbent Minister of Health, Enoch Powell, gave an undertaking that in return for this group's collaboration with the CSD, the ABPI would have access to the Committee at all times and would be invited to participate in the evaluation of criteria by which safety factors would be assessed.[41] The strategic importance of this collaboration cannot be overstated. Firstly, it affected the distribution of work between the CSD subcommittees, so that the emphasis was on processing applications rather than monitoring safety. As a former chairman, Wade later recalled:

Looking back I see only one error in our performance. We were so aware of the enormous co-operation we received from the drug industry that the main Committee made every effort it could to see that the submissions from firms were handled as quickly as possible—as a result, Frazer's sub-committee (on Toxicity) and Hunter's sub-committee (on clinical trials and efficacy) had a much higher priority for staff than did the Adverse Reactions sub-committee, and I think the work of that committee suffered.[42]

Secondly, it influenced the Dunlop Committee's interpretation of its terms of reference. The latter quickly displayed its unwillingness to take up the interventionist mantle as arbiter of efficacy.[43] At the ABPI's suggestion, the CSD introduced an abridged, less rigorous procedure to speed up the process of licensing products containing known or established substances.

The obvious success of the CSD (products were marketed without approval on only two occasions) and its relative speed and flexibility meant that voluntary co-operation and negotiated standards were elevated to the status of a model regulatory relationship. The Labour government's 1967 White Paper, introducing Cohen's proposed statutory scheme, promised to preserve at least the spirit of co-operation and informality, even if the regulatory relationship would be cast in a different legal form.

The introduction of a statutory licensing system with sanctions necessarily involves making detailed requirements with regard to the particulars to be supplied, the conditions to be satisfied, the provisions attached to licenses and the circumstances in which licenses can be refused or revoked, but the intention is to retain the flexible administration which has been so effective under the voluntary scheme ... with cooperation and mutual confidence, legal proceedings should be exceptional.[44]

The subsequent Medicines Bill, however, incorporated a number of key changes advocated in the Sainsbury Report which threatened to make further inroads into the industry's commercial autonomy. Its Parts V and VI, on the regulation of labels, leaflets, and promotion, will be examined in detail in Chapter 8. Part I, which dealt with the proposed Medicines Commission and the expert committees, stipulated that the Commission would be primarily an advisory, appellate body and not, as the Sainsbury Report had recommended, an independent executive and regulatory authority. That report had also recommended that the Commission draw up and implement a British Classification of Medicines, based on efficacy,[45] but the fate of this proposal was not decided until the second reading of the Bill.[46]

The thorny issue of therapeutic efficacy had meanwhile surfaced on another front. In 1963 a new committee—the MacGregor Committee—replaced the former Joint Standing Committee on Prescribing. Its task was to classify products with a view to encouraging economy in prescribing. It recommended that a fundamental distinction should be made between drugs containing a single active ingredient with an acceptable degree of efficacy and those containing a fixed ratio of active substances, the so-called 'fixed-combination drugs', which were only to be made available in limited circumstances.

The ABPI had vigorously opposed this system of classification but had not convinced the Minister to abandon it. Paradoxically, the passage of the Medicines Bill gave the Association a renewed opportunity to lobby against it. The Minister had already assured the industry that the new efficacy test would not be a comparative one,[47] and at a subsequent meeting the ABPI impressed upon the Minister the redundancy, from the point of view of any benefit to doctors engaged in prescribing, of any further system of classification based on efficacy. The MacGregor Committee was abolished. The Conservative opposition secured an amendment to the Bill 'to put it beyond doubt' that comparative efficacy would not be a determining factor in licensing decisions, although the government modified the wording at the report stage of the Bill to ensure that comparative efficacy could still be taken into account where product safety was concerned.[48] The threat of comparative classifications or tests appeared to have been neutralized, and it was not until 1973 that the CSD's successor, the CSM, began to demand some positive evidence of efficacy.[49] When the Act came into force in 1971, some 30,000 products already on the market were granted automatic licences of right, without any requirement to substantiate the claims made for them.

A comparison of the pre-regulatory periods in the UK and France

There are evident similarities between the legal nature of the 'pre-regulatory' period that preceded the introduction of product-safety licensing in the UK and France and the approach to price control discussed in Chapter 3. In the UK the preference was once more for self-regulation and informal co-operation between the industry and the CSD. In France a formal system of registration emerged at a much earlier date, but its primary aim was protectionist rather than regulatory. The visa system itself formed only part of an extensive regulatory framework. In France, unlike the UK, some form of licence or permit was required at every stage of manufacturing, wholesaling, and distribution.[50] The award of any one of these licences was made dependent on the presence in the licensed firm of a fully qualified, licensed pharmacist, originally in the capacity of owner[51] but later in various *postes de direction*, including that of managing director.[52] These rules, a product of the dispensary-based origins of the French pharmaceutical industry, were eventually reformed in 1968 to bring French law into line with that of the EC,[53] but they are nevertheless typical of French regulatory law and practice, founded on the notion of a unilateral *autorisation de police* in the public interest.[54] In exchange for carefully regulated monopoly rights, the pharmacy profession was expected to execute its activities in the public interest and to assume legal responsibility for them.[55] In essence, the nascent pharmaceutical industry was assimilated into this decentralized regime of control, originally designed for dispensing chemists. The pharmacist gave way to the concept of the 'expert', itself an invention of industry, allowing for a certain continuity of the passive, decentralized style of safety control which typified the earlier visa regime.

The early British system, although voluntary, involved a *centralized* elaboration of standards, so that in practical terms the transition to a statutory licensing regime did not involve a major change in regulatory philosophy. In addition, the industry had participated actively in the process of setting standards. There are obvious parallels with the early licensing controls and the self-regulatory approach to price control reviewed in Chapter 3. This pre-regulatory period undoubtedly allowed the industry, through extensive co-operation, to extend and consolidate a similar relationship of interdependence with government. At the same time, however, even at this early stage important differences in national approaches to safety control were evident. As we shall see in the following sections, the centralizing tendencies inherent in the British system have developed further, creating potentially greater problems for British-based firms. Their French counterparts have not had to confront a similar proactive or anticipatory system of regulation.

The Administration of Product-Safety Regulation: A Case of Regulatory Capture?

Even if its support for some form of pre-marketing regulation endures, industry must endeavour to ensure that the regime does not become too onerous, or intrude unduly on its commercial freedom. National governments, always attentive to the international competitiveness of their home-based firms, are constrained to ensure that their regulatory regimes, while guaranteeing certain standards in the public interest, are not unduly burdensome to the industry. Once again the regulator is faced with the search for policy trade-offs, and with the need to balance and bargain.

In practice the implementation of the three basic concepts of modern drug-regulation, discussed in the first section of this chapter, appears eminently susceptible to bargaining. The concepts of safety, quality, and efficacy are relative rather than absolute; no product can be completely without risk. Regulatory authorities are therefore involved in a risk/benefit analysis. Perceptions of risk and benefit must, inevitably, change over time, as regulatory knowledge and expertise develop. Initial reluctance to introduce the contentious concept of comparative therapeutic efficacy into the risk/benefit equation may partly be explained by gaps in the relevant scientific knowledge.[56] That a status quo has apparently been maintained, however, despite the gradual accrual of the necessary expertise to execute comparative efficacy tests, would suggest that deference to industry's commercial freedom appears to have prevented current use of such tests. In the remainder of this chapter I examine the mechanisms by which the apparent maintenance of this status quo has been accomplished.

Exponents of the various forms of capture theory discussed in Chapter 1 identify three particular factors which may act as vehicles or incentives for an agency's identification with the interests of its client group, and therefore for the maintenance of the status quo. Firstly, the role of key personnel in the agency may facilitate the assimilation of the interests of client groups;[57] secondly, excessive reliance on data supplied by industry, to the exclusion of that compiled independently or supplied by other interest groups, may contribute to a pro-industry bias;[58] finally, the extent of the regulatory authority's isolation or autonomy from related government departments or personnel may contribute to capture by its clientele. I will examine the present organizational structure of the French and British licensing authorities and their decision-making processes and consider whether 'incentives' to capture are present in each system.

The licensing process in UK

Under the 1968 Act, the licensing authority in the UK is legally constituted by the Minister for Health.[59] The administrative aspects of product licensing are now executed by the Medicines Division at the DHSS, which also handles applications for manufacturing and wholesale licenses. In addition, the Division advises the Minister on the exercise of his or her considerable powers to issue regulations and orders under the Act. This Division, comprising some 320 staff, processes all licence applications, which must be submitted to it, in approved form, in the first instance.

The prospect of future, and usually more lucrative, employment with the firms is often seen as an incentive for civil servants to identify with industry and eventually to seek jobs there. The Medicines Division has always suffered from chronic shortages of skilled staff. The most famous case of 'keeper turned poacher' was the move by a former Permanent Secretary at the Medicines Division, John Griffin, to the directorship of the ABPI. It is also highly autonomous from other divisions within the DHSS which have pharmaceutical responsibilities. The complexity of its licensing and regulatory tasks, as well as the commercial confidentiality attached to much of the information with which it deals, has perhaps in itself fostered a close identification with the interests of its clientele group. Relations between the Division and the industry are generally conceded to be good, and many firms acknowledge the willingness of Department officials to give informal advice on applications.[60]

If a product application is not a 'minor one'—that is, if it relates to a new chemical entity or a new presentation, or if it raises particular problems—the application is referred to the Committee on the Safety of Medicines, an advisory body set up under the Medicines Act 1968.[61] The Committee is made up of nineteen external experts drawn from various branches of medical science, who are appointed for a period of 4 years. The Medicines Division receives annually an average of 1,000 applications for product licenses (PLs), of which the CSM considers 150 on average. The CSM in turn works through four special subcommittees.

If the CSM advises that a licence should not be granted, the company may appeal to another advisory body, the Medicines Commission, which comprises external, medically qualified experts, as well as four industrialists and two members with legal qualifications. The Commission is responsible for advising on general policy matters, including proposed regulatory developments.[62] Although this body may recommend that a particular licence should not be issued, the final decision rests with the Minister, and should he or she propose to reject an application contrary to the advice of the CSM, there is the possibility of a further appeal to a 'person appointed' for that purpose.[63] The applicant has the opportunity to make written submissions or to appear in person at any stage of the appeal process,[64] but the Act makes no provision for public hearings to which rival producers or consumer groups might be invited, except in the case of the 'person appointed' procedure.[65] This procedure has been used on one occasion following the Minister's equivocation over the CSM's recommendation for a PL for Upjohn's long-term contraceptive drug Depo-Provera. The company chose to exercise its right to hold the hearing in public, and although consumer and health groups were invited to attend and submit written evidence, the 'person appointed' refused to allow either the presentation of oral evidence or the cross-examination of witnesses.[66]

It is often argued that one of the factors contributing to the relative flexibility of the British approach to safety regulation and to the comparative speed with which decisions are taken is the small size of its permanent bureaucracy and the permeation of independent medical expertise via these various permanent and *ad hoc* committees.[67] On the other hand, critics of the system argue that these experts are not in fact independent but are all too frequently in the current or past employ of the industry. In 1986, for example, five members of the Medicines Commission were drawn from the pharmaceutical industry, while at least four members of the CSM held consultancies with drug companies. Moreover, as Collier argues, it 'can safely be assumed that almost all the physicians on the committees will have worked with the drug companies on research projects'.[68] Indeed, following controversy over the independence of a former chairman of the CSM, who had been involved in research on, as well as the subsequent licensing of, benaxoprofen, an antirheumatic product which is alleged to have produced considerable adverse effects in elderly patients, the DHSS proposed that members of the Committee declare their connections with the industry in a public register.[69]

It is clear from the above description of the British licensing procedures that the Medicines Division is dependent on scientific and technical data supplied by companies, data which at no stage in the procedure can be challenged by third parties. It has no independent testing or laboratory facilities of its own.

French safety-regulation: The role of the expert

A general bias towards client identification by regulatory bodies has been well documented in French studies on government and industry relations. Divisions of ministries are traditionally highly autonomous in comparison to their British counterparts.[70] Interchange of personnel between government and industry occurs frequently in France. The phenomenon of *pantouflage*, the movement of senior civil servants into industry and perhaps back into public service through employment in a ministerial cabinet (private office), is seen by many commentators as a key to understanding the development of close links and shared understandings between government and industry.[71] It is not entirely unknown in the Ministry of Health.

There are, however, two distinctive features of the administration of product-safety control which suggest that organizational factors are of particular importance in this area of government activity. In the first place, the *Direction de la pharmacie et du médicament* (DPHM) at the Ministry of Health is especially self-contained. It is administratively responsible for every aspect of pharmaceutical regulation, and not just matters relating to product safety. The DPHM is, however, much smaller than the Medicines Division and has a permanent staff of just over 30, who are responsible for its entire range of administrative tasks. This can be explained by the second feature of the French system: applications for marketing authorizations are generally assessed 'out of house' by specially appointed experts and rapporteurs.

The tradition of the expert, which dates back to the 1941 legislation discussed in the second section of this chapter, is a major difference between the British and French approaches to safety regulation.[72] The expert's original role was to furnish the Ministry of Health with documentary evidence to support the manufacturer's claims for his product's qualities. The objectivity of these reports was assumed, rather than guaranteed by any legal provisions prohibiting financial inducements and so on. The expert, who was not necessarily specialized in any particular branch of medicine, was selected and paid by the firm, and the form and method by which the visa application was validated was left entirely to his or her discretion.

The expert has remained central to the French procedure of product authorization. Reforms in 1959 introduced the concept of the *expert agréé*—that is, an expert nominated and remunerated by the firm but selected from a general list of recognized experts established by the Ministry of Health.[73] In theory these reforms provided for greater central direction over safety controls. Prior to the issue of a visa, reports were scrutinized by an informal advisory body, the *Commission du visa*, which could appoint specialist rapporteurs to advise on individual applications. In practice this commission made no attempt to design test protocols or to guide the experts' work, nor was there any real control over the objectivity of the latter. The Commission lacked the administrative resources and the political weight necessary to conduct a sufficiently thorough critique.[74]

The adoption of EEC directive 65/65 forced the Ministry to abandon its traditional passive approach and to adopt a more interventionist stand. An ordinance of 1967[75] replaced the old visa with a new marketing authorization (*autorisation de mise sur le marché*—AMM), and a series of subsequent decrees[76] introduced for the first time officially designed, if highly generalized, test protocols. Experts were officially recognized as competent to perform only particular types of test, depending on their specialism, and could no longer be nominated by firms as general experts. The names of the designated experts were to be notified in advance of testing, putting an end to the widespread practice of only using favourable expert reports in support of an application.[77]

A new advisory committee, with statutory powers, the *Commission d'autorisation de mise sur le marché des médicaments* (Commission on Marketing Authorizations),[78] replaced the informal commission. It now comprises twenty-eight members, drawn primarily from the medical profession; in addition, two representatives of the industry, one consumer representative, and a representative of the health insurance funds may participate in deliberations but may not vote. Article R.5141–2 CSP denies full membership to anyone who is in receipt of payment or who benefits financially, directly or indirectly, from the industry. The AMM Commission, unlike the CSM, considers all applications for product licences, however minor. In consequence, it deals annually with about 500 original applications and 1,700 applications for modification. It also deals with the review of existing licences. The Commission was set up 'to pursue an active policy in licensing',[79] but companies still nominate and pay experts of their own choice to prepare the licensing application. The Commission may appoint its own rapporteurs and experts to examine and verify individual applications.[80]

While these reforms were undoubtedly a step in the direction of more centralized control, a number of important lacunae remained. The independence of the experts was doubtful, and allegations of corruption were not unknown. Although a decree of 1972 specified that experts could not be salaried employees of the firm seeking marketing authorization, this provision was never enforced, and it was eventually abolished in 1979.[81] The Minister, who retains ultimate responsibility for licensing decisions, may now also appoint his or her own experts, the *experts désignés*, to examine files. Three separate lists of *experts agréés* are now maintained. Depending on the nature of their expertise, the latter are authorized to validate only certain types of tests.[82] Test protocols have been greatly tightened up.

Despite the shift towards centralization and the technical improvements made over the last decade, the expert, who is usually an employee of the applicant, remains pivotal in the French system. Although the 1979 law prohibits an expert from having any direct or indirect financial connection with the marketing of the product, there seems nothing to prevent him or her from holding shares in, or being employed by, the firm concerned. Even if the Ministry and the Commission now appoint their own experts and rapporteurs, the force of circumstance created by the rather backward state of clinical research in France implies that these must be drawn from a restricted pool which has established ties with industry. An official rapporteur on one AMM request may also act as an expert for a company in another application. In this way, close co-operative links between industry and the administration are maintained.[83]

It will be readily apparent that in the French licensing system not only is the industry the primary source of all data supplied to the licensing authority, but the latter, unlike its British counterpart, has insufficient centralized resources to process that data. The experts themselves undertake the tests, on the basis of a contract of employment with the applicant firm, are responsible to that firm for the execution of their tasks,[84] and are obliged to maintain a high degree of confidentiality.[85]

Finally, it should be added that although consumer representatives and other non-medical experts participate in the licensing process via their membership of the AMM Commission, hearings and appeals against a refusal to recognize an expert[86] or to refuse[87] or revoke[88] an AMM are never held in public.

Although extensive provision is made for a *recours gracieux* or administrative review,[89] and for a subsequent *recours contentieux* or judicial review of a decision to refuse[90] or revoke[91] an AMM, the AMM Commission has in fact developed its own system of informal hearings, involving a number of its own members, the applicant, and the experts and representatives of the DPHM. The Commission has stressed the importance of this development:

La Commission considère comme prioritaire l'établissement d'une concertation permanente avec l'Industrie Pharmaceutique pour définir une politique du médicament ... Outre les recours gracieux prévus par la réglementation de nombreux échanges de vue ont eu lieu aux diverses étapes d'instruction d'un dossier entre les responsables des laboratoires et les membres de la Commission et ses rapporteurs.[92]

Incentives for 'agency capture' undoubtedly exist in the British and, more especially, the decentralized French regime. Nevertheless, it is difficult to reconcile the notion of a 'captured agency' with the increased density and growing complexity of legal norms governing the manufacture, distribution, sale, and marketing of pharmaceutical products. The French CSP alone contains some 100 'legislative' articles, supplemented by almost 1,000 executive provisions. Capture theory fails on three further counts. Firstly, it cannot explain why the various 'incentives' to capture were initially incorporated into the licensing framework, or why such strikingly different national approaches have been evolved. Secondly, it cannot explain why these differences have persisted. The enduring place of the expert in the French system is the most obvious example. Sporadic instances of *pantouflage*, 'revolving doors' between civil service and industry, or occasional links between industry and advisory committees do not in themselves provide conclusive evidence of capture, nor do they explain the predominance of a particular

approach to implementation. At most, these processes are suggestive of client identification, but not necessarily of client influence.
Thirdly, as capture theory focuses primarily on actors within
national agencies, it offers little scope for an understanding of
'external' developments, in this case the adoption of a series of
directives at European level. A more nuanced approach is needed,
based on an analysis of the way in which each regulatory framework has functioned to accommodate the type of bargaining and
policy trade-offs which have been necessary to ensure that the
implementation of this increasingly complex body of legislation on
product safety has not been entirely inimical to industry's interests.

The Licensing Systems in Operation

On the basis of the discussion, in the second section of this chapter,
of the origins of the two systems, it might legitimately be concluded
that despite profound differences in the legal origins and form of
safety regulation, each system did in fact provide a framework for
the accommodation of industry influence. Nevertheless, these very
differences have proved important, firstly as a source of very different sets of regulatory tensions within each country, and
secondly, and relatedly, in shaping the subsequent development of
each regime. British firms, having contributed to the setting-up of a
more vigorous, centralized system of controls in 1968, have been
faced with the task of ensuring that it continues to serve their ends
and that too much power does not accrue to the regulators.
Although the industry continues to make an active contribution at
the level of general issues relating to licensing policy—usually
through liaison between its own *ad hoc* working parties and official
bodies—it does not enjoy the same input into individual licensing
decisions as its French counterparts; product, clinical trial, and
manufacturing licences are all subject to formal regulation. At the
same time, many important aspects of manufacture and marketing
remain subject to a variety of forms of self-regulation by the
industry.[93] On the one hand, it is possible to find 'mandated self-
regulation',[94] as in the case of advertising, where the ABPI—subject
to government approval—drafts, monitors, and enforces its own
code of practice.[95] On the other hand, there are a number of non-
binding instruments used by the Department of Health to regulate
certain aspects of testing and manufacture. Codes of good laboratory

practice or good manufacturing practice, for example, have been drawn up by the DHSS, in concertation with the industry, but are policed in the first instance by the individual firm, whose compliance is in turn monitored by the Department's Medicines Inspectorate. In addition, mention should be made of the various codes of practice or guidance notes drawn up by the industry association without any active or formal input from the governmental authorities. Self-regulation by the industry of Phase IV clinical trials, reviewed in Chapter 8, is an example of this form of control.

The more decentralized French approach to product licensing and to risk/benefit analysis was frequently characterized as inefficient and too lenient. Its modernization has not only been required by more recent developments in European law but has been actively welcomed by French industry as necessary to improve the standing of its products on export markets.

Two case-studies

The durability of the early patterns of regulatory interdependence has been put to the test by a number of developments, including the increasingly stringent requirements of European law and the accretion of the skill and expertise of national regulators.

In the first place, the adoption of the second EEC directive, 75/319, required further adjustments at the national level.[96] The Commission's plans to introduce automatic mutual recognition of national licences had in fact met with considerable opposition from the member states. As I have indicated, the first directive, 65/65, was concerned only with the initial harmonization of administrative procedures. A second draft directive was aimed at achieving the harmonization of the substantive evaluation criteria on which licences were to be based, while a third draft laid down the basis for an automatic mutual recognition procedure.[97] Negotiations were blocked for almost a decade, largely because of the substantial divergence in national regulation of the pharmacy profession, whose members were to play a key role as designated 'experts' in the draft directives. Furthermore, West Germany—the largest pharmaceutical producer in the EC—proved reluctant to abandon its own liberal system unless the other member states agreed to introduce automatic mutual recognition simultaneously with the Commission's proposed stricter requirements on testing. The remaining original five member states, reluctant to abandon their own protectionist systems, advocated a more gradual harmonization, to allow time for adjustment to the new licensing procedures. The deadlock was finally broken in 1973, prior to the UK's entry into the EC, when the Commission proposed to postpone the adoption of the procedure for mutual recognition, to drop a further proposed draft directive on advertising, but to combine the remainder of the second and third drafts into the so-called second directive, 75/319, on proprietary medical products of May 1975. An additional directive, 75/318, laid down the basis for harmonized general standards and protocols to be incorporated into clinical tests and trials.[98] Directive 75/319 made provision for experts to prepare reports which would assess the results of the tests specified in broad terms in 75/318 (Article 2).

As a further step towards mutual recognition, Chapter IV of the directive laid down various general principles for manufacturers' licences, thus eliminating the practice of systematic checks on quality on all products manufactured in another member state. Finally, Article 39(2) required the progressive application of the directive to products already on the market by 1990. This provision in effect required each member state to *review* and update the documentation submitted in support of licences issued prior to 1975. The manner in which this was to be undertaken was, however, left entirely to the discretion of the member states, the Council having originally failed to agree on an obligatory timetable for the review procedure or on any alternative mechanisms of co-ordination.[99]

The review process in the UK and France

To comply with these provisions, British products awarded an automatic licence of right in 1971 had to be subject to a full review if they were to remain legally on the market after 1990. Products marketed under the old 'visa' system have also been reviewed in France. I will compare the problems encountered and their attempted resolution in each country.

In the UK a special Committee on the Review of Medicines (CRM) was set up in 1975 to supervise the arrangements made to meet the Community deadline and to examine the documentation which companies were now obliged to supply in support of the claims made for their products. It began its task with a systematic examination of the major therapeutic substances, each of which covered a large number of products. Separate subcommittees scrutinized data culled from scientific publications, supplemented by company data. Provisional general recommendations on the value of the substance were then issued by the Committee. Following a two-month consultation period, a definitive recommendation on the substance was issued as a prelude to the formal review of the individual products in which it was contained. This multi-stage process proved slow and cumbersome. Problems were exacerbated when the CRM proceeded to the review of individual products. Whilst the companies were prepared to co-operate with the CSM in order to obtain a licence, they were understandably reluctant to aid a body which threatened to withdraw, revoke, or vary existing licences. Producing and updating documentation in support of old, well-established products, and conducting tests on these, was a burdensome and expensive task. The CRM was forced to use statutory powers to obtain the information necessary to fulfil its functions,[100] and the firms in turn made considerable use of the statutory procedures for appeal against the CRM's recommendations,[101] further straining the already overstretched resources of the DHSS.

To remedy this situation, the Minister instituted an accelerated review, bypassing the consultation procedure, for products judged by the CRM to present special hazards. Relations between the CRM and the industry finally drifted into 'an adversarial attitude'[102] over the accelerated review of psychotropic drugs. Many of these products were of the fixed-combination variety, and the CRM had expressed considerable doubt over their safety and particularly their efficacy. An unprecedented 200 'Section 28' notices were dispatched, recommending the revocation of licences of right for barbiturates.[103] The British subsidiary of the American multinational Squibb, with the full support of the ABPI, took the highly unusual step of seeking judicial review, on the basis of insufficient justification, of the CRM's decision to revoke the licences for two of its products.[104] Although the company's application for review failed on the somewhat predictable legal ground that as the CRM was only an advisory body, it need not give full reasons for its decision,[105] the judgment itself revealed the extent of the shift in the balance of power which the review process had entailed. The company claimed that the CRM had formed its opinions on the basis of its own internal, secret report on psychotropics, ignoring the company's own oral representations and written data. Because the CRM had taken the therapeutic class to which Squibb's product belonged as its starting-point, it had in fact compared the product with a similar version marketed by a rival manufacturer. The comparative efficacy test had been brought in through a back door. This in turn prompted the company to resort to confrontational tactics and, for the first time in the history of product licensing, to pursue its complaint in the courts.

Although Squibb ultimately lost its case, the government, anxious to avoid further confrontation in the courts and to restore something of the former balance between regulator and regulated, overhauled the review system in late 1981. A special *ad hoc* group comprising scientific experts and ABPI representatives was constituted to review the review procedure. At a time when cuts in public expenditure were holding down staff levels, and efficiency studies were being instituted in most governmental departments, including the DHSS, it was obviously in the interests of both parties to find the quickest and cheapest method of completing the review if the 1990 target date were to be met. The systematic reviews of therapeutic substances ceased, and revocation orders were confined to exceptional cases, so that products could be withdrawn with minimum publicity. Product licences are now reviewed on renewal, in accordance with a two-stage timetable based on numbers of company licences. Although it appears that the review process will be completed in time, it is certainly less rigorous than originally intended. The onus is now on the applicant to produce updated information on safety, based on modern clinical testing methods; efficacy is assumed from the product's past successful marketing record.

In France the review of older products did not commence until 1985, although discussions on how the problem should be approached began in 1980 and the AMM Commission was given responsibility for the *validation* of older products.[106] If the large volume of French medicines, many of which had obtained licences on the basis of little documentation, were to remain on the market after 1990, it was obvious that the review had to be executed with speed and efficiency. A working party comprising representatives of the Commission, the DPHM, and the industry met at regular inter-

vals to identify 'critical problems of mutual interest'.[107] In particular, the industry was concerned that the speed of the review process
would be slowed down if the administration were required to
review and validate data relating to the so-called *médicaments
doux* or herbal remedies, which fall into the widely defined category of a medicinal product but the claims for many of which
cannot be substantiated by modern scientific drug-evaluation techniques. Some 1,100 herbal remedies featured on the list of reimbursable products in 1985.[108] The DPHM has responded, firstly by
postponing the review of a large number of herbal remedies until
1989, and secondly by accepting that a past record of safe usage of
such products should be sufficient justification for continued
marketing, even if efficacy cannot be demonstrated in accordance
with scientific tests.[109]

Products requiring review are divided into three categories. Category I includes drugs registered after 1968 which have obtained an
AMM and for which some data relating to quality, efficacy, and
safety is already on file. These may be validated on the basis of an
abridged application without further scientific study. Category II
comprises older products, licensed under the visa system, whose
files need updating in line with current international standards.
Guide-lines on these standards for different therapeutic groups of
drugs have been defined by one of eleven subcommittees of the
AMM Commission—comprising members of the latter, administrators, and representatives of industry—and have been sent as
monographs to firms, which use them as a basis on which to update
their files. Updated files are then submitted to the AMM Commission, in accordance with a phased timetable,[110] and products are
moved from Category II to I or III. Category III comprises drugs
which do not fulfil the criteria for quality, efficacy, and safety and
which therefore must be removed from the market within a period
of 18 months.[111]

In contrast to what has happened in the UK, the review process in
France has not provoked antagonism from industry, which has co-
operated actively in its design and execution. Again, limited central
administrative resources necessitated such an approach. Further
flexibility has been guaranteed by the fact that, unlike most aspects
of French drug-regulation, the review procedures have not been
embodied in legal rules but have been set out in a series of *avis* and
letters issued by the DPHM to the industry.

Clinical trials

A further illustration of the contrasting performance of the two systems is found in the regulation of the first crucial phases of a product's commercialization—the clinical trial. In the British case, this offers indications of the tensions that have emerged within the more centralized system, and of the way in which the continued reliance on self-regulation has offered a means to their resolution. Clinical trials are conventionally divided into four phases. Phase I involves the initial introduction of drug into man, following toxicological study in animals. Phase II includes early controlled clinical trials on a small number of patients, in order to establish a product's safety and efficacy. Phase III trials are expanded controlled and uncontrolled trials which are intended to yield additional evidence on efficacy and adverse effects. Phase IV or post-marketing trials are used to control adverse effects in a wider section of the population and to determine morbidity and mortality. Regulation of Phases I and II has proved particularly problematic, involving as it does ethical problems, as well as issues of scientific and clinical freedom.

Sections 31 and 32 of the UK Medicines Act regulate Phases II and III.[112] Phase IV, which is partially regulated, will be dealt with in the context of promotion in Chapter 8. The conduct of clinical studies at Phase I, on healthy human volunteers, is not directly regulated under the Medicines Act. Test protocols and results must be submitted in support of an application for a clinical trial certificate (CTC) or a product licence (PL), so that there is, arguably, some a posteriori control. Indeed, the DHSS maintains an informal 'blacklist' of contract laboratories in the UK and elsewhere and will advise companies on the acceptability of proposed trials.[113]

Phases II and III are subject to both statutory and non-statutory controls. On the one hand, the ethical aspects of trial protocols, that is, their medical value and therapeutic justification, are the province of local ethical committees. These are informal advisory bodies set up by hospital authorities. On the other hand, assessment of the safety and efficacy of clinical trials is the task of the Licensing Authority (Section 31(3)), which has wide powers to stipulate the manner and form in which applications must be made, as well as the supporting information to be supplied (Section 36(1)). These two sets of control are therefore supposed to be complementary.

Whereas most European agencies, including the French, only require notification that Phase II and III trials are about to commence, shortly after the introduction of statutory licensing, the British Licensing Authority demanded the submission of increasingly detailed and complex data prior to granting a CTC. By 1979 it was alleged that the average work and time spent on an application was four times greater than required elsewhere in Europe. In 1973 the average application took some 30 weeks to compile and process, but by 1979 this had increased to 130 weeks.[114]

This regulatory burden was allegedly driving research elsewhere, with detrimental effects on the development of clinical pharmacology and industrial R. & D. An estimated 80 per cent of new medicines in the UK were being sent abroad for clinical testing.[115] The publication by the DHSS of stringent new guide-lines on fertility and reproduction studies in 1978[116] prompted renewed protests from the medical profession and the industry. In response, the Conservative Health Minister set up an *ad hoc* working party on clinical-trial data, chaired by Professor Grahame-Smith, a senior member of the CSM. The CSM itself also explored ways of reducing processing time, while an ABPI working group operated in parallel and exchanged papers with the official working party.[117] In his final report, Grahame-Smith suggested that the reasons for delays in processing could be attributed in part to the poor standard of initial applications,[118] but that standards had undoubtedly become more rigid: guide-lines were applied as rules, or at least precedents, a development which a senior ABPI official attributed to the views on pre-clinical testing held by several CSM members.[119] Grahame-Smith largely accepted the ABPI group's recommendation that a phased approach to trial procedures and data submission should be adopted, but suggested in the alternative that the Medicines Division take a more active part in assisting with—as opposed to merely supervising—the compilation of data by industry. The DHSS opted for the former solution,[120] and the clinical trial exemption (CTX) scheme was introduced in March 1981.[121]

Under the CTX scheme, applicants are required to generate the same data as for a CTC, but they need only forward a certified summary of it to the Medicines Division, which, without reference to the CSM, 'negatively vets' the summarized data[122] and can make objections to the proposed trials.[123] If exemption is refused, the application for a full CTC can be made, and this will be referred to the CSM. It would seem that in the period prior to the introduction of the new scheme the Medicines Division was more receptive to industry's interests than the CSM, liberally interpreting a statutory provision exempting doctors from the need to hold a CTC.[124] The number of these applications had increased considerably in the mid-1970s, when the CTC scheme was at its most onerous, but has fallen away following the introduction of the new scheme.[125] The industry acknowledges that this exemption procedure was used as a way of getting around the CTC scheme.[126]

Although direct statutory regulation of Phase I trials has been under discussion for some time in the UK, it has never been introduced. Following the deaths of a number of healthy volunteers in 1982 and 1983, the Health Minister referred the issue to the Royal College of Physicians (RCP), which in turn set up a working party of industry representatives and experts in 1985. The Medicines Commission concluded in its 1984 report that a system of prior notification to the CSM or a registration system would be unwieldy and unduly burdensome for industry and would result in unwarranted constraints on medical and scientific practice. Instead, the combined protection offered by the industry's self-regulatory codes of practice, its guide-lines on compensation, professional medical ethics, and the provisions of the common law were considered to be a sufficient guarantee that a volunteer would not be exposed to undue risk.[127] The RCP's report, published in October 1986, recommended that research companies or other organizations which carry out clinical trials on healthy volunteers should be willing to have their facilities open to inspection, and that physicians involved should declare any financial interest to the DHSS. These suggestions have not been taken further,[128] even although the new CTX scheme puts increased pressure on hospital and local ethics committees, which are entrusted with informally 'vetting' trials on volunteers. The committees protest that they can no longer rely on official assurance that products are reasonably safe.[129] The CTX system puts considerable trust in the individual company, a practice which the industry's critics question. Although there is no firm evidence so far of increased hazard to patients participating in clinical trials,[130] deaths of healthy volunteers have been attributed to the relaxation of regulatory requirements for the later stages of testing.[131] Inspection of research facilities in the USA, where the

FDA enjoys substantial monitoring powers over all four stages of drug testing, has revealed a number of alarming irregularities, even among the more reputable firms.[132]

Clinical trials in France are also divided into four separate stages, but only the execution of Phase III trials by clinical experts are subject to detailed regulations. As mentioned in the previous section, the reforms of the 1970s did not go beyond the requirements of European law, nor perhaps could they, since the French authorities lacked the necessary resources and expertise to draw up their own protocol for standard tests. An *arrêté* of 1976 literally transposed into French law the test protocols annexed to EEC directive 75/318 of 1975. The fact that the directive was taken as a blueprint for control is indicative of the poor quality of clinical research in France, especially in the vital areas of toxicology and clinical pharmacology.[133] The recent introduction of bio-availability and mutagenicity tests, as required by EEC directive 83/570, have created particular difficulties.[134] As late as 1982 there were only two research establishments in France capable of carrying out the full range of tests envisaged in the 1975 directive. The AMM Commission has in fact indicated that the standard of clinical trials and expert reports has not always been sufficiently high to allow for a proper assessment of a product's therapeutic efficacy.[135]

These reforms[136] were deliberately silent, however, on whether controlled clinical tests may be carried out on patients or on healthy volunteers, reflecting the dubious legality of medical experimentation on healthy volunteers in French civil and criminal law. Experimentation other than for the direct therapeutic benefit of the particular subject is technically illegal,[137] so that, strictly speaking, Phase I and II clinical trials are not within the law in France.[138] Many larger firms have preferred to conduct Phase I trials abroad, while the smaller national firms have relied on clandestine tests.[139]

As a result, the development of French clinical pharmacology has suffered. The AMM Commission is forced to rely on expert reports of trials conducted abroad and over which it has no real control, while trials in France are left largely unregulated. The Dangoumau Report, commissioned by the Minister of Health in 1981, revealed the latter type of trial to be relatively widespread but outside the cognizance or control of local hospital ethics committees.[140] On the basis of this report and as a result of recommendations issued by the newly created *Comité consultatif national d'éthique* (National

Advisory Committee on Ethics) in 1984, the Socialist government introduced a bill to legalize medical experimentation on healthy volunteers and to provide for its detailed control. The bill, however, was lost as a result of the change of government in 1986 and has not subsequently been revived.[141] In the meantime, data generated from Phase I and II trials conducted in France are accepted 'unofficially', while the DPHM has concentrated on improving the quality of Phase III trials and has provided financial incentives for the development of specialized research teams at specialized centres throughout France.[142]

A further indication of the persistent passivity of the French system is its very belated efforts to regulate adverse reaction monitoring, or *pharmacovigilance*, for products already on the market. This had been left almost entirely to the private efforts of the medical profession and the industry.[143] A law of 1980 amended Article 605 of the CSP to allow the Minister of Health to regulate adverse reaction monitoring,[144] and, following a detailed critique of the existing system,[145] a new *Commission nationale de la pharmacovigilance* was set up in 1982 to co-ordinate adverse reports, to advise on individual products, and to propose inquiries into groups of drugs.[146] A legal obligation to report all side-effects was not imposed upon industry and doctors until 1984.[147] Once more, the development of a reputable system of adverse reaction monitoring, increasingly viewed internationally as an indispensable adjunct to pre-marketing testing, was considered vital if French exports were to compete on the American and European markets.[148]

Conclusion

Given the divergent development of French and British product-safety regulation reviewed in this chapter, the reader may well ask whether these regimes do in fact represent a continuation of the patterns of price-control regulation, discussed in Chapter 3. The case-studies of development and change in two particular phases of the licensing process illustrate the underlying tensions in the British regulatory system, tensions which were not present in the regulation of prices and are certainly not to be found in French product-control. It is certainly simplistic to characterize UK product-licensing as 'captured'; industry has at most a substantial influence over it. Indeed, the British Licensing Authority has acquired the skill and resources to impose both stricter safety-testing requirements[149] and even, as the early implementation of the review process demonstrated, surrogate comparative efficacy tests, both of which have proved inimical to industry's interests. This is in marked contrast to the DHSS's approach to profit regulation, discussed in the previous chapter. Nevertheless, the nature of the bargaining framework which emerged in the early phase of safety control, and on to which the 1968 Act was superimposed, has nurtured and preserved a degree of interdependence—albeit of a different order from that discussed in Chapter 3. This has allowed the industry, via the offices of the ABPI, not only to persuade the government to alter course on several occasions but also to participate actively in drawing up alternative forms of control, bringing the implementation of the Medicines Act more closely into line with the philosophy of the former voluntaristic system operated by the CSD. A combination of self-regulation and an established tradition of consultation over, as well as participation in, studies evaluating licensing policy has therefore assured British-based firms a considerable influence over the general direction of licensing philosophy, though not over its routine implementation. The British pharmaceutical industry has not been co-opted into the actual processes of decision-making on the licensing of individual products to the same extent as its French counterpart, a factor which perhaps explains the sporadic but recurrent criticism by industry of the British licensing system, and the relative absence of any dissatisfaction on the part of industry with the French scheme.

If the centralized, formal approach to product licensing in the UK contrasts with its system of profit regulation, the same is true for France. Irrespective of the reforms of the 1970s, the French licensing system has continued to be administered, according to the AMM Commission, in an 'esprit incitatif et non répressif'.[150] Informal concertation has developed within the formalistic licensing framework. As the implementation of the review process demonstrates, the AMM Commission has created various working groups, comprising specialists drawn from industry and the medical fields, to develop test procedures and protocols. Informal *groupes de réflexion* of similar composition examine emerging regulatory issues and also make recommendations—for example, on the problems involved in licensing products derived from biotechnological processes.[151]

This approach is to be contrasted with the administration of French price-controls. And yet the very absence of tensions over the implementation of legislation on product safety in France is arguably also evidence of a certain continuity of regulatory style. The French licensing system has never been used as a supplementary method of stimulating competition on the domestic market; surrogate forms of comparative efficacy tests have yet to emerge in France. There are arguably three reasons for this, two of which reflect the particular legal tradition surrounding the implementation of regulation in France as discussed in Chapter 3. Firstly, average prices remained low throughout the 1970s. Secondly, the administration has continued to adopt a largely passive stance on licensing issues, an approach not dissimilar to that taken to price control. Hence it was unlikely to interpret licensing criteria in a way that would involve a more 'activist' approach to regulatory issues. A final and related point is that the fragmentation of regulatory power both between ministries and across the advisory committees, as discussed in Chapter 3, has also produced a strict division of regulatory competences, much in the same way as for price control. As we shall see in Chapter 7, once the AMM Commission had assumed powers under the 1976 legislation to deal with questions of product efficacy in the context of safety regulation, the SNIP successfully convinced the Ministry of Health that the social security reimbursement committee need no longer occupy itself with this issue in relation to product pricing.[152]

Even if there is some evidence of continuity of regulatory styles in the administration of product safety and price regulation in each country, it is important to recognize that the two very different forms of industry participation in product-safety licensing discussed in this chapter are distinct, and that the bargaining frameworks in which matters of safety policy are negotiated are appreciably different from those in which pricing policy is debated. These differences have significant implications for the resolution of the new sets of conflicts which have characterized the process of regulation in the 1980s. In the next Chapter I will seek to demonstrate that the structure of the pharmaceuticals market has gradually altered. Different forms of competition are emerging, creating new tensions with the licensing system, and in turn imposing new strains on the existing patterns of relations between government and industry.

Notes

1. M. Dukes, *The Effects of Drug Regulation* (The Hague: MTP Press, 1985), 7.
2. The Food and Drugs Acts 1909–49 regulated quality and fraudulent claims; the Therapeutic Substances Act 1956 Part I regulated the manufacture, importation, and sale of therapeutic substances the purity or potency of which could not adequately be tested by chemical means. Part II of the Act regulated penicillin and other therapeutic substances, which were capable of causing danger to the health of the community if used without proper safeguards.
3. *Financial Times*, 10 Aug. 1971.
4. H. Teff and C. Munro, *Thalidomide: The legal aftermath*, (Farnborough: Saxon House, 1976).
5. For an account of the early negotiations, which lasted over two years, see Y. Champet, *Revue du Marché Commun*, (1965), 210–19.
6. EEC Council directive 65/65, OJ (1965), no. 22, 369.
7. Art. 1(1) limits the scope of the directive to 'proprietary medicinal products', that is 'any ready-prepared medicinal product placed on the market under a special name in a special pack'.
8. Art. 601, ordonnance 67-827 of 23 Sept. 1967 in JO, 28 Sept. 1967, the full text of which reads: 'Cette autorisation peut être assortie de conditions adéquates. Elle n'est accordée que lorsque le fabricant justifie: (1) Qu'il a fait procéder à la vérification de l'innocuité du produit dans des conditions normales d'emploi et de son intérêt thérapeutique, ainsi qu'à son analyse qualitative et quantitative, (2) Qu'il dispose effectivement d'une méthode de fabrication et de procédés de contrôle de nature à garantir la qualité du produit au stade de la fabrication en série' (Arts. L.601 and R.5136, CSP). Arts. R.5137 and R.5239 on the renewal, suspension, or withdrawal of an AMM use the term *effet thérapeutique*. In fact the terms *intérêt thérapeutique* or *effet thérapeutique* have been used interchangeably in the French legislation since 1968, and most commentators argue that there is no significant difference between them. See I.-M. Auby and F. Coustou, *Droit pharmaceutique*, (Paris: Librairies techniques, 1980), fasc. 34, 10.
9. M. Granat, B. Jordal, and I. Sjoblom, 'The Processing of Applications for the Registration of Medicines in Nordic Countries', *Journal of the Society of Pharmacists*, 1 (1983), 34–44.
10. Although the scope and detail of the French and British regimes have been greatly expanded by ministerial regulation, order, and circular, even these tend to trail behind actual practice and are constantly supplemented by a stream of administrative notices, letters, and guidance notes which flows from the regulatory authority to industry. In France the latter take the form of *avis*, published in the Ministry of

Health's official bulletin, while in the UK developments in departmental practice are notified in the monthly Medicine Act Information Letters (MAIL).

11. D. C. Quantock, 'The effect of regulation on international drug development', in A. W. Harcus (ed.), *Risk and Regulation in Medicine* (London: Association of Medical Advisers in the Pharmaceutical Industry, 1980), 99–108.

12. The study of licensing of cromolyn sodium by Dukes is a rare example (Dukes, *Risk and Regulation*, p. 47). Some studies have attempted more generalized comparisons. For example, in a five-country comparison over the period 1960–81, Hass *et al.* found that, of the new molecules introduced in one or more of these countries, some 68 per cent were marketed in France, only 46 per cent in the UK, and, after some delay, 32 per cent in the USA. They also found that the French and British authorities took about the same time to process a drug application. It was largely as a result of these sorts of studies that French product-safety regulation became tainted with the 'second order' label in comparison to the stricter British and American regimes. A. E. Hass, L. D. McCormick, and S. Aspel, *A Historic Look at Drug Introductions on a Five-Country Market* (Maryland: Food and Drug Administration, 1982).

13. S. Peltzman, 'An Evaluation of Consumer Legislation', *Journal of Political Economy*, 81 (1973), 1046–91.

14. Details of the amount of paperwork submitted in support of a product licence, which runs to several thousand pages, can be found in *R. v. Licensing Authority, ex parte Smith, Kline and French Laboratories* [1988] 3 CMLR 301.

15. D. Taylor, *British Medicines Research* (London: ABPI, 1988).

16. L. Langle and R. Occelli, 'Le coût d'un nouveau médicament', *Journal de l'économie médicale*, 1 (1983), no. 2, 113–21.

17. M. N. Baily, 'Research and Development Cost and Returns: The US Pharmaceutical Industry', *Journal of Political Economy*, 80 (1972), 70–85.

18. R. Chew, T. Smith, and N. Wells, *Pharmaceuticals in Seven Nations* (London: Office of Health Economics, 1985), 28.

19. D. Kennedy, *A Calm Look at Drug Lag* (Maryland: Food and Drug Administration, 1981).

20. N. A. Ashford and G. R. Heaton, 'Regulation and Technological Innovation in the Chemical Industry', *Law and Contemporary Problems*, 46 (1983), 115.

21. Massachusetts Institute of Technology Center for Policy Alternatives, 'Environmental/Safety Regulation and Technological Change in the US Chemical Industry' (Cambridge, Mass.: MIT, 1979).

22. P. Quirk, 'The FDA', in J. Wilson (ed.), *The Politics of Regulation* (New York: Basic Books, 1980), 138–69. J. E. S. Parker, 'Regulating Pharmaceutical Innovation', *Food, Drug and Cosmetic Law Journal*, (1977), 163–79.

23. That is, products not approved for government purchase. Unfortunately, the government rarely purchased medicines, and although the term lacked meaningful definition, the commercialization of 'patent medicines' was nevertheless technically illegal. Any agreement relating to their sale was therefore a nullity. By some quirk of fiscal law, these same illegal products were made subject to a tax in 1916, a contradiction which was exploited to the full by the emergent industry and was eventually remedied by the *de facto* legalization of the sale to the public of all products prepared and packaged in advance (decree of 13 July 1926).

24. The courts had declared 'mixed' companies to be invalid: Cass. 21 June 1943, *Recueil Sirey*, D.1808.

25. L. F. Haber, *The Chemical Industry 1900–1930* (Oxford: Clarendon Press, 1981), 83; J. Sigvard, *L'Industrie du médicament* (Paris: Calmann-Levy, 1975), 75.

26. The *exposé de motifs* stated that Part II of the legislation was aimed at the 'réorganisation corporative et administrative de l'État français': Esmein, *Gazette du Palais*, (1941) 2 Dec.

27. P. Rougevin-Banville, *Droit social*, (1959), 518–24.

28. Art. 41 and ministerial instruction of 30 Aug. 1943.

29. Stalinon, Tribunal Correctionnel de la Seine. 19 Dec. 1957. *Gazette du Palais*, (1957) no. 257, n. Gollety.

30. Conseil d'État 4 Dec. 1954, Société des Laboratoires Geigy, *Recueil Dalloz*, (1955), J.130.

31. Law of 22 May 1946. In addition, pharmacists could sell certain products by generic name only under their own guarantee (*sous cachet*) at any time.

32. Art. 596 CSP.

33. OECD, *Gaps in Technology* (Paris: OECD, 1969), 43, for figures on exports and imports between 1955 and 1966.

34. This was essentially the reason that the drug Stalinon slipped through the 'visa' controls without examination of its supporting documentation; loc. cit.

35. ABPI, *Annual Report 1959–60*, (London: ABPI, 1961), 8.

36. Ministry of Health, *Final Report of the Joint Standing Committee on Prescribing* (London: HMSO, 1963).

37. Lord Sainsbury, *Report of the Committee of Enquiry into the Relationship of the Pharmaceutical Industry with the NHS*, Cmnd. 3410 (London: HMSO, 1967).

38. Committee on the Safety of Drugs, *Annual Report for the year ending 1964* (London: HMSO, 1965).
39. Committee on the Safety of Drugs, *Annual Report for the year ending 1969* (London: HMSO, 1970).
40. O. L. Wade, 'The Review of Medicines', in BIRA, *Fifth Annual Symposium on Regulatory Affairs* (London: BIRA, 1984), 4.
41. ABPI, *ABPI Yearbook 1962–63* (London: ABPI, 1963), 11.
42. 'The Review of Medicines', p. 3.
43. See D. Dunlop, 'The Assessment of the Safety of Drugs and the Role of Government in their Control', *Journal of Clinical Pharmacology* (1967) July–Aug., 184–92.
44. Cmnd. 3397 (London: HMSO, 1967), para. 143.
45. Sainsbury Report, Cmnd. 3410, p. 81.
46. R. Lang, *The Politics of Drugs*, (Farnborough: Saxon House, 1974), 274.
47. ABPI, *Annual Report 1967–68* (London: ABPI, 1968), 9.
48. Hansard, 20 June 1968, vol. 766, cols. 1433–40.
49. Committee on the Safety of Medicines, *Annual Report for the year ending 1972* (London: HMSO, 1973), 6.
50. Law of 11 Sept. 1941, incorporated in 1951 into the Code de la pharmacie and in 1953 into arts. L.596–600 and arts. R.5105–5116 of the CSP.
51. The ordinance of 23 May 1945 stipulated that registered pharmacists must retain the majority shareholding in any firm engaged in production, wholesaling, or distribution. These provisions were modified by a decree law of 20 May 1955 which abolished the majority rule for companies with a capital of over 50 million (old) francs.
52. The ordinance of 4 Feb. 1959 required that qualified pharmacists should constitute a majority on the firm's administrative council. A decree of 13 Sept. 1961 substantially altered this rule and reduced the statutory number of pharmacists on the council to two. The requirement that the PDG (*président-directeur général*) had to be a qualified pharmacist was also abolished. This decree was subsequently challenged by the Conseil national de l'ordre des pharmaciens on the grounds that art. L.596 of the CSP provided that companies had to remain under the *control* of pharmacists. The decree was annulled by the Conseil d'État as an abuse of power (*excès de pouvoir*). CE 17 Dec. 1965, Conseil nationale de l'ordre des pharmaciens et Monsieur Vigan, *Recueil Lebon*, 698.
53. Ordinance of 23 Sept. 1967.
54. A. de Laubadère, *Traité de droit administratif*, 1, 8th edn. (Paris: Librairie générale de droit et de jurisprudence, 1980), no. 560, 347; E. Picarde, 'La notion de police administrative', thesis Université de Paris II, 1978).

55. See V. J. Moreau 'De l'interdiction faite à l'autorité de police d'utiliser une technique d'ordre contractuel', *l'Actualité juridique (Droit administratif)*, 1 (1965), 3.

56. Dukes, points out that it was not until the mid-1960s that the growth of clinical pharmacology during the 1960s and 1970s both demonstrated the inadequacy of existing evidence and provided the tools with which to determine whether a drug was truly effective in man or not. *The Effects of Drug Regulation*, p. 12.

57. Quirk, 'The FDA', pp. 138–69.

58. R. Baldwin and C. McCrudden (eds.), *Regulation and Public Law* (London: Weidenfeld and Nicolson, 1987), 10.

59. Medicines Act 1968, sect. 6.

60. This view was repeated to the author by ABPI officials and by a number of company executives and regulatory affairs officers from British and foreign multinationals operating in the UK.

61. Section 4(i) enables the Minister to establish, by order, one or more advisory committees. The CSM was set up by the Medicines (Committee on the Safety of Medicines) Order 1970, S.I. no. 1257.

62. Sects. 2 and 3 of the Act.

63. Sect. 21 (5).

64. Sect. 21.

65. Sect. 21(7)(b).

66. *Guardian*, 12 July 1984.

67. Parker, 'Regulating Pharmaceutical Innovation', pp. 163–79.

68. J. Collier, *The Lancet*, 17 Aug. 1985, 379.

69. *Scrip* no. 1350, 27 Sept. 1987, 4.

70. J. E. S. Hayward, *Governing France: The One and Indivisible Republic* (London: Weidenfeld and Nicolson, 1983).

71. P. Birnbaum, *Les Sommets de l'État* (Paris: Seuil, 1977), 42 ff.; E. Sulieman *Elites in French Society* (Princeton, NJ; Princeton University Press, 1978), 176–84.

72. Law of 11 Sept. 1941.

73. Ordinance of 4 Feb. 1959 and its implementing decree of 5 Apr. 1960.

74. J.-P. Dupuy et S. Karsenty, *L'Invasion pharmaceutique* (Paris: Seuil, 1974), 171 ff.

75. Ordinance 67-827 of 23 Sept. 1967 in JO 28 Sept. 1967.

76. 30 Apr. 1972; 27 Apr. 1972; 16 May 1972; 26 June 1972; 21 Nov. 1972.

77. Decree of 21 Nov. 1972.

78. Arts. R.5140 and R.5141 CSP and decrees of 9 Feb. 1978 and 26 Apr. 1984.

79. Decree of 9 Feb. 1978.

80. Art. R.5141-3 CSP.
81. Decree of 21 Mar. 1979, bringing France into line with the require-
    ments of the second EEC directive on proprietary medicinal prod-
    ucts, 75/319.
82. Art. R.5118 CSP. Again, this reform may be attributed to the require-
    ments introduced by EEC directive 75/319.
83. Interviews with officials from the DPHM, Paris, May 1986.
84. See Auby aᵣ d Coustou, *Droit pharmaceutique*, fasc. 33.
85. Art. R.5122 CSP, para. 4 provides that 'Les experts sont tenus au
    secret professionnel en ce qui concerne la nature des produits essayés,
    les essais eux-mêmes et leurs résultats.'
86. Art. R.5119, CSP, para. 3.
87. Art. R.5136 CSP.
88. Art. R.5139 CSP.
89. Art. R.5140 CSP.
90. Art. R.5136 CSP.
91. Art. R.5139 CSP.
92. Commission d'autorisation des médicaments, *Rapport du Président
    1980*, (Paris: Ministère de la Santé, 1981), 5.
93. A. Page, 'Self-Regulation: The Constitutional Dimension', *Modern
    Law Review*, 49 (1986), 141–67.
94. J. J. Boddewyn, 'Advertising Self-Regulation: Organisation Struc-
    tures in Belgium, Canada, France and the United Kingdom', in W.
    Streeck and P. Schmitter (eds.), *Private Interest Government: Beyond
    Market and State* (London: Sage, 1985), 34.
95. See further chap. 8.
96. Council directive 75/319, OJ 1975, L 147/13.
97. See OJ 1968, C 14/4 and OJ 1968, C 248/3.
98. Council directive 75/318, OJ 1975, L 147/1.
99. N. Bel, 'Horizon 1990: L'AMM à visage multiple?', unpublished
    speech, Paris, 28 Mar. 1984.
100. Medicines Act 1968, Sect. 44(i).
101. Medicines Act 1968, Sect. 21(1).
102. R. Hurley, 'The Medicines Act: Is it Working?', *Journal of the British
    Institute of Regulatory Affairs*, 2 (1983), 1–3.
103. Sect. 28 provides that the powers to suspend, revoke, or vary licences
    can only be exercised on certain stated grounds, which include a
    decision by the licensing authority that the product can no longer be
    regarded as safe or efficacious for the purposes indicated in the
    licence.
104. R. v. *The Committee on the Review of Medicines, ex parte E. R.
    Squibb and Son*, 8 Apr. 1981, unreported.
105. *Franklin* v. *Minister of Town and Country Planning* [1948] A.C.87.

106. Art. R.5133 CSP.
107. M. Legrain, 'The Medicines Review Process: The French Approach', in BIRA, *Fifth Annual Symposium on Regulatory Affairs: Medicines Review Worldwide* (London: BIRA, 1984), 31.
108. CES Report, *L'Industrie pharmaceutique*, p. 69.
109. Commission d'autorisation des médicaments, *Rapport du Président* 1984–5 (Paris: Ministère de la Santé, 1986), 30.
110. Nine separate *tranches* are envisaged, covering different therapeutic categories. The first *tranche*, covering neurological and psychiatric products, had to be submitted by 31 Dec. 1985, and the remaining eight *tranches* would be completed in six-monthly phases, ending in Dec. 1989.
111. See further: Ministère de la Santé, DPHM, 'Avis aux fabricants de spécialités pharmaceutiques relatif à l'application de l'article 39 (point 2) de la directive 75/319/CEE', circular reproduced in *Annuaire IP 1986* (Editions de santé; Paris, 1986).
112. Sect. 31(1)(a) defines a clinical trial as 'an investigation consisting of the administration of one or more medicinal products of particular description by or under the direction of a doctor to a patient ... where there is evidence that the medicinal product may be beneficial to the patient(s) in question'. This definition excludes healthy volunteers.
113. Interview with DHSS officials, Oct. 1985.
114. B. J. Cromie, 'Testing New Medicines in the UK', *Journal of the Royal Society of Medicine*, 73, (1980), 312–17. Only about one-third of CTC applications referred to the CSM were granted without request for further information. The number of CTCs issued had fallen from 170 in 1972 to 87 in 1980.
115. C. J. Spiers and J. P. Griffin, 'A Survey', *British Journal of Clinical Pharmacology*, 15 (1983), 649–55.
116. MAIL, 21 Sept. 1978.
117. ABPI, *Annual Report 1981–82* (London: ABPI, 1982), 6.
118. A similar criticism has been made by F. G. Farell, 'Clinical Trials and their Monitoring', BIRA, *Third Annual Symposium* (London: BIRA, 1982) 57, who also argues that clinical studies were generally the least acceptable part of the data reviewed by the authorities.
119. Interview with senior ABPI official, 4 Nov. 1985.
120. DHSS, MLX no. 130, 21 Jan. 1981; E. S. Snell, 'The Regulatory Authorisation of Clinical Trials', *British Journal of Clinical Pharmacology*, 15 (1983), 625–7.
121. The Medicines (Exemption from Licences) (CTX) Order 1981, S.I. no. 164.

122. Art. 4 (2) of S.I. no. 164 allows the authority to extend the period by a further 28 days.
123. Art. 4(1)(a)(i) and sched. 1.
124. Sect. 31(5) and The Medicines (Exemption from Licenses) (Special Cases and Miscellaneous Provisions) Order 1972, S.I. no. 1200.
125. Spiers and Griffin, 'A Survey', pp. 649–55.
126. Interview, Dec. 1985, source withheld.
127. The common-law offence of criminal trespass. For a review of the existing law see, *Report of the Royal Commission on Civil Liability and Compensation for Personal Injury*, Cmnd. 7054 (London: HMSO, 1978).
128. *Scrip* no. 1145, 13 Oct. 1986, 5.
129. These committees have in turn been extensively criticized. Their size, composition, standards, and procedures vary considerably, and there is substantial confusion over whether their role is supervisory or merely advisory. Few have the resources to monitor clinical trials effectively. A DHSS circular makes some recommendations on membership, but there is no accepted definition of a 'properly constituted ethical committee' as referred to in S.I. no. 164. See also work by Thompson *et al.* 'Research and Ethical Committees in Scotland', *British Medical Journal*, 282 (1981), 717–20.
130. J. M. Royle and E. S. Snell, 'Medical Research on Normal Volunteers', *British Journal of Pharmacology*, 21 (1986), 548–9.
131. A Conservative MP complained to the *Pharmaceutical Journal* that old people in his constituency were being offered £40 per day to participate in clinical trials (see *Pharmaceutical Journal*, 10 Aug. 1985, 180). The death of two students while participating in two quite separate sets of clinical trials also prompted concern. See further *The Times*, 11 Nov. 1985.
132. J. Braithwaite, *Corporate Crime and the Pharmaceutical Industry*, (London: Routledge & Kegan Paul, 1984), but, *contra*, P. Cardon and F. Dommel, 'Injuries to research subjects', *New England Journal of Medicine*, 295 (1976), 650–4.
133. L. Velluz, 'La Recherche pharmaceutique: Rapport de la Commission d'étude', in *Pour une politique de la santé*, A, vol. 5 (Paris: La Documentation française, 1975), 130–67.
134. OJ 1983, L 322/1.
135. Commission d'autorisation des médicaments, *Rapport du Président 1982–83*, (Paris: Ministère de la Santé, 1983), 34–5.
136. JO, 11 Jan. 1976.
137. See Tribunal Correctionnel de Lyon, 15 Dec. 1859, D. 1859 II, 87; Aix, 22 Oct. 1906, D.1907 II, 41, n. Merinhac. The validity of this jurisprudence was confirmed in an opinion of the Conseil

d'État (section sociale) of 10 Apr. 1962 and is reflected in art. 19 of the French medical profession's code of ethics. Nevertheless, France has adhered to the International Declaration on Civil and Political Rights of 1981, art. 7 of which forbids medical and scientific experimentation without the subject's consent. Some commentators therefore argue that where the volunteer consents to the experimentation, the clinical trial should be considered legal under French law (J.-M. Auby, 'Les essais de pharmacologie clinique sur l'homme sain sont-ils dorénavant licites?', *Labo-pharma*, Mar. 1981.

138. F. Coustou, 'Les pré-essais cliniques', *Rev. sc. techn. pharm.* Feb. 1983, 47.

139. *Libération*, 1 Nov. 1987.

140. A. Langlois, 'Les Comités d'éthiques locaux en France', *Revue française des affaires sociales*, 3 (1986), 91–103.

141. For a detailed description of the provisions of the Bill see, J.-M. Auby, 'Les essais de médicaments sur l'homme sain: l'état actuel du problème', *Revue de droit sanitaire et sociale*, 3 (1985), 316–27. At the time of writing, a draft bill has been submitted by Prof. C. Huriet in the Senate which would legalize properly conducted Phase I and II trials. *Libération*, 13 Oct. 1988.

142. CES Report, *L'Industrie pharmaceutique*, p. 49.

143. In 1973, the SNIP, together with the medical profession, formed its own Centre national de pharmacovigilance. A ministerial order of 1976 subsequently set up regional monitoring centres in hospitals and created a central Commission technique de pharmacovigilance to advise the Minister (*arrêté* of 2 Dec. 1976, as amended and replaced by an *arrêté* of 10 April 1978, in JO, 10 May 1980.

144. Loi Talon, 7 July 1980.

145. Le Rapport Dangoumau, Feb. 1982. This report, prepared by the director of the DPHM was never published, but its principal recommendations may be found in *Consommateurs actualité*, 344 (1982), 3–7.

146. Decree 82-682 of 30 July 1982, in JO, 4 Aug. 1982.

147. Decree 84-402 of 24 May 1984, in JO, 25 May 1984, incorporated as arts. R.5144-1–R.5144-11 of the CSP.

148. CES Report, *L'Industrie pharmaceutique*, p. 54.

149. For example, the stricter reproduction and carcogenity tests laid down in MLX no. 130, 21 Jan. 1981.

150. Commission d'autorisation des médicaments, *Rapport du Président 1978–79*, (Paris: Ministère de la Santé, 1980), 10.

151. Commission d'autorisation des médicaments, *Rapport des Présidents*

des commission 1983–84, (Paris: Ministère de la Santé, 1984), 38.

152. Interview, SNIP, May 1986.

5

The Impact of European Law and Policy

In this chapter attention is switched from the national regulatory arena to that of the European Community. My intention here is not to enter into a detailed analysis of the application of Community law to the pharmaceutical sector but to discuss European policy and the relevant case-law of the Court of Justice in the context of this study. There are three factors which make the impact of European law and policy of central importance to an understanding of recent developments in national government–industry relations. In the first place, as Chapter 2 indicated, the European market, if unified, is potentially larger than the Japanese and American markets. As yet, however, 32 years after the signature of the Treaty of Rome, that market is not a unified one; a considerable number of barriers to free trade remain.[1] As noted in Chapter 4, substantial legislative efforts have been made with respect to harmonizing safety rules, but as long as automatic mutual recognition of national product-safety licences is postponed, the complete free movement of pharmaceuticals cannot be secured. In its 1985 White Paper on the completion of the internal market, the European Commission committed itself to securing a unified market for the pharmaceutical sector by 1992, and has set out a timetable for future action.[2] The first section of this chapter examines recent developments on safety harmonization.

In the past decade, price differentials within the Common Market have widened considerably as member states have adopted more rigorous policies of price control and cost containment, and the relative absence of Community action has become the target of criticism.[3] Until recently, divergences in national systems of price control had been conveniently ignored by the Commission, an attitude which was perhaps understandable if one considers the immense problems involved in reconciling on the one hand the *laissez-faire* approach to drug prices in West Germany, where there

is no control over manufacturers' prices and where prices are consequently among the highest in the EC, and on the other the interventionist strategies of France, Belgium, and now Spain, Portugal, and
Greece. Had the Commission continued to procrastinate on price
control, the market for drugs would have been in danger of becoming even more fragmented. Consequently, as part of the Community's renewed commitment to completing the internal market
by 1992,[4] and in the light of recent case-law on pharmaceutical
pricing and containment schemes, the Commission has now formulated a broad policy on price control, set out in a legally non-
binding communication on pharmaceutical pricing in December
1986[5] and supplemented by its directive on transparency on
pharmaceutical pricing, first submitted to the Council in 1987.[6]
These developments are reviewed in the third section of this
chapter.

   A second reason for analysing European developments is that the
gradual harmonization of product safety and, eventually, of
national controls on pricing and reimbursement has important
implications for competition within the sector. It was argued in
Chapter 2 that product-based competition is primarily a national
phenomenon. If territorial barriers are successfully removed, then
price-based, or at least intensified product competition may
emerge. As this chapter will illustrate, the Commission's current
attempts to complete the internal market for pharmaceuticals are
fraught with problems. First, it must persuade member states to
surrender complete sovereignty over safety regulation in a highly
sensitive policy area. Secondly, if it attempts to intervene in
controls over prices or national reimbursement rules, it risks
trespassing into the general economic policies, as well as the health
policies, of the member states. In the meantime, as this chapter will
argue, the existing competitive distortions within the Community
have been exacerbated by the disparate progress on the harmonization of the former, but not the latter, set of national rules. As the
third section demonstrates, this has facilitated the emergence of
new forces of competition, from generic producers and parallel
importers.

   The third and final reason for a detailed analysis of at least some
of the complexities of Community law in this area is that not only
does Community legislation restrict the sovereignty of national
legislators, but European law has come to provide industry with a

distinct and separate set of legal resources with which to oppose national policies. This is because Community law is capable, in certain defined circumstances, of conferring *directly effective* rights on individuals, rights to which national courts must give effect.[7] In this chapter I will describe the nature of those rights, and in Chapters 6 and 7 I will discuss their importance for these new entrants to the European pharmaceutical market, and consider the implications of their deployment on the implementation of national regulatory policy.

Harmonizing Controls on Product Safety

As noted in Chapter 4, by 1975 the Commission had made some progress towards mutual recognition of national product-licences in a series of directives which aimed to harmonize administrative procedures. Automatic mutual recognition, however, has not been achieved. As an interim solution, a cumbersome advisory procedure was introduced in 1975, which provided that firms wishing to market their products in five or more member states could submit their documentation to a special Committee on Proprietary Medical Products (CPMP), which would then advise national authorities as to whether a product should be licensed. The Committee's opinion had no binding effect, but the Commission hoped that the CPMP procedures would promote a gradual convergence of the substantive scientific criteria employed by the various national authorities.[8] As the CPMP was itself forced to acknowledge, however, the general nature of the standards and protocols for clinical tests 'could guarantee neither the uniformity of the experimental work done in the different Member States or the harmonization of decisions taken by national authorities',[9] so that the approval of each of the relevant licensing authorities proved hard to secure. Indeed, several member states had failed to implement directives 75/318 and 75/319 within the required period, obliging the Commission to initiate enforcement proceedings.[10] The procedure was not popular with the industry—the applicant had no right to be heard—so that there was no scope for the type of informal negotiation which, as Chapter 4 illustrated, had become an integral part of national licensing procedures. As a means to co-ordinate national techniques of risk/benefit evaluation, the CPMP procedure had failed,[11] and indeed, in the first 4 years of its existence only eight multiple applications had been filed under the CPMP procedure.[12] Every application was in fact referred back by at least one of the member states to the Committee, thus providing evidence of the wide national divergence in approaches to the substantive evaluation of a product.

If the decentralized route to mutual recognition was eventually to succeed, the scientific and medical principles, as well as the methodology of testing-procedures, had to be more closely harmonized. To this end, the Committee set up three expert panels: on the safety of drugs, on the efficacy of drugs, and on plant-derived substances. These panels, which comprised national experts, liaised closely with representatives of the pharmaceutical industry before finalizing their recommendations to the Committee. The Committee itself was reticent on the legal form which these recommendations should assume. It was evident firstly that national pharmaceutical associations feared that legally binding requirements could come to represent an aggregation of the strictest national practices, and secondly that as long as national authorities remained politically and even legally responsible[13] for the final decision to issue marketing authorizations, undue interference from the EC authorities would not be welcomed.[14] Plans to incorporate the findings of the expert panels into binding directives were therefore abandoned and were instead issued as legally non-binding recommendations.[15]

The 1983 directive and the revised CPMP procedures

In the light of the evidently slow pace at which harmonization was progressing, the Commission was obliged to consider once more whether full harmonization could be achieved only by a centralized Community registration procedure, rather than by decentralized mutual recognition. Recent experience with the Benelux registration had hardened industry's opposition to a supranational system which it regarded as unduly severe and inflexible. These views were supported by the 'exporter member states', who continued to lobby for the immediate introduction of decentralized procedures for mutual recognition. A number of consumer organizations, backed by the 'importer' member states, opposed this latter strategy on the grounds that, in view of the wide variations in national practices, it would enable a company to conform only to the least onerous set of national requirements, thus diluting safety standards throughout the Community.

The Commission, while considering the extension of the CPMP procedure inadvisable, continued to oppose a centralized Community registration system as politically and legally impracticable.[16] A draft directive, published in 1979, advocated a system of automatic mutual recognition for products containing a *new* active substance which had already been marketed in one member state. The CPMP would play an arbitral role where national decisions clashed. The proposal also aimed at closer co-ordination of national evaluation techniques. A product summary or data sheet, containing a synthesis of the product's qualities and defects as recognized by the competent authorites, was to provide the basis on which manufacturers could supply information to the professions and to the general public. Originally, the Commission hoped to promote greater market transparency by requiring the inclusion of economic particulars, including pricing, but this was abandoned following criticism from industry. Nevertheless, mention of the product's non-proprietary name was eventually made compulsory.[17]

This new set of proposals, although generally welcomed by the industry, met with a great deal of hostility from those member states who considered that harmonization of testing procedures was insufficiently advanced to allow for adequate confidence in another state's practices. The consumer organizations criticized the partial nature of a programme which facilitated product marketing but did little to harmonize surveillance of adverse reactions, the criteria for withdrawal of licences, and the information provided to patients or doctors.[18] After 3 years of further negotiation, directive 83/570[19] postponed the introduction of mutual recognition until 1990[20] but in the meantime strengthened and improved the multi-state procedure and introduced various mechanisms to enhance administrative co-ordination.

The basic features of the revised multi-state procedure[21] are as follows: a company applies for a licence in one of the member states, submitting a variety of documentation in compliance with the form laid down by the three directives. In considering the application, this first country undertakes a full review and compiles an *assessment report*, commenting on the company dossier. This allows other authorities to become more closely acquainted with different national evaluation techniques. The firm can then apply for an extention of the authorization to two or more member states, using the same basic dossier. The relevant licensing authorities are under a duty to take the original authorization into due consideration, although they are not bound by it. If objections are raised, the case is referred to the CPMP for an advisory opinion. This procedure is not compulsory, and companies are free to use the normal national licensing route.

The industry's European association, the EFPIA, as well as most national associations, have continued to exhibit an ambivalent attitude to the CPMP procedure, which they see as a poor substitute for mutual recognition. On the one hand, it is feared that it might facilitate the emergence of a Pan-European pro-regulatory bias.[22] The industry was also concerned that the assessment report (Article 13), would function as a vehicle for the transfer of one regulatory authority's prejudices to another. Originally, the Commission envisaged that this report would be compiled by, and remain totally confidential to, the licensing agencies, so that the individual firms would not have an opportunity to comment upon it. An early draft of the directive had made provision for the exchange of national reports on assessment prior to a national authority's decision to suspend or revoke an authorization, but this proposal was eventually dropped, as a result of industry pressure, from the final version (Article 12). In practice it would appear that industry is responsible in the first place for compiling the report, to which the authorities will append their own comments, and the entire dossier becomes part of the normal national licensing procedure, and therefore subject to appeal under national law.[23] Furthermore, Article 14 extends the applicant's procedural rights before the CPMP.

On the other hand, at a time when national governments are finding it difficult to attract civil servants of a sufficiently high calibre to evaluate complex scientific applications, the industry has been forced to recognize the value of centralized procedures as more efficient. To date, the fear that a Pan-European bias might emerge appears to be groundless, as the CPMP has formed an adverse opinion in very few cases. Of the first twelve opinions issued under the new procedure, only two were negative.[24]

There was also concern that the procedures might become a short cut for the marketing of established rival products, and in fact the CPMP has been used as a way of queue-jumping in national procedures for licensing. Several national authorities have complained to the Commission that the compulsory time-limit of 120 days is too short, so that priority has to be given to multi-state over national applications. This suggests that licensing bodies are reluctant to rely upon the first authority's assessment of the application and are therefore conducting full investigations of their own, as opposed to the limited appraisal originally intended by the Commission. Such diligence reflects not only divergent medical traditions and practices but also the reluctance of one licensing authority to shoulder the moral, political, and possibly legal, consequences of another's risk/benefit calculations.

The 1987 harmonization package

Directive 87/19,[25] adopted after 2 years of discussion, attempts to remedy this situation. It aims to improve the co-ordination of the revision of national requirements on testing through the creation of a new Committee on the Adaption to Technical Progress of the Directives on the Removal of Technical Barriers to Trade in the Proprietary Medicinal Sector.[26] Directive 87/22 sets up a more centralized co-ordination procedure for medicinal products derived from biotechnology and for certain other high-technology products. This new procedure, which is compulsory for the former category only, entails discussion by the CPMP of all decisions on marketing, withdrawal, or suspension, in parallel with assessment at the national level. It is designed to resolve questions of principle at the earliest stage, but the final licensing decision still rests with the member states. This procedure, while fundamentally national, is seen by the Commission as a significant step in the direction of a single evaluation procedure applicable throughout the Community and as a way of pooling expertise to deal with increasingly technically complex dossiers.[27] It is likely to be extended to *all* new products when the CPMP procedures are next reviewed, in 1990.

In the final event, it would appear that the modified CPMP procedures have not fulfilled the original expectations, in particular the hope that movement of genuinely innovative products would be facilitated. Co-ordination of evaluation techniques does not appear to have proceeded at the pace intended by the Commission, and it has been insufficient to surmount the considerable divergences in national scientific and medical traditions, of the type discussed in Chapter 4. The present partial approach to harmonization has continued to draw fire from consumer organizations, who argue that the emphasis is almost entirely on facilitating the marketing of drugs, at the expense of monitoring and other forms of post-marketing control. A product which can no longer be legally marketed in one member state may nevertheless remain on the market in the remaining eleven. The Commission protests that the directives make ample provision for informal liaison over national decisions to withdraw, but the consumers have criticized the secrecy which surrounds these and many other decisions relating to pharmaceuticals policy, as well as the close identification of the relevant directorate-general, DG III, with industry's interests. In particular, the Bureau of the European Union of Consumers (BEUC), the European umbrella consumer-association, has pointed out that this is one area where the consumer organizations are given no official status in consultation procedures, whereas industry has been afforded increased opportunities to collaborate extensively in the work of the CPMP.[28]

As all harmonization measures on medicinal products are now based on Article 100A[29] of the EEC Treaty, which allows for the adoption of directives by a qualified majority as opposed to a unanimous vote, it is conceivable that the Commission's task of completing the internal market for pharmaceuticals by 1992 might prove less difficult than in the past. It must be pointed out, however, that Article 100A(4) allows a member state, under certain circumstances, to disregard a majority decision of the Council and to introduce national provisions which, under certain restrictive conditions, may derogate from harmonized Community law.[30]

The case-law of the European Court of Justice

Even if mutual recognition of product licences is realized by 1990, it is unlikely that every aspect of pharmaceutical marketing and manufacture will be harmonized by that date, or even by 1992, the appointed date for the overall completion of the internal market, and disparities between national regulation are likely to remain.[31] In particular, the Community definition of a medicinal product is not on all fours with national legislation;[32] the rules on product suspension, withdrawal, and revocation are not fully harmonized; nor indeed are all aspects of marketing, including distribution.[33] National rules on the provision of information for patients and doctors, as well as on advertising, are particularly diverse. Given continuing divergence, member states are likely to assert, and probably enjoy, limited sovereignty in matters relating to health.[34] For example, they may continue to restrict the importation of, or may even ban, products which do not confirm to national laws on labels or leaflets or advertising.[35]

Given that the harmonization of regulations on product marketing is incomplete, the scope for member states to retain sovereignty will be determined on the basis of the case-law of the Court of Justice on free movement of goods, and in particular Articles 30–6. This jurisprudence is also of vital significance to the present attempts of parallel importers who seek to circumvent national restrictions on free trade in pharmaceuticals.

The prohibition of so-called quantitative restrictions on imports and of measures having equivalent effect in Article 30 of the EEC Treaty is widely defined and is subject to only limited exceptions. Following the decision of the Court in *Dassonville*,[36] it is clear that national legal and administrative rules regulating marketing are capable of falling within the definition of measures having equivalent effect to quantitative restrictions on trade, even where those rules are not directly related to frontier restrictions. In its subsequent case-law, the Court has repeatedly stressed that all rules enacted by member states which are capable of hindering, directly or indirectly, actually or potentially, intra-Community trade are to be considered as measures having equivalent effect. The case-law on Article 30 suggests that its terms might *imply* the concept of mutual recognition or mutual acceptance, and not only the prohibition of restrictions on trade between member states.

Certain exceptions to this concept are recognized, however, including the right to take measures to protect public health, as enshrined in Article 36, and the so-called 'rule of reason', developed by the Court of Justice in its jurisprudence on the interpretation and application of Article 30. In essence, the Court, by using this latter concept to fill in gaps in the Treaty pending the adoption of harmonizing measures by the Community, has recognized the rights of member states, in the absence of legislative guarantees at Community level, to protect certain interests, including those of consumers.[37]

According to current case-law, the member states may no longer derogate from the principles of free movement and invoke either

Article 36 or the rule of reason when Community law provides an 'unconditional set of assurances'[38] or 'a complete and exhaustive set of guarantees'[39] for the general interest. In the case of complex medicinal products, the inherent risks of which can never be totally eliminated, it might be doubted if such a high standard could be obtained, especially as harmonization of substantive testing criteria has proved problematic.[40]

The Community rules on free movement were expressly applied to national pharmaceutical licensing in case 104/75, *De Peijper*, a case concerning the importation of valium into the Netherlands by an independent importer. The valium was lawfully marketed in both countries, as the product had been duly licensed by its manufacturer, Hoffmann-La Roche. Dutch legislation, however, laid down certain safety requirements in the case of imports of medicinal preparations, which included the presentation of documentation verified by the manufacturer. Centrafarm, the independent importer, argued that it could not rely on co-operation from Hoffmann-La Roche to obtain this documentation and was therefore prevented from importing its products. The Court, on a reference from the Dutch courts, ruled that national practices which resulted in the channelling of imports in such a way that certain traders could effect these imports while others could not, constituted a measure having equivalent effect to quantitative restrictions on trade. It went on to recognize that while member states were entitled under Article 36 to enact legislation protecting public health, these measures were limited to those which were *necessary* to achieve that objective and which did not constitute an arbitrary restriction on trade.[41] In this instance, the product in question had been licensed in both countries and, furthermore, was in every respect similar to the product which had been imported through the manufacturer's authorized channels. In the Court's view, there existed alternative ways of protecting public health, including active co-operation between the national administrative authorities or between the latter and the original holder of the licence.

Three aspects of this case are of note. Firstly, the Court did not expressly consider the compatibility of the national licensing requirements with EC law *per se*, but only a single aspect of them. It is clear from the judgment that, in the absence of harmonizing measures, product-licensing regimes were not in themselves con-

ᴉitted under Article 36, as
ʳreaty objectives. The scope
ᴉh in Article 36 is therefore
ᴉres must be justifiable and
or disguised restriction on
ʳ with products which were
ʳhich had already received
ries concerned. Import and
which did not satisfy these
gnition of national require-
t therefore be established on
of harmonized rules, member
at level of health protection
ruling, and particularly the
should actively co-operate to
ᴉy beyond the requirements of

estrictions on imports, but it is
ʾs subsequent case-law that so-
—that is, national rules apply-
oducts alike—are capable of
amounting to measures having equivalent effect if they affect the
prospects of importing products from other member states. Rules
affecting the marketing and manufacture of pharmaceuticals may
therefore be considered prima facie contrary to Article 30 if their
practical effect is to restrict the volume of imports.[45] In its judgment
in the landmark case 120/78, *Cassis de Dijon*, which concerned the
legality of marketing restrictions on alcoholic drinks lawfully
marketed in another member state, the Court addressed itself not to
any intention to discriminate but to the protective effect, and then
to the justification for national restrictions:

There is no valid reason why, provided that they have been lawfully produced and marketed in one of the Member states [alcoholic beverages] should not be introduced into another Member State.[46]

This reasoning seemed to open the door to automatic mutual
acceptance, irrespective of the stage reached by the Community in
formulating harmonization measures—an interpretation endorsed
by the Commission in its Communication of 1980 on the consequences of the case.[47] It can be argued, however, that in fact the

Court not only recognized the validity of national restrictions, pending the adoption of appropriate Community guarantees to protect the interests concerned, but went on to justify new derogations when it ruled that:

Obstacles to movement within the Community resulting from disparities between national laws relating to the marketing . . . must be accepted in so far as those provisions may be recognized as being necessary in order to satisfy mandatory requirements relating in particular to the . . . protection of public health . . . and the defence of the consumer.[48]

As Mortelmans has suggested, the Court's approach can best be understood as an attempt to reconcile the very broad definition of a measure having equivalent effect and its narrow interpretation of the permissible exceptions under Article 36, which do not always allow for an adequate balance to be struck between Community and national interests.[49] As a result, the Court has tended to search for equitable solutions to individual cases. Its jurisprudence in a series of cases concerning restrictive national measures on public health under Article 30 or 36 does not readily yield general principles. Nevertheless, I would suggest the Court's jurisprudence reflects the same broad distinction which is evident in the Community's pharmaceutical harmonization programme: between administrative or procedural requirements on the one hand, and substantive criteria on the other.

Where administrative procedures have been harmonized, the Court, applying the principles of proportionality and the prohibition against arbitrary discrimination, has struck down a variety of national health-controls, particularly those relating to foodstuffs. Thus, for example, where goods had already been subject to health checks in the exporting member state, a requirement by the importing state that they undergo further (·rols was found to be disproportionate, and this is especially the case where, as in case 132/80, *United Brands* v. *Belgium*,[50] t..e first checks were carried out in accordance with partially harmonized rules, applicable also in the country of destination.[51] Similarly, the Court has struck down, for lack of justification, a restriction allowing only persons established in the national territory to apply for marketing approvals for pesticide products.[52] It has also condemned similar national rules on the safety of pharmaceutical products, including regulations requiring that the person responsible for placing the goods on the market should be resident in that country[53] and a requirement that enterprises supplying domestic retail chemists directly must maintain premises locally.[54] It is also clear from its judgment in case 28/84, *Compound Feeding Stuffs*,[55] that where manufacturing and marketing is governed by a coherent and complete set of harmonizing directives, as in the case of this type of feeding stuffs, questions of public health are regulated exhaustively by those directives, and member states are precluded from unilaterally introducing new testing procedures. It will be obvious that the directives relating to the safety of pharmaceutical products do not yet aspire to these standards.

However, in its subsequent case-law on claims of equivalence, or on mutual recognition of complex requirements in regard to scientific testing, the Court has erred on the side of caution, leaving the actual determination of equivalence to the national courts.[56] The greater the scientific uncertainty surrounding the methodology employed or the results rendered, the more willing the Court has been to allow member states to adopt different approaches. Thus in case 97/83, *Melkunie*,[57] a case concerning food additives, it held that where the available scientific findings did not make it possible to lay down precise common standards, it was up to member states to set their own criteria, subject always to the principle of proportionality.[58] The Court has also allowed member states to insist on additional testing or to apply different criteria to take into account national variations in diet[59] or climatic conditions. Where the product's particular qualities meet a real need, however, especially a nutritional one, the member state must authorize marketing.[60]

Much will depend on the nature of the tests and the nature of the standard of safety to be ensured, although it is clear that mere differences in national safety standards cannot be relied upon in themselves as sufficient justification to exclude an import. Justification must be made out for each product,[61] and even where member states are authorized in specific directives to subject products such as vitamins to pre-marketing procedural controls, the substance of these controls will be reviewed, to ensure that the principle of proportionality is respected.[62]

Where partial harmonization has been achieved, the Court is more demanding, as for example in case 274/84, *Motte*.[63] This case involved Belgian restrictions in respect of foodstuffs to which two particular colourants had been added. The Court ruled that where an importing state applies specific controls to a product lawfully marketed in another member state—in this case West Germany—in so far as there are uncertainties in the present state of scientific research, it is for member states to decide the level of protection they intend to assure, having regard to the requirements of free movement. It went on to add, however, that the member states must also take into account the non-binding recommendations of the relevant Community scientific committee. Although the latter's opinions could not 'abrogate the responsibility of national authorities for the protection of health in the absence of binding rules and effective supervisory measures at the Community level', these opinions must be taken into account in assessing the risk represented by a particular colourant.[64] The Court has further clarified this requirement in several recent cases and has ruled that member states are bound to take international standards into account.[65]

As long as Community provisions on the substantive scientific criteria and protocols on which licences for medicinal products are based are not fully harmonized, it is conceivable that a member state might be justified in relying on Article 36 either to ban unilaterally a product in the future or to restrict the conditions of its use, subject always to the proportionality test, the necessity criterion, and the need to pay due regard to non-binding Community standards.[66] In the meantime, the stricter approach to restrictive administrative requirements, particularly in the aftermath of the *De Peijper* case, has been of considerable benefit to parallel importers. As the burden of proving that a product is dangerous, and thus that the refusal to allow marketing is justified, lies with the authorities seeking to refuse importation or marketing, parallel importers have made significant use of so-called Eurodefences in national proceedings dealing with the illegal importation of medicinal products.[67]

European Law and Policy on Pricing Controls

A preference for co-ordinating the procedural or administrative aspects of national price-controls, as opposed to the substantive criteria on which they are based, has also come to dominate the Commission's approach to harmonization of divergent national controls. The Commission has been notably reluctant to interfere with national regimes which serve goals of industrial as well as of health policy.

The harmonization of national price-controls undoubtedly presents the Commission with a rather particular set of legal and political problems. At present there is no consensus on the proper role of the public authorities in regulating pharmaceutical prices or pharmaceutical consumption within the Community. Countries which are highly dependent on imports, such as Greece, Spain, Portugal, and Belgium, tend to give a higher priority to the strict regulation of pharmaceutical price, while countries with a well-established domestic pharmaceutical industry, including the UK and West Germany, have tended towards a more liberal approach. As a consequence, there are large differences in the levels of prices and in the number of products on the market in each member state. According to a recent study of price variations commissioned by BEUC, taking an average Community price of 100, the level of prices within the member states varies from 61 in Spain to 152.8 in Germany. Variations in pharmacists' margins exacerbate these differences.[68] In Spain and West Germany, some 11,000 products were classified as reimbursable by the relevant insurance funds in 1985, but only 9,500 products were theoretically available in the UK and France, and as few as 4,500 in the Netherlands.[69] Furthermore, there are substantial differences in the levels of reimbursement in each member state. In Denmark, for example, the patient must bear a cost six times higher than that borne by a patient for the same medicines in the Netherlands.[70]

The Commission's past hesitance over price controls is therefore best explained not in narrow doctrinal terms but on the basis of straightforward political expediency. From the perspective of policy, the crux of the problem is finding the correct balance between the Community's interest in the free movement of goods and the legitimate budgetary concerns of the national governments. From a legal perspective, the task is made more complex by the deficiencies in the Treaty of Rome regarding the general problems of state intervention in the economy. According to the doctrine of legislative pre-emption, member states are free, in the absence of Community provisions, to adopt legislation to control prices within their own territories, provided they do not contravene Community law.[71] Although the Court is clearly of the opinion that 'it is part of the Community authorities' task to eliminate factors likely to distort competition between Member States, in particular by the harmonization of national measures to control prices',[72] the correct legal basis for such measures is open to dispute.[73] The Court has also ruled that the directives harmonizing procedures and principles for granting marketing authorizations cannot be invoked as a basis for price-related controls.[74]

In practice the Commission, and to a certain extent the Court, have been exceedingly cautious about trespassing into the realm of economic policy-making. It is perhaps the search for a compromise between Treaty goals and the realities of national interests which explain, on the one hand, the Commission's reluctance to condemn certain discriminatory practices and, on the other, the somewhat erratic jurisprudence of the Court regarding controls on pricing and profits. To date, the Court has relied primarily on Article 30 as the basis for supervising national pricing policies in general. Article 2 of Commission directive 70/50, on the application of the rules on free movement, defines offending measures as those which lay down less favourable prices or discriminatory methods of calculating different margins for imported products as against domestic products,[75] but the Court has consistently refused to rule that they automatically constitute measures having equivalent effect; material discrimination or disadvantage must be demonstrated. This caution can be discerned in a series of cases involving maximum prices and profit margins,[76] minimum prices and profit margins,[77] and price freezes.[78] At the risk of generalization, it is possible to distil a number of broad principles from these cases.

(a) A maximum price or price freeze applicable without distinction to domestic and imported products does not necessarily constitute a measure having equivalent effect, but might do so when prices are fixed or frozen at such a level that the marketing of imported goods becomes either impossible or more difficult than the marketing of national products. A prima-facie case of such discrimination can be made where traders wishing to import the products in question can only do so at a loss.[79]

(b) In cases of price controls or price freezes providing for separate systems for imported and domestic products such rules will constitute measures having equivalent effect wherever they are capable of hindering the sale of imported products in any way.

(c) Maximum profit margins should not be calculated in such a way as to preclude the effect of price movements and cost increases in the country in which the imported good is produced.[80] The application of these general principles to pharmaceutical pricing had until recently remained unclear. On the one hand, they are based on decisions concerning homogeneous commodities such as sugar, and involving only relatively straightforward, direct methods of price control. Their potential application to heterogeneous products, the price of which in any one member state is not fixed according to the usual laws of the market, is highly complex. On the other hand, because of the peculiarities of the pharmaceutical market, member states can influence prices in a number of indirect ways.

In case 181/82, *Roussel*,[81] the Court had its first opportunity to apply its existing general principles to pharmaceutical price controls. It was asked to rule on a Dutch scheme imposing maximum limits on the prices of imported medicines. Prices of imported medicines were fixed by reference to the price charged by the manufacture for sale in the country of origin, subject to certain increases to cover overheads and taxes, but the prices of nationally produced medicines, representing some 20 per cent of final consumption, remained subject to an earlier decree, which fixed prices by reference to a different system, which in effect guaranteed higher prices for domestic goods. Ten drug companies brought an action against the Dutch government, claiming that the legislation infringed Article 30. Their principal argument was that low price levels in certain member states were caused by national legislation and that producers in those states were sometimes unable to cover their costs. Given that this legislation discriminated directly against imports, it is not surprising that the Court found for the manufacturers. Two aspects of the decision deserve further comment, however. Firstly, both the Commission and the Advocate General (Rozes) considered that short-term restrictions on free movement for example, cost-containment measures— could be justified under Articles 36 and 103, although the Court itself has consistently refused to accept economic necessity as justification for restrictions to trade.[82] The Dutch government contended that in the absence of common rules member states were in principle free to regulate the production and distribution of goods on their own territories and to take measures to compensate for the distorting effects of price controls applied elsewhere. The Court itself chose not to follow either line of reasoning; it did not advert to the problem of justification at all. Secondly, *Roussel* would appear to be authority for the proposition that Article 36 cannot be used to justify national measures which seek to achieve budgetary objectives—such as a reduction in the cost of publicly funded health-care—if imports are placed at a disadvantage. In this respect, the judgment would appear to serve as valuable ammunition to drug companies seeking to oppose the imposition of cost-containment measures which could adversely affect their profitability.

The practical difficulties which confront the Commission in policing national pharmaceutical price controls are well illustrated by the judgment of the Court of Justice in its recent ruling on the legality of the Italian pharmaceutical pricing system. The Court reasoned that a system of calculating prices which allowed manufacturers to include the major part of those costs realized in Italy but which made no provision for the inclusion of costs of importation amounted to a breach of Article 30. As the Commission had failed to provide concrete evidence of material discrimination against imports, however, the regime could not be considered an infringement of Community law.[83] A major problem for the Commission or for a rival firm who believes that a competitor is receiving favourable treatment is, of course, the need to obtain concrete evidence of discrimination.[84] An explicit aim of the new directive on transparency is to close this 'information gap'.

At the national level, the judgment of the British Court of Appeal in the case of *Bomore* provides further evidence of the practical difficulties of applying these principles to a sector where the margins of distributors as well as manufacturers are subject to control.[85] A number of small companies and independent wholesale pharmacists, taking advantage of price differentials within the Community, began importing popular products from low-priced EC countries and supplying them to chemists at large discounts. As chemists are reimbursed under the NHS at a fixed price, they could buy imported products at large discounts but retain a considerable profit when eventually reimbursed by the NHS.

As a consequence, the DHSS devised a 'higher discount' scheme, which obliged chemists who had obtained a product at a discount of more than 12 per cent to endorse prescription forms 'HD'. These would eventually be reimbursed at 80 per cent of the tariff price. As all domestic drugs were offered at less than 12 per cent and all imported products at more than 12 per cent, the change only affected imports. To entice chemists to accept their products, importers would be obliged to offer discounts of more than 20 per cent, forcing them, in some instances, to trade at a loss. Bomore contended therefore, that the HD scheme amounted to a breach of Article 30. Applying the reasoning in the *Cullet* case, the Court of Appeal found that the HD scheme prevented the parallel importers from passing on the advantages of their lower costs, and therefore that the competitive advantage resulting from lower cost-prices had been neutralized. Hence the scheme fell foul of the prohibitions set out in Article 30.[86]

Restrictions on reimbursement

Case 238/82, *Duphar*,[87] concerned a Dutch ministerial order instituting a negative list to be applied by the health funds. The list was divided into two parts, the first listing products which could not be reimbursed by the funds, and the second listing those which could only be supplied subject to certain conditions. Duphar BV and twenty-two other drug companies challenged the legality of the order under national and Community law, arguing that although the order applied to domestic and imported goods alike, sales of the latter had been adversely affected by these measures, and they produced 'clear evidence' to support their contention.[88]

The Court confined its judgment to an interpretation of whether the term 'measure having equivalent effect' could be construed to cover negative lists. In approaching this question, the Court appears to have adopted the Dutch government's proposition that in this instance the state, via the social security system, acted in its capacity as a consumer, an argument which the Advocate General had dismissed as 'far-fetched'. It recognized that the member states had a legitimate interest in keeping down drug costs, and in view of the special nature of the trade in pharmaceutical products, namely the fact that social security institutions are substituted for consumers as regards responsibility for the payment of medical expenses, legislation of the type in question could not necessarily be regarded as constituting a restriction on the freedom to import guaranteed by Article 30.[89] The Court went on to stress that 'for such legislation to be in conformity with the Treaty, the choice of the medicinal preparations to be excluded must be free of any discrimination to the detriment of imported medicinal preparations'. Hence certain conditions in the preparation of such a list had to be met:

1. There must be no discrimination as to the origin of the products.
2. Medicines must only be excluded on objective and verifiable grounds such as the existence on the market of an equally effective but less expensive product, or the fact that a product could be bought without a prescription.
3. It must be possible to amend the list of excluded products in accordance with published criteria chosen to take account of changing circumstances.[90]

Duphar is undoubtedly an important precedent. By expressly recognizing cost criteria as a valid consideration for national authorities, the Court has perhaps limited the constraints imposed on governments by the *Roussel* judgment, even if it did lay down rather strict procedural conditions under which these lists should be drawn up. These principles were subsequently incorporated into the 1986 Communication on prices and have now found expression in the transparency directive.[91]

The directive on transparency in pharmaceutical pricing

The new transparency directive is in many ways a cautious, if not disappointing, measure. It is limited to the co-ordination of procedural aspects of intervention and is undoubtedly a first step on the very long road to complete harmonization of controls on pricing and reimbursement. By endeavouring to make controls more transparent, the directive aims essentially 'to enable all concerned to verify that the requirements of Community law are being respected by laying down a series of rules regarding time limits, the reasoning and publication of decisions, etc. which would be directly effective so that those concerned can defend their interests in the national courts'.[92]

In its initial version, the Commission's draft directive had provided for greater co-ordination of national decisions by the creation of the Consultative Committee on Pharmaceutical Pricing and Reimbursement, which would function as a Community forum on major issues such as transfer pricing and harmonization of national criteria on therapeutic efficacy. Article 8 also envisaged a substantial delegation of powers to the Commission to adopt new directives or issue guide-lines on these matters. Following criticism of vagueness in the drafting from the other European institutions,[93] and industry opposition to a centralized Pan-European classification of therapeutic efficacy,[94] as well as opposition from several member states,[95] a compromise text was proposed. Although the final version retains the obligation to notify the Commission of the criteria adopted in classifying products and in calculating transfer prices, it abandons any substantial delegation of powers to the new Committee. Similarly, the proposal that this body should have responsibility for formulating a Community policy on pharmaceutical pricing and reimbursement has also been dropped.

Profit controls

The shortcomings of this limited approach to harmonizing price controls, which, I have argued, concentrates on co-ordinating national administrative procedures rather than the substantive criteria on which allowable prices are calculated, is at its most evident in relation to national controls over *profits* as opposed to individual prices. It is significant that the Commission's December Communication dealt primarily with controls on prices and reimbursement rather than systems of profit control such as the British PPRS. Article 5 of the transparency directive merely requires national authorities to publish information on the methods used to define profitability and return on capital or sales. It does not attempt to impose a Community method of calculation.

The compatibility of profit controls with European law is somewhat difficult to establish, especially when those controls are not directly linked to margins allowed for individual products, as discussed above, but relate to the general levels of profit earned by individual firms. In principle, schemes such as the British PPRS, which link a firm's allowable rate of profit to its contribution to national economic well-being, could operate to impede free movement of imports and exports. It could also be argued that these schemes distort competition within the EC by providing greater incentives to nationally based firms. These three aspects will be discussed separately.

i. Free movement

A particular problem with the application of the rules on free movement to profit-related controls is that the latter relate primarily to production whereas the rules themselves deal mainly with trade. Despite the Court's broad interpretation of Article 30, national restrictions on production have rarely been condemned, unless they are overtly discriminatory, as this would involve the Community in matters of national economic or industrial policy.[96] This cautious approach is particularly evident in the case-law on Article 34, which deals with quantitative restrictions on exports. In *Duphar* the plaintiff pharmaceutical companies contended that by excluding certain nationally produced medicines from reimbursement, the national measure altered the structure of production in a way that affected exports. The Court chose to interpret Article 34 narrowly, in accordance with its earlier case-law:[97]

Article 34 concerns national measures which have as their specific object or effect the restriction of patterns of export and thereby the establishment of a difference in treatment between the domestic trade of a Member State and its export trade in such a way as to provide a particular advantage for national production or for the domestic market of the State in question.[98]

Negative lists compiled for purposes of reimbursement will be unlikely to constitute a restriction on exports unless it could be shown that they were compiled with the specific intention of distorting trade.

ii. Competition

A determined application of the EEC Treaty's rules on competition might furnish the Commission with an alternative method of tackling profit controls. These rules are discussed in detail in Chapter 9. Significantly, however, the Commission makes no reference in its 1986 Communication to the application of the Treaty's provisions on competition[99] to systems of profit control which promote nationally based firms.

The application of the rules on competition laid down in Articles 85 and 86 is somewhat problematic in voluntary schemes such as the PPRS, where the distinction between public and private conduct is rather blurred. These articles are addressed to undertakings and not to member states. There is, however, a school of thought which argues that all voluntary agreements between national governments and firms, whether formalized or not, should be treated as quasi-cartels and therefore subject to Article 85, which outlaws agreements between undertakings eliminating or restricting competition. Governments are also under a general duty to ensure that competition is not distorted (Article 3(f)), and to abstain from any measure which could jeopardize the attainment of the Treaty's general objectives (Article 5). If these general duties are read in conjunction with the rules on competition, then a so-called 'mixed situation' may arise that is, a situation where government agencies and private firms act in close co-operation—through, for example, a government-sponsored cartel arrangement—to achieve a result which would otherwise be prohibited. In what is very much a developing area of its jurisprudence, the Court has suggested that, subject to certain restrictive conditions, such situations could be subject to Treaty rules.[100]

Firstly, for Article 85 to apply, there must be some element of agreement between the parties, or a significant degree of involvement or participation by industry.[101] Secondly, 'mixed situations' will be condemned only if they contravene clearly-defined Commission policy and decisions, otherwise the Court will look relatively favourably on national measures.[102] Thirdly, the Court will apply a remoteness test—do the measures at issue actually result in restrictions in competition between enterprises?[103] Where all three conditions are satisfied, government-sponsored cartels could be subject to the normal rules on competition and could be challenged by either the Commission or a private concern.

iii. State aids

Profit controls which encourage nationally based research might also be attacked as a form of state aid, prohibited by Article 92(1) of the Treaty. While the pharmaceutical industry receives few direct subsidies from national governments, Article 92 prohibits 'any aid granted by the State or through State resources in any form whatsoever which distorts or threatens to distort competition by favouring certain undertakings or the production of certain goods'.[104] It is immaterial whether government authorities grant aid directly or through the agency of some private or public body. The Court has said that 'in applying Article 92 regard must primarily be had to the effects of the aid on undertakings or producers favoured and not the status of the institutions entrusted with the distribution and administration of the aid'.[105] Hence Article 92 could be used as a basis to attack a hidden element of subsidy in a system of administered control on prices or profits, as in the Commission's recent action against a Belgian pharmaceutical pricing scheme which, via contractual agreements, granted subsidies to firms locating research facilities in Belgium.[106]

As a follow-up to its 1986 Communication, the Commission began enforcement proceedings against Italy, Belgium, and Greece. Yet these are all countries where prices have been held down, in the interests of health expenditure. The Commission has yet to display similar enthusiasm in challenging profit-related schemes, which, in the interests of national industrial policy, tend to protect locally based firms. This seems at odds with its declared intention to ensure that a 'rigorous policy is pursued ... so that public resources are not used to confer artificial advantage on some firms over others'.[107] It is, however, quite conceivable that member states may use public expenditure on pharmaceutical products either to attract foreign investment into their national territory or to further the interests of nationally based firms.

While the adoption of the directive on pricing transparency undoubtedly represents an important step in the development of a Community policy on pharmaceutical pricing and reimbursement, the real test of its usefulness will, of course, be found in the use which the Commission makes of the information it receives and its willingness to apply its primary powers under the Treaty.

In this context, it might be useful to draw an analogy with the Commission's reluctance to interfere with certain member states' protectionist policies on oil and gas. It prevaricated for a period of 20 years over certain aspects of French licensing policy on petroleum which were clearly intended to favour the domestic refining industry.[108] It failed to issue a complaint to the United Kingdom over a clause contained in all offshore licences prohibiting direct export of oil and gas won in the North Sea, and it was reluctant to challenge broadly similar concessions in Dutch offshore-production licences.[109]

This hesitation to enforce Community law is best explained by the absence of a coherent Community policy which might displace disparate but—in national and, by implication, Community terms at least—necessary controls. Although the Commission considers it

important to encourage the development of an innovatory pharmaceutical industry, it does not have the necessary instruments to
pursue this goal. The same can be said of cost-containment policies.
In the absence of coherent Community policies on health or
industry, the Commission defers to national interests and permits
divergent forms of control. Yet it must be acknowledged that as
long as the Commission restricts the harmonization of controls on
prices and reimbursement to administrative as opposed to substantive criteria, it is unlikely to succeed in narrowing the pricing gap
between the different member states, at least by 1992. In the meantime, however, scope for parallel importing will increase.

The Impact of Community Rules on Market Structure

As the first section of this chapter made clear, automatic mutual
recognition of national safety-measures has not yet been achieved.
The existing directives, together with the case-law of the Court,
have nevertheless facilitated the movement of two particular classes
of pharmaceutical products—generics and parallel imports—trade
in which has been made all the more attractive by the failure to
arrive at a Community policy on pricing. In this section I will
examine the nature of this trade and its impact on the structure of
the Community's pharmaceutical market.

Parallel imports

The term 'parallel import', not being a term of art, is difficult to
define in the abstract. In general, however, it is used to describe two
types of situation:

(a) A manufacturer in the UK exports to France, where, because of
price controls, the selling price is lower. A third party buys the
goods in France and re-exports them to the UK, undercutting the
manufacturer in the home market.
(b) Instead of continuing to manufacture products for the French
market in the UK, the manufacturer sets up a French subsidiary. A
third party buys the goods in France and sells them at a lower price
in the UK.

In economic terms the result in either case is the same; from the
point of view of public health, however, the situation in (b) is rather

different, in that the parallel import is manufactured by a different person from the domestic product and may not be therapeutically equivalent to it.

The European Court and Parliament have tended to regard type (a) parallel imports as essentially legitimate where they tend to break down artificial barriers to trade created by the manufacturers themselves. The Court has not distinguished between barriers created by governmental measures and those created by company policies; it has looked primarily at the effects of restrictions on the functioning of the Common Market.[110] Parallel importing in general is economically attractive when substantial price differences prevail and when transport costs are low. Pharmaceuticals satisfy both criteria, and, unsurprisingly, parallel trade within the Community is considerable. The pharmaceutical industry protests, however, that it must bear the economic brunt of market divisions which are not of its making but result from national legislation on price control and rules regarding social security reimbursement. The governments of the major exporting countries, particularly West Germany and the UK, share the industry's broad concern about the detrimental effects of parallel importing on company investment in research and development.

The Commission has been more equivocal, partly because it initially did not consider that industry's case had been made out and partly because the doctrine of parallel imports is so enshrined in Community law that, in practice, the legal margin for manoeuvre is extremely limited. In the wake of the confusion caused by the De Peijper ruling, however, the Commission, in an attempt to ensure a consistent implementation of the judgment, submitted a draft directive to the Council on parallel imports[111] which would have established, inter alia, a common system of simple registration for parallel imports. The importer would not be required to establish a product's safety, efficacy, or quality, as these would already have been substantiated in the original file. This proposal was eventually abandoned following harsh criticism both of its drafting and of its economic implications, and instead the Commission issued a non-binding communication on parallel imports in which it reiterated the De Peijper principles and endorsed each member state's right:

1. to verify that there is therapeutic equivalence between the domestic and imported product; and therefore to ensure

2. that batches of imported goods conform to the particulars in the dossier; and to request

3. additional information relating to the parallel importer's own business, and on the proposed packaging and leaflets.

The authorities of the member states are nevertheless under a duty to comply with Community law and to make legal provision for parallel importation.[112] In low-price countries such as France, however, which are primarily parallel exporters, there appears to be little justification in practice for any special scheme on parallel imports.[113] In 1982 the UK, in marked contrast, moved from being a net exporter to a net importer, when higher domestic prices and currency fluctuations made the latter activity more attractive. Importation without a product licence was technically an infringement of Section 7(3) of the Medicines Act. Pharmacy wholesalers sought successfully to rely on a loophole in the existing regulations,[114] and, in view of the position under Community law, the DHSS was reluctant to institute proceedings.

In December 1983 the DHSS, after length negotiations with the ABPI and the medical and pharmacy professions, finally announced the introduction of a new Product Licence (Parallel Import) scheme (PL(PI)), which would provide essentially for an abridged application procedure for products which were therapeutically identical to those covered in an existing UK product licence.[115] In its final version, and largely at the behest of the ABPI, the new scheme[116] imposes substantial requirements on the parallel importer to provide information on the source of the imported product and on any repackaging and labelling which has been carried out.[117] Wherever possible, the UK authorities, in accordance with De Peijper, will make a presumption of conformity with the specifications of the medicine in relation to batch controls.[118] However, the PL(PI) scheme also requires that therapeutic equivalence be substantiated with full details both of the product's formulation and of the composition of its active ingredients. The former is usually considered to be commercially confidential information, and the DHSS therefore indicated that the necessary supplementary information would be sought from other licensing authorities, there being no legal basis in UK law to compel disclosure by the original manufacturer. This scheme met with the Commission's broad approval, although the latter expressed some reservation about the absence of an appeal mechanism.

Two months after the scheme came into force, the DHSS Medicines Division had received over 300 applications for PL(PI)s. A significant number were rejected, however, on the grounds that the import was not therapeutically equivalent to the licensed product. Initially, it was DHSS practice to issue a standard refusal, without reasons, unless the applicant made further enquiries. While this might have been legitimate under British administrative law,[119] the fact that it potentially placed an excessive burden on the importer might have had implications under European law, as discussed above,[120] and a formal appeal mechanism was eventually introduced.[121] As we shall see in Chapter 6, the PL(PI) scheme has given rise to a considerable number of legal problems.

In the meantime, it remains open to the original manufacturers to frustrate the practice of parallel importing by other means, particularly through the assertion of their intellectual-property rights in the product itself, where this is under patent,[122] in its trade mark,[123] its 'get-up', its packaging,[124] and its product literature.[125] Community law imposes certain restrictions on the *exercise* of these private rights, through the application of the doctrine of exhaustion.[126] This doctrine has been developed by the Court to reconcile the Treaty's express recognition of national property rights (Article 222) and national rules governing intellectual-property rights (Article 36) with the rules on free movement. This means that the proprietor's exclusive rights are deemed to be exhausted once the products are put into circulation elsewhere in the Common Market. The original manufacturer cannot then rely on these rights to oppose parallel imports. National regimes relating to intellectual property which facilitate product differentiation and which have not been fully harmonized at the European level undoubtedly contribute further to the emerging process of market segmentation between research-based products and generics, discussed in Chapter 2, an issue which will be taken up at the end of this chapter.

Generics

At the time of writing, non-branded or 'pure' generics are not yet covered by the Community directives, which apply only to branded products, which may themselves be either originals or copies.[127]

Older products for which patent rights have elapsed and which have obtained marketing authorization in compliance with directive 75/318 may, however, benefit from an abridged licensing procedure. Article 4(8) of directive 65/65, as amended, provides that, without prejudice to the laws relating to the protection of industrial and commercial property, the applicant need only provide the analytical dossier. The results of clinical trials and pharmacological and toxicological tests need not be submitted if it can be demonstrated that the product is essentially similar[128] to an existing licensed product, and that the original holder of the licence has consented to the original file's being used in the present application; or if it can be demonstrated by detailed reference to published scientific literature[129] that the product has a well-established medical use, with recognized levels of safety and efficacy.[130]

However, Article 1 of directive 87/21[131] introduced important limitations on the use of the abridged procedure which were designed to clarify the conditions under which the 'second applicant' may rely on information already submitted to the licensing authorities. In the light of De Peijper, where the Court held that national authorities might consult the file lodged by the original manufacture, this was an area of Community law which remained unclear. The preamble to directive 87/21 stresses that while it is in the interests of public policy to avoid unnecessarily duplicative tests, innovative firms should not be placed at a competitive disadvantage. Article 1 provides that full details of all tests and clinical trials will be required, up to the point where the product has been on the market for a specified period, which is 10 years in the case of products derived from biotechnology or certain other high-technology products, and 6 years from the date the product was first authorized in the case of other medicinal products. This six-year period may be extended to 10 years at the option of the member states, and is without prejudice to the original manufacturer's patent rights.[132]

It is too early to say what the impact of these new restrictions will be, but it is perhaps worth noting that, prior to their enactment, the Commission and a number of member states had expressed concern, if not surprise, about the number of abridged applications submitted via the multi-state application-procedure discussed above.

Conclusion

In this chapter I have contended that progress towards a harmonized single market for pharmaceuticals will be slow as long as member states remain reluctant to surrender sovereignty on matters of public health and industrial policy, and as long as the European pharmaceutical industry remains suspicious of the possible emergence of Pan-European regulatory bodies which might impose uniform criteria not only for safety standards but also for the evaluation of therapeutic efficacy.

I have also argued that even if the principle of mutual recognition of national licences is established by the target date of 1990, a number of aspects of the procedures for pharmaceutical safety-licensing will not have been harmonized, and substantial variations in technical criteria will be likely to remain, so that a single, internal market for pharmaceuticals is unlikely to be created by 1992.[133] At the same time it must be recognized that some progress has been made towards speeding up the administrative aspects of mutual recognition, with the result that different rules apply to different categories of drugs: different procedures now apply to the movement of generic products, parallel imports, high-technology goods, and 'ordinary medicinal products'. Indeed, the Commission appears to be devoting most of its efforts to approximating the scientific testing requirements and evaluative criteria for high-technology goods. Nevertheless, parallel importers and generic manufacturers have been able to rely upon the general principles of Community law to enforce their right to compete with the original manufacturers on their national territories.

It might therefore be argued that whereas the Common Market had hitherto been compartmentalized along national boundaries, a new form of market stratification has emerged from the Commission's harmonization efforts, a segmentation involving innovative products on the one hand, and more traditional products on the other. There is a marked trend towards applying different regulatory procedures to different classes of drugs; and the separation of research-based or innovative medicines from generic or established products would appear to be confirmed by the extension of increasingly centralized Community procedures to the former category of product, while the licensing of the latter will continue to be dealt with at the national level. I have also argued that the latest Community measures on pricing are inadequate to deal with national regimes of profit control and that scope therefore remains for national governments to use these systems of control to discriminate in favour of home-based firms producing innovative drugs. The implications of these developments on the existing pattern of product competition and its regulation at the national level are, however, complex and will be examined in detail in the following two chapters.

Notes

1. The cost of non-Europe for pharmaceuticals has been estimated at 0.5 per cent of the Community's GNP. Commission of the EC, *Research on the Cost of Non-Europe, Basic Findings*, vol. 15 (Luxembourg: European Communities, 1988), 8.

2. Commission of the EC, *White Paper on the Completion of the Internal Market*, Com (85) 310 (Luxembourg: Commission of the EC, 1985), Annex, 17–18.

3. Case 104/75 *Officier van Justitie* v. *De Peijper* [1976] ECR 613. For the relevant data, see chap. 2, Table 3.

4. Commission of the EC, Com (85) 310, para. 156.

5. OJ 1986 C310/7.

6. Commission of the EC, Com (86) 765: 'Proposal for a Council Directive relating to the transparency of measures regulating the pricing of medicinal products for human use and their inclusion within the scope of the national health insurance system'.

7. For a straightforward introduction to this concept see J. Steiner, *A Textbook on European Law* (London: Blackstone, 1989).

8. S. Forch, 'Probleme des freien Warenverkehrs von Arzneimittelversorgung in den europäischen Gemeinschaften', in *Wettbewerb in Recht und Praxis*, (1981), 71–7.

9. Commission of the EC, 'First Commission Report to the Council on the Functioning of the Committee for Proprietary Medicinal Products and its Impact on the Development of Intra-community Trade, 1977–1978', Com (79) 59 final, 22 Feb. 1979.

10. Case 145/82, *Commission* v. *Italy* [1983] ECR 711; Case 102/79 *Commission* v. *Belgium* [1980] ECR 1473.

11. Closer collaboration between national experts on techniques of drug monitoring was, however, evolving—partly because of the obligation imposed on national authorities by arts. 30 and 33 of directive 75/319, as amended by art. 8, directive 89/341, OJ 1989, L 142/11, to communicate to the Committee all decisions to authorize or to

refuse or revoke a licence. See Commission of the EC, 'Fourth Commission Report to Council', Com (82) 787, final, Dec. 1982.

12. Commission of the EC, 'Third Commission Report on the Approximation of the Laws relating to Proprietary Medicinal Products', Com (80) 789, final, 28 Nov. 1980, p. 4. By 1982 this number had increased to 28, covering a total of 179 national applications (Com (82) 787).

13. The tortious liability of licensing authorities following the licensing of a product which causes harm is by no means clearly established in the existing jurisprudence in either the UK or France, although an action may well lie in the case of evidence of *faute lourde* on the part of the French authorities. See further J.-M. Auby and F. Coustou, *Droit pharmaceutique* (Paris, 1980), fasc. 43.

14. Commission of the EC, 'Third Commission Communication to Council', Com (80) 789.

15. Council recommendation 83/571, OJ 1983, L 322/11; Council recommendation 87/816, OJ 1987, L 73/1. Council directive 87/19, OJ 1987, L 15/31, provides for a new method for revising existing guidelines and for issuing new ones. The Commission now submits a draft to the Technical Committee, which can act by qualified majority. If the Committee is not in favour of the measures, the Commission can refer them to the Council.

16. Com (80) 789, p. 10.

17. Commission proposal, OJ 1980, C 335/4.

18. N. Reich, 'Commercialisation du médicament dans la CEE', unpublished conference paper. See also the minority opinion of the Economic and Social Council of 26 May 1981, OJ 1981, C 19/45.

19. Council directive 83/570, OJ 1983, L 322/1.

20. Art. 15(2) of directive 83/570 provided that the Commission shall, not later than 4 years after the entry into force of the directive, submit to the Council a proposal containing appropriate measures leading towards the abolition of any remaining barriers to free movement. The directive came into force on 31 Oct. 1985.

21. Chap. III of directive 83/570.

22. Interview, EFPIA official, Jan. 1986.

23. See, for example, DHSS, *Pharmaceuticals and the EEC: Symposium Proceedings*, (London, 1985). Similar observations were made to the author in the course of interviews with officials in the French Ministry of Health in May and June 1986.

24. R. Hankin, Speech to the Annual Meeting of Medical and Research Directors, ABPI, 4 Nov. 1987, unpublished.

25. OJ 1987, L 15/31.

26. Art. 5 of directive 87/22 brings pharmaceutical products into the

ambit of the so-called standstill regime, obliging member states to communicate to the Commission proposed new technical regulations (OJ 1987, L 15/40), in compliance with arts. 8 and 9 of Council directive 83/189, which established a procedure for the provision of information in the field of the regulation of technical standards (OJ 1983, L 109/8).

27. Com (88) 143.

28. Interview with T. Venables, Director of BEUC, Jan. 1986.

29. This is the case for the latest package of measures on generics, radio-pharmaceuticals and vaccines, adopted in Council on 3 May 1989 (Council directives 89/341, 89/342, 89/343, OJ 1989, L 142/11–15).

30. Only national measures which are justified on the grounds referred to in art. 36 and the major needs criteria may continue to be applied. Such measures must be verified by the Commission as not being arbitrary or disguised restrictions on trade. As yet, the legal consequences of the latter's refusal to confirm national derogations are unclear. It should be noted that art. 100A(5) provides that the Community may, in appropriate cases, insert a safeguard clause in the harmonization measure, based on art. 100A(1) to allow individual member states to take provisional measures for one of the reasons referred to in art. 36. These measures must also be subject to a Community control procedure. There is some controversy over whether art. 100A(5) prevents para. 4 from being involved. See Glaesner 'Die einheitliche europäische Akte', *Europa Recht*, 20 (1985), 119, at 134, and C. D. Ehlermann, 'The Single European Act', *C. M. L. Rev.* 24 (1987), 361–404.

31. It should be noted that although in its original working paper the Commission had intended to back up the obligation on member states to achieve the internal market by 31 Dec. 1992 with a provision that after that date all unharmonized national restrictions would be automatically recognized, this approach was eventually abandoned, and art. 100B now confers upon the Council the power, but not the duty, to designate national provisions as equivalent. See C. D. Ehlermann, 'The Single European Act', p. 401.

32. Case 227/82 *Van Bennekom* [1983] ECR 3388. Here the Court ruled that the Community definition of a medicinal product is based on the criterion of 'presentation', which is designed to cover not only medicinal products with a genuine therapeutic or medical effect but also products which, in view of their presentation, would be presumed to have such an effect by consumers. Thus products such as vitamins, which are not indicated by recommended expressly as having curative or preventive properties may nevertheless constitute substances presented for the treatment or prevention of disease, within the

meaning of directive 65/65. However, the classification of a product as medicinal within the meaning of the second part of the definition in directive 65/65 must be carried out case by case, having regard to the pharmacological properties of the product, to the extent to which they have been established in the present state of scientific knowledge. National measures which subject 'borderline' products such as vitamins to the procedures laid down in 65/65 are therefore justified in principle on the grounds of public health, even if member states have adopted different solutions in that regard. See also Case 35/85 *Procureur de la République* v. *G. Tissier* [1986] ECR 1207.

33. See the observations of the Advocate General Mancini in Cases 87–88/85, *Pharmacie Legia* v. *Minister for Health* [1986] ECR 1707.
34. Case 27/80, *Fietje* [1980] ECR 3839; and Case 53/80 *Officier van Justitie* v. *Koninklijke Kaasfabriek Eyssen BV* [1981] ECR 409.
35. Case 27/80 *Fietje*, [1980] ECR 3839.
36. Case 8/74 *Procureur du Roi* v. *Dassonville* [1974] ECR 837.
37. Case 120/78 *Rewe Zentralfinanz* v. *Bundesmonopolverwaltung für Branntwein* [1979] ECR 649.
38. Case 72/83 *Campus Oil* [1984] ECR 2751.
39. Case 28/84 *Commission* v. *Germany* [1985] ECR 3123.
40. J. Currall, 'Some Aspects of the Relation between Articles 30 and 36 of the EEC Treaty', *Oxford Year Book of European Law*, 4 (1984) 169–206. In Case 28/84, *supra*, the Court places considerable emphasis on the coherence of the Community system for regulating feeding stuffs. The proposed West German measures, which introduced new composition standards for a *general class* of foodstuff, would have derogated from the division of power laid down by the directives in question. Again, this would suggest that where harmonized procedural arrangements have been established, the Court will be more willing to intervene and strike down national measures than it will be in cases where there is dispute over the nature of the substantive criteria to be applied in determining equivalence.
41. [1976] ECR 613.
42. See further the Advocate General's Opinion in Case 32/80 *Kortmann* [1981] ECR 1980. See also L. Gormley, *Prohibiting Restrictions on Trade within the EEC* (Amsterdam: Elsevier, 1985), 157.
43. In the EEC Treaty art. 36, first sentence, the justification has to be made out and the second sentence examines its use and effects (*De Peijper*, [1976] ECR 635; Case 152/78 *Commission* v. *France* [1980] ECR 2316).
44. J. Azéma and A. Benoit-Lévy, 'Droit Communautaire de la pharmacie', in Auby and Coustou, *Droit pharmaceutique*, fasc. 90-30, p. 9.
45. Case 268/81 *Oosthoek's Uitgeversmaatschappij BV* [1982] ECR 4575.

46. Case 120/78 *Rewe*, [1979] ECR 649, para. 14.
47. 'Any product imported from another Member State must in principle be admitted to the territory of the importing Member State if it has been lawfully produced, that is conforms to rules and processes of manufacture that are customarily and traditionally accepted in the exporting country, and is marketed in the territory of another.' OJ 1980, C 256/2.
48. Case 120/78 *Rewe*, [1979] ECR 649, at recitals 8 and 9; See also R. Barents, *C.M.L. Rev.* 18 (1981), 271.
49. K. Mortelmans, 'The Campus Oil Case', *C.M.L. Rev.* 21 (1984), 405–12.
50. [1981] ECR 995.
51. The duty on member states to bring about a relaxation of administrative controls was underlined in Case 272/80 *Biological Products*, [1981] ECR 3277, which involved the importation of Driol, a substance used to fumigate sugar silos. Driol had been legally marked in France and subsequently imported into the Netherlands without a proper licence. The Court ruled that where the results of the requisite tests were available to the importing authorities, they could not unnecessarily insist on duplicate testing.
52. Case 152/82 *Commission* v. *Belgium* [1983] ECR 531.
53. Case 247/81 *Commission* v. *Germany* [1984] ECR 111.
54. Cases 87–88/85 *Pharmacie Legia* v. *Minister for Health* [1986] ECR 1707.
55. Case 28/84 *Commission* v. *Germany* [1984] ECR 1111.
56. Case 22/78 *ICAP* v. *Beneventi* [1979] ECR 1163.
57. [1984] ECR 2367.
58. The Commission, on the other hand, had argued that the lack of scientific justification for the tests was evidence of their discriminatory nature. See further the Court's recent judgment in Case 54/85 *Mirepoix* [1986] ECR 1067.
59. Case 53/80 *Essen* [1981] ECR 409.
60. Case 174/82 *Sandoz* [1983] ECR 2463; Case 54/85 *Mirepoix*, [1986] ECR 1067; Cases 176/84 *Commission* v. *Greece* and 178/84 *Commission* v. *Germany* (the 'beer cases') [1986] ECR 1203 and 1262.
61. Case 251/78 *Denkavit* [1979] ECR 3369 and Case 174/82, *Sandoz*, [1983] ECR 2445.
62. Case 227/82 *Van Bennekom*, [1983] ECR 3388.
63. [1985] ECR 3887.
64. Ibid. pp. 3094 and 3096.
65. Case 304/84 *Muller and Kampfmeyer* [1986] ECR 1511 and Cases 176/84 and 178/84 *Commission* v. *Greece* and *Commission* v. *Germany* 1986] ECR 1203 and 1262.

66. Case 247/84 *Motte* [1985] ECR 3887.
67. Case 251/78 *Denkavit* [1979] ECR 3369, but see Case 174/82 *Sandoz*, which suggested that authorities may ask the importer to give them such information as he has in his possession concerning the technical composition of the product and the technical or nutritional reasons for adding the vitamins or other additives [1983] ECR 2465.
68. BEUC, *The Consumer and Pharmaceutical Products in the EEC*, BEUC Report, 258/84 (Brussels, 1984).
69. COFACE, *The Community Pharmaceutical Market*, statistics quoted in *Agence Europe*, 4975, 15 Mar. 1989, 13.
70. These statistics are drawn from a study commissioned by BEUC in 1989 on the single market for pharmaceuticals. The study confirmed wide price differentials of up to 500% between low-cost countries such as Portugal and high-cost countries such as West Germany (*Agence Europe*, 5033, 10 June 1989, 13).
71. In particular the binding Treaty obligations under arts. 3, 5, 85, 86, 90, 92, and 30–6. It is highly unlikely that the Community would ever assume direct interventionist powers, even if it did have the competence to do so, something which is a matter of academic debate rather than a practical eventuality.
72. Case 15/74 *Centrafarm* v. *Sterling Drug* [1974] ECR 1164.
73. In theory arts. 103(1), 104, and 145 leave intact the right of each state to take whatever economic measures it deems necessary, but only in the short term. For the Commission's view, see answer to European Parliament Written Question 185/80, OJ 1980, C 316/1.
74. Case 301/82 *Clin Midy* v. *The Belgian State* [1984] ECR 251.
75. As noted earlier in this chapter, the Court, in its jurisprudence on art. 30, has extended its application to include measures applicable without distinction to domestic and imported products where these have the effect of making the sale of imported products more difficult. Case 8/74 *Dassonville* [1974] ECR 865.
76. Case 75/75 *Tasca* [1976] ECR 291; *SADAM* v. *Comitato Interminiseriale dei Prezzi* [1976] ECR 291.
77. Case 82/77 *Van Tiggele* [1978] ECR 25.
78. Cases 16–20/79 *Openbaar* v. *Danis* [1979] ECR 3327; Case 188/86 *Ministère Public* v. *Lefèvre* [1989] 1 CMLR 2.
79. P. Oliver, *Free Movement of Goods in the EEC* (London: ESC Publications, 1982), para. 7.57. See further the case of *R.* v. *Secretary of State for Social Services, ex parte Bomore Medical Supplies*, [1986] 1 CMLR 228.
80. In two recent decisions on regimes fixing maximum profit margins, in other words regimes similar to the former French *cadre de prix* system, the Court threw some light on the legality of these more indirect

methods of price control. In Case 78/82 *Commission* v. *Italy* it was asked to rule on an Italian law which fixed retailers' profit margins on tobacco products at a certain percentage but left manufacturers free to determine the basic price. Applying the general principles discussed above, it held that these controls did not infringe Community law so long as producers remained free to determine their own retail prices and thus take advantage of their lower production costs [1983] ECR 1955. In Case 231/83, *Cullet*, however, the Court ruled that in calculating profit margins for the retailing of petrol a system which reflected the cost structure of the domestic refining industry effectively put imported products at a disadvantage and was therefore discriminatory [1985] ECR 305.

81. [1983] ECR 3849.

82. Case 7/61 *Commission* v. *Italy* [1961] ECR 1625.

83. Case 56/87 *Commission* v. *Italy* [1989] 3 CMLR 707.

84. It will be recalled that in its recent judgment in Case 56/87 *Commission* v. *Italy* [1989] 3 CMLR 707, the Court refused to condemn the Italian system as an obstacle to free trade because the Commission had not furnished sufficient proof of discrimination.

85. R. v. *The Secretary of State for Social Services, ex parte Bomore Medical Supplies* [1986] 1 CMLR 228.

86. The Court of Appeal's decision in Bomore has been roundly criticized, not least by officials of the European Commission (interview, source withheld). On the one hand, it ignored a basic principle of Community law, namely that it is not the intention of art. 30 to give the importer better or greater rights than the distributor of domestic products. There was no obligation on the DHSS to implement or continue to implement the discount scheme in a way that protected parallel trade. On the other hand, the Court of Appeal appears to have overlooked the peculiar features of the market for pharmaceuticals, and confounded the interests of the DHSS as paymaster with those of the ordinary consumer. If, however, it had followed the European Court's reasoning in *Duphar*, examined below, it ought, with respect, to have reached a different conclusion.

87. [1984] ECR 523.

88. Once again the Advocate General argued for a broad reading of the derogations listed in art. 36, contending that the exception in regard to public health should be interpreted to include not only restrictions relating to safety but also indirect measures such as financial restrictions, an approach which was at odds with the Court's previous, restricted interpretation of the scope of the exception relating to public health in Case 251/78 *Denkavit* [1979] ECR 3369, where it

held that the provision 'cannot be relied on to justify rules or practices which, even though they are beneficial, contain restrictions which are explained primarily by a concern to lighten the administration's burden or reduce public expenditure, unless, in the absence thereof this burden or expenditure clearly would exceed the limits of what can reasonably be required'.

89. Case 238/82 *Duphar* [1984] ECR 523, para. 20.
90. Ibid. paras. 22–4.
91. OJ 1989, L 40/8.
92. Com (86) 765, p. 10.
93. P. Lataillade, *Report of the Commission's Proposal for a Directive on Pharmaceutical Pricing Transparency*, (European Parliament, Doc. A2-261/87).
94. EFPIA, Statement 11 Feb. 1987, reproduced in *Scrip*, 1203, 8 May 1987, 7.
95. See the DHSS's submission to the House of Commons Select Committee on European Legislation, 15th Report, 1986–7, HC 22–XV.
96. Commission directive 70/50, interpreting the scope of art. 30, expressly refers to restrictions on marketing and makes no mention of restrictions relating to production which could operate in favour of domestically produced goods, indirectly affecting prices. See also Cases 3, 4, and 6/76 *Kramer* [1976] ECR para. 27.
97. In essence following its earlier ruling in Case 19/79 *Groenveld* [1979] ECR 3409.
98. Case 238/82 *Duphar* [1984] ECR 523, para. 26.
99. Arts. 3(f), 5, and 85–94 EEC.
100. Case 13/77 *GB Inno-BM* v. *Atab* [1977] ECR 2115. The Court will also have to address these questions when it examines the Dutch Nefarma's challenge to a recent Commission decision on the application of art. 85, registered as Case 166/89 *Nefarma* v. *Commission*.
101. If the public authorities retain ultimate responsibility for fixing prices, art. 85 cannot apply, although art. 30 probably does (Case 231/83 *Cullet* v. *Leclerc* [1985] ECR 305; Case 29/83 *Leclerc* v. *Au blé vert* [1985] ECR 1; Commission decision 86/596 (Meldoc), OJ 1986 L 348/50; Case 66/86 *Saeed*, judgment of 11 Apr. 1989, not yet reported).
102. Case 72/83 *Campus Oil*, [1984] ECR 2751; Case 311/85 *Vereniging van Vlaamse Reisbureaus* [1989] 4 CMLR 213; Cases 202–213/84 *Ministère Public* v. *Lucas Asjès and others* [1986] ECR 1425. For a useful discussion of these cases, see L. Gyselen, 'State Action and the Effectiveness of the EEC Treaty's Competition Provisions', *C.M.L. Rev.* 26 (1988), 33–60.

103. Cases 240–2, 261, 262, 268, and 269/82 *Stichting Sigaret-tenindustrie* [1987] 3 CMLR 661.
104. Case 61/79 *Amministrazione delle finanze dello stato* v. *Denkavit* [1980] ECR 1205.
105. Case 78/76 *Firma Steinike und Weinlig* v. *Germany* [1977] ECR 595.
106. OJ 1986, C 312/6. The potential application of art. 92 to an agreement between the Spanish health authorities and the Spanish pharmaceutical industry association is due to be considered by the Court of Justice, following a reference from the Spanish courts, *Farma Industria* v. *Consejeria de Salud*, registered as Case 179/89.
107. Commission of the EC, *White Paper on Completing the Internal Market*, 1985, p. 31.
108. Commission of the EC, *Ninth Competition Policy Report* (Luxembourg: EC Commission, 1981); but see Case 172/82 *Inter-Huiles* [1983] ECR 555.
109. T. C. Daintith and L. Hancher, *Energy Strategy in Europe: The Legal Framework* (Berlin: De Gruyter, 1986), esp. chaps. 6 and 7.
110. Case 8/74 *Dassonville*, [1974] ECR 837; Case 104/75 *De Peijper*, [1976] ECR 613.
111. OJ 1980, C 143/1.
112. The Commission's 1986 communication makes it clear that it will not hesitate to bring art. 169 proceedings where there is a failure of that duty.
113. Prior to the suppression of the *autorisation de débit* by the decree of 21 Nov. 1972, importation of finished products into France was impossible. Nevertheless, the French CSP makes no express provision for imports, but arts. R.5128 and R.5129 of the CSP require supporting documentation which can only be obtained with the consent of the original manufacturer. This would appear to restrict imports to the company's authorized channels.
114. The Medicines (Exemption from Licences) Importation Order 1978, S.I. no. 1461 allows for the importation of medicines not already available in the UK as long as they are for specific patients. However, these terms appear to have been sufficiently loosely defined to allow for parallel importation, and the DHSS intimated that it would not prosecute (*Pharmaceutical Journal*, 26 Feb. 1983).
115. DHSS, MAIL, MLX no. 150, 1983.
116. Medicines Act (Licensing Regulations) 1984 S.I. no. 673, 1984.
117. In any event, anyone who assembles medicinal products is required to obtain the necessary licence.
118. See Clarke's statement to the House of Commons, 16 May 1984, Hansard, May 1984, vol. 60, col. 157 W.
119. Sect. 20(5)(b) provides that where, on an application for a licence, the

licensing authority refuses to grant a licence and the applicant requests it to state reasons, the authority must serve a notice stating the reasons for its decision.

120. Case 272/80 *Biological Products*, and art. 4(8) of directive 87/22 EEC, discussed below.
121. S.I. no. 1761.
122. Case 15/74 *Centrafarm* v. *Sterling Drug*, [1974] ECR, 1147.
123. Case 16/74 *Centrafarm* v. *Winthrop* [1974] ECR 1184.
124. Case 102/77 *Hoffmann-La Roche* v. *Centrafarm* [1978] ECR 1139; Case 3/78 *Centrafarm* v. *American Home Products* [1978] ECR 1823.
125. Case 1/81 *Pfizer* v. *Eurim-Pharm* [1981] ECR 2913.
126. The doctrine of exhaustion was first elaborated by the Court in Case 78/70 *Deutsche Grammophon* v. *Metro* [1971] ECR 487 and more fully developed in Case 15/74 *Centrafarm* v. *Sterling Drug*, [1974] ECR, 1147.
127. Com (87) 697, final, 4 Jan. 1988, on the extension of the pharmaceutical directives to products not yet covered, included a proposal that henceforth Community pharmaceutical legislation should simply refer to 'medicinal' products rather than proprietary medicinal products. This proposal was adopted by the Council in May 1989 (EEC directive 89/341, OJ 1989, L 142/11).
128. For the purposes of this provision, a product will be regarded as essentially similar if it has the same qualitative and quantitative composition in terms of active principles, if the pharmaceutical form is the same, and if, where necessary, bio-equivalence has been demonstrated by appropriate bio-availability studies carried out in accordance with the principles set out in Annexe X to recommendation 87/176, Com (87) 697.
129. Presented in accordance with art. 1 of directive 75/318.
130. Art. 2(c) of directive 75/319 provides that the experts must clearly state the grounds for using published references.
131. OJ 1987, L 15/36. These issues are further examined in Chap. 6.
132. The following member states have notified the Commission of their intention to apply a ten-year period in respect of all products marketed on their territory in the interest of public health: Germany, France, Italy, and the UK. In Denmark the six-year period will not apply beyond the date of expiry of a patent protecting the original product. Greece, Spain, and Portugal have until 1992 to apply the directive.
133. The commission has now sent to the Council a package of draft directives on the labelling of medicinal products of human use and on package leaflets (OJ 1990, C58/21); on the legal status of medicinal products for human use (OJ 1990, C58/19); and for the wholesale distribution of medicinal products for human use (OJ 1990, C58/16).

6

Cost Control in the 1980s: Reappraising Health Costs in the UK

In this and the following chapter I review and compare the emergence and subsequent fate of recent initiatives for the containment of health costs in the UK and France. Each chapter will offer a comparative account of the genesis and performance of these policies, and attempt an explanation for their limitations in institutional and legal terms. It will be argued that while the techniques of regulation reviewed in Chapters 3 and 4 have provided a framework for the negotiation of the new strategies, they have also acted as an important constraint upon the bargaining position of each government and of their respective industries.

There are a number of factors which explain the renewed impetus to reduce pharmaceutical expenditure in the UK and France in the 1980s, as elsewhere in Europe. First, the inflationary impact of the second oil shock of 1979, which prompted a reappraisal of levels of welfare spending in general, provoked a reassessment of priorities in health spending and of expenditure on drugs. In France the Ninth Plan predicted that to commit further resources to health care at existing levels of growth would endanger other areas of economic and social provision.[1] In the UK, where the proportion of GNP devoted to expenditure on health care over the previous three decades has remained relatively low in comparison with France and other EC member states, wider constraints on public-sector borrowing necessitated financial stringency. At the same time, the demands made upon health-care systems have increased, partly as a result of the availability of improved, and therefore more costly, forms of care or methods of treatment, but also as a result of demographic change. An increasingly elderly population consumes a disproportionate amount of expensive drugs.[2]

Secondly, the existing controls on pharmaceutical expenditure did not appear to be working. Despite, or perhaps because of, the operation of the systems of price control reviewed in Chapter 3, average prices for drugs rose steadily in the last decade. In France payments for drugs and appliances increased by 42 per cent between 1977 and 1982, compared with increases of 34 per cent in payments to hospitals and 36 per cent in the cost of medical and other services.[3] In the UK in the period 1978–82 drug costs rose more sharply. Taking an index of 100 for the base year of 1975, an OECD survey revealed an increase to 153.3 in 1978, 196.9 in 1980, and 248.7 in 1983. Comparable figures for the same period in France were 116.4 in 1975, 134.1 in 1980, and 161.1 in 1983.[4] In its report on the government's expenditure plans, the British Social Services Committee of the House of Commons found that pharmaceutical price increases at 2.5 per cent above inflation were being automatically incorporated into NHS budget projections for 1982.[5]

To reduce health expenditure in absolute terms is, of course, a politically difficult, if not impossible, goal. In consequence, the leitmotif of health policy in the 1980s has been the search for efficiency in the utilization of scarce and, in real terms, declining resources: the quest for the maximum value for the minimum amount of money. To this end, proposals for major financial and administrative reforms in the health sector featured in successive French pluriennial plans[6] and were adumbrated in the British Conservative Party's manifestos of 1979, 1983, and 1987. Subsequent reform, particularly in the hospital sector, has largely been in the direction of greater centralization of controls over expenditure and the imposition of cash limits on spending. This process was accomplished without too much difficulty in the UK. The 1980 Health and Social Services Act imposes a statutory duty on health authorities, but not the FPS, to comply with annual targets set by the Secretary of State. Although France has in fact adopted an essentially similar strategy of cash limits, it has been tailored to suit a very different set of institutional arrangements. Decentralization or *départementalisation* has meant delegation to regionally based teams of professionals and administrators who determine spending priorities.[7]

The transposition of the strategy of cash limits to control spending by practitioners has, however, proved problematic in both countries. There are two possible reasons for this. Firstly, cash limits may constitute an infringement on the medical profession's clinical freedom to prescribe the drug of their choice, irrespective of cost. Secondly, the ability to devise satisfactory mechanisms to control 'demand determined' costs at their point of origin appears questionable.[8] Significantly, the independence of the British FPS from the other decentralized NHS bodies was reinforced in 1984, arguably strengthening the position of the DHSS to determine 'fixed costs', including capital expenditure on surgeries and expense allowances.[9] As I will argue in this and the subsequent chapter, both governments have attempted to introduce surrogate forms of cash limits on pharmaceutical expenditure. It is in this context that the two recent major changes in policy—the adoption of the Limited List in the UK, discussed in this chapter, and the French Socialist government's experiment with 'contractualization'— should be understood. Although the design of each of these strategies reflects profound ideological differences, this should not be allowed to obscure the continuing influence of the institutional and legal factors reviewed in Chapter 3 and the nature of the constraints which they have imposed both on the industry and on French and British government.

The remainder of this chapter is devoted to a detailed analysis of the British situation. The first section examines the impact of the British tradition of self-regulatory controls over profits on the formulation and implementation of the new policy on costs. It traces the failure of the system of voluntary price control to hold down price rises. It also examines the gradual emergence of a 'two-tiered' drug market in the UK, where competition from parallel importers and generic manufacturers has developed. Whereas product competition continues to dominate in the research-based or innovative tier of the market, price competition in the market for older drug products, most of which are now out of patent, is evident. As the structure of the market has altered, however, the role of some of the other barriers to entry, discussed in Chapter 2, has begun to change. In this context, the second section examines recent developments in the administration of product-safety licensing in the UK. It examines government attempts to accommodate the interests of the research-based industry within the existing bargaining framework, a policy framework which has been put under strain by the emergence of new market-entrants.

Cost Controls in the UK and the Adoption of the Selective List

The circumstances leading up to the introduction of the Selective or Limited List in April 1985 must be understood in the context of the failure of the Sixth Pharmaceutical Price Regulation Scheme, negotiated in 1978, to contain price increases. The change in nomenclature, with the omission of the term 'voluntary', reflected the changed nature of industry's commitment to the scheme.[10] Although the DHSS's negotiating position appeared to have been strengthened by an accretion of indirect formal legal powers,[11] in a number of fundamental respects the bargaining framework remained unaltered, allowing for continued flexibility in the negotiation of company profits. To a certain extent, this flexibility enabled the Labour government and its Conservative successors the scope to exploit the nascent changes in market structure to obtain concessions from the industry. In particular, now that many leading products were no longer under patent, the prospect of introducing price competition by stimulating competition among generic manufacturers had become an attractive and feasible option. However, a joint statement issued in the spring of 1978 by the DHSS and the British Medical Association (BMA) on prescribing costs,[12] urging doctors to prescribe generically, seemed to confirm a continued preference for exhortation over regulation. The entire question of compulsory generic prescribing by doctors or generic substitution by pharmacists was conveniently shelved by the Labour government, pending publication of the final report of the Royal Commission on Health in 1979.[13]

The sixth PPRS in operation

In reality it was a commitment to effective *product* rather than price competition which lay at the core of the sixth PPRS. Its major innovation was to differentiate between firms and to reward those with good investment records with higher rates of profit. It was, in other words, an experiment in fine tuning. A fixed formula for allowable advertising expenditure was introduced into the scheme for the first time, but in every other respect flexibility remained at the heart of the new approach. An individual firm's profit target, although linked to an overall 'industry-wide rate', in fact reflected the DHSS's 'view of the merit of the company, having regard to its contribution to the economy, its investment, research and development expenditure and value added in manufacture in the UK, and by the value of its exports'.[14]

Prices for individual products had to be notified and would be approved by the DHSS provided that it was satisfied that the company's profit would remain within its target rate. On the assumption that the primary objective of most of the firms in the PPRS was to make themselves more efficient, the DHSS allowed individual firms a margin of tolerance—the 'grey area'—of up to 10 per cent over and above the overall target. This meant that certain firms could, and indeed did, earn an average rate of return of up to 33 per cent, although the scheme provided that where a firm exceeded its target rate plus the grey area, the DHSS could either demand a cash rebate or could refuse future price increases. In addition, this flexibility allowed firms the possibility of offsetting the adverse financial consequences of generic competition. Where a company could demonstrate that the export earnings of a product with a newly expired patent would be badly affected by price competition, the DHSS could be persuaded to maintain prices at artificially high levels on the home market.[15]

As an attempt at fine tuning, the PPRS was bound to fail. Its substantive terms perpetuated the two major weaknesses common to its five predecessors: an absence of real powers and resources to implement the scheme and an absence of objective criteria by which to evaluate performance. The Department claimed that its negotiating position had been greatly strengthened, firstly by an amendment requiring companies to submit forecast financial returns, which would be compared with audited financial returns for each year;[16] and secondly by the introduction of a power to claw back excess profits or refuse to grant future price increases under the PPRS. Together these powers allowed officials to make a prospective judgement about profitability, considered vital in an inflationary period, and theoretically to make retroactive adjustments.[17] With a staff of only twelve, the Industry Division at the DHSS was constrained to rely heavily on each firm's own estimate of its out-turn of sales, costs, and profit on NHS business for each year.

Furthermore, where the performance of individual firms was assessed on largely subjective criteria, these new powers were unlikely to be used to much effect. The DHSS appears to have been both unable and unwilling to devise objective criteria of efficiency for the sixty-five adherents to the scheme, whose performance 'varied acutely'.[18] The broad assumption that because the majority of firms were internationally competitive their performance at national level was also efficient continued to hold. And yet allowable pharmaceutical R. & D. costs, always high, increased steadily under the PPRS, from £82 million in 1978 (12 per cent of NHS sales) to £247 million by 1983 (18 per cent of NHS sales).[19] The Industry Division limited its task to comparing estimated profits with out-turns, its entirely non-medical staff not being equipped to investigate the scientific value of any particular item of R. & D. expenditure.[20]

Significantly, the scheme made no advance over any of its predecessors on the sensitive issue of transfer pricing. Companies were asked to use 'best endeavours to inform the department of any profit margins or contributions contained within the transfer prices of significant items' (para. 9.1). As the calculation of 'reasonable profits' was based on a percentage of capital employed for all firms with NHS sales of over £1.5 million, an accurate allocation of capital to NHS business was more crucial than ever, but in the absence of access to the supplying affiliates' financial records, the DHSS had no real power to assess the reasonableness of these calculations. This weakness was acknowledged—but not tackled—by the Department when the scheme was introduced. Instead, there was a commitment to review the problem at the end of the five-year period, an approach which evoked some scepticism from the CPA, which estimated that in 1983 alone profits on NHS sales were understated by over £200 million—a sum equivalent to the official adjusted profits allowed under the scheme.[21]

The DHSS was also generous in its treatment of firms who overshot their target, and as such it appeared unwilling to take full advantage of its monopsonistic power and position. After all, a firm anticipating a series of annual negotiations on profits and prices would surely find it in its own interests to act reasonably. If its forecast profits appeared excessive, the DHSS could either require prices to be adjusted immediately or could ask for retrospective adjustment when the AFRs were submitted. In fact the DHSS gave industry the benefit of the doubt and relied upon the latter course: in each of the first 4 years of the scheme's operation sums of only £1.3 million, £1.6 million, £0.5 million, and £3.2 million were repaid. While an alleged average of £11 million per annum in price increases had been disallowed, there was no evidence to suggest that the prices initially requested were anything more than a bargaining gambit. Between 1979 and 1985 the total costs in medicines of the FPS had risen by almost 90 per cent.[22] The pharmaceutical companies' average rates of return on capital had risen to around 26 per cent by 1982—in other words, 9 points higher than the rate of return allowed on other government contracts, a rate itself estimated to be higher than average industrial profitability. International and European comparative studies indicated that the UK had moved from near the bottom to around the middle of league-tables on pricing,[23] a trend confirmed by the rise of parallel importing from mid-1981 onwards.[24] Unsurprisingly, the NHS market grew more attractive to industry, accounting in 1984 for 48 per cent of its total sales, as opposed to 42 per cent in 1978.[25]

Immediate reactions to the failure of the sixth PPRS

In this context, it is understandable that neither the Comptroller and Auditor General, who reported on the scheme in early 1983, nor the Committee of Public Accounts, which, after a decade of silence, examined the PPRS in 1979 and in three consecutive sessions between 1982 and 1984, were satisfied that the NHS was obtaining drugs at reasonable prices. The CPA's findings received considerable publicity. Against a background of general expenditure cuts, it was clear that the PPRS would require major amendment when it came up for renegotiation, but the form it would take remained an open question. The government's response to scepticism about the scheme and to the rising costs of drugs to the NHS is an interesting demonstration of the endurance of existing linkages with the industry.

In the first place, the very informality and flexibility of the scheme allowed the DHSS, under pressure from the Treasury, to react in a prompt, if pragmatic fashion to higher drug prices and company profits. In August 1983 a 2.5 per cent cut and a price freeze, backdated to April 1983, were unilaterally imposed on all NHS sales, yielding savings to the NHS of some £25 million. In December 1983 the Minister, Kenneth Clarke, announced that, following 'extensive discussion with industry's representatives', the target rate of return would be cut to 21 per cent, with a reduced 'grey area' of 7 per cent, and that the price freeze would continue into 1984–5. The amount of expenditure allowed on advertising under the scheme was reduced from 10 to 9 per cent, and companies overshooting this ceiling were asked to repay excess expenditure to the DHSS immediately.[26]

The government anticipated savings of £65 million from this package of measures, even although industry's average rate of return remained some 5 points above the recommended ROR for government risk-contractors. Individual RORs, which are never made public, allegedly continued to fluctuate between wide margins: from the 4 per cent allowed to Hoechst in 1984 to the 33 per cent reputedly enjoyed by Fisons.[27] In January 1985 further reductions in the overall ROR were announced for 1985–6, and companies were asked to reduce their prices to reflect the lower profit target and promotional allowance. Savings of up to £45 million were anticipated.[28] The very flexibility of the scheme had seemingly allowed the Conservative government to achieve the goal which had eluded ministers since 1954—the alignment of the drug industry's profits with those earned by other contractors to government.[29]

It is also important to note that these various measures were instituted without any question of official recourse to the various indirect powers discussed in Chapter 3. Instead, the government chose deliberately to refrain from exposing the industry to increased competition, either from cheap parallel imports or from generics as a quid pro quo for industry's agreement to the 1983 price cuts. In early 1982 the government had referred the question of prescribing costs to an *ad hoc* committee of medical and pharmaceutical experts under the chairmanship of Dr P. R. Greenfield. The industry was not represented, nor did it have the opportunity to put its views to the Committee. Although it concluded its deliberations in late 1982, the Greenfield Committee's report was not published until the following year. When it became clear that the Committee had come out in favour of generic substitution as the most effective means of saving an estimated £35 million per annum on costs, ministers were quick to allay the respective fears of industry, the medical profession, and the pharmacists.[30] The practical and legal problems associated with generic substitution, as well as its wider implications for the international competitiveness of British-based industry, convinced the Health Minister not to proceed on this front. In Chapter 5 it was noted that the ABPI was extensively involved on the proposed licensing scheme for parallel imports, the final version of which was not enacted until 1984 and which accommodated most of the demands of the larger research-based firms in terms of the information required from importers. The readiness with which the ABPI accepted price cuts in August 1983 no doubt helped to reinforce the prevailing view that an alternative solution to increased exposure to price competition could be found within the terms of the existing bargaining framework.

Nevertheless, the industry reacted vehemently to the further round of cuts in 1985 and continued to protest that the alignment of the average ROR to that allowed for other government contracts, although adequate for production-based industry, was far too low for a technology-based sector. Relations between the two sides did not break down, however, in the way in which they were to do in France, where, as we shall see in Chapter 7, the SNIP's board resigned in protest at a price freeze imposed in July 1984. Individual firms continued to negotiate on product prices, and the ABPI, anticipating a renewal of the scheme, reconstituted its PPRS negotiating committee in the summer of 1985. For the individual firm, the incentive to continued negotiation was the very real possibility of being alloted a higher target rate, but for the industry as a whole, as represented by the ABPI, the stakes were much higher.[31] If the PPRS was to retain its non-statutory, non-binding character, a continued and visible commitment to its underlying consensual philosophy was paramount. It is perhaps for this reason that individual firms consented voluntarily not only to reduce prices but, when the issue of transfer pricing attracted public and parliamentary notice, to allow DHSS officials access to records of transactions between parent companies and subsidiaries.[32] While ABPI officials conceded that relations with the DHSS had undoubtedly deteriorated, this period in the history of the PPRS was depicted as one of instability rather than hostility. It can also be seen as a period of a succession of 'victories' by the government.

The introduction of the Limited List

Unfortunately for the industry, other changes were afoot which would disrupt the existing pattern of relations with government still further. The various adjustments to the PPRS had undoubtedly resulted in short-term savings, but if significant long-term economies were to be achieved, some attention had to be given to the wider issue of competition. Although the generic market was the most obvious source of competition, the government was clearly concerned about the impact of compulsory generic prescribing or generic substitution by pharmacists on the international position of its home-based industry. The DHSS continued its search for alternative means to economize, but its quest was pre-empted by the results of the Treasury's 1983 Public Expenditure Survey, which revealed an overshoot on FPS spending targets—which, it will be recalled, were not cash-limited—of some £100 million for that year. It was up to the DHSS to make up the shortfall from savings on the NHS drugs bill,[33] and on 8 November 1984 during the debate on the Address, the Minister announced that from 1 April 1985 a limited list of medicines restricting the availability of 'minor remedies and tranquilizers' would be enforced. Although he made it clear that 'we do not intend to move over to a policy of indiscriminate generic substitution', he went on to add 'I see no reason ... why in the two groups that I have set out, the NHS should not limit itself to providing only the cheaper generic alternatives.'[34] The traditional methods of exhortation and persuasion, although still favoured, were no longer considered sufficient in themselves.[35] Although the Minister indicated that proposals were only in rudimentary form, and that the final version would be the result of anticipated negotiations with the professions and the industry, a brief consultative letter which followed the announcement made it plain that only the form, and not the principle, of the list was negotiable.

The announcement met with predictable hostility on all fronts, and antipathy was only strengthened by the government's refusal to disclose details of which drugs would remain prescribable, as well as the mechanisms by which the process of selection was to be made. In particular, the legal mechanism by which the list would be introduced was not made clear. This was due in part to the DHSS's own equivocation over the merits of a positive or white list, specifying those products which would be reimbursed, as compared with those of a negative or black list, which would simply ban various branded products. Initially, the proposal took the form of a rather restricted white list. The government wished to introduce the provisions by way of amendment to the terms of service for doctors, and it became clear that while a black list banning the prescription of some products could be introduced quietly by way of statutory instrument, a positive list would require legislation[36] and might also be incompatible with European law.[37] Under the present scheme, only the black list has the force of law, the white list being merely advisory.

Legal challenges to the Limited List

Such was the political controversy and furore unleashed by the announcement of November 1984 that the main groups which were affected not only refused to follow the traditional consensual path and enter into negotiations on the composition of the list but also articulated their opposition to it by legal or confrontational means. Indeed, the volume of legal activity was unprecedented, even if the scope for effective judicial challenge was limited. According to the city analysts Greenwells, the foreign multinationals were likely to be the most adversely affected by the list, while the British firms with a research base were expected to be little affected, mainly because of their broadly based product-ranges and their large interests in generic drugs or OTC sales. A possible legal challenge to the list was explored by several of the British-based American and European subsidiaries. The Council of the BMA, in a resolution of 9 January 1985, suggested that the list was contrary to the spirit, if not the letter, of the Minister's general statutory duty 'to continue the promotion of a comprehensive health service'.

It was, however, highly unlikely that a court would find the introduction of a cost-cutting measure, and in particular a limited, negative list which restricted choice but did not preclude treatment, sufficiently 'unreasonable' as to amount to a breach of this duty or as *ultra vires* under the 1946 Act.[38] When confronted with policy decisions of this type, the English judiciary has undoubtedly erred on the side of caution.[39]

At first sight, the potential offered by the supposed failure to consult meaningfully seemed the most promising and sustainable course of challenge in the light of recent developments in British administrative law, but the very informality of past patterns of negotiation worked against the individual firms. In the important case of CPSU v. *Minister for Civil Servants*,[40] the House of Lords had only recently held that an aggrieved person was entitled to invoke judicial review if he or she showed that a decision of a public authority deprived him or her of some benefit which he or she could legitimately expect to continue to enjoy unless given reasons for its withdrawal and an opportunity to comment on those reasons. The legitimate expectation arising from the existence of a regular practice of consultation which could be reasonably expected to continue gave rise to an obligation to act fairly. It would appear that the drug firms in question were advised that their own situation was sufficiently distinguishable. The enabling legislation, the National Health Service Act 1977, makes no provision for the extensive consultation required as, for example, under the Medicines Act 1968. The thirty-year course of dealings between the industry and the DHSS on prices had not been conducted under the auspices of either legislative framework.[41] Furthermore, the Minister had invited consultation; the industry had refused to co-operate.[42]

European law, however, offers a potentially wider scope than British administrative law for an aggrieved individual to challenge an act of government. Not only may a sustainable legal action lie against national governments for breach of a Community obligation, but the judiciary have expressed a willingness to go beyond the traditional narrow confines of judicial review and to evaluate the facts on which a ministerial decision was based.[43] Hence a number of individual companies, the ABPI, and the EFPIA all considered the European route. As the Court's judgment in *Duphar* in 1984 had sanctioned the principle of the limited lists based on cost considerations, a successful challenge would have to rest upon breach of one of the conditions laid down in the judgment. The DHSS was, of course, well aware of the implications of *Duphar* and had consulted the Commission on the compatibility of their proposed list.[44] The decision to set up the non-statutory Advisory Committee, the task of which was to update the list and ensure that drugs met all clinical needs at the lowest cost, appears to have been one result of these discussions.[45] The Commission, in a series of replies to questions in the European Parliament indicated that, prima facie, the final version of the list complied with *Duphar*. The main criterion for inclusion on the 'black list' was that of price in relation to therapeutic need. The procedures and principles on which decisions were based very objectively verifiable, and there was a procedure to amend the list at regular intervals.[46] In addition, a successful challenge to the inclusion of a product on the list would require proof of discrimination on the basis of origin.[47] Although both the ABPI and the EFPIA compiled evidence on the volume of imported business which would be affected by the list, and the latter made a formal complaint to the Commission, neither succeeded in persuading it to initiate proceedings.

Alternative strategies of challenge

With the option of legal challenge to the decision to introduce the list foreclosed, the industry, both collectively and individually, continued their opposition through other channels, including a high-profile advertising campaign by the ABPI and extensive lobbying of government by individual firms. In addition, delegations from other national interest-groups, most notably the American Pharmaceutical Manufacturers Association (PMA), sought to protest to the Prime Minister in person. This strategy too proved unsuccessful, and the list duly became law on 1 April 1985.[48] The companies were therefore constrained to pursue a campaign of damage limitation, now fought on two distinct fronts.

In the first place, it was important to ensure that decisions to 'black' products were made on the basis of cost alone, and not according to the subsidiary criterion of real clinical need. The systematic application of the latter could mean the introduction of the long-opposed comparative efficacy or needs test. The announcement of a non-statutory advisory committee, staffed by medical experts, some of whom were not entirely dissociated from the industry,[49] and serviced by the Family Practitioner Services Division of the DHSS, offered a glimmer of hope. After its initial meetings, the latter made it clear that the only real criterion for inclusion on the black list would be cost, and indeed companies who informally agreed to lower prices would not have their products included. Within several months relations between the Committee and the industry were reported to be satisfactory by both sides.[50]

In the second place, the companies set about minimizing the impact of lower prices by attempting to suppress competition from rival firms. Legal arguments once again provided bargaining power when all else failed. This strategy was pursued by firms such as Glaxo, which already marketed generic lines. Glaxo attempted to counter the adverse effects of the list by marketing its own lines of branded generics, the 'Gx' range. Other firms, including Wyeth and

Duphar, lowered the price of their blacklisted product to the tariff price for the permitted generic compound and remarketed the compound under its generic name. But not every product listed was out of patent, so not all had a generic equivalent, even if the DHSS anticipated that this would only be a temporary state of affairs.[51]

Other companies invoked European law to protect their brand names. Arguably, once a price has been adjusted, a company has an automatic right to have its product *prescribed* by its brand name. The current view in the Department and at the Commission, however, is that so long as there is nothing to prevent the product being *dispensed*, by whatever name, then European law will not be breached,[52] an interpretation favoured by the English High Court in the *Schering* case in 1986. Schering sought judicial review of the refusal to list its product Noctamid by its brand name on the white list. It claimed that the product was the same price as, and therapeutically equivalent to, its 'comparator', and that the brand names of other products were not blacklisted. Hence the decision to exclude the trade mark was a measure having equivalent effect to a quantitative restriction on trade, contrary to European law.[53] The company also 'convincingly asserted that their sales (were) reduced by the refusal to list their brand name'.[54] The trial judge found no merit in the assertion that generic prescribing as such put the applicants at a competitive disadvantage, and ruled that the exclusion of the trade mark was not discriminatory. Although the reasoning in this decision has been criticized,[55] the result is probably now good law, as it would seem to reconcile the principle that a trade mark represents an important guarantee of origin to the consumer with the special conditions under which a medicine is selected by a doctor.[56]

This flurry of legal activity therefore produced little by way of direct concrete result. The government claimed to have saved around £75 million in the first year of the list's operation. In 1988 generic prescriptions accounted for some 39 per cent of all NHS prescriptions. In the meantime, however, the ABPI has opted for a quite different strategy to promote the orthodoxy of product competition and to exploit the emergence of a two-tiered market within the NHS.

Renegotiating profit regulation

Despite the fact that it pressed ahead with the list, the Conservative government was obviously alarmed by the industry's vehement reactions to it and to the other inroads on its profitability. A ministerial reshuffle in June 1985, followed by repeated promises that the list was not 'the thin end of the wedge' of compulsory generic prescribing and by an explicit commitment to a period of stability for the industry probably helped to clear the air initially. ABPI pressure for the DHSS's sponsorship function to be transferred to the Department of Trade and Industry was abandoned,[57] and negotiations on the renewal of the PPRS began in earnest.

The PPRS and the Limited List

An important and probably unforeseen consequence of the adoption of the Limited List was that it made untenable a major assumption on which previous versions of the VPRS had been constructed: that where almost all prescribed medicines sold in the UK were bought by a single purchaser, if a company's overall costs and profits in supplying such medicines were reasonable, the prices of individual medicines were not in themselves significant. If the list were to reduce costs in the long term, however, manufacturers could not be allowed to offset their lower profits on generic products against higher prices on other NHS products. Either a method of excluding the former from profit calculations for PPRS purposes had to be devised or individual product costs had to be more carefully examined, an approach not particularly welcomed by the industry as long as the related, but equally problematic issue of transfer pricing remained unresolved.

If the government did not want to lose the little ground it had gained in recent years, the industry was equally determined to restore the balance in its own favour. Several firms had already made it clear that the UK market was sufficiently small for them to begin reducing the scale of their operations there, especially if generic competition were encouraged. Some companies had cancelled investment projects, and others were publicly contemplating switching operations to other locations in Europe. The ABPI claimed that in total £138 million of capital investment had been cancelled or deferred and 2,000 jobs lost.[58]

Negotiations were protracted, lasting until August 1986, and were conducted in the utmost secrecy. It is not easy to identify the processes by which compromises were reached between the DHSS and the ABPI negotiating team, and within the latter's membership. One can only compare the end result with what went before. Various leaks to the trade press suggested that the large firms had divided, at least temporarily, into nationalist camps. The German firms were allegedly prepared to test the legality, under European law, of various draft clauses linking allowable profit to research and development expenditure in the UK. The American Pharmaceutical Manufacturers Association kept a close watch on the formulation of the proposed controls on transfer prices.[59] For a number of foreign-owned firms, the PPRS was allegedly 'a very British deal', based on a substantial element of trust. They were concerned that a loosely drafted PPRS could be manipulated by a tough-minded official to suit future government interests, irrespective of any purported commitment to fair play and good faith on all sides.[60] All were united in their opposition to formal control, and none seemed committed to price negotiation on an individual basis. With voting on the ABPI's Board of Management now weighted to favour the larger, British-based companies, unanimous acceptance by the Board guaranteed the endorsement of the renegotiated scheme by ABPI membership.[61]

The implementation of the seventh PPRS in a changing market

The renegotiated package is somewhat hard to classify. It remains legally non-binding, but its substantive terms are much more detailed than those of any of its predecessors. A broad requirement to consult with industry on 'trends and developments in the NHS pharmaceutical market' ensures that industry will be consulted prior to the introduction of any major change in policy on prescribing and pricing, therefore preventing the type of situation which arose over the introduction of the list.[62] Mechanisms for the resolution of conflicts between the DHSS and individual firms are spelled out, and although the scheme stops short of a formal appeals procedure, third party arbitration by either the ABPI (para. 9.3) or an independent 'adviser' is envisaged (para. 13.3). In the Department's view, the new PPRS is simply an extension of the previous scheme: it does not envisage a 'rule book' approach, and it sees the more detailed arrangements as providing it with a wider range of options if companies do not comply voluntarily. Indeed, at one stage in the negotiations on the scheme, officials protested that as the PPRS was no more than an outline agreement, there was little point in bargaining over its general provisions when there was scope for adjustment during negotiations on individual AFRs.[63]

It would be a mistake to assume that the seventh PPRS is simply a refinement of all that went before. The market in the UK is no longer made up principally of branded, patented ethicals: generics and parallel imports now hold significant shares of the market; there are also whitelisted and blacklisted products, all with different pricing requirements. In fact, closer examination reveals significant changes in the philosophy underpinning the scheme, changes which, taken altogether, suggest that although the DHSS and the Treasury had won the battle over the List and over the subsequent exclusion of generics from the scheme (para. 3), the industry had won the war over the more fundamental issue of who should determine the parameters of its new competitive environment and by what means.

In the first place, the new PPRS is about long-term planning in the age of fast-changing health priorities. It is about providing the required stability for the expansion of research-based industry. The scheme is couched in terms of support for, rather than control of, these firms.[64] In order to offer stability, and in keeping with government planning on expenditure and normal commercial and budgeting arrangements, the aim is to give companies a firm indication of the level of NHS spending for the forward year and a provisional indication for the following years. It also provides the research-based firm with an input into shaping the direction of cost-containment policy. The twenty largest suppliers of NHS medicines will actively assist the Department in monitoring costs and other trends by furnishing it with annual sales projections. If the latter indicate that increases in the aggregate cost of NHS medicines are higher than general inflation, the ABPI, whose own negotiating role is considerably strengthened, will participate actively in formulating cost-containment measures. In place of blanket price-reductions or freezes, the new approach guarantees discrimination in favour of companies whose innovative products have contributed to a reduction in the overall cost of health care: 'the Industry undertakes to participate jointly with the Department in an examination of the overall cost of such medicines. Any such examination will include, inter alia, the effect of medicine use and development on the overall economics of NHS health care provision, and trends in and projections of the cost and efficiency of medicines supply' (para. 1.5).

The new PPRS is also about promoting and rewarding efficiency. As from October 1988, the overall ROR was linked not to the rate allowed to government risk contractors but to the more generous Financial Times 500 index. Individual target rates reflect a company's investment record. An additional 'grey area' allowance of up to 50 per cent of the target permits the retention of profits, if, for example, these can be attributed to improved efficiency, the launch of a new product, etc. (para. 6). Arguably, excessive profits can always be adjusted retrospectively, but the scheme provides that new products introduced following a major application for a product licence may be priced at the discretion of the company, echoing the days of the old 'freedom period'.[65] Now that domestic prices are no longer consistently lower than foreign prices, the old export criterion has finally been abandoned. Incentives for new, innovatory products are also found in the rules on advertising. Throughout the negotiations, the DHSS had refused to abandon limits on advertising expenditure, even when its intransigence brought negotiations to a temporary halt. Research-based companies are now allowed extra expenditure of up to £1 million over 2 years to promote new chemical entities or similar products. This is further discussed in Chapter 8.

As the new PPRS only came into operation in October 1987, it is too early to appraise its effectiveness. Two important question marks hang over the scheme, however: the calculation of allowable R. & D. costs and the control of transfer pricing.

The permitted level of R. & D. support will now be negotiated, *inter alia*, on the basis of the company's world-wide spending on this item. The scheme also provides, perhaps for the benefit of the EC Commission, that the overall pattern of investment in the UK is only one of the factors to be taken into account in calculating prices. Officials accept that although the current allowance, at a ratio of around 20 per cent on NHS sales, is more than generous, this is in recognition of the industry's character world-wide. The Department will not, and probably cannot, 'audit' a firm's expenditure to ensure that the British taxpayer is subsidizing genuine, innovative research carried out in the UK.[66] When asked what information he had about the principal areas of research and development carried out by the pharmaceutical industry in each of the last 5 years, the Minister replied that he was unable to provide any.[67] The new rules on transfer pricing hardly offer reassurance that this aim will be realized. The R. & D. element in transfer prices of semi-finished goods is to be allowed in addition to the general allowance for research expenditure,[68] but it is unclear from the scheme how this is to be assured.

It was over the renegotiation of the transfer-pricing issue, however, that the DHSS met with greatest resistance. Following the recommendations of the Binder Hamlyn Report,[69] the DHSS was initially committed to an assessment of individual product prices on a 'cost-plus' basis, that is, prices would be broken down into their component manufacturing and commercialization costs, and a mark-up added. This approach met with opposition not only from the industry but from other government departments, including the Treasury, the Foreign Office, and the Technical Division of the Inland Revenue. All objected to any departure in principle from the commitment to the 'arm's length' approach enshrined in OECD guide-lines for the taxation of multinationals.[70] In ascertaining arm's length prices, the authorities look for evidence of prices in similar transactions between economically independent parties who are in fact operating at arm's length.[71] The 'cost-plus' method was considered unsuited to a research-based industry, which was forced to expend considerable sums on products that were never commercialized.[72]

In the final event, political pressure from the American TNCs, anxious to prevent the UK establishing an awkward precedent on greater transparency over pricing, secured an 'accommodation' on the issue.[73] In this connection, representatives from the US Department of Trade, from the PMA, and from the DHSS had crossed the Atlantic on several occasions.[74] The 'arm's length' principle is now taken as the point of departure for the calculation of transfer prices, although the problem of identifying comparable, uncontrolled prices for products subject to world-wide patents is notorious.[75] Where the company is unable to satisfy the DHSS that the prices are at arm's length, 'the Department will discuss with the company the information needed to enable it to satisfy itself that costs and profits are reasonable' (para. 13.1). In other words, there are no firm and formal rules on what data an affiliated company should produce, nor is there any indication of what standard the Department will apply, although the scheme now requires the Department to take into account rulings by the Inland Revenue.[76] The scheme further provides that the 'additional information will reflect aggregated cost and profit data relating to NHS medicines and (except by mutual agreement) will not be on an individual product basis'. As an incentive to companies to comply, the DHSS reserves the right to deny the company any increase in product prices and to adjust the company's target return on capital (para. 13.5). Nevertheless, firms retain considerable flexibility in apportioning costs, both between the domestic and foreign operations and between their NHS and private domestic sales. A private member's bill which required companies to maintain separate accounts for NHS sales, and which was introduced in early 1987, failed to become law.

A DHSS memo circulated in 1986 to ABPI members indicated the way in which the scheme would be implemented. It reflected the Department's preference for a flexible, negotiated solution, with a gradual adjustment in cases where change was justified. Its stated aim was not to take a 'rule book' approach but to ensure, for example, that levels of profit in transfer prices were not seriously disproportionate to the levels allowed within the PPRS as a whole.[77] In a subsequent letter to the ABPI, the DHSS's chief negotiator promised that where cost information was not forthcoming, the profits element would be calculated at the mid-point of the ROR range.[78] However, even where an unco-operative company was penalized, its final target profit rate might still be adjusted to reflect its wider contribution to the economy.

DHSS officials have privately confessed to being far from happy with these provisions on transfer pricing, which will in fact govern the appraisal of 20 per cent of total NHS pharmaceutical expenditure. As a number of studies on transfer pricing have pointed out, it is impossible to pay more than lip service to the 'arm's length' principle. In practice most prices are negotiated. Their reasonableness is a reflection of negotiating strengths and available administrative resources.[79] The DHSS cannot avail itself of trained specialists. It is also isolated. It is denied access to specific information on a company's affairs held by either the Inland Revenue or Customs and Excise,[80] and, unlike tax officials who deal with transfer pricing, it cannot officially liaise with foreign pricing authorities to check prices charged by parent companies. The seventh PPRS gives ample scope to companies for 'creative accounting'.

The economic logic of the seventh Scheme is also questionable. It implies a continued acceptance of the view that product competition based on innovation and not regulation will ensure reasonable price levels. The scheme finally abandons any attempt at comparative testing. Indeed, the compartmentalization of the NHS into two separate markets—for 'innovative' products and for generics—means that the Department is prevented from making good use of vital comparative data, which, for the first time in 30 years, might make comparative costing tests feasible. With so many drugs now out of patent, production and marketing costs are becoming sufficiently transparent to act as a useful bias for the compilation of efficiency indicators, a development that industry feared, but which the rift with government over the Limited List offered it an ideal opportunity to subvert.

Recent Developments in Product-Safety Licensing

The changing structure of the British pharmaceutical market has had important implications for the implementation of regulations on product safety. If the research-based industry was to continue to assert control over its competitive environment, some attention had to be directed to this issue, particularly as a number of adverse developments appeared to be emerging in this regulatory arena. Two separate trends can be identified. First, as Chapter 5 indicated, as a consequence of the increased demands for parallel-import licences and the improved European procedure for multi-state applications for product licences,[81] a number of firms marketing established or older products have jumped the queue in the national licensing process. National authorities must adhere strictly to the timetable laid down in the directives—120 days—and have been forced to divert their limited resources away from processing regular, purely national applications for NCEs. Second, the ABPI alleged that 'an increase in regulatory conservatism engendered by a fear of a wrong decision',[82] had followed public outcry over the licensing authority's failure, in 1982, to detect the dangerous side-effects induced by the antirheumatic drug, benoxaprofen, to which severe adverse reactions were later attributed. For example, in the early 1960s it took ICI 31 months to push Inderdal, a new heart-drug, through all the regulatory hoops. In 1980 it took the same company 108 months to win approval for Tenormin, a chemically related drug.[83]

The British authorities are now considered by industry to be the most demanding in the European Community. A combination of this increased conservatism, the procedures for product review, and the growth in the number of licensing applications for parallel-import licences produced average delays of up to 20 months in processing applications. The Department of Health deals with all licence applications in strict chronological order, resisting ABPI demands that applications for an important new substance should be 'fast-tracked' through the licensing system. The ABPI, and in particular its larger, research-oriented members, also question the methods by which the Medicines Division has handled certain types of licence applications, especially those submitted by generic manufacturers and parallel importers.

The government has been quick to respond to the industry's complaints about the slowness of the system. In 1987 the Department of Health instituted a major review of the operation of the Medicines Division. As on previous occasions involving a review of licensing policy, the industry was actively involved. Unusually, however, the review was jointly chaired by a former civil servant and a past chairman of the ABPI. Although the idea that licensing might be hived off to a non-governmental institution was briefly mooted at an early stage, in the final event the review recommended that if independence from industry was to be assured, responsibility for the control of medicines should remain in the Department. It did, however, advocate a number of major organizational changes, in particular, a new Medicines Control Agency, whose work would be organized into functional teams, under the control of a single director, and the cost of which would be met entirely from licence fees levied on the industry. A functional division of labour would also facilitate a greater reliance on outside experts, along the lines of the French system, a development welcome to the UK-based industry.[84] The review also recommended the creation of a budget committee — comprising representatives of government and industry — to ensure value for money in licensing activities.[85] This would have allowed the larger, research-oriented firms to have a greater input into the allocation of administrative resources between different types of licence applications. The Health Minister, while accepting most of the review's recommendations as furthering 'our objective of promoting investment by research-based pharmaceutical companies in this country', nevertheless considered that the proposed budget committee would detract from the new Agency's independence and instead proposed to consult regularly with industry on fee structure and management perform-ance.[86] In this way, industry should have at least some informal input into the new Agency's priorities in regard to the allocation of resources.

In the meantime, it had also become evident that the so-called 'abridged' application procedures for licensing were especially beneficial for generic manufacturers and parallel importers. This shortened licensing procedure for products derived from substances whose safety, quality, and efficacy have already been fully substan-tiated was originally devised by the former CSD to benefit licence holders who wished to market a new formulation of a licensed product. It was subsequently retained under the statutory system, although no clear or detailed procedural requirements were ever specified in law: the Medicines Division exercised considerable dis-cretion in deciding which products would qualify for the procedure and the exact form which the procedure would take.[87]

Prior to the adoption of EEC directive 87/21, discussed in Chap-ter 5, a so-called 'second applicant'—that is, the generic manufac-turer—was not required to produce the results of additional tests for safety and efficacy in the case of a known product if the appli-cant produced a bibliography of published research relating to such tests, or where the originator of the product gave consent to the use of his files. Directive 87/21 introduced the further limitation that the second applicant would only be exempted from such tests if the product was 'essentially similar' to a licensed product which had been licensed for 6 years or more. It is for the second applicant to *demonstrate* essential similarity, but the means by which this is to be accomplished, and in particular the relevance of the original applicant's data, is not made clear. In the past the Medicines Divi-sion handled this aspect of the procedure in a somewhat *ad hoc* fashion, claiming limited rights to refer to the original applicant's data where the second applicant's data were incomplete, even in the absence of the former's consent. This practice, and in particular the limited use of the original data to ensure 'essential similarity', was considered justified by the Licensing Authority in the light of its general duty under the Medicines Act to ensure that products were safe to the general public.[88]

In late 1987 the American company Smith, Kline & French, whose patent on its world market leader Tagamet was about to expire in the UK, sought judicial review of this interpretation of the law. It claimed in the first instance that it was for the second applicant to demonstrate essential similarity, without any reference whatsoever to the original file and, in the alternative, that the DHSS had an obligation of confidentiality towards information submitted to it.[89] Giving judgment in the High Court, Justice Henry found that the licensing authority had misdirected himself in law by presupposing that the test demanded by European law required comparison with the original file. The burden of proving similarity is to be placed on the second applicant, and the DHSS must be satisfied that that burden has been discharged without referring to the original file.[90] Justice Henry also found that the information submitted in support of the original product was confidential, even although the continued availability of generic products was in the public interest.[91]

As a consequence of this ruling, the Department might have been exposed to substantial claims for damages in respect of misuse of confidential information, and the ruling undoubtedly made the process of obtaining licences for generics more complex. Whereas directive 87/21 sought to restrict access to tests of safety and efficacy contained in the original file for a period of 6 years—or 10 in the case of high-technology goods—the SK&F judgment would have extended the scope of protection indefinitely, by denying the Medicines Division access to the original applicant's file to establish 'essential similarity' at any time. The Department subsequently appealed, and the Court of Appeal's reversal of the High Court ruling was confirmed by the House of Lords. It is interesting to note that Lord Templeman, giving the leading speech in the Lords, firmly admonished the company for harassing the Licensing Authority by taking action in the Courts.[92]

The terms on which the special product licenses for parallel imports, discussed in Chapter 5, are issued have also been the subject of legal challenge. Once again, the research-based companies have sought to ensure that the mechanics of the licensing process do not conflict with their commercial interests and have asserted various intellectual-property rights in their products. The DHSS's practice of issuing single parallel licences to cover products designated by more than one trade mark in different EC countries was the subject of challenge in the case of ex parte *The Wellcome Foundation Ltd.*[93]

Wellcome marketed a drug under the name Septrin in the UK, Spain, and Portugal, but as Eusaprim in the remainder of the EC. The product licences granted to importers identified the licensed product as Septrin/Eusaprim, allowing them to import from anywhere within the EC. Wellcome alleged this practice to be an infringement of their registered trade mark. It sought judicial review of the Licensing Authority's failure to consider trade-mark rights when dealing with an application for a parallel licence, claiming it to be both unreasonable and *ultra vires* under the Medicines Act. The company succeeded at first instance in its contention that trade-mark rights were a relevant consideration which no reasonable decision-maker could ignore.[94] For imports from Spain and Portugal, where full patent protection for medical products is not available, the Medicines Division had in fact issued a circular letter to the effect that, in accordance with Community obligations imported into the Medicines Act by Section 20(1)(b), parallel licences would not be issued.[95]

On appeal, the Master of the Rolls took a much narrower, pragmatic view of the limits of the Licensing Authority's duty to take trade-mark rights into account, including the considerable demands that would be made on DHSS resources if the Licensing Authority were to become embroiled in issues relating to trade marks.[96] Trade-mark rights were private rights which could be enforced accordingly and were not a matter for the Licensing Authority.[97] This ruling was subsequently affirmed by the House of Lords.[98]

Parallel import licences issued for identical products marketed under different trade marks provoked further litigation in 1987. The products involved included several of the most commonly prescribed drugs, representing a lucrative share of the NHS market. Parallel-import trade in these products began to decline substantially, however, following a press campaign by home-based companies and wholesalers. The Licensing Authority subsequently endorsed an official statement issued by the Pharmaceutical Society, the professional body responsible for pharmacy in the UK, reminding members that a pharmacist was legally precluded 'from substituting any other product for a specifically named product even if he or she believes that the therapeutic effect of the other product is identical', and that these provisions applied to imported products. Pharmacists who formerly dispensed, for example, Eusaprim against a prescription for Septrin were therefore in danger of being removed from the professional register under the Pharmacy Act 1954. The importers' association, the API, contended that this statement amounted to a measure having equivalent effect to a quantitative restriction on imports, contrary to Article 30 of the Treaty of Rome. This case was subsequently referred to the European Court, which has now confirmed that in the particular case of parallel products which have been licensed as being therapeutically equivalent to a domestic product, the rule prohibiting substitution could amount to a measure having equivalent effect to a restriction on trade. The Court, however, considered that a member state was entitled to rely on the public health exception in Article 36 to justify such a restriction.[99]

An Overview

The various developments of the last decade in British regulatory policy on pharmaceutical prices might suggest a number of divergences from the earlier pattern of government relations reviewed in Chapters 3 and 4. In the first place, it has been the government which has taken advantage of the informal nature of that relationship on three successive occasions: firstly with the imposition of price cuts and freezes; secondly with the subsequent introduction of the Limited List; and thirdly to process abridged licences for generic rivals. In the second place, the industry itself has been increasingly prepared to use either formal legal challenge or the threat of such challenge in its attempts to frustrate the introduction of the list and to contest certain practices of the Medicines Division.

Must it therefore be concluded from these developments that the former, informal patterns of regulation through negotiation and persuasion is past history? I would argue that such a conclusion would be a mistaken one; the dominant informal, negotiated style of government–industry relations in the UK has not only persisted but has itself accommodated change, and appears even to have been reinforced by it. The events of the mid-1980s must be understood above all in the context of the changes in the market for pharmaceuticals in the UK. That market is no longer homogeneous; it now comprises generics, parallel imports, blacklisted and non-blacklisted as well as traditional branded products. By the same token, the economic actors within this market are more diverse; the interests of the 'new entrants', the generic manufacturers and parallel importers, do not necessarily coincide with those of the traditional manufacturers.

Chapter 3 argued that the industry, in co-operation with the DHSS, had erected and sustained an informal framework within which policy on the control of profits was negotiated. Considerable interdependence between the two sides had developed. The Limited List was not negotiated within this framework, but its effects have nevertheless been accommodated within it. If a relationship based on interdependence is to be sustained, each party to it must bear certain costs. For the government, this has entailed the acceptance of a two-tiered market: for research-intensive, patented products on the one hand, and for cheaper generics on the other. In the seventh PPRS it has committed itself to the support and promotion of 'first tier' companies, on the basis of the latter's own evaluation of the nature, direction, and value of their research. These firms must also tolerate one of the largest generic markets in Europe, and consequently lower prices within that tier of the market. As long as cost-containment measures are confined to this second, generic tier, however, the industry can retain control over the pace and nature of product competition in the market for branded products. The final terms of the renegotiated PPRS suggest that, at least in the case of profit regulation, it has accomplished this goal. In 1988 the total expenditure on pharmaceutical services rose to £1.9 billion, outstripping the cost of the doctors who write the prescriptions.[100]

Indeed, the larger innovative firms are now assured an important influence over the future direction of policies on profit control and cost containment by the very terms of the seventh PPRS, which now elevate the twenty largest companies, together with the ABPI, to a privileged bargaining role. In 1988 the ABPI reported that the scheme was working to its satisfaction and 'in general there was a large measure of good will and common sense employed by both the DHSS and the ABPI member companies' and 'investment confidence in the UK . . . has regained its old buoyancy as a result of improved relations with Government'.[101] The exclusion of generic products from the seventh PPRS has also meant the effective exclusion of independent generic manufacturers and parallel importers from this privileged negotiating forum.

While the eventual fate of cost-containment measures cannot be attributed entirely to questions of legal form, the persistence of the established, informal or non-legal patterns of government–industry relations described in Chapter 3 is significant. Firstly, the absence of a formal system of price regulation has been of considerable importance to the bargaining framework in which profit control has been adapted. All negotiations on the scheme were conducted in the utmost secrecy, with little opportunity for public or parliamentary discussion on even its general orientations. It is conceivable that a parliamentary select committee will review the implementation of the scheme *ex post facto*, but any of its recommendations will only be considered on the scheme's renegotiation in 1991. An opposition amendment to the Health and Medical Services Bill 1988 which sought to make generic substitution compulsory, thereby saving an estimated £100 million per annum, was heavily defeated in April 1988. The government spokesman on the bill vigorously defended the economic contribution of the research-based industry.[102]

Secondly, the nature of the scheme, which is not legally binding, has itself facilitated, as on previous occasions, a gradual but imperceptible shift in its underlying philosophy. We have argued that the purpose of the new PPRS is not so much to contain profits but to promote and reward innovation. As a consequence, future cost-containment measures will be restricted to the generic tier of the market. It is perhaps for this reason that the government's most recent cost-containment initiative, in the form of proposed 'indicative drug budgets' for prescribing doctors (to be introduced in 1991),[103] has elicited a somewhat muted response from the ABPI. In evidence submitted to the House of Commons Social Services Committee, the ABPI expressed some concern on the impact of the proposals for innovative drugs and for costly treatments for the elderly and chronically sick, but in general it has adopted a markedly low profile, leaving the medical associations to orchestrate most of the protest against the government proposals.[104]

Thirdly, the informal arrangements have perpetuated the appearance of co-operation between government and the industry when in fact consensus over profit control appears to rest on a rather fragile basis, shored up by a mutual unwillingness to embrace formal controls, and the absence of effective legal remedies

to safeguard existing positions. Past reliance on informal arrangements that were not binding in law effectively precluded potential
legal challenge by the firms to the procedures attending the
introduction of the list. Even if judicial review had been available, it
would have been of little use to industry in the longer term: the
option would always be open for the government to reintroduce the
list, using the correct procedures.[105]

If it is arguably in the industry's long-term interests to maintain
the existing interdependent relationship, a continuation of the
informal arrangements has also suited government. On the one
hand, it is inherently difficult to draft effective formal controls over
inherently open-ended and complex matters such as transfer pricing.[106] On the basis of the experience at the Inland Revenue's Technical Division, a special unit which deals with transfer pricing for
taxation purposes, negotiated prices appear an inevitability in an
industry where 'arm's length' or objective, uncontrolled costs are
virtually impossible to establish. On the other hand, such controls
would be expensive to administer and implement, and it is
inconceivable that the Department of Health's staff at the Industry
Division would be augmented at a time when the civil service as a
whole is being cut back. The PPRS has the further advantage that
its incompatibility with European law is much harder for either
non-British-based firms or the Commission to establish, due to the
very absence of hard and fast rules.

Finally, as further evidence of the way in which the existing
patterns of relations have been maintained, it is possible to establish
the emergence of new 'compensatory' adjustments to related
regulatory regimes, arguably designed to offset more intrusive profit-control measures. In this way, the government can ensure that
the cumulative impact of regulation, discussed in Chapter 1, is not
augmented. In the first place, the government manifested its support for the research-based industry in the manner in which it chose
to implement the EEC directive on product liability,[107] which
introduces into UK statute law the concept of strict liability,
without proof of negligence, for defective products, including
pharmaceuticals. The government had the option, under the terms
of the directive, to introduce a so-called 'developments risk'
defence, whereby a producer was not held liable if, as stated in the
directive, the state of scientific and technical knowledge was such
that the defect could not have been discovered prior to the prod-

uct's being put on the market. The ABPI had argued that if the defence had been excluded, the effect would have been to inhibit innovation, and indeed the defence was included in the subsequent Consumer Protection Act 1987, implementing the directive. In the second place, the government has gone some way to accommodate industry's demands for the extension of patent life. This issue is discussed further in Chapter 9.

If industry's victory over its new competitive environment was to be complete, however, it could not afford to ignore the impact of related regulatory developments, which indirectly affected its pro-fitability. As Chapter 2 suggested, other forms of regulation, in particular product-safety regulation, structure the market for pharmaceuticals and the processes of competition within it. If the introduction of the Limited List, in conjunction with the changes at the European level, have contributed to the segmentation of the pharmaceutical market, the growth in size and significance of each of the 'market tiers' discussed in this chapter may be affected by the impact of these controls. Since 1985, the industry has been occupied with two issues: firstly the streamlining of the product-licensing process, to ensure that the marketing of research-based products is not delayed by unduly cumbersome procedures; and secondly the prevention of the use of the more flexible aspects of the licensing process to the commercial advantage of importers of parallel products or generic manufacturers. It is now therefore necessary to recast our initial conception of safety regulation, in terms of its potential function as a barrier to entry into the different segments of a stratified market and its role in suppressing competi-tion between the different tiers of the market. In this way, the stricter enforcement of product-safety regulations, via the courts, has become a potential resource for the research-based industry.

The legal framework within which policy on product-safety licensing has been negotiated is, as Chapter 4 argued, somewhat different from that governing price control. Although there is undoubtedly interdependence between regulator and regulated, the more legally formal and centralized nature of the licensing process has limited the impact of that interdependence to facilitating nego-tiation over the direction of general policy. In the 1980s the pharmaceuticals market has grown more complex; the economic actors within it are more diverse. The informal nature of British drug-price regulation allowed the research-based industry to exclude the newcomers from the benefits of this interdependence with relative ease. Given that policy on product licensing is expressed and implemented through formal regulatory instruments, a similar strategy of exclusion could not be easily accomplished without the adoption by the ABPI and its members of a more adversarial or confrontational stance in its dealings with government over issues of fundamental importance to the future direction of policy on product safety. The growth of legal challenge here should therefore be seen not as a potential threat to the existing pattern of government and industry relations in the UK but as an important strategy òn the part of large research-based firms to maintain the existing status quo.

It should also be stressed that in the course of this period each side has been forced to accept certain costs of interdependence. For the government this has entailed a commitment to a two-tiered market and to the promotion of innovative companies on the basis of the latter's own evaluation of the nature, direction, and value of their research. As a result, NHS expenditure on drugs has continued to rise, and there is no assurance that the government is getting 'value for money' in return. For the industry it has entailed the acceptance of one of the largest generic markets in Europe and consequently of lower prices within that tier of the market. As long as limited lists and other cost-containment measures are confined to this second, generic tier, however, the large firms can retain control over the pace and nature of product competition in the key market for branded products. The final terms of the renegotiated PPRS appear to suggest that, at least for controls on profits and prices, it has accomplished this goal. As I have argued in this chapter, the informal, non-legal nature of the bargaining framework within which profit control is negotiated has made a significant contribution to its success.

Notes

1. JO, 1983, Avis 164, 17 July 1983, 88.
2. OECD, *Measuring Primary Health Care* (Paris: OECD, 1985). In the UK, for example, successive White Papers on public expenditure have assumed that, on the basis of past trends, an annual spending increase of 0.7 per cent is required to cope with the growing needs of an ageing population, while a further 0.5 per cent is needed to cope with the consequences of technological change.

3. B. Abel Smith, *Cost Containment in Health Care: The experience of Twelve European Countries (1977–1983)* (Luxembourg: Commission of the EC, 1984), 49.

4. OECD, *Measuring Primary Health Care*, p. 53.

5. *Second Report on 1982 Public Expenditure White Paper* (London: HMSO, 1983) para. 25.

6. For the Ninth Plan, see JO 1983, Avis 164, 17 July 1983, p. 88.

7. Law 82-6 of 7 Jan. 1982 in JO, 9 Jan. 1980 and law 84-5 of 3 Jan. 1984 in JO, 4 Jan. 1984. Cash limits for hospital care were introduced in rudimentary form by the third Monoroy government in 1978, and were systematically refined under the Socialist administration: decree 83-744 of 11 Aug. 1983 in JO, 12 Aug. 1983.

8. R. Klein, 'Health Policy 1979–83: The Retreat from Ideology?', in P. Jackson (ed.), *Implementing Government Policy Initiatives* (London: Royal Institute of Public Affairs, 1985), 118–35.

9. C. Ham, *Health Policy in Britain*, 2nd edn. (London: Macmillan, 1985). R. Chew *et al.*, *Pharmaceuticals in Seven Nations*, (London: Office of Health Education, 1984).

10. J. Sargent, 'The Politics of the Pharmaceutical Price Regulation Scheme', in W. Streeck and P. Schmitter (eds.), *Private Interest Government: Beyond Market and State* (London: Sage, 1985) 105–27.

11. Namely the NHS Act 1977, sect. 57, which consolidated legislation on emergency pricing, and the Health and Public Services Act 1968, sect. 59 which extended the concept of Crown Services for the purpose of working compulsory patents to the General Practitioner Services.

12. Hansard, 19 Apr. 1978, vol. 949, cols. 415–6.

13. *Report of the Royal Commission on the NHS*, Cmnd. 7615 (London: HMSO, 1979).

14. Para. 5.2 of the sixth PPRS. See further Committee of Public Accounts, 'Dispensing Drugs in the NHS', *10th Report for the Session 1982–83*, (London: HMSO, 1983), para. 6.

15. Interview, source withheld.

16. Committee of Public Accounts, *25th Report for the Session 1979–80*, (London: HMSO, 1980), para. 4149.

17. Ibid. para. 4175.

18. Committee of Public Accounts, *Dispensing Drugs in the NHS*, para. 15.

19. J. Collier, *The Lancet*, 13 Apr. 1985.

20. Compare the industry's own figures on increases in R. & D. in general from £79 million or 7.3 per cent of gross output in 1975 to £251 million or 11.4 per cent in 1980, £431 million or 13.1 per cent in

1983, and £500 million or 13.7 per cent in 1984 (at 1984 current prices). ABPI, *Annual Report 1985–86*, (London: ABPI, 1986), 20. For 1987 the estimated figures are £668 million at current prices or 13.7 per cent of gross output. ABPI *Annual Report 1987–88*, (London: ABPI, 1988), 10.

21. Hansard, Nov. 1983, vol. 49 col. 477.

22. DHSS, *Green Paper on Primary Health Care*, Cmnd. 9771 (London: HMSO, 1986).

23. OECD, *Measuring Primary Health Care*; BEUC, *The Consumer and Pharmaceutical Products in the EEC*, BEUC Report 258/84, (Brussels, 1985).

24. Scrip, *Parallel Imports and the UK Pharmaceutical Market: A Status Report* (Richmond: PJB Publications, 1984).

25. Committee of Public Accounts, Dispensing of Drugs in the NHS', *Twenty-Ninth Report for the Session 1983–84* (London: HMSO, 1984).

26. Hansard, Dec. 1983, vol. 50, col 137.

27. *Guardian*, 27 Mar. 1985, 24.

28. Committee of Public Accounts, 'NHS Supplies and the PPRS', *Twenty-Third Report for the Session 1984–85* (London: HMSO, 1985). Memo submitted by the ABPI, 25–33.

29. Ibid. para. 1455.

30. Hansard, 21 Nov. 1984, vol. 68, col. 205W.

31. In fact there were two reported instances where company targets increased: Committee of Public Accounts, 1984, 'Dispensing of Drugs in the NHS' (1984), para. 1550.

32. Ibid. para. 1498.

33. Interview, J. Long, Assistant Secretary, DHSS, Jan. 1986.

34. Hansard, Nov. 1984, vol. 68, col. 226.

35. The Junior Minister, John Patten, announced the introduction of cost comparison charts in Nov. 1984.

36. Terms of service are set out in sched. 3A to NHS (General Medical and Pharmaceutical Services) Regulations 1974, S. I. no. 160. These may be amended by statutory instrument in accordance with sects. 29, 41, and 42 of the NHS Act 1977.

37. Case 182/82 *Roussel* [1983] ECR 3849.

38. As H. W. R. Wade points out, where a power is granted to a minister responsible to Parliament, the courts do not readily assume that Parliament intended his discretion to be limited, an attitude which is further reinforced if the regulations subject to challenge must be laid before Parliament. Only in cases of manifest unjustness (*Kruse* v. *Johnson* [1898] 2 Q.B. 91) or an arbitrary use of power (*Commissioners of Customs and Excise* v. *Cure and Deely Ltd.* [1962] 1 Q.B.

340 will the courts exercise controls over the legality of delegated legislation (*Administrative Law*, 5th edn. (Oxford: Clarendon Press, 1982), 753). As MacPherson, J. commented in the only case on the list to reach the courts, 'It would plainly be difficult if not impossible to mount an attack upon the Secretary of State's decision in terms of "Wednesbury" unreasonableness or upon the traditional grounds upon which judicial review is available.' *R.* v. *Schering Chemicals Ltd*, 1 (1987) CMLR 227.

39. See more generally C. Harlow and R. Rawlings, *Law and Administration*, (London: Weidenfeld and Nicolson, 1984), 47–52.

40. [1984] 3 All E.R. 935.

41. Interview with company lawyer, Sept. 1986.

42. *Grunwick Processing Laboratories* v. *ACAS* [1978] A.C. 277.

43. *R.* v. *Minister of Agriculture, Fisheries and Food, ex parte. Bell Lines Ltd* [1984] 2 CMLR 502.

44. Hansard, 19 Apr. 1984, vol. 60, col. 221W.

45. Interview and private communication with Commission official, Jan. 1986.

46. European Parliament Written Question 1211/87, Seligman, OJ 1987, C 93/49.

47. See, for example, the recent Case 56/85 *Commission* v. *Italy*, [1989] 3 CMLR 707, where the Court placed a heavy onus on the Commission to justify its allegation that the Italian system of pharmaceutical price control discriminated against imported products.

48. NHS (General Medical and Pharmaceutical Services) Regulations (Amendment) 1985, S.I. no. 290. See further K. MacMillan and I. Turner, 'The Cost-Containment Issue', in S. Wilks and M. Wright (eds.) *Government and Industry Relations in Major OECD Countries*, (Oxford: Clarendon Press, 1986), pp. 117–47.

49. J. Collier, *The Lancet*, 10 July 1986.

50. Interview with DHSS official, Apr. 1986.

51. Ibid.

52. Answer given by Lord Cockfield to European Parliament Written Question 1211/87 on the Noctamid case, OJ 1987, C 93/49.

53. Case 228/82 *Duphar* [1984] ECR.

54. *R.* v. *Secretary of State for Social Services, ex parte Schering Chemicals* [1987] 1 CMLR 227.

55. It is submitted that MacPherson J., misinterpreted the well-established principle of European law that the object or intent of a measure is irrelevant; it is its discriminatory effect which is important. The learned judge found that 'discrimination implies a state of affairs where a person deliberately takes up a position which is to the detriment of others upon discriminatory grounds'. It followed, on this

reasoning, that if the intention of the scheme was to reduce costs and not to hamper imports then it was not discriminatory.

56. Case 102/77 *Centrafarm* v. *Hoffmann-La Roche* [1978] ECR 1139. See also the 'API' case, discussed below.
57. MacMillan and Turner, 'The Cost-Containment Issue', pp. 117–47.
58. *Financial Times*, 12 June 1985.
59. *Scrip*, 1128, 13 Aug. 1986, 1.
60. *Scrip*, 1124, 30 July 1986.
61. *Scrip*, 1138, 17 Sept. 1986, 1.
62. DHSS, *The Seventh Pharmaceutical Price Regulation Scheme* (DHSS, 1986), para. 1.3.
63. *Scrip*, 1117, 7 July 1986, 5; and interview with DHSS official, May 1987.
64. Para. 12.1, for example, on R. & D, states that the level of support will be negotiated individually with each company.
65. Seventh PPRS, para. 9.1. The 'freedom period' is discussed in Chapter 3.
66. Interview with DHSS official, May 1987.
67. Hansard, 23 June 1986, vol. 99, col. 65.
68. Paras. 12.2 and 12.3.
69. This report, prepared by the financial consultancy firm Binder Hamlyn was never published. A summary of its main recommendations can be found in *Scrip*, *The UK Pharmaceutical Market* (Richmond: PJB Publications, 1984).
70. OECD, *Report on Transfer Pricing* (Paris: OECD, 1979) and in its Model Double Taxation Convention (arts. 7 and 9).
71. This is the explanation of the term provided by the UK Inland Revenue in its memorandum *The Transfer Pricing of Multinational Enterprises*. (London, 1980).
72. Interview with R. Thomas, Inland Revenue, 7 Apr. 1986.
73. Interview with J. Long, DHSS, Jan. 1986.
74. *Scrip*, 1127, 11 Aug. 1986, 4.
75. See US General Accounting Office, *Report to the Chairman, House Committee on Ways and Means*, 30 Sept. 1981.
76. In deference to para. 44 of the OECD guide-lines, *Report on Transfer Pricing*.
77. *Scrip* 1127, 11 Aug. 1986, 4.
78. *Scrip* 1117, 7 July 1986, 5.
79. R. Murray, chaps. 1 and 10, in Murray (ed.), *Multinationals Beyond the Market* (London: Harvester, 1981), 1–14 and 147–72.
80. Lord Keith, *Report of the Committee of Inquiry into the Enforcement Powers of the Revenue Departments*, vols. 1 and 2, Cmnd. 8822, (London: HMSO, 1979).

81. EEC Council directive 83/570.
82. *Scrip*, 1213, 12 June 1987, 3.
83. *The Economist*, 4 Feb. 1989, 64.
84. Interview with ABPI official, Nov. 1985.
85. For details, see *Pharmaceutical Journal*, 30 Jan. 1988, 146.
86. T. Newton, written reply to parliamentary question, 14 Apr. 1988, reported in *Pharmaceutical Journal*, 23 Apr. 1988, 528.
87. Interview with R. Cox, Assistant Secretary, Medicines Division, Oct. 1985. The abridged procedure must, of course, conform to European law, in particular the requirements of art. 4 of directive 65/65, which requires submission of certain supporting documentation.
88. Thus public authorities should not be fettered in the exercise of their functions by the introduction of confidentiality concepts more appropriate to private law. *Bushell* v. *Secretary of State for the Environment* [1981] A. C. 75.
89. R. v. *Licensing Authority, ex parte Smith, Kline & French Laboratories Limited, and others*, [1988] 2 CMLR 883. Reversed on appeal: R. v. *The Licensing Authority, ex parte Smith, Kline & French Laboratories*, [1988] 3 CMLR 301.
90. This case concerned rival generic manufacturers based in the United Kingdom, but if imported products had been at issue, it might, with respect, be supposed that this strict interpretation of art. 4 (8) places an undue burden on the applicant and appears to run counter to the ruling in the De Peijper case. See generally L. Gormley, *Restrictions on Free Movement of Goods in European Law* (Amsterdam: Elsevier, 1985).
91. *Ex parte Smith, Kline & French*, [1988] 3 CMLR 301.
92. R. v. *Licensing Authority ex parte Smith, Kline & French (HL)* [1989] 2 CMLR 137, 153.
93. R. v. *Secretary of State for Social Services, ex parte The Wellcome Foundation Limited*, [1987] 3 CMLR 333.
94. Ibid. p. 345.
95. Circular dated 12 Feb. 1986, reprinted at pp. 338–9 of the judgment.
96. [1988] 3 CMLR 333. The Court held that even if the Licensing Authority had addressed the trade-mark issue, it would have acted reasonably if it considered that it need not take it into account in its final decision. In consequence, where the substance of the final decision was not in practice affected by failure to take these rights into account, it could not be impugned. Donaldson stressed earlier in the judgment that the scope of judicial review 'is a supervisory jurisdiction of an essentially practical nature' (para. 71). In recent years the courts appear to have been reluctant to impugn the decisions of overstretched

government departments and local authorities. See generally D. Feldman, 'Rationing Judicial Review', *Public Administration*, 66 (1988), 109–21.

97. On the specific issue of trade marks, considerable reliance was placed on the case of *Clin-Midy* v. *The Belgian State*, where it was held that marketing authorizations must be granted on conditions relating solely to the protection of public health (Case 301/82 [1984] ECR 251).

98. *R.* v. *Secretary of State for Social Services, ex parte Wellcome Foundation Ltd.*, (HL) [1988] 3 CMLR 95. These cases are discussed further in L. Hancher, 'The European Pharmaceutical Market', *European Law Review* 15 (1990), 9–33.

99. *The Queen and the Royal Pharmaceutical Society of Great Britain, ex parte the Association of Pharmaceutical Importers and others* (the 'API' case), unreported, 16 May 1989.

100. *The Economist*, 4 Feb. 1989, 29.

101. ABPI *Annual Report 1987–88* (ABPI: London, 1988). For a detailed list of new investments, see p. 23.

102. Hansard, May 1988, vol. 132, cols. 525–99 and Apr. 1988, vol. 131, cols. 257–70.

103. Secretary of State for Health, *Working for Patients* Cm. 555, (HMSO: London, 1989); Secretary of State for Health, *Promoting Better Health*, Cm. 249, 1988.

104. *Scrip* 1396, 22 Mar. 1989, 1.

105. The case of *Padfield* v. *Minister of Agriculture, Fisheries and Food* [1968] 2 WLR 924 vividly illustrates this point. The Minister merely referred the issue to the appropriate advisory committee, but then declined to follow their recommendations. (HC Parlt. Deb. vol 781, cols 46–7W). See further Harlow and Rawlings, *Law and Administration*, pp. 327–30.

106. The precedent here is the Oil Taxation Act 1975, Sched. 4, para. 2, which limits allowable expenditure to the expenditure incurred by the connected person (as defined by the Income and Corporation Taxes Act 1970 sect. 533). There is therefore no arm's length rule. See further T. C. Daintith and G. Willoughby, *Manual of UK Oil and Gas Law* (London: Sweet and Maxwell, 1984).

107. EEC Council directive 418/85 on the approximation of laws, regulations, and administrative provisions of the member states concerning liability for defective products, OJ 1985, L 210/29.

7

Cost Control and Contracts: The French Experiment

Further insight into the importance of legal and institutional factors in determining the fate of governmental attempts to restrict health-care expenditure can be gained through a comparison of the British cost-containment initiatives with those adopted in France. The problems facing French regulators in the late 1970s were at once of greater magnitude and of greater complexity than those of their British counterparts. The French pharmaceutical sector was not performing well at an international level. Its products were not achieving the same level of penetration as those of its principal European rivals, the United Kingdom and West Germany,[1] a matter of some concern to the Ministries of Industry, Finance, and the Budget. The decline in the rate of introduction of NCEs[2] was particularly worrying at a time when France's overall record on industrial innovation was considered poor.[3] Inadequate communication and co-ordination between publicly funded and privately organized establishments dealing with basic and applied research was seen as a major obstacle to better and faster scientific progress, a problem which preoccupied the DICTD at the Ministry of Industry.[4] Expenditure on health in general and on drugs in particular was growing rapidly, as per capita consumption increased annually at a higher rate than in most other EC member states.[5] The growing deficit in the social security budget troubled the Ministers of Health, Social Security, and, of course, Finance and the Budget.[6]

The constant dilemma faced by successive governments and their responsible ministers has been to find a way of stimulating competition in the long term while keeping the social security budget under control in the short term. Unlike their British counterparts, however, French regulators have been unable to exploit a changing market structure to encourage industry to accept new initiatives on cost containment. This fundamental difference in the structure of the French and British pharmaceutical market cannot be over-emphasized.

In Chapter 3 it was argued that a persistent and fundamental problem of pharmaceutical price-control policy in France has been the absence of interministerial agreement on, and co-ordination of, overall objectives and initiatives. In the absence of cohesion over basic policy aims, loosely structured compromises, or even conflicting policies, have been implemented in a fragmented, piecemeal fashion, via a plethora of regulatory instruments. This chapter argues that these controls have had the effect of suppressing rather than stimulating product competition on the domestic market. As a result, policies adopted since the end of the 1970s attempted to introduce greater generic competition into the French market. The failure of that initiative coincided with the election of the Socialist government in 1981 and the nationalization of 25 per cent of pharmaceutical production. As part of its new industrial strategy, the Mitterand government attempted a more global approach to the pharmaceutical sector, through its contractualization policy. This chapter assesses the intended aims and actual results of this ostensibly radical departure in government–industry relations in the sector and goes on to analyse the change in policy following the return of the centre-right government in 1986.

The Structure of the Market for Pharmaceuticals in France

Product competition and price competition

The adverse impact of an incoherent pricing policy on research and innovation in France—that is, on product competition—had been well documented in the early 1970s.[7] A further unwanted and unintended consequence of the policy of low prices was the almost total suppression of price competition. In particular, there was no incentive for rival firms to engage in this form of competition when a product's patent expired. Consequently, a market for pure generics never really developed in France.[8] Low prices similarly discouraged parallel imports. France has therefore become a major source of, rather than a destination for, the latter. Paradoxically, the 'cost-plus' system of price control, in conjunction with high domestic rates of consumption, provided a 'gilded cage' for national producers and distributors. The extensive monopoly of the pharmacists over the sale of borderline, parapharmaceutical, and prescription products consolidated this situation by suppressing competition in the OTC market.

Attempts at reform

The performance of the French pharmaceutical sector appears to have caught the Giscard administration's attention in the mid-1970s. A combination of the publication of a number of attacks on industry profits on allegedly worthless drugs, increased penetration of foreign multinationals which devoted a very small percentage of their profits to R. & D. spending in France,[9] and the overhaul of regulations on product safety between 1972 and 1976 prompted ministers to take a closer look at the French-based pharmaceutical industry.

Initially, the French financial press had predicted that pharmaceuticals would be subjected to a version of the state-imposed restructuring programme which had just been completed in the computer and electronics sector. However, this was to underestimated the complexity of the task.[10] An *ad hoc* interministerial council on the industry, set up in mid-1976, while confirming the adverse effects of price control, and in particular the overall decline in the industry's profitability and efficiency, also revealed the extent of the dissension on how to proceed with fundamental reforms on the pricing issue. The Minister of Industry, d'Ornano, called for a total liberalization of pharmaceutical prices, bringing the sector into line with changes in price regulation elsewhere in the economy, but this proposal was vigorously opposed by Madame Veil, then at Health and Social Security.[11] The latter initiated her own inquiry into the reimbursement system in 1975, chaired by M. Guinard, to report on ways of improving existing controls and in particular to recommend methods of distinguishing between new, genuinely innovative products and mere copies or fixed-combination drugs.[12] In the same year a parallel inquiry, chaired by M. Villain, was set up by the Ministry of Finance.[13]

The reports of both inquiries attributed France's deteriorating record on drug innovation to the impact of the pricing system on R. & D. Both advocated the stimulation of product competition by means of a liberalization of price controls and a more selective use of the reimbursement system. The Villain Report recommended that prices of new, innovative products should either be totally liberalized or set at a high level. The Guinard Commission, however, advocated the retention of the system of fixed controls on profit, with sufficient flexibility to reward research undertaken in France. The proliferation of copies could be discouraged by low prices and/or restricted reimbursement for older products.

Although the Minister of Health maintained her opposition to a total liberalization of prices, some concession had to be made to the inflationary pressures of the period if industry was to recoup its rising real costs. In the absence of interministerial agreement on far-reaching reforms, an incremental approach was preferred. In 1977 the price-scale system was modified to allow for systematic increases in price (*hausses conjoncturelles*) at a predetermined, uniform rate negotiated between the SNIP and the Ministry of Finance; and in 1978 the principle of *modulation* or variation permitted manufacturers to vary, without prior approval, the prices of individual products at different times as long as overall profits remained within the prescribed limits. Prices of new products remained subject to approval. In practice, the level and frequency of these periodic increases depended largely on the SNIP's ability to compile persuasive dossiers on rising real costs for submission to the Ministries of Finance and Health. The system itself had no legal basis, it was simply the result of a process of concertation between government and industry. Altogether some six *hausses conjonc-turelles*, allowing for annual increases of between 4.5 per cent in 1978 and 8 per cent in 1980, were permitted.[14] Individual price rises no longer had to be approved by the Coudrier Commission but merely notified to the DPHM.

The Guinard inquiry's recommendations on older products were in fact incorporated into the reimbursement system. A decree of 1977[15] divided prescription products into three main categories: products deemed particularly costly and unique were reimbursed at 100 per cent, products deemed to be of general usefulness at 70 per cent, and minor or 'comfort' products at only 40 per cent. Products were allocated to each category by the Health Minister, on the advice of the Coudrier Commission, responsible for reimburse-ment. In the meantime, in August 1978, the Minister of Health issued an administrative instruction to the latter Commission requiring it to review all newly inscribed products after a period of

2 years, with a view to establishing whether the marketing of the products in question had led to real benefits or merely to undue increases in consumption levels.

The third Barre government's general programme on the liberalization of administered price-controls prompted a further reappraisal of pharmaceutical pricing policy, in 1978. An inter-ministerial consensus on the future direction of pricing policy appeared finally to be emerging, although the SNIP's proposals to inject a degree of price competition into the system through the total separation of manufacturing and reimbursement prices were not accepted.[16] Instead, M. Barrot, the new Minister of Health, was entrusted with drawing up a system which would reimburse innovative products at manufacturers' real prices but would also retain controls over the volume of copies or 'me-too' products coming on to the market. This compromise solution reflected the opposition of the Ministry of Finance to substantial modifications to the existing system of control. A proposal to hold down prices for products containing a substantial quantity of imported active ingredients was rejected on the grounds that it might be contrary to EC law.[17]

The major problem confronting the Health Minister was by no means novel: to devise a satisfactory means of distinguishing the genuinely new product from the improved copy. To this end, the Coudrier Commission was disbanded and replaced by a new com-mittee, which was to advise on each product's innovative quality and make recommendations on its cost-effectiveness.[18] This new body, the *Commission de la transparence* would also issue lists for doctors which provided comparisons of transparency and price. The government simultaneously announced its intention to pro-mote generic prescribing for established products.[19]

M. Barrot also attempted to co-ordinate policy-making. He pro-posed to set up an advisory Drug Innovation Committee compris-ing representatives from the various ministries, the chairmen of the administrative committees, and the directors of the two state research institutes, INSERM and CNRS.[20] The DICTD at the Ministry of Industry was to assume responsibility for research and foreign investments, while the Finance Ministry would lose its hold on drug prices but would monitor the industry to ensure com-pliance with general rules regarding competition.[21] Finally, an annual meeting of an *ad hoc* interministerial committee would review the overall level of prices for new products, on the basis either of profit rates or of return on capital.

Had these various reforms been implemented as planned, many of the industry's long-standing demands would have been met.[22] The emphasis would have shifted away from price control, at least for new products, towards a more global approach to profit control, similar to the British system. In turn, it was hoped that the *ad hoc* committee, in which the Ministry of Health was to take the lead, would function as the much-lobbied-for single forum within which a long-term, coherent policy for the pharmaceutical sector could evolve.[23]

Price liberalization

In true French regulatory style, an *arrêté* of 1980 authorized manufacturers to set their own price levels for new products, subject to the provisions of the Social Security Code.[24] The initial selling price of innovative and non-innovative products would be negotiated through the reimbursement system, and future price adjustments would still be regulated indirectly in the context of the Minister of Finance's general supervisory powers over prices. The frequency with which these proposed adjustments would take place was not decreed, as the government wished to retain maximum flexibility. M. Barrot had suggested that they might be linked to fluctuations in the costs of the health insurance funds, but this did not come about. In reality regulatory power remained as fragmented as ever.[25]

To compensate for price liberalization, several other methods of controlling the growth in the health funds' deficit were devised. Industry had pressed for all price controls to be lifted on 'comfort' products, reimbursed at 40 per cent. Many of these were out of patent and could be subject to price competition. Fearing spiralling consumption rates, the government preferred to retain controls on volume, some of which fell on industry and some on the consumer. A decree of 1980[26] revived the so-called *ticket modérateur d'ordre public*, preventing private insurance funds—including the mutual health funds—from reimbursing the entire value of the *ticket*.[27] As a deterrent to consumption, the patient was to bear at least 20 per cent of the cost, and those suffering from long-term or chronic illness would no longer have their medical expenses reimbursed in

full.[28] If costs continued to rise, manufacturers were expected to
refund some of their excess profits to the health funds via a contractual discount scheme introduced in 1979.[29] The scheme provided
for the conclusion of binding agreements between either individual
firms or the SNIP and the CNAMTS, the terms of which were to be
based on model clauses and approved by the Ministries of Health,
Social Security, the Budget, and Industry. The discount system was
supposed to offer a mechanism by which to correct retrospectively
erroneous budgetary forecasts. The number and level of the general
rounds of price increase mentioned earlier would depend on the
successful conclusion of these agreements.

The promotion of competition between generics

This largely untried package of reforms was inherited by the Socialist government following its election victory in May 1981. By this
date not one agreement between industry and the CNAMTS had
been signed. Industry resented their *dirigiste* character and also
feared that joint agreements on rebates might be caught by Article
85 of the Treaty of Rome.[30] Following the protestations of the
mutual insurance funds, the planned *ticket modérateur* was
abandoned before ever being tried. The Socialist government consequently shifted its attention to the generics market. At least fifty of
the most frequently prescribed products would be out of patent by
1985, and many of these were currently being marketed by foreign
TNCs. 'A co-ordinated policy on generics'[31] became a central plank
in their three-point programme for the pharmaceutical sector: the
promotion of national research and innovation, a reduction in the
costs of the health service, and greater equality in access to
treatment.

The emergence of generic competition had in fact begun to look
promising when, in late 1979, one of France's largest pure-pharma-
ceuticals groups, Clin-Midy, announced the setting up of the
Laboratoire français de produits génériques (LFPG). LFPG was
granted reimbursement approval for generic versions of a number
of leading products—including Beecham's Clamoxyl, Boerhinger
Ingelheim's Persantine and Wellcome's Eusaprim—at prices about
30 per cent below those of the originals. The products were sold
under the name ES (Économie Santé) plus the generic name.
Unfortunately for LFPG, the former government was not prepared

to introduce a policy of compulsory generic prescribing or substitution. Within 20 months the company was put into liquidation, and the promotion of generic competition was abandoned as an official strategy.

The promotion of generics met with formidable resistance both from the industry and from the medical and related professions. The former had always protested that prices were already too low to withstand further competition. The smaller, national firms expressed a positive interest but were forced to buy the active ingredients from the market leader at grossly inflated prices, which, they argued, could not be recouped because generics prices were too low. Several cases of refusal to supply were eventually condemned by the competition authorities, but this had little effect on the immediate situation in respect of supply.[32]

The French regulatory framework itself gave ample scope for the realization of the opposition to generics. There was no need for French firms to bargain with government to counter the threat of generic competition, as their British counterparts were to do in 1983. Initially, the manufacturers of the original product took advantage of the system of *modulation* in order temporarily to lower their prices in the face of competition, but they also exploited to great effect the rigidities of the reimbursement system itself. The Transparency Commission did not commence operations until early 1981. In the meantime, it fell to its predecessor, the Coudrier Commission, to set reimbursement prices. The essential aim of its available controls, specified in the 1967 decree, was to impose limits on volume. A subsequent ministerial circular of 1977[33] had stipulated that a generic copy would be reimbursed only if it represented a cost saving. In consequence, reimbursement prices for generics were automatically fixed at 10 per cent below that of the market leader,[34] an inflexible approach which in retrospect was naïve in the extreme.

On receipt of information that a rival was about to market a cheap copy, the market leader, or one of its subsidiaries, being in possession of all the necessary data on safety, could quickly apply for an abridged product-licence[35] and proceed to manufacture its own copy, which would be reimbursed at 10 per cent below the price of its own leader. This procedure could be repeated several times, so that a fifth or sixth subsidiary was marketing the product for up to half the original price. The rival producer, whose reimbursement price was consequently fixed at 10 per cent below this price, was either squeezed out of the market or was faced with an effective boycott by the retail pharmacists, whose own profit margins were linked to this price. This procedure was even used to great effect by Sanofi, who acquired Clin-Midy, and therefore a controlling interest in LFPG, in 1980. By manipulating the reim- bursement system in this way, Sanofi succeeded in maintaining its original market share for its anti-epileptic product Depakene.[36]

In fact it was the pharmacists who drove the final nail into the coffin of generic competition. Threatened with an erosion of their own profit margins, and yet legally obliged to stock a complete range of products, they organized a boycott of all Clin-Midy prod- ucts, under the aegis of various pharmacists' associations, including the Federation of French Pharmacist Associations (*Fédération des syndicats pharmaceutiques de France*). Clin-Midy lodged a com- plaint with the Competition Division at the Ministry of Finance in early 1981, but it was only when the National Federation of Con- sumers (*Fédération nationale de coopératives de consommateurs*), a long-standing advocate of generic prescribing, took up the issue following the change of government that the Minister finally took decisive action and referred the matter to the competition authori- ties.[37] In the meantime, the entire question of the distribution of medicines and the pharmacists' fee structure was subjected to an exhaustive inquiry by Senator Sérusclat. The Socialists and their centre-right successors proved equally reluctant to attack the monopoly position of a politically powerful profession, and in the final event no reforms were introduced.[38]

For its part, the medical profession also resented generics, which they viewed, mistakenly, as leading to an unnecessary proliferation of wasteful copies.[39] Indeed, a number of studies suggested that branded, but not necessarily 'pure', generics actually fuelled con- sumption rates.[40] Obviously, a major obstacle here was poor infor- mation, a problem which Rallite, the Communist Health Minister envisaged could be tackled by a programme of education, implemented by his High Council on Medicines, a broad policy forum established in the summer of 1982.[41]

The fate of the short-lived pro-generics policy can be attributed in part to its lack of real coherence and in part to the institutional rigidities of a highly regulated sector which offered little or no scope for a bargained or negotiated solution to expenditure problems. The SNIP, reflecting the interests of the large firms, had always maintained that price competition and price control were incompatible. The bigger firms manipulated the reimbursement mechanisms to demonstrate the point. With the instruments of competition policy very much in their infancy at this stage,[42] the anti-competitive practices of the firms and the pharmacists attracted only belated, and therefore ineffective, sanction. In the French context, a successful pro-generics policy requires the re-education of prescribers and patients, as well as the recasting of the pharmacists' fee structure and an overhaul of the system of regulating prices and competition. The striking paradox of the French situation is that as long as the French market remains insulated from the changing competitive forces which have altered the structure of the market in the UK, there is little incentive for industry to alter the status quo. Furthermore, the implementation of a successful pro-competition policy, such as the promotion of generics, requires a highly co-ordinated interventionist strategy on the part of government. Yet the very fragmentation of regulatory instruments has always militated against the possibility of such co-ordination.

Nationalization, Pharmaceuticals, and Industrial Strategy

The pharmaceutical sector featured prominently in the new Socialist government's planned industrial strategy, thus providing ministers with renewed opportunity to develop an alternative set of instruments to control prices and stimulate competition. A detailed exploration and explanation of the fate of the Socialist government's grand design is beyond the scope of this book.[43] The subsequent direction of industrial policy in fact altered course at several junctures between 1981 and 1986, switching from Pierre Dreyfus's emphasis on managerial autonomy for the newly nationalized industries to Chevènement's interventionist ambitions—to be implemented by a MITI-style super ministry—through to Laurent Fabius's renewed emphasis on managerial autonomy and profitability, the so-called *normalization fabiusienne*, eventually to turn full circle with Edith Cresson's programme of liberalization and privatization. Ministerial changes, and consequently changes in policy, were also frequent at Health, and at Social Security and National Solidarity. Indeed, the only constant factor throughout this period appeared to be the growth in the deficit in the social security budget. Despite the changes in style and emphasis of the policies pursued by four consecutive Industry Ministers, the pharmaceutical sector remained relatively immune from direct intervention.

The extension of public ownership: Rhetoric and reality

The most radical development in government–industry relations in France following the election in 1981 was the transfer of legal ownership to the state of some 25 per cent of French industry's entire productive capacity, including 25 per cent of pharmaceutical production, and the subsequent conclusion of various types of pluriennial planning contracts (*contrats du plan*) with the newly nationalized firms. This in turn provided the framework for a new, contractually based approach to pharmaceutical price control which promised sufficient flexibility to encourage R. & D. and export growth but which would also contain health costs. The impact of these developments on pharmaceutical price control must be assessed in the particular context of the French programme of nationalization, a context which is best understood by drawing a firm line between rhetoric and reality.

In the rhetoric of the government, the new public-sector companies were to provide the technological and innovatory lead that would restore France to an internationally competitive position.[44] The purpose of taking the pharmaceutical industry, or part of it, into public ownership was to promote greater innovation and higher profitability and had little to do with the principle of the socialization of ownership *per se*. The new industrial strategy included a commitment to the 'co-ordinated autonomy' of the public sector, a programme of investments for modernization, and the development of coherent, integrated industrial networks (*politique filière*). The public-sector firms were to function primarily as 'poles of development', or the '*fer du lance*', for the rest of industry. Their own commercial interests would be reconciled with the state's broader economic and social interests through the planning contracts. Under the terms of the latter, the firm would agree to embark upon an agreed programme of investment and modernization while guaranteeing employment levels and price restraint; in return the government would guarantee the firm's managerial autonomy and provide a certain amount of financial support.

In reality the nationalization programme attained few of these goals. One cannot do justice here to the complex debate over the relative success or failure of the Socialist industrial policy or policies, but most commentators are unanimous in their verdict on its failure to influence the firms' own internal commercial strategies. As Cohen and Bauer have argued, given the constraints of the French financial market, nationalization was the only way to amass the enormous injection of cash necessary to modernize companies or free them from the burden of long-term indebtedness.[45] In effect, the state socialized the costs of modernization and cushioned disinvestment in declining sectors, which in turn led to an accelerated liberalization of economic controls and, by late 1984, to an overt programme of privatization, in addition to the covert privatization of the subsidiaries of state-owned firms.[46] The nationalization programme also provided government with the opportunity to initiate a number of managerial changes, even if these were largely symbolic. The company's supervisory boards (conseils d'administration), on which ministerial representatives sat, were not considered the real locus of decision-making power.[47] Firms like Sanofi, for example, are holding-companies with shareholdings in over sixty legally distinct companies established under private law. In reality the scope for influence through representation on the board of the holding company was limited.

The state already owned a stake in the pharmaceutical sector, acquired in 1973 via the 60 per cent holding in Sanofi which the state-owned oil holding-company SNEA had obtained. Following its restructuring in 1976, it was understood that the SNEA and its subsidiaries would operate as a 'normal industrial enterprise with complete commercial and financial autonomy'.[48] This independence was seen as necessary to allow the company to compete internationally. In the past, Sanofi's executives claimed that there had been 'no privileged relations either way',[49] a situation which they did not envisage would change under the new administration. Its chief executive was not replaced. In fact Sanofi's management welcomed the contracts as the first step to establishing a coherent strategy for the sector, and the company was one of the first to sign the contracts on pharmaceutical prices in 1983.[50]

Roussel and repatriation

The Socialist government's declared aim of protecting national patrimony did not in reality constitute a significant departure in policy style. Previous administrations had successfully blocked private-sector companies from merging with foreign multinationals.[51] Nevertheless, given the high level of foreign penetration into the pharmaceutical sector, the attempted repatriation through public ownership or through the relocation of production and research facilities was a high priority. An obvious target for repatriation through nationalization was Roussel-Uclaf, the third-largest and most profitable manufacturer in France—and now a world leader in new-generation antibiotics—which had been taken over by the German company Hoechst in 1976.

After protracted negotiations led by the Prime Minister, Mauroy, first with Hoechst and subsequently with the West German government, the French government failed to gain a controlling interest in Roussel-Uclaf. Hoechst, understandably reluctant to surrender control in this highly profitable subsidiary, convinced the French government that the company's international standing was substantially due to Hoechst's financial backing for research into, and commercialization of, new products and that its future profitability could not be assured if these resources were to be withdrawn. The government agreed to take a compromise minority stake of 34 per cent in return for a controlling position on the company's supervisory board.[52] Plans to extend this stake to 51 per cent were shelved as research spending rose by 24 per cent and consolidated profits jumped some 150 per cent in the following year.[53] Under the terms of the agreement, both Hoechst and the government proclaimed a commitment to common strategic direction but guaranteed Roussel's freedom from intervention.[54] The government also agreed not to sell any part of its holding to a rival chemical company, a concession which effectively pre-empted Rhone-Poulenc's later attempt to acquire a stake in its rival.[55]

Rhone Poulenc and the restructuring of the chemicals sector

The nationalization programme also brought Rhone-Poulenc into public ownership. This was the largest chemical and pharmaceutical group in France and the eleventh-largest in world terms. The overhaul of the basic-chemicals sector was seen as one of the most urgent tasks facing the Socialists in May 1981. Huge losses had been sustained by the two leading private companies, Rhone-Poulenc (2,000 million francs in 1980 and 587 million francs in 1981) and the metals and aluminum group PUK (1,700 million francs in 1981). The total losses of the existing public-sector companies CDF-Chimie (1,200 million francs in 1981) and ATO-Chloe (300 million francs) on heavy chemicals exceeded the Ministry of Industry's entire projected annual budget for selective intervention in industry as a whole. The sector's weak financial standing adversely affected the capacity of a diversified company such as Rhone-Poulenc to undertake expensive pharmaceuticals research. A large portion of its profits on drugs were being siphoned off to underwrite losses and pay huge financial charges. The chemical sector's growing dependence on foreign imports of fine chemicals and the prospect of further foreign control if PUK carried out its pre-election threat to sell out to the American company Occidental Petroleum compelled the Industry Minister to intervene.[56]

The saga of the various efforts of three successive Industry Ministers to impose order on the French chemical sector has been well documented elsewhere.[57] It is a saga which graphically illustrates the considerable power and managerial autonomy which certain large, profitable public-sector companies—for example, Elf—can wield to frustrate government plans, and it is perhaps indicative of the general character which relations with the newly nationalized sectors were subsequently to assume.[58] An early plan to merge all state holdings to form a single giant chemicals holding-company was abandoned in the face of the absolute refusal by the national oil-company Elf to take over Rhone-Poulenc and PUK's loss-making heavy-chemical activities. When Rhone-Poulenc and PUK, along with the latter's pharmaceutical subsidiary, Pharmuka, were nationalized in March 1982, the restructuring question remained unsolved. Following the demise of Chevènement and of his ambitious plans for the sector, his successor, Fabius, eventually persuaded the chairmen of the various companies involved to accept, in June 1983, a restructuring around three main poles: Rhone-Poulenc got the profitable fine chemicals, agrochemicals, and pharmaceuticals; fertilizers and the loss-making end of petrochemicals went to CDF-Chimie; while Elf took the rest of the pickings.[59]

The contractualization policy and price and reimbursement control

In the spirit of the February 1982 nationalizations, ownership was not meant to imply outright managerial control, but the mechanisms by which a general influence or direction could or would be secured over the newly nationalized firms remained an open question. The Minister of Industry, Dreyfus, did not even replace their chairmen. The head of Rhone-Poulenc, Jean Gandois, departed in June 1982 following a disagreement with Chevènement over the group's strategy for reconstruction and in particular over the latter's refusal to sanction foreign investment and collaboration.[60] After further disagreements with the other public-sector chairmen, it was Chevènement who was replaced.

It was in fact the new planning contracts, or bilateral agreements between government and firms, which were to form a link between the various sectoral objectives enunciated in the Ninth Plan and individual managerial goals in the public and private sector.[61] In assessing their impact, it is once more important to distinguish rhetoric from reality: as Zinsou has observed, these agreements were neither contracts nor plans, nor indeed were they planning contracts.[62]

Pharmaceuticals had not received explicit mention in the Ninth Plan, although biotechnologies came under a modest programme of resource mobilization,[63] and a small goal-oriented research programme for chemicals was instituted on the recommendations of the plan's special working party on the chemical sector. This body also recommended a freeing of the price of pharmaceutical products destined primarily for the export market.[64] As one of the eleven newly nationalized firms under the tutelage of the Ministry of Industry, Rhone-Poulenc signed a separate, general planning contract in 1982.[65] However, the general orientations of a 'global pharmaceutical policy', the principles of which were to be incorporated into individual contracts with firms in both the public and private sectors, were thrashed out in a special interministerial committee—chaired by François Gros, Mitterand's personal scientific adviser—which met in March 1982.[66] Future policy was to be based around four axes: R. & D., exports, investment, and employment. Firms would be encouraged to draw up a programme of action along these lines and submit it to the DICTD at the Ministry of Industry, which would monitor their implementation. It was

hoped that these contracts would allow French regulators to emulate the flexibility of the British PPRS, and would stimulate innovation and encourage exportation.

These goals of industrial policy were to be reconciled with the
budgetary constraints resulting from the expanding deficit in social
security by means of a policy of cash limits; the interministerial
committee was to allocate a specific sum from the social security
budget to finance drug spending—the *enveloppe budgétaire*—
which would then be distributed among the contracting firms on
the basis of merit. Hence 'European prices' would be sanctioned for
new, innovative products if, in return, firms committed themselves
to creating a fixed number of jobs, invested a specific amount in
new plant or in a new product-line, and restricted promotional
spending to 16 per cent of turnover.[67] For products already on the
market, biannual contractual price increases (*hausses convention-
nelles*) of around 2 per cent were to supplement the existing rounds
of general price-rises (*hausses conjoncturelles*). Awards of the
former, like the latter, were purely discretionary.

General price increases as well as prices awarded for new products negotiated within the context of the planning agreements had
nevertheless to be linked to the provisions of the Social Security
Code on reimbursement. These procedures were already more flexible as a result of the 1980 reforms, which had also modified the
criteria for inscription to be applied by the new advisory body, the
Transparency Commission.[68] The manufacturer is now required to
submit an economic dossier and a separate technical dossier. The
firm's *dossier technique* should demonstrate the product's pharmacological qualities and is designed to fulfil the first of the positive
criteria for selection for reimbursement, i.e. that the product
represents progress in general health-care (*amélioration du service
médical*): a product's therapeutic efficacy is now presumed to have
been established in the course of the AMM procedure.[69] The economic dossier should justify the price claimed and, where the product is not new, should show that it represents a saving on the cost of
health care. Initially, both dossiers were to be appraised by the
Transparency Commission, which would then advise the Minister
on a price. (This advice was not binding on the Minister—Article
8.)

On the introduction of the contractualization policy these procedures were altered slightly. Where the product does not offer a

therapeutic advance, the DPHM's section on economic affairs, at
its discretion, negotiates a price on the basis of the average price of
products considered comparable by the Transparency Commission.
If the latter considers the product an innovation, the firm's
requested price is assessed by an informal administrative committee
(*comité restreint*), comprising representatives from four separate
ministerial divisions.[70] The subsequent inclusion of a representative
from the Ministry of Foreign Trade and Commerce in 1984 suggested that this committee would look favourably on products with
a large export potential. Its opinion is only advisory, and in the
final event a price is negotiated between the Minister(s) of Health
and Social Affairs and the firm.[71] This complex negotiation procedure has been known to take up to 2 years, although on average
agreement is reached within about 10 months.

The contracts policy and market structure

In Chapter 6 it was argued that British cost-containment measures
have led to market segmentation. The French policy of contractualization arguably provoked a different form of market stratification—between firms as opposed to products. There is sufficient
evidence to suggest that the terms of the contracts were highly
favourable to the large firm, whether public or private, as long as it
was export-oriented. The first 'wave' of new contracts was signed
in February 1983. The three public-sector companies and some
sixteen medium-sized firms, that is almost 40 per cent of the French
pharmaceutical industry, shared out some 350 million francs
between them. A further sixty-four medium-sized firms participated
in the second round, worth only 250 million francs, in 1985.

Despite their terminology, the contracts themselves were legally
non-binding declarations of intent, unenforceable by either party.[72]
Their terms remained highly confidential, but the individual contracts were said to be closely drafted documents. In theory, it was in
the interests of the firms to comply if they wanted favourable prices
in future years. The imposition of anti-inflation controls, including
an economy-wide price freeze in the summer of 1982,[73] the subsequent cancellation of the second stage of the drug industry's
annual round of price rises, and the restrictions imposed on the
modulation system demonstrated that bilateral agreement would be
preferable to unilateral control. The only price increases allowed in

the subsequent 18 months were awarded under the *hausse conventionnelle* system.

As the public-sector firms accounted for at least 75 per cent of total turnover of the firms included in the first 'wave', it was not difficult to work out who benefited most.[74] For example, at Rhone-Poulenc Santé (RPS), the health division of Rhone-Poulenc, the self-declared mission was firstly to reconquer the national market—to counter the foreign 'colonization' of the production of the principal active ingredients for many of the country's leading products, and secondly to increase the presence of French industry in foreign markets, particularly those of Japan, West Germany, and the USA. Effective foreign control over the supply of important active ingredients allegedly ranged from 60 per cent for tranquillizers and antirheumatics to up to 95 per cent of the market for cardiovasculars, anti-infectives, and anti-asthmatics. This strategy, although certainly in line with the contractualization policy, had been adopted internally a year prior to Rhone-Poulenc's signature of its general planning contract.

Funding the company's ambitions was another matter, however. From the outset the firm made it very clear to its new owners that given its meagre record on profitability and the high cost of financing its long-term debts, it would be looking for state assistance in realizing these ambitions.[75] And indeed the government lived up to its duties as a shareholder, and later as a contractual partner, ploughing some 1.7 billion francs in capital injections and 1.3 billion francs in soft loans into Rhone-Poulenc between 1982 and 1985.[76] Under the terms of the planning contract, the company was expected to devote some 60 per cent of this sum to investment in fine chemicals.[77] By 1985 Rhone-Poulenc was France's third most profitable chemicals company.[78]

Sanofi also benefited from the contractualization policy, taking the opportunity to restructure its biotechnology interests. The Dutch government's attempt to link the price of imported pharmaceutical products to the country of origin, which eventually led to the litigation in the *Roussel* case,[79] gave Sanofi the opportunity to threaten the French government that it would move all its export business to its foreign-based subsidiaries if it did not get 'European prices' for its products. If the Dutch government's scheme had not been found contrary to European law, the lower French prices would have been taken as the reference price for drugs imported into the Netherlands. It was therefore in Sanofi's interests to switch production to countries such as the UK, where profit controls are not as stringent. Given that almost 50 per cent of its production was already located outside France this was no hollow threat. Between 1983 and 1985 the company's group profits increased by over 50 per cent.[80]

Private companies and the contractualization policy

The more specific policy on contracts for the pharmaceutical sector also benefited a number of the larger private-sector companies, especially the subsidiaries of foreign multinationals. Companies exporting more than 40 per cent of their turnover were granted 'European prices' for their products.[81] In consequence, export-oriented firms such as Glaxo, Wellcome, and Merck Sharpe and Dome were awarded especially favourable prices in exchange for investment and employment commitments which, given the weakness of the franc in this period, were not especially onerous. All three made record profits in 1983–4.[82] The larger independent French firms Synthelabo, Servier, and L'Air Liquide also exploited the 'European pricing policy' to their own advantage by marketing only their most innovative and most expensive products in France.[83]

Smaller companies (generally defined as those with a turnover of less than 50 million francs) who were not major exporters were *de facto* excluded from both the contracts policy and the *hausse conventionnelle* system. They also failed to reap much benefit from the *hausse conjoncturelle*, which was based on average weighted prices. As we have seen in Chapter 3, these firms had been penalized under the old system of price control, so that their existing price levels were already low. Initially they were compensated by means of a special price rise in 1983.[84] In view of the government's failure to repeat the exercise the following year, these companies formed their own organization in late 1984 to press for change. The SNIP, in response to this loss of membership, voted at its annual conference in 1985 to refer to the EC Commission the question of the compatibility of the contracts policy with European law. It was argued, *inter alia*, that the contracts system amounted to an indirect barrier to trade, as it discriminated against companies who had to rely on imported active ingredients and who were therefore not awarded sufficiently high prices to meet costs. Although the Commission requested further information from the French government, in the light of the latter's decision to abandon the policy in 1985, the matter was not pursued. It is conceivable that if the Commission had been able to adduce evidence of systematic discrimination against importers, on the basis of the case-law reviewed in Chapter 5, infringement proceeding might have been initiated against the French government.

Legal challenges to the nationalization programme

The possibilities for a rival company to challenge the legality of the nationalization programme itself, and the privileged access to public capital that it allowed to public-sector firms via the contractualization programme, appeared highly restricted. The Nationalization Law of 11 February 1982, taking the assets of private firms into public ownership,[85] concerned only the appropriation of private property and not the subsequent organization of the sector or its relations with government. The constitutionality of these appropriation procedures had been affirmed by the Constitutional Council.[86]

The scale of capital injections by the French government into Rhone-Poulenc and other nationalized firms prompted a number of rival firms to complain to the EC Commission. The Commission subsequently examined the aid element in capital transfers to state companies in a survey published in 1987, but it expressly exonerated the government's purchase of new equity in Rhone Poulenc after nationalization.[87]

The current position of state holdings and transfer of capital under European law is complex. The Commission recognizes the right of member states under Article 222 of the EEC Treaty to take holdings in companies, but it has consistently argued that this right does not justify the adoption of measures incompatible with the prohibitions on state aids in Articles 92 and 93 of the Treaty. If the special nature of the acquisition, as indicated by its terms, purpose, or duration revealed that it was intended to give a firm an unfair competitive advantage, then a question of aid could arise, a view endorsed by the European Court.[88] Both the Commission and the

Court work from the principle that aid is involved unless a member state has acted as would a normal investor in a market economy; a principle easier to state than to apply. A major weakness of the Commission's position is that it has no method of calculating the amount of aid represented by the acquisition of capital holdings. This might in part explain the Commission's reticence to challenge the financing of the French nationalization programme.

An assessment of the contractualization policy

Two sets of factors conspired to ensure that despite its successful launch, the contractualization policy did not, and indeed could not, live up to the expectations of either side. In the first place, the large international companies continued to outmanoeuvre the administration, frustrating its hopes of controlling costs. Neither the DPHM nor the DICTD had the necessary resources, skill, or personnel to police compliance with the contractual terms.[89] In any event, the contractualization policy's goals for research and development could only be realized in the long term; other objectives, including the commitment to preserve employment levels, increase capital investment, and improve efficiency, were viewed by the firms' chairmen as mutually incompatible.[90] It is generally agreed that most drug companies failed to honour their particular commitment to reduce promotional expenditure in return for higher prices.[91]

In the second place, the continuing fragmentation and uneven dispersal of regulatory power between the ministries prevented the emergence of a stable framework for bargaining within which a coherent policy could be negotiated. On the one hand, the SNIP alleges that the internationalization of cost-containment measures resulted in the adoption of reference prices, based on French prices, by over fifty francophone countries. Some 60 per cent of the French industry's total exports go to these same countries, so that in 1984 alone, according to SNIP's estimates, the industry lost 1,700 million francs in profits and the French revenue some 800 million francs in tax revenue.[92] On the other hand, the Minister of Finance claimed that by the end of 1983 a record 15 per cent overall rise in the price of pharmaceuticals had not been matched by the necessary effort in investment and exports; the distribution of the 1984 *enveloppes budgétaires* was blocked until 1985, after which the system was finally abandoned. The SNIP's Council resigned in protest following the cancellation of the *hausse conjoncturelle* in July 1984.

The return to price freezes

As early as October 1982 the Ministry of Finance, as part of general anti-inflation policy, had ordered compulsory price reductions on nine leading products whose consumption patterns had outstripped initial predictions.[93] Given the breadth of the Minister's discretionary powers under the 1945 ordinance, a subsequent legal challenge by the SNIP proved ineffectual.[94] Again, the larger companies were able to outmanoeuvre government. Sanofi's world best seller, Tilcid, was originally included in this measure, although the company was able to negotiate a reprieve on the basis of its export record. Bayer withdrew its product Mintacol from the market in the knowledge that its immediate competitor, Specia, could not produce a cheaper substitute in sufficient quanities to meet demand; following complaints from doctors, the Minister of Health was obliged to renegotiate prices.[95]

In November 1982 the Health Minister ordered a compulsory reclassification to the 40 per cent category of over 1,200 products previously reimbursed at 70 per cent. A subsequent survey revealed that the savings from this measure was cancelled out by the sudden increase in the numbers qualifying for total reimbursement under the so-called 'twenty-sixth illness' criteria.[96] It was hoped that large savings would be yielded by further major reclassification of five therapeutic classes, involving over 370 products, in June 1985, together with a stricter surveillance over doctors' prescribing patterns.[97] The former measure is now the subject of a challenge by the SNIP before the Conseil d'État for *excès de pouvoir*. SNIP alleges that insufficient warning was given, that consultation was inadequate, and, further, that the Minister's power to recategorize products is to be exercized following the appraisal of individual products, and not according to therapeutic category.[98]

The Minister also began to make imaginative use of the powers under the 1980 decree regulating reimbursement, to develop further a posteriori controls over product prices. Since 1982 it has become common practice to list a new product for a period of 2 to 3 years only; the renewal of reimbursement approval is conditional on 'mutually acceptable' modifications of current prices. The Transparency Commission compares the product's actual usage with the firm's initial projections for it, and if consumption levels are in fact higher, it can recommend a compensatory reduction in price. The firms argue that the system penalizes successful, innovative products, and they have threatened to challenge the legality of the practice of systematic limitations on the period for which drugs are selected for reimbursement, which they allege is not provided for in the decree.[99] The Minister has also threatened to make fuller use of discretionary powers to remove products from the reimbursement list when he or she considers prices are too high.[100]

In response to these various developments, the SNIP claimed that by 1986 there were no longer any bench-marks in the system of price control; everything depended on the economic clout of the individual firm. The health insurance funds have contended that the lack of consistency in pricing decisions is alarming; the price of two essentially similar products can vary by up to 40 per cent.[101] The president of the Transparency Commission, in evidence to the Economic and Social Council in 1985, recognized the difficulties of obtaining sufficient and accurate information on the use of a particular drug and on its comparative benefits. As a consequence, the Commission has adopted rather general criteria in its assessment of a product's usefulness.[102] Although aggrieved companies are legally entitled to seek judicial review of a ministerial decision refusing or withdrawing reimbursement status, scope for effective legal challenge remains limited. The Conseil d'État has consistently refused to review the substance of the decisions of either the Minister or the relevant advisory body when complex technical factors are involved.[103]

The gradual erosion in value of the general rounds of price rises has renewed the incentive for firms to bring out new versions of old products in order to avoid adverse effects on profits at home and abroad. In this context, it is hardly surprising to discover that in France spending on drugs has continued to grow at a faster rate than in most European countries, even if the net rate of growth has declined slightly in recent years.[104] The persistent irony of the French system is that almost every attempt to control prices has had a perverse impact on the volume of consumption.[105] Both the number of products used in daily prescribing and per capita consumption rates remain among the highest in Europe.[106]

Pharmaceutical Price Control under the Chirac Government

Privatization and deregulation

The French pharmaceutical sector's hopes that the return of a centre-right majority in the legislative elections of March 1986 would lead to major policy reforms were soon dashed. Given the degree of managerial autonomy which they had enjoyed under the previous administration, the public-sector firms did not envisage that the proposed privatization programme would bring about major changes, although Rhone-Poulenc and Elf, the state oil company which holds 60 per cent of Sanofi, were included in the list of sixty-five candidates for privatization.[107] With the agreement between the French government and Hoechst due to expire at the end of 1986, the future of the former's stake in Roussel-Uclaf was also uncertain.[108] Group profits had declined somewhat dramatically in 1985 and 1986 following the expiry of patents on three major products and the impact of the weak dollar on exports, but share prices had leapt from 300 francs in 1982 to 2,000 francs in 1987.[109] Hoechst was allegedly threatening to relocate the company's investments in biotechnology abroad if the renewed agreement proved unfavourable to its interests.[110] A new six-year agreement was finally negotiated in the summer of 1987. The French government has retained its 36 per cent shareholding in the company—no part of which may be sold to any competitor, whether public or private—but has lost its majority on the administrative council.[111]

As part of its declared policy to abandon *dirigiste* price controls and strengthen the instruments of competition policy, the Chirac government repealed the ordinances of 1945 in December 1986. The new ordinance 86-1243 reserves the right to retain controls over public-sector pricing, to reimpose controls in the event of excessive price rises or 'manifestly abnormal market developments', and to maintain certain price-control regimes for a transitional period.[112] Thus the price of drug products remains subject to control through the reimbursement system. The Minister of Finance retains his or her powers to approve general rounds of price rises and may, by way of a decree, reintroduce direct controls over pharmaceutical prices. An industry-wide price increase of 2 per cent had in fact been granted in May 1986.

In accordance with pre-election commitments to phase in a

liberalization of pharmaceutical prices, the new Minister of Health, Madame Barzach, set up an *ad hoc* committee comprising representatives of the various interested ministries, the SNIP, and the CNAMTS, to review the situation and make recommendations.[113] The industry, supported by the health funds, continued to press for the total separation of prices from reimbursement controls. It argued that if drug prices were left to the market and if the doctor and consumer were fully exposed to the real cost of medicines, of which only a predetermined proportion would qualify for reimbursement, the total bill for drugs would eventually fall.[114] The government's initial willingness to embrace such a plan was tempered by two factors. In the first place, the predicted social security deficit for 1986 amounted to almost 23 billion francs and was expected to rise to 30 billion in 1987 and to 40 billion by 1988.[115] Although pharmaceuticals accounted for only 3.5 per cent of this budget, French drug-prices were now estimated to have fallen to some 30 per cent below the European average,[116] so that a complete liberalization would have a considerable impact on the already precarious financial situation of the health funds. Complete freedom in pricing was therefore predicated on a prior fundamental restructuring of the social security regime, a recategorization of reimbursement products, and the implementation of measures to

Table 5. Index of Prices of Pharmaceuticals in France (1970 = 100)

	Reimbursable	Non-reimbursable
1970	100	100
1975	107.7	118.4
1978	122.1	137.6
1980	134.6	177.0
1982	160.0	245.6
1984	168.8	287.4
1985	175.7	298.9
1986	177.2	312.1
1987	180.3	349.1

Source: SNIP, *L'Industrie pharmaceutique: ses réalités,* 1988

reduce the volume of expenditure, including greater competition from OTC products.

In the second place, the experience of pricing freedom for non-reimbursable products, introduced in 1978, was not encouraging. Average annual prices of these products had increased by 13 per cent in 1979 and 18 per cent in 1982, when controls were temporarily reimposed,[117] a trend confirmed by INSEE statistics published in 1987.

The Health Minister preferred to proceed cautiously and announced that the total liberalization of prices could not be achieved in the short term but would be accomplished over a five-year period, provided co-operation from the industry was forth-coming.[118] As the industry pointed out, however, neither concrete proposals for reform nor any clear timetable for liberalization had been spelled out.

The return to incrementalism

In the meantime, the government reverted to incremental reforms. The modulation system was reintroduced, and smaller firms were awarded a special price increase.[119] A priori controls on advertising, and the special tax on pharmaceutical publicity were abolished in 1987.[120] Finally, a renewed attempt to promote generic competition was made in late 1987 with the announcement that prices of drugs sold to hospital pharmacies would be deregulated.[121] The Minister also announced that new, innovative products and products with significant export potential would be reimbursed at 'international' prices. Negotiation procedures were to be facilitated by placing sole responsibility for pricing matters with the DPHM.[122] At the same time, as part of the government's plans for the rationalization of social security, some 1,100 products were transferred from the 70 per cent to the 40 per cent reimbursement category, while a number of vitamin-based products were excluded altogether. The SNIP estimated that the exclusion of these products would result in major losses of profit for a number of medium-sized firms.[123] In addition, the provisions relating to the 100 per cent reimbursement of drugs used in the treatment of long and costly illnesses were modified, so that only certain categories of patient or certain types of product would qualify.[124] These measures were expected to save some 3 billion francs.

These piecemeal changes did little to alleviate the SNIP's pre-occupations about the long-term future of French-based industry, especially after 1992, when French firms will be more exposed to competition from their European partners. The net deficit on trade in intermediate products had continued to worsen, rising from 1,887 million francs in 1980 to 2,018 million in 1985. The percentage of total turnover devoted to investment and R. & D. remains lower than that expended by British- or German-based industry,[125] and by 1987 France could no longer claim representation among the world's top twenty-five companies.

The return of a Socialist majority in the legislative elections of 1988 brought an end to the privatization programme, but no clear alternative industrial strategy has so far emerged, and there is no indication that planning contracts will be revived. Shortly after his appointment, the new Minister of Health, Claude Évin, referred the entire question of the quality and funding of health provision in France to a group of experts and, on the basis of its recommendations, announced a large-scale programme of reform. No firm indications on future pharmaceutical pricing policy were announced, however, but a further report on the state of the French-based pharmaceutical sector, jointly commissioned by the Ministers of Industry, Health, and Research, concluded that a series of radical reforms were urgently required if French firms were to meet the increased competitive pressures in the European market. In particular the Dangoumau-Biot Report, as this study is known, advised that prices for reimbursement should be separated from selling prices, with an immediate and total deregulation of the latter. It also suggested that the industry should benefit from a combination of subsidies and tax relief in order to salvage its declining research base. The Health Minister has since alluded to a tentative plan to introduce a reimbursement system based solely on comparative efficacy tests, but not to price deregulation.[126] In recognition of the relatively precarious international competitive position of the French-based industry, however, the Minister suggested that a dual-scale reimbursement system might be retained, at least in the short term.[127]

Conclusion

Despite a commitment to common goals in the UK and France, two distinguishing features of the background to French cost-containment initiatives conspired to force French regulators to adopt a rather different strategy in regard to reconciling the conflicting aims of public-expenditure restraint and industrial policy from that pursued by their British counterparts. In the first place, the net effect of 40 years of stringent price control has not only suppressed competition internally but has effectively insulated the French market from the impact of the changing competitive forces which have assailed the British pharmaceuticals market. The absence of a potential generics market, and therefore the possibility of exposing the industry to greater price competition, weakened the bargaining position of the French government. Industry had no real incentive, for example, to accommodate itself to the anti-inflation controls and resultant price freezes of 1985. In the UK the threat of exposure to increased generic competition compelled industry to accede voluntarily not only to price cuts but to repayment of excess profits. The French-based industry had, in comparison, little to gain from participating in the various negotiating committees formed during this period. Furthermore, whereas I have argued that a two-tiered market is gradually emerging in the UK, I have argued in this chapter that if any division has occurred within the French pharmaceutical sector, it is between the large, international export-oriented firms, who could use their individual bargaining power to obtain 'European prices' for their products or to win concessions from the government, and the smaller, rationally based firms, who had to depend upon the regular official rounds of price increases. Collective action, via the SNIP, was not a necessary part of this process.

In the second place, it will be recalled that, whereas the Conservative government in the UK was compelled to introduce a radically new measure of cost containment, the Limited List, similar types of instruments had been at the disposal of the French authorities since the socialization of health care in 1948. In theory, the introduction of stricter cost-containment measures should have been accomplished more easily, by means of a 'sharpening-up' of these existing policy instruments. The enduring irony of the French case is that the very proliferation of unwieldy, formal controls has systematically frustrated attempts to arrive at the co-ordinated approach to reform that, in the French system at least, is a precondition of promoting effective competition on the domestic market. This chapter has demonstrated that, despite the reforms to the price system in 1968 and 1980, the power to control the prices and the conditions for reimbursement has remained fragmented, and little clear logic has evolved from the system.

In consequence, a vicious circle has resulted. Piecemeal or incremental reform has remained the only option open to the French government in the absence of ministerial consensus on a general policy for the pharmaceutical sector, and yet, in the meantime, with the system of price control — and therefore also the structure of pharmacists' fees and the pharmaceutical distribution system — essentially unaltered, French pharmaceutical prices have continued to fall below the European average. The option for deregulation or price liberalization therefore appears an impractical and expensive course for any government to pursue as long as the deficit in the social security budget gives cause for concern. At the same time, the legacy of formal legal control is such that, despite several attempts to emulate the more flexible and discretionary PPRS, effective reform of the system of price control has eluded a succession of governments. In effect, a thorough overhaul of the French regime of pharmaceutical price regulation and distribution is urgently required. Paradoxically, this would appear to require the very type of 'state-led' solution which, as I have argued in this chapter, the institutional setting of French pricing policy has effectively precluded for the past 40 years. Such an interventionist strategy would require a coherent and co-ordinated approach to the sector, an approach which has so far proved impossible because of the continuing impact and legacy of a highly formalized system of regulation.

Notes

1. M. L. Burstall, *The Community's Pharmaceutical Industry*, (Luxembourg: Commission of the EC, 1985), 92.
2. See P. Lataillade, *The Commission's Pharmaceutical Price Transparency Proposals*, European Parliament Doc. A2-261/87 (Luxembourg, 1987), 29.
3. OECD, *Innovation Policy in France* (Paris: OECD, 1986), 3.
4. INSERM/DPHM, *Le Contrôle des médicaments* (Paris: DPHM, 1984).
5. OECD, *Trends in Health Care* (Paris: OECD, 1985).
6. CES Report, *L'Industrie pharmaceutique*, p. 32.
7. J. Boutet, *L'Industrie pharmaceutique* (Paris: La Documentation française, 1975), 106.

8. CES Report, *L'Industrie Pharmaceutique*, p. 75 estimated this market at about 2.7 per cent of drugs reimbursed in France.

9. It was alleged that large firms such as Hoffmann-La Roche and Sandoz were devoting as little as 4 per cent of their overall research budget to the development of drugs in France (*Le Monde*, 10 Jan. 1977).

10. *Les Échos*, 15 July 1976.

11. *Le Monde*, 16 Aug. 1976.

12. *La Vie Économique*, 26 Apr. 1976.

13. *Le Monde*, 10 Jan. 1977.

14. For a detailed breakdown see DAFSA, *L'Industrie pharmaceutique en France* (Paris: DAFSA, 1984).

15. Decree 77-593, in JO, 12 June 1977.

16. *Le Monde*, 19 Feb. 1980.

17. *Scrip* 467, 1 Mar. 1980, 5.

18. Arts. 3 and 7 of decree 80-786 of 3 Oct. 1980, in JO, 4 Oct. 1980.

19. *Le Monde*, 9 Feb. 1980.

20. *Le Figaro*, 7 Mar. 1980.

21. *Scrip* 470, 12 Mar. 1980, 5.

22. *Le Monde*, 2 Dec. 1977.

23. *Le Monde*, 7 Mar. 1980 and *Le Figaro*, 7 Mar. 1980.

24. *Arrêtés* 80-50/A and 80/51A of 10 July 1980; BOCC, 12 July 1980.

25. *Scrip*, 470, 12 Mar. 1980, and 474, 26 Mar. 1980.

26. Decree 80-24 of 15 Jan. 1980, in JO, 17 Jan. 1980.

27. Provision for the *ticket modérateur* had in fact been made by ordinance 67-707 of 21 Aug. 1967 (art. 20).

28. Patients were expected to pay 80 fr. per month when they incurred expenses of over 100 fr. per month: decree 80-08, 8 Jan. 1980, in JO, 10 Jan. 1980.

29. Law 79-1129 of 28 Dec. 1979, in JO, 29 Dec. 1979, adding art. L.266-2 to the Code de la securité sociale.

30. F. Mercereau, *La Securité sociale*, (Paris: Fondations Sciences Politiques, 1987).

31. C. Ducol et J. Ralite, *Retour de la France*, (Paris: Éditions sociales, 1982), 191.

32. Décision no. 83-4-DC du ministre relative à la situation de la concurrence sur le marché des médicaments et specialités pharmaceutiques à base de dipyridamole, BOCC, 31 Aug. 1983, 249-53. See also SNIP, *Rapport sur les génériques*, Jan. 1979.

33. BOSP, 31 Aug. 1977—fasc. 36 of 4 Sept. 1977.

34. This was the so-called *désescalade* procedure, implemented under art. 3 of decree 67-441 of 5 June 1967.

35. Art. R.5133 CSP.

36. *Scrip*, 1100, 7 May 1986.

37. J. Semeler-Collery, 'Tous droits de reproduction non réservés: les médicaments génériques', *Coopération*, 6 (1980), 3–8.
38. F. Sérusclat, *La distribution du médicament en France*, Rapport au Premier ministre, (Paris: La Documentation Française, 1983), 37-38.
39. A. Jemain, 'Comment soigner la Pharmacie?', *Le Nouvel Économiste*, 18 Feb. 1980, 3–7.
40. *Le Quotidien du médicin*, 2151 (1980), 7.
41. *Le Monde*, 12 July 1982.
42. The history and development of French competition policy will be more fully explored in chap. 9.
43. For a comprehensive overview, see E. Cohen and M. Bauer, *Les Grandes Manoeuvres industrielles* (Paris: Belfond, 1985).
44. For an exposition of the philosophy, see Projet Socialiste, *Pour la France des années 80s* (Paris: Club socialiste du livre, 1980). See also the declarations of the Prime Minister on the public sector's mission: JO, Débats parlementaires, Assemblée nationale, 9 July 1981, 46 ff. and JO, Débats parlementaires, Assemblée nationale, 16 Sept. 1981, 1031 ff.
45. Cohen et Bauer, *Les Grandes Manoeuvres*.
46. Commission des finances du Sénat, *Rapport du Sénat*, no. 8, 1985 (Paris: Journal Doc. Sénat, 1985).
47. See the evidence of Laurent Fabius to the Haut Conseil du secteur public, *Rapport 1984*, 92: *La Gestion du secteur public* (Paris: La Documentation française, 1984), 411–12.
48. *Le Monde*, 24 June 1976; M. Durupty, *Les Entreprises publiques* (Paris: PUF, 1984) vol. 1, 334.
49. See interview with René Sautier, *Informations chimie*, 157 (1976), 208.
50. *Le Matin*, 16 Feb. 1983.
51. For example, under the earlier Liberal administration, the chemical and pharmaceutical company Rhone-Poulenc had been forced to buy out a French fertilizer company which was to be sold to the Dutch DSM, but RP as a public company was allowed to sell the same company to Norsk Hydro in 1983. RP was also permitted to sell Chloe to BP in furtherance of its attempts to rationalize French heavy chemicals. See generally, E. Cohen, 'Nationalisations: Une bonne leçon de capitalisme', *Le Revue politique économique*, Apr. 1986, 12–16.
52. *Le Monde*, 24 Feb. 1982.
53. *Financial Times*, 11 Apr. 1985.
54. *Le Nouveau Journal*, 25 Feb. 1982 for the full text of the communiqué.
55. *Le Monde*, 20–1 May 1984.
56. Cohen and Bauer, *Les Grandes Manoeuvres*, p. 88.

57. Ibid. See also L. Zinsou. *Le Fer du Lance* (Paris: O. Orban, 1985), 84.

58. For a case-study of the consumer electronic sector following the nationalization of Thomson, see, A. Cawson, G. Shepherd and D. Weber, 'Governments, Markets and Regulation in the Western European Consumer Electronics Industry', in L. Hancher and M. Moran, *Capitalism, Culture, and Economic Regulation* (Oxford: OUP, 1989), 109–35.

59. Zinsou, *Le Fer du Lance*, p. 90.

60. *Le Monde*, 4 June 1982 and *Le Monde* 7 Aug. 1982 for full text of letter of resignation.

61. *Les contrats du plan*, (Paris: La Documentation française, 1983).

62. Zinsou, *Le Fer du Lance*, p. 101.

63. OECD, *Innovation Policy in France*, p. 89.

64. Groupe de stratégie industrielle, *Rapport du synthèse; Situation et Perspectives de la chimie française*. Cahiers de GSI, no. 5, 1983 (Paris: La Documentation française, 1983), 61–74.

65. For the broad orientation of this contract, see Haut Conseil du secteur publique, *Rapport 1984*, 92; *La Gestion du Secteur Public* (Paris: La Documentation française, 1984), 264–76.

66. *Le Monde*, 12 Mar. 1982.

67. M. Tisseyre-Berry and G. Viala, *Législation et déontologie de l'industrie pharmaceutique* (Paris: Masson, 1983), 129.

68. Decree 80-786 of 2 Oct. 1980 in JO, 4 Oct. 1980.

69. J.-M. Auby and F. Coustou, *Droit pharmaceutique* (Paris: Librairies techniques, 1980). Fasc. 39, p. 6. Under the 1967 regulations a product had to lead to an improvement in therapy ('amélioration à la thérapeutique').

70. DPHM; Social Security; DICTD; and the Direction générale de la concurrence.

71. See text of letter from J. Dangoumau to SNIP, 27 Mar. 1983, reproduced in *Annuaire IP*, (Paris: Éditions Santé, 1986).

72. See M. Fleuriet, *Les Techniques de l'économie concertée* (Paris: LGDJ, 1974), 199; J. Dutheil de la Rochère, 'Les régimes conventionnels des prix, engagements de stabilité et contrats de programme', AJDA, (1967), 597–601; A. de Laubadère, 'Interventionnisme et contrat', *Revue française de l'administration publique*, 12, (1979), 485–93; M. Mazex, 'Les contrats de plan entre l'État et les entreprises publiques', AJDA, (1984), 101–9.

73. *Arrêté* 82-17/A, of 14 June 1982, in BOCC, 16 June 1982, extended by *arrêté* 82-95/A of 22 October 1982, in BOCC, 23 Oct. 1982.

74. *Le Monde*, 17 Feb. 1983.

75. *Les Échos*, 29 Apr. 1982.

76. *Le Figaro*, 27 Feb. 1986.

77. M. Durupty, *Les Entreprises publiques*, vol. 2 (Paris: PUF, 1986), 391.
78. *Financial Times*, 1 Nov. 1985. The extent to which this new-found success could be attributed to the general international recovery and to Gandois's earlier efforts is disputed.
79. Case 182/82.
80. *Journal des finances*, 13 June 1985: 'Sanofi n'a pas fini d'étonner'.
81. *Scrip*, 1087, 24 Mar. 1986, 11.
82. See generally *Le Courrier du Parlement*, 700, Mar. 1984, 38–9 and 57.
83. DAFSA, *L'Industrie Pharmaceutique en France*.
84. *La Vie française*, 21 Nov. 1983.
85. Law 82-155 of 11 Feb. 1982 in JO, 13 Feb. 1982.
86. Decision of the Constitutional Council, 11 Feb. 1982 in JO, 14 Feb. 1982. See L. Favoreu. 'Les Décisions du conseil Constitutionnel dans l'affaire des nationalisations', *Revue de droit public et de la science politique en France et à l'étranger*, (Apr. 1982), 84–98, and D. Linotte, 'Chronique législative', *Revue de droit publique* (1982), 120–5.
87. Commission of the EC, *The State Aid Element in Capital Transfers* (Brussels: Commission of the EC, 1987), 150–2.
88. In Case 323/82 *Intermills* [1984] ECR 3809 the Court ruled that no distinction should be drawn between aid granted in the form of loans and aid granted in the form of a holding acquired in the capital of an undertaking. It was unnecessary on the facts of this case for the Court to define the circumstances in which this may be the case. Some guidance can be found in the Advocate General's Opinion in Joined Cases 296 and 318/82 *The Netherlands* v. *Leeuwarder Papierwaren-fabriek BV* v. *Commission* [1985] 3 CMLR 380. The Commission's views are set out in its *Fourteenth Report on Competition Policy* (Brussels, 1986), point 198. For a full discussion of European law and state acquisitions, see K. Hellingman, 'State Participation as State Aids'. C.M.L.Rev, 23 (1986), 111–19. In Case 40/85 *Belgium* v. *Commission* [1988] 2 CMLR 301 the European Court ruled that two large injections of capital into a company making heavy annual losses was an investment that no private investor would have contemplated and therefore amounted to state aid.
89. See the submission of the Minister for Industry and Research to the Haut conseil du secteur publique, *Rapport 1984*, pp. 404–14.
90. Cohen et Bauer, *Les Grandes Manoeuvres*, p. 91.
91. Interview with the Minister of Finance, Paris, May 1986.
92. See SNIP, *Médicaments remboursables aux assurés sociaux* (Paris, 1986), 57.
93. *Arrêté* 82-92/A of 15 Oct. 1982 in BOCC 16 Oct. 1982.
94. Conseil d'État, 1982. The Council of State did, however, declare void

arrêté 76/14P of 5 Feb. 1976, BOCC, 6 Feb. 1976 on grounds of procedural irregularities. A number of pharmaceutical firms, as well as the SNIP, sought review of the Minister's decision to lower the prices of their products without first consulting the special commission comprising representatives of the health funds and the industry (art. 593 CSP). Although this commission never met, the Council ruled that the Ministry of the Economy ought to have constituted such a commission prior to ordering the price reductions. The *arrêté* was therefore void (*Laboratoires Allard et autres*, 8 Jan. 1979, Doc. Pharm. 2582, 197), 9.

95. *Le Nouvel Observateur*, 28 June 1986.
96. *Scrip*, 1026 19 Aug. 1985, 5.
97. *Arrêté*, 17 June 1985.
98. *Scrip*, 1023, 7 Aug. 1985, 4.
99. Interview, SNIP, May 1986. Art. 5 of the decree of 1980 provides as follows: 'peuvent être rayés de la liste par arrêté du ministre de la Santé et de la Securité Sociale, les médicaments qui ne sont pas régulièrement exploités ou qui ne sont plus indispensables à la thérapeutique ou qui ne peuvent plus figurer sur la liste en vertu des dispositions des articles 3 et s'. The general tenor of this article would appear to enable the Minister to exert certain a posteriori controls as opposed to exercising a priori limitations.
100. Art. 4 of decree 80-786 of 3 Oct. 1980.
101. See in particular the results of the survey compiled by M. Teulaude of the Fédération nationale de la mutualité française, *Bulletin de Droit et Pharmacie* (Vie Juridique), 12 (1985), 12-4.
102. CES Report, *L'Industrie pharmaceutique*, p. 71.
103. In *Societé des Laboratoires Beytout* (CE 22 Mar. 1968, Doc. Pharm. 506) the Council of State upheld the Minister's decision to remove a product from the reimbursement list where proof of its therapeutic efficacy could not be conclusively demonstrated. In *Métadier* (CE 23 Feb. 1953, Doc. Pharm. 209) the Council of State had refused to consider an application for review of the Minister's assessment of a product's active substances. This was a matter reserved to the Minister's sole discretion. While this jurisprudence is somewhat dated, most French commentators are of the opinion that it is still good law. See J. M. Auby and F. Coustou, 'Les médicaments spécialisés et les institutions sociales' *Droit pharmaceutique*, fasc. 39, 16.
104. CES Report, *L'Industrie pharmaceutique*, p. 61.
105. Commission des comptes de la sécurité sociale, *Rapport annuel 1982–83* (Paris, 1984), estimated the annual growth in volume to be 4.1 per cent in 1982, 5.4 per cent in 1983, and 5 per cent in 1984.

106. T. Lecompte, *La Consommation pharmaceutique: Structure, prescription et motifs* (Paris: CREDES, 1984).
107. Loi d'habilitation économique et sociale, 87-793 of 2 July 1986, in JO, 3 July 1986.
108. Art. 7(1) of the enabling law 86-783 provided that where a company had been taken into the public sector by legislation, any transfer of majority or minority participations held directly or indirectly by the state had to be authorized by a law, in accordance with art. 34 of the French Constitution. Where the state holds less than 50 per cent, directly or indirectly, any transfer would have to be authorized by decree.
109. *Le Figaro*, 25 May 1987.
110. *L'Humanité*, 2 Apr. and 5 May 1987.
111. *Le Monde*, 27 June 1987. The government's shareholding in Roussel is now to be transferred to Rhone–Poulenc. *Financial Times*, 5 Mar. 1990.
112. Ordinance 87-1243 of 1 Dec. 1986, in JO, 3 Dec. 1986, art. 61. *Arrêtés* 83-9/A of 4 Feb. 1983, 84-55A of 29 June 1984, and 86-31/A of 10 July 1986 *relatifs aux prix des médicaments remboursables aux assurés sociaux* are maintained in force. See decree 86-1309 of 29 Dec. 1986 on the implementation of ordinance 86-12423, in JO, 30 Dec. 1986.
113. *Le Monde*, 3 July 1986.
114. See also J. J. Rosa, 'Lois du Marché et innovation', *Prospective et Santé*, 36 (1985/86), 103-8.
115. *Le Nouvel Économiste*, 588, 17 Apr. 1987.
116. *Les Informations Chimie*, special issue on the pharmaceutical sector, June 1986.
117. A. Jeunemaitre, *Revue française des affaires sociales*, 3 (1986), 81.
118. *Scrip* 1128, 13 Aug. 1986, 5.
119. *La Tribune de l'Économie*, 10 May 1987.
120. This is discussed in detail in chap. 8.
121. *Scrip* 1261 27 Nov. 1987, 1.
122. *Bulletin de droit et pharmacie*, (Vie Juridique), 10 (1987), 49.
123. *Le Monde*, 19 Nov. 1986.
124. Decree 86-1377 of 31 Dec. 1986, modifying R.322-9-1 CSS and giving entitlement to 100 per cent reimbursement of drugs listed in D.322-1 CSS. (Further modified by decrees 88-915 and 88-917 of 7 Sept. 1988 in JO, 8 Sept. 1988).
125. *Scrip*, 1129 17 Aug. 1986.
126. *Le Monde*, 5, 8, 13, and 15 Apr. 1989.
127. *Libération*, 13 Apr. 1989.

8

Regulating Pharmaceutical Promotion: An Impossible Task?

In earlier chapters I have emphasized the enduring importance of product competition to the drug industry. This chapter, which examines the regulatory controls over a crucial component of product competition—the promotion of branded ethical or prescription drug-products—returns to this theme and contrasts the different approaches to the sensitive issue of control on pharmaceutical advertising in the UK and France. The first section discusses the significance of advertising for the process of product competition and presents a brief overview of the various types of promotion common to the sector. It examines some of the common difficulties confronting regulators. The second section compares the French and British approaches to the regulation of the quality and content of advertising material. The third section examines a related issue, the control of expenditure on pharmaceutical promotion. In one sense, these two sets of controls serve related functions. Levels of advertising expenditure influence the quantity of products prescribed by doctors as well as the quality of prescribing: 'the more widely and exuberantly a medicine is marketed, the less effective it will be in some users and the less safe it will be, because marketing and reliable user information are antipathetic'.[1] Nevertheless, expenditure control and quality control are subjected to very different techniques of regulation, which are best examined separately.

As in preceding chapters, the aim here is not to present a detailed or exhaustive exegesis of the current regulations of every aspect of advertising but to examine the way in which each country's diverse legal and administrative arrangements offer different solutions to regulatory problems and yet allow accommodation and compromise over the conflicting aims and objectives of advertising control.

The Significance of Advertising: Conflicting Aims and Objectives

The danger to the public from fraudulent claims for medical products has long been recognized, and controls over the marketing of various remedies have operated in both the UK and France for many years. Even before the rise of 'consumerism' and the development of the modern pharmaceutical industry, drug products were recognized as inherently dangerous, and the very existence of controls over their promotion to the public set them apart from other products. The earliest form of control was the restriction of their sale to pharmacies, and by the end of the Second World War the requirement of a prior prescription from a medical practitioner further restricted their purchase. The doctor's role in the process of selecting a product for a patient has thus become pivotal. It is therefore of the utmost importance that doctors be kept informed of the products available and of their advantages and disadvantages.

The socialization of health care has brought with it the additional problem that this selection is often made with little regard for cost. Pharmaceutical companies aim to convince doctors of the superior quality of their product rather than of its economic attributes. Chapter 2 explained how the structural features of the pharmaceuticals market gives promotion its peculiar significance. In particular, it will be recalled that competition within existing therapeutic submarkets is assured not by price cutting but by product differentiation, a process in which advertising plays a crucial role. I have argued that both the French and British governments have failed to stimulate price competition, and instead rely primarily on product-based competition as the motor of the industry. However, that form of competition must be efficient: the freedom of rival drug-firms to promote new brands is necessary to break the temporary monopoly enjoyed by a market leader, ensuring the continued competitiveness of the industry as a whole. With fewer new active ingredients being brought on to the market, and with the erosion of patent protection, marketing and promotional activities are of even greater importance to the drugs industry. The sheer volume of expenditure which drug companies devote to promoting their products to doctors is in itself eloquent testimony to the vital role of advertising. It has been estimated that in France the

industry devotes a total of 16.9 per cent of its turnover to information and publicity, 12.5 per cent of turnover being spent on promoting products to the medical profession.[2] In 1985 the industry
spent an estimated 4 billion francs on all forms of advertising.[3]
Expenditure on drug advertising in the UK currently accounts for
an estimated 11 per cent of turnover, or some £200 million.[4]

At a certain point, however, promotional expenditure must cease
to further competition and become merely extravagant wastage,
which can be passed on by the companies to the NHS in the UK, or
to the health insurance funds in France, and indirectly to the taxpayer or the insured, thus inflating overall health-costs. The problem for the regulator is firstly to establish where the threshold
between the two should lie, and secondly to devise methods of
determining at what point that threshold has been crossed.

Advertising and information

If the role of the doctor in providing information to patients about
the potential benefits and side-effects of a drug is pivotal, it is of the
utmost importance that he or she be kept well informed about
products which have been on the market for some time. It is equally
vital that he or she receive 'objective' information. While products
can be marketed only if they have received a product licence or an
AMM, the safety criteria on which licences are issued are relative,
not absolute. The incidence of adverse effects will often become
apparent only when the product has been in widespread use. It
would thus appear incumbent on the licensing authorities to ensure
that doctors are provided with adequate and accessible prescribing
information about each product's known advantages and disadvantages, and to ensure that that information is kept accurate and up to
date. The question is, how can the quality of this information be
best guaranteed?

Overt and covert promotion

In selecting methods to ensure the objectivity and accuracy of prescribing information, regulators face two obstacles: hostility from
the medical profession, who resent any encroachment on their clini-

cal freedom, and hostility from the drugs industry, which resents
intrusion on its commercial freedom. There has been a marked
reluctance to 'police' the prescribing patterns of individual doctors,
and although powers exist to penalize particularly wasteful practices, these are rarely used.[5]

The French and British governments have both considered, and
summarily rejected, suggestions to create independent government
agencies with sole responsibility for providing the necessary information to doctors.[6] Instead, they have preferred to let the industry
assume primary responsibility, at the same time endeavouring,
through regulatory control, to ensure that purely commercial considerations do not dictate the quality, quantity, and content of that
information. These controls have been supplemented by the provision to doctors of 'objective' information from independent
sources. In France, for example, government publishes *fiches de
transparence* (transparency notes), designed to provide doctors
with comparative prescribing information, and distributes free two
government-sponsored magazines, *La Lettre Médicale* and
Prescrire.

The amount of resources devoted to these official activities is tiny
in comparison with the industry's spending. The Department of
Health is estimated to spend around £2 million a year on this sort
of literature—approximately 1 per cent of the industry's promotional budget. More resources are being devoted to training medical
students in clinical pharmacology and therapeutics, in the hope that
this will lead to improved prescribing standards, at least in the long
term.[7]

In the meantime, doctors still look primarily to commercial
sources of information.[8] Company literature, advertisements and
features in medical journals, and visits from medical representatives
are the main sources. In the UK it has been estimated that in each
month a typical GP will be exposed to over 1,300 advertisements
for some 250 drugs. Doctors in France seem to attach considerable
importance to information received from company representatives,
and in consequence the industry devotes some 60 per cent of its
promotional budget to this form of advertising. It has been
estimated that a French doctor receives between 1,200 and 1,300
visits per year, or between five and six per day.[9] In addition to
expenditure on these forms of 'overt promotion', the industry
spends considerable sums on 'covert promotion'.

Covert promotion includes scientific and medical research sponsored by drug companies, the funding of post-graduate education and university posts, subsidized conferences, research seminars and symposia, and the sponsorship of scientific journals. As public funding for scientific and medical research has declined,[10] educational and research bodies rely increasingly on industry finance. It has been estimated that one-sixth of the staff of British academic departments of clinical pharmacology are directly sponsored by industry. In the UK professional associations of doctors and physicians also enjoy financial support from drug companies. The priming fund of £105,000 from Glaxo, Wellcome, and Beecham was central to the establishment of the Royal College of General Practitioners in the early 1950s.[11]

A second form of covert promotion can occur through the careful use of the public media — for example, to exploit public interest in the discovery of new cures or to announce the imminent arrival of some wonder drug such as a cure for AIDS. Such tactics offer drug firms a means of bringing patient pressure on doctors who might otherwise be slow to change their prescribing habits.

A third form of covert promotion takes place through the proffering of financial inducements to doctors to engage in so-called 'seeding' or Phase IV trials. These are controlled trials on products which have already received official authorization for marketing but on which the company wishes to carry out further investigations. With each of these methods of covert promotion the problem facing regulators is one of drawing a line between genuine informational activities and disguised publicity.

Regulatory controls over promotion

This profusion of possibilities open to drug companies to promote their products is almost matched by the proliferation in the UK and France of legal and administrative controls and self-regulatory codes governing the quality and quantity of advertising materials. Although it is important to note that advertising controls do not comprise formal statutory regulations alone but are in reality a patchwork of overlapping formal legal and informal voluntary controls, the gaps in each regime should not be overlooked.

In the first place, there are formal statutory or regulatory controls over the quality of some, but not all, forms of overt promotion in both countries. These are contained in Part VI of the UK Medicines Act 1968 and in the regulations made under it, and in Chapter V of the French *Code de la Santé publique*. An important distinction must be drawn in the way in which these controls are implemented. In France, until September 1987, all advertising material, in whatever form, had in theory to be submitted for the prior approval of the *Commission de contrôle de la publicité* (Commission on Publicity Control).[12] In the UK, however, the statutory controls are supplemented by the industry association's own code of practice, first drafted in 1958, and implemented by its Code of Practice Committee (CPC). Adherence to the ABPI's code of conduct is a condition of membership of the Association, and the breach of its provisions may lead, and indeed has led, to expulsion.[13] Non-member companies may also agree to be bound by the code, although it is unclear whether any real sanction lies against them.[14] The CPC is appointed by the ABPI, in consultation with the Department of Health. Since 1978 it has comprised twelve senior industry representatives, a chairperson with legal qualifications, who has a casting vote, and, as a result of pressure from the Labour government of the day, two independent medical members. The CPC never vets promotional material. The code's substantive provisions intentionally duplicate most of the statutory regulatory controls, but they also go beyond them to include restrictions on the activities of medical representatives, as well as on the distribution of gifts and samples, matters which are covered by formal regulation in France.

Shortly before the introduction, in 1977, of the first set of comprehensive regulations on advertising to the professions, the British government made clear its intention to continue to seek compliance primarily through the existing self-regulatory mechanisms which had been in operation since 1958. Statutory powers would be limited to 'reserve powers'.[15] Control over promotional material, whether by the CPC or by the Medicines Division at the DHSS, is always a posteriori.

The severity of the former French regime set it apart from its European partners. Yet at the same time we have seen that the vagaries of the French pricing system have impelled the industry to promote 'me-too' types of product as a way of securing higher prices. Does this mean that the French system is particularly constraining for industry? The industry association, the SNIP, campaigned vigorously for the abolition of the a priori controls and for their replacement with a posteriori controls, or even self-regulation. It finally met success with the former, but not the latter, of these demands. In 1982, together with the *Ordre des pharmaciens* and the *Union des annonceurs*, it drew up a code of good marketing practice,[16] monitored and updated by an ethical committee with a membership drawn from all three associations (*Commission d'éthique professionnelle sur l'information du médicament*— CEPIM). Neither the Socialist government nor its successor were sufficiently impressed with the concept of self-regulation to elevate it to the status it enjoys in UK.

The most striking difference in the controls imposed on advertising content in each country is therefore the presence of a high degree of 'mandated self-regulation'—that is, government-induced self-regulation—in the UK and the outward formalism of the French regime, a pattern of contrast which is evident in every aspect of pharmaceutical regulation discussed in this book.

In comparison, controls over levels of expenditure on promotion appear to bear a closer similarity, being largely of a discretionary, non-statutory nature in both countries. This aspect will be dealt with in the third section of this chapter, which will show that the regulation of expenditure is linked to, if not incorporated into, the mechanisms for the regulation of prices and profits.

Controls over the Quality of Promotional Material

The following review of quality controls in the UK and France is divided into two parts: first, control over the selection and presentation of name and ingredients, and second, a comparison of current techniques of control over the presentation of information about the drug, including contra-indications and side-effects. This review is followed by an appraisal of the way in which controls are monitored and enforced.

Perhaps one of the most basic controls on overt promotion is that relating to the selection of a product's name. A discrete drug-substance may be known by three types of names: its chemical name, which simply lists every part of its molecular structure; its generic name, which abbreviates the components but still informs the doctor of its chemical composition, and finally the trade or brand name, which links the drug with a particular manufacturer but which contains little information about its composition. In principle, the manufacturer's right to choose a product name is sovereign; the selection of a trade mark which is sufficiently suggestive of a product to make a lasting impression is an important stage in a product's commercialization. It is not uncommon for several manufacturers to market the same drug under different trade names, or for a firm to promote a new branded version of an existing product, leading to possible confusion.

The British Medicines Act 1968 empowers the Licensing Authority to refuse to grant a product licence if the CSM considers that the proposed name could give rise to hazard, but it has no power to select a brand name,[17] nor does it have powers to prevent companies acquiring a proprietorial interest in a generic name. In France the Minister may refuse to issue an AMM if the proposed name might be confused with that of other products, or if it is a misleading description of the product's qualities.[18] The Transparency Commission may also raise objections to names likely to lead to an 'excessive demand' for a product.

Any promotional literature, data sheets (or their French equivalent, the *fiches signalétiques*), leaflets, or labels, as well as any packaging used or issued in connection with a product, must include the product's non-proprietary name, where it exists, and active ingredients must also be listed by their 'appropriate' non-proprietary names. Lists of generic or international non-proprietary (INN) names for products and ingredients are devised by the World Health Organization and by the European Pharmacopoeia. In addition, in the UK, monograph names and British Approved Names (BANs) are devised and compiled by the British Pharmacopoeia Commission (BPC)—a standing committee appointed under the Medicines Act—for use as headings of monographs which appear in the British Pharmacopoeia.[19] These monographs are primarily concerned with quality standards, and it is an offence to sell or supply a product by reference to a BAN if the product, or its active ingredients, does not comply with the specified standard.[20]

In France the application for an AMM must include a separate request for approval of the proposed generic name (*dénomination commune*). This request is transmitted to the *Commission de nomenclature* of the National Pharmacopoeia Commission for its opinion.[21]

In both countries the regulations governing advertising to the professions require the conspicuous display of non-proprietary names alongside brand names. Theoretically, failure to comply used to entail refusal of a publicity visa in France.[22] In the UK, however, the industry's reluctance to give prominence to generic names in its promotional literature was made apparent in 1978, when the ABPI refused to include obligations relating to the position and type-size of information on active ingredients in its code of practice. Although the CPC has acted in the past upon complaints from the DHSS that companies had failed to list active ingredients in a journal advertisement,[23] it would not act on a complaint relating to the positioning of the information.

As the patents on a number of important products have begun to lapse, several British-based companies have sought to promote or secure brand loyalty, either by promoting proprietary names for generic products or by attempting to acquire a proprietorial interest in a generic name, or a shortened version of it. These practices appear to have been exacerbated by the rise in parallel importing and the introduction of the Limited List in April 1985, causing the director of the BPC to propose a voluntary code of practice for the industry on the selection and use of trade marks. The BPC and the Licensing Authority were of the opinion that neither the Medicines Act 1968 nor the Trade Marks Act 1938 provided adequate regulatory powers to prevent confusion and avoidance of possible hazards.[24] The ABPI was not particularly receptive to this idea, which would give third parties the opportunity to involve themselves in disputes over matters relating to trade marks, and might also further delay the processing of product-licensing applications. In the Association's view, the normal commercial process of selecting a product name militated very effectively against the choice of potentially confusing names. However, it indicated that it might be prepared to deal with problems by way of guide-lines, which would not have to be policed.[25] In the final event, the DHSS in 1988 issued *Guidelines for the Construction of Pharmaceutical Trade Marks*, the final version of which, in deference to the ABPI's wishes, no longer included proposals that the assignment of a trade mark to a generic product should be discouraged.

Article 3 of the French law of 31 December 1964 on trade marks stipulates that marks consisting exclusively of the generic name will not be recognized as pharmaceutical trade marks. However, Article R.5128 CSP does recognize the use of the generic name plus the

name of the manufacturer as a proprietary name. The recent jurisprudence on pharmaceutical trade marks is somewhat inconsistent,
but the courts appear to be quite lenient in their interpretation of
Article 3 and have permitted marks to be registered where they bear
a closer resemblance to the generic name, but not where they are
suggestive of the drug's composition.[26]

The presentation of prescribing information: A posteriori versus a priori controls

Controls over the way in which companies present information
about their products to doctors constitute perhaps the most sensitive aspect of advertising control. On the one hand, most experts
agree that there can be no such thing as a completely 'true' or
'objective' account of a product's properties; different schools of
thought will produce different accounts. The pharmaceutical firm,
on the other hand, will be tempted to base the claims it makes for
its products on perceived gaps in the market as much as on the basis
of clinical evidence. The promotion of Thalidomide is the most
infamous example.[27] The compromise position adopted in the UK
and France has been to let the industry prepare its own literature
but to impose certain minimum requirements on content and style
of presentation. Ideally, company information should indicate
whether a drug is new, and if so what makes it new, how the drug
will fit into the doctor's medical practice, how it differs pharma-
cologically from existing products, and whether there are any particular clinical circumstances in which it should or should not be
used.[28] It has been suggested that even though the initiative remains
with industry, the strict French approach to the regulation of
advertising led to an 'officialization' of information between 1976
and 1987.[29] Controls were at once comprehensive and severe, and
most promotional literature, whatever its form, was subject to
administrative scrutiny prior to circulation or publication.[30] The
preference for a priori as opposed to a posteriori controls has
obvious implications for the way in which the relevant regulations
on advertising have been implemented in each country.

In the first place the British approach is permissive. The industry
is free to promote its product claims subject to certain statutory
restrictions. The controls themselves are directed at overt promotion. General controls on advertising to the medical professions are

contained in Part VI of the Medicines Act 1968. Section 93 makes it an offence for a commercially interested party to issue advertisements or to make 'promotional' representations which falsely describe a product or which are likely to mislead as to the nature or quality of a drug, or as to its uses or effects. The purposes for which the product may be recommended—its authorized recommendations—are limited to those specified in the licence, the terms and conditions of which are not published.

In France, following the major overhaul of advertising controls in 1976[31] by the Minister of Health of the time, Simone Veil, the starting-point of the regulatory regime is prohibition: promotional activities (*publicité*) are permissible only in accordance with the conditions fixed by decree of the Conseil d'État.[32] Prior to 1976 most advertising to the professions was exempt from a priori control, this method being reserved for direct advertising to the public.[33] Under the terms of the 1976 decree, no promotional material, in whatever form, for any medicine, medical device, or product, or for any product presented as having curative properties, could be distributed either to the medical professions, the pharmacists, or the public without prior ministerial approval.[34] These provisions are sufficiently wide in scope to apply to all forms of promotion, covert and overt. The 1976 decree was also the first to regulate the activities of medical representatives.

In particular, the 1976 decree amending the CSP dropped the qualifying word 'commercial' so that, in theory, all information supplied by a firm or by a third party in connection with a product could be put into circulation only if it had received prior approval. The incumbent Minister of Health, Mme Veil, appears to have intended to exercise the greatest possible control over the industry's promotional activities, which had come in for considerable public criticism at that time. The position of genuine scientific articles and publications, however, was now dubious if the regulations were strictly interpreted. In consequence, the Minister of Health submitted a series of questions on the scope of the regime to the Conseil d'État. The latter was of the opinion that although each case had to be judged on its own merits, the regime actually applied to every publication—issued by the firm or otherwise, whether delivered free or otherwise—promoting the attributes of a product.[35] The Minister of Health declared that this *opinion* would be treated as guidance. Special procedures for vetting press articles were subsequently developed by the DPHM.[36] However, this system was widely criticized on two counts. First, the logic of the *opinion* suggested that pejorative scientific articles would escape control while laudatory reviews would not; and second, it made inadequate distinction between genuine information and publicity.[37]

The 1976 decree provided that the Minister could only issue a publicity visa after he or she had obtained the advice of the *Commission de contrôle de la publicité*, a body comprising twenty-three representatives drawn from the medical and pharmacy professions, representatives from the various ministries concerned with the industry's affairs, a consumer representative, and an industry representative.[38] Although this advice was not legally binding on the Minister, it has always been followed. The Commission's terms of reference were to ensure that the material presented neither danger nor inconvenience to public health, and that it was true, fair, verifiable, and in complete conformity with the terms and conditions of the AMM, to which the Commission has access.[39] Furthermore, the Commission could appoint specialist rapporteurs to assess claims made for a product. Although the Commission published a 'guidance document' of 250 pages on its working methods, it had no fixed operating rules and decided each case on an *ad hoc* basis.

The principal instrument of a posteriori control in the UK is the data sheet. The Medicines Act provides that prior to the delivery or publication of any promotional literature, or prior to a visit by a medical representative, the practitioner must receive a data sheet relating to the product.[40] Regulations made under Section 95 of the Act further provide that all advertisements in journals should include a succinct statement of the entries on the data sheet relating to side-effects, precautions, relevant contra-indications, and conditions of use. This information should be presented in a clear and legible form and positioned in such a way that its relationship to the claims made for the product are readily apparent to the reader.[41] The current edition of the ABPI code essentially mirrors these provisions.

Although the data sheet is the foundation-stone on which all other a posteriori controls rest, there are a number of reasons to doubt its efficacy. The concept itself was originally modelled on the Sainsbury Report's proposed 'control documents', to be issued by the Licensing Authority as a source of objective advice about a product and as an independent reference against which to judge a manufacturer's claims. In fact data sheets are treated as advertisements for the purposes of the Medicines Act.[42] They are prepared by the individual firm and published annually, in compendium form, by the ABPI. Regulations prescribing the content and layout of data sheets were introduced in 1972, and while copies of sheets had to be deposited with the Licensing Authority, a requirement that a draft data-sheet should accompany a submission for a product licence—with a view to being subjected to official scrutiny and approval—was introduced only as late as 1980.[43] Studies conducted in the UK show that there are often considerable variations in the data sheets prepared by different companies for substantially similar products, or in those prepared by the same company for different national markets.[44] When the Medicines Act came into force in 1971, some 31,000 products already on the market received automatic product licences of right, so the accuracy of the claims made for these products had never been assessed until the review process began in 1975.

In addition, there are often gaps in the prescribing information, which, although technically accurate, may in practice be too scanty to offer real guidance. Warnings, precautions, and notification of adverse effects may be conscientiously listed, but without estimates of their frequency: 'The mechanism by which the drug exerts its therapeutic effect is often explained but information can seldom be found on the pathogenesis of adverse effects.'[45] It was only as a result of the large number of deaths alleged to be associated with the antiarthritic drug benoxaprofen (Opren) that the Licensing Authority specified that information on prescribing for the elderly was to be incorporated into a data sheet.[46] Similar problems attend the amount of information included in advertisements. In the regulations, reference is made to a succinct description of the products indications and contra-indications, but there is no legal definition of the meaning of the term. The Department suggests that the statement should include 'the most important points' in a statement of between seventy-five and 150 words. Under the current regulations on the standard provisions for licences, the Medicines Commission may issue a formal notice to a licence holder requiring the inclusion of serious warnings about the product in all advertisements. Where such a warning has been issued, an abbreviated or 'reminder' advertisement may not be issued. In the absence of such a notice, it may be assumed that a warning, even though it appears on the data sheet, is not one which need necessarily be shown in other promotional material.[47] Again, the French provisions are much wider: it is necessary to indicate 'undesirable effects' as well as side-effects.[48]

Finally, there are significant lacunae in the coverage of the provisions of the Medicines Act and the implementing regulations. Publications which are intended for pharmacists or nurses are covered by the general provisions of the Act and by the code but not by the more detailed provisions of the regulations. Only doctors and dentists need receive a data sheet. Part VI of the Act is not applicable to products such as medical devices, which may be sold without a product licence, and yet misleading claims as to their properties are not entirely unknown.

This somewhat partial approach to control in the UK is in marked contrast to the all-embracing nature of the French regime, which applies to all forms of products and all forms of publicity, irrespective of their addressee. In France commercial prescription-guides or handbooks are subject to the scrutiny of a special *Commission de contrôle des dictionnaires de spécialités* and must contain a certain amount of minimum information, presented in a particular format, while their British equivalents not only escape official scrutiny but are also exempt from a number of regulations.[49] The *fiches signalétiques*, now known as product summaries, are the principal method, indeed the only method, of ensuring the accuracy of information conveyed by medical representatives, and the 1976 decree requires that they must be presented on each visit.[50] These summaries are considered to be advertising material and must be submitted to the DPHM for prior authorization by the Minister.[51] Not only must the summaries conform strictly to the terms of the AMM, but they must contain certain obligatory information, set out in accordance with the layout of the monographs adopted by the official guide or dictionary of prescription products, the VIDAL.

Finally it might be noted that the Medicines Act does not regulate the provision of gifts or samples—this being a matter for the ABPI code. In theory, Articles L549 and R.5051 of the French CSP prohibit gifts and financial advantages, but abuse is considered to be widespread.[52] Regulatory restrictions on the provision of samples were introduced in France in 1963, in response to complaints by doctors that they were being inundated with products. Samples could be delivered only on receipt of a written request. The 1976 decree considerably reinforced these restrictions.[53] It provides that free samples should be made available only in the first 2 years after a product is marketed.[54]

Phase IV trials

Perhaps one of the most striking examples of the divergence in the British and French approaches to advertising regulation is the treatment of so-called Phase IV or post-marketing clinical trials. A firm will request a doctor to monitor its product in a controlled study in return for some form of financial inducement, supposedly to cover administrative costs and to compensate for general inconvenience. Such trials may well be nothing more than disguised promotional exercises, although the value of a properly controlled study, with an adequately specified protocol, is now widely recognized by regulatory authorites; the continued monitoring of products in a wider cross-section of the population may reveal unwanted side-effects which were not apparent in the smaller groups used at the pre-clinical stage. Industry is also keen to promote responsible Phase IV monitoring as an alternative to a prolonged licensing procedure.

The most obvious method of ensuring that a trial is for a genuine clinical purpose and not for disguised promotion is to establish some means of 'vetting' the protocol. This is the French approach. Test protocols potentially fall within the wide definition of publicity, and copies must be deposited with the DPHM for authorization. The question of payment for doctors remains problematic in France, and there is no obligation to submit tests to local hospital ethics committees.[55]

The British-based industry and medical profession succeeded in resisting government attempts to regulate Phase IV trials until 1984, when, following 3 years of negotiations, the ABPI was eventually persuaded to draw up a code of practice for licensed products. A principal stumbling-block in these negotiations was the issue of payments to doctors. The ABPI had been reluctant to draw up a code in the first place, preferring instead to issue guide-lines on the matter. The DHSS insisted that a watch-dog body should be entrusted with the code's enforcement. The final version is a compromise: it does not deal with the question of payment, this being left to a set of non-mandatory guide-lines. These guide-lines are not even referred to in the ABPI's general code of practice, and failure to observe them will not necessarily result in an unfavourable decision by the CPC. In fact, in a recent complaint involving financial inducements for a Phase IV trial, the CPC did not once refer to the guide-lines.[56]

Monitoring and enforcement

As mentioned, many of the provisions of the ABPI's code of practice on promotion intentionally mirror the requirements of the regulations, a state of affairs which is directly attributable to the DHSS's assurance to industry during the negotiations on the proposed regulatory package, which began in 1976, that self-regulatory mechanisms would always be used in the first instance. Health ministers have repeatedly stressed their faith in the system of voluntary compliance, which they consider flexible and capable of rapid application to complex technical cases, as compared with the cumbersome enforcement procedures which attend formal regulation.[57] Until recently it was impossible to judge the accuracy of this claim, as the CPC did not commence publication of its decisions until 1983.

Currently the Committee disposes of an average of fifty cases per annum at its two-monthly sittings. Most cases involve fairly minor technical breaches. Complaints may be submitted by a member of the public, a doctor, or, most commonly, a rival firm. In addition, the Department of Health and the ABPI each employ staff to scrutinize medical publications. Although the claims made by manufacturers for sophisticated and highly specialized products are difficult to assess, neither the Department nor the CPC appear to have the necessary skill, expertise, or resources to conduct searching investigations. Twelve of the CPC's members are appointed from industry, on the basis of seniority rather than on medical qualifications. The ABPI added two independent doctors only when put under pressure to do so from the Labour government in 1978, and in 1983, following widespread criticism of the industry over the Opren scandal, it appointed a full-time in-house medical expert to its permanent secretariat for the first time.[58] Unlike the French Commission, it has no access to the original product licences to check that claims are an accurate reflection of the latter, nor does it have any link with the procedure for monitoring adverse reactions. Unlike the French Commission, it cannot employ specialists to undertake further investigations. Significantly, the CPC failed to screen out some of the more notorious advertisements which have appeared in recent years, especially those associated with the discredited antiarthritic drugs Opren, Flosint, and Zomax. Nor has it reacted to the increasingly numerous complaints of illegible prescribing information.[59]

The French Commission on Publicity Control estimated that one in every three submissions was rejected in the first instance, and that it found irregularities in 10 per cent of journal advertisements, which it monitored. Approximately 15 to 17 per cent were eventually refused visas by the full Commission.[60] It would seem fair to conclude that the British CPC apparatus is best suited to policing unfair commercial practices whereas the French system was designed more to police the scientific content of promotional material and information.

The British regulatory authorites, unlike the French Minister of Health, have no power to compel a company to issue corrective advertising, a technique considered to be very effective in countering misleading promotion. The standard provisions incorporated into all product licences issued in the UK do allow the Licensing Authority to prohibit the publication of a particular advertisement or to require modifications, including the addition of specific warnings, but these are enabling provisions, which come into force only when specifically invoked. To date, they have never been used. It is perhaps indicative of British regulatory techniques that the present government has not chosen to avail itself of the general option to require publication of corrective statements, as provided for in the recent EEC Council directive on misleading advertisements.[61]

A general problem of a posteriori control is that it will usually be enforced too late, after a promotional campaign based on potentially misleading information has drawn to a conclusion. Nevertheless, one alleged advantage of self-regulatory controls is their relative speed of operation. As the recent case of *The Queen* v. *Roussel* indicates, criminal sanctions are an absurdly inappropriate, costly, and complex method of controlling misleading drug-promotion. A total of 42 months elapsed between the first appearance of the offending advertisement and the commencement of criminal proceedings.[62] On the other hand, it will take, on average, 3 months before the CPC reaches a decision, but the code envisages immediate suspension of an advertisement only in limited and unusual circumstances. These include the receipt of a complaint by the Licensing Authority, together with a request that the advertisement be withdrawn. Where a firm chooses to appeal against the CPC's initial ruling, the Committee may request the temporary withdrawal of the material in question, but this is considered highly unusual. It might be 6 months before the offending publicity is eventually halted, ample time in which to realize and consolidate an effective campaign.

In fact the CPC has few real sanctions at its disposal and will normally content itself with delivering a mild and, until recently, anonymous rebuke to the company. The ultimate sanction available to the CPC is to request the ABPI's Board of Management to expel a member company. Such a course of action is unlikely to appear attractive to a body comprised solely of industrialists, drawn from an organization which depends on membership fees for financial support.[63] In 1986, however, the Board took the highly unusual step of suspending the German firm Bayer, following allegations in the media that it had used questionable methods to promote its best-selling heart drug Adalat. Bayer's expulsion from the ABPI does not appear unrelated to an unusual display of interest by the Director-General of the Office of Fair Trading, who was actively considering an investigation under Section 2(1) of the Competition Act, which prohibits anticompetitive practices. Once a company has been expelled, it is not immediately obvious why, as the ABPI seems to expect, it should continue to accept the responsibilities of membership. Interestingly, in the case of 'illegal' gifts, a possible 'intermediate' sanction—a direction by the CPC that the offending material be withdrawn—was until recently available only for promotional materials. Gifts distributed as part of a promotional exercise are treated as inducements, and the CPC was precluded by the code from recovering such items.

The reform of advertising control in France

The French drug-industry's principal objection to the a priori control system was its time-consuming nature, which further eroded the period when a product could be marketed under patent. Visas

were valid for only 2 years and had to be renewed. The French
Ministry of Health went some way to accommodate industry's complaints before actually abolishing the visa outright, in September
1987. In January 1983 the various working groups which considered
the different publicity visas were instructed not to give advice or to
consult informally with individual firms with a view to rectifying
dossiers, but to reject non-complying submissions immediately,
thus saving time.[64] Rejections were, however, to be accompanied by
a reasoned decision. An informal appeal could be made to the full
Commission on Publicity Control. Firms also looked for guidance
to the Commission's annual reports, and to the guide published by
it, as well as to the circulars and letters emanating from the
Ministry. These have become considerably more numerous over the
years and represent an informal dialogue between the administered
and the administration, complementing—and even subverting—the
formal regulatory provisions. Administrative 'guidance' was of particular importance in stipulating the procedures to be followed in
the numerous cases where the requirement to obtain a publicity visa
was jettisoned.[65] In fact the number of exceptions outweighed the
instances where a visa was required: in 1983–4 there were 2,060
applications for exemption and 1,381 for visas, and in 1984–5
2,246 and 1,197 respectively.[66] Such material had to be submitted
for prior authorization by the Minister, who in this instance was
advised not by the Commission but by an *ad hoc* departmental
group of experts and officials. If no objection was made within 15
days, it could be assumed that permission has been granted.

   The form which this internal procedure took and the criteria on
which it operated were left almost entirely to the discretion of the
Minister and his or her officials. Unlike 1979 he or she was not even
obliged to give reasons for refusing authorization.[67] By and large,
the system worked to industry's benefit, as it was used to speed up
authorization procedures and to relax formal rules in its favour.
Some indication of the way in which the system functioned in
practice is given in the correspondence between the Minister and
the president of the SNIP. For example, in 1976 the Minister wrote
to the SNIP indicating that 'genuinely scientific material' which was
in no way an incentive to prescribe a particular product need not be
submitted to any form of procedure, while that which was could
benefit from the faster procedures for authorizing circulation (*autorisation de diffusion*).[68]

Despite the flexible way in which the formal controls appear to
have been administered, the system of a priori controls attracted
considerable criticism from industry, and, in the absence of any
progress on the promised abolition of price control, it was eventually repealed by Michèle Barzach in autumn 1987, for prescription
as opposed to OTC products.[69] The Commission on Publicity Control continues to vet advertisements for the latter but only monitors
promotional literature and campaigns relating to the former.[70] The
Dangoumau-Biot Report on the French pharmaceutical industry,
published in April 1989, suggested that the sanctions for misleading
information were being insufficiently enforced.[71]

Controls on Promotional Expenditure

The drug industry's ability to devote sizeable budgets to the promotion of their products and, in the final result, to pass on the costs of
the exercise to the public purse has been a constant source of
concern to regulators in all countries, and yet, surprisingly, there
has been little attempt to exert formal legal control over pharmaceutical expenditure. This is not to say that drug firms have an
unfettered discretion to allocate vast sums to promoting their
products.

In the UK the Minister of Health currently imposes non-statutory
ceilings, via the PPRS, on the amount of promotional expenditure
which firms can offset against the profits they earn on their NHS
sales. The use of expenditure ceilings is a recent development, but
its effectiveness should not be overestimated. In the first three versions of the VPRS, in the opinion of the Committee of Public
Accounts, the machinery for investigating the relationship between
advertising expenditure and drug prices was totally inadequate,
despite widespread allegations of wasteful and profligate
practices.[72]

In 1967, on the basis of financial returns prepared for it by
independent consultants, the Sainsbury Committee confirmed this
view. On average, firms were devoting some 14 per cent of the
total value of their NHS sales to promotional activities, although
there were significant variations.[73] The Committee also commissioned a number of studies on the quality of advertising material
and its impact on the medical profession.[74] Its solution to the
problem of excessive expenditure and wasteful product-differenti-

ation was a rather drastic one—the abolition of brand names. Instead, product names would be designated by the proposed Medical Commission, although patent protection would continue to be available.[75]

It is perhaps unsurprising that the Labour government, still smarting from the 1967 devaluation of sterling, was sufficiently receptive to the ABPI's grim prognostications as to the effect of such a measure on international competitiveness to ignore Sainsbury's recommendations. Nevertheless, the new system of AFRs, incorporated into the fourth VPRS, allowed for closer surveillance of separate items of expenditure. In 1968 the Minister announced that substantial reductions in advertising costs would be realized through the introduction of a graduated formula, linking allowable expenditure to sales or capital.[76] In fact he met with massive opposition, not only from the industry but also from the civil servants at the Ministry. Past methods of calculating reasonable levels of profit had been so subjective that the information available to the Ministry was quite insufficient to allow it to estimate a reasonable ratio of capital to promotional expenditure. The Minister resigned, leaving his successor, Richard Crossman, to appease the industry by abandoning the formula-based approach altogether.[77]

A formula-based approach to allowable expenditure on sales promotion was finally included in the fifth VPRS, negotiated by the Labour government in 1976. An aggregate ceiling of 12 per cent of turnover was initially imposed, to be reduced to 10 per cent in 1979. Nevertheless, certain concessions were made to the industry's commercial interests. The initial communication to the ABPI on the new advertising restrictions coincided with the publication of the White Paper on the reform of patent law, designed to give effect to the recommendations of the Banks Committee. Banks had recommended the repeal of Section 41 of the Patents Act 1949, which allowed the Comptroller of Patents to grant compulsory licences for food and medicines. The previous Conservative government had made clear its intention to implement this proposal, but the White Paper stated that the incumbent government considered these compulsory licences a valuable adjunct of price control.[78] In the final event, following several consultative meetings with the Minister, the ABPI succeeded in having the relevant clause, Clause 49, deleted from the bill at its committee stage, and the government spokesman on the bill gave a strong hint that should the discussions on advertising controls be brought to a successful conclusion, the clause would not be reintroduced at a later stage in the legislative process.

In 1983 the expenditure ceiling was further reduced to 9 per cent for the fiscal year 1985–6, and despite rumours that it would be lowered once more in the seventh PPRS, this level has been maintained.[79] Nevertheless, the DHSS has a considerable discretion in the way in which it calculates promotional expenditure. The term 'sales promotion' is distinguished from 'sales information' under the PPRS. This latter category includes medical samples, data sheets, and financial support for symposia, whereas spending on gifts, hospitality, and other samples is not an allowable charge. Expenditure on informational items is not included in the calculation of the allowance for sales promotion. It would appear, however, that there are no hard and fast rules for distinguishing between any of these three categories.

If a company did exceed the ceiling, the DHSS could, at its discretion, adjust the manufacturer's disclosed profits by adding back the disallowed expenditure. However, as we have seen in Chapter 6, most companies benefited from a generous 'grey area', which was added to their target rate of return. Consequently, the DHSS would only obtain a cash refund for excessive promotional expenditure when the company's adjusted profit-rate exceeded this higher rate, so that aggregated promotional expenditure was kept within the stipulated limit only 'in very broad terms'.[80]

As part of the package of financial stringency measures introduced in autumn 1985, companies could be asked to repay immediately any sum exceeding the ceiling at the time of submission of their AFR. The companies protested that this was a form of double taxation, as the disallowed expenditure was added to profits. Although this provision has been retained in the seventh PPRS, the industry's protests have been accommodated in two ways. First, a company will be allowed to spend an additional £1 million over 2 years to promote a new chemical entity, over and above their allowance, and second, expenditure and allowances may be averaged on a rolling two-year basis, in order to accommodate difficulties in planning promotional expenditure.[81]

In conclusion, the current PPRS operates to restrict the cost of promotional expenditure to the NHS on a purely aggregate basis, and therefore does not greatly intrude on commercial freedom. There is nothing to prevent a company's concentrating a large percentage of its allowance on a single product. The Swiss company Eli-Lilly is estimated to have spent several million pounds on the aggressive promotion of Opren, a campaign which influenced doctors to write 1.47 million prescriptions, at a cost to the DHSS of £13.5 million.[82] At the same time, successive governments appear to have evaded the difficult task of drawing a line between the promotion of competition and the elimination of wasteful expenditure; rather, as has so often happened, they have delegated the task to the firms themselves.

If the UK appears, at least in theory, to have moved closer to a formula-based approach to control on promotional expenditure, France has moved in the opposite direction—that is, towards a more discretionary or *ad hoc* form of control. The two methods of price control—the price framework and price scale—discussed in Chapter 3 allowed the government to monitor the percentage of promotional overheads attributed to each product. Because costs for basic materials were inflated, this system did not prove particularly effective, and companies were estimated to devote some 14 to 17 per cent of their sales to promotional activities but only 8 to 10 per cent to research.[83] Some 60 per cent of the budget was devoted to expenditure on medical representatives. Under the present regime, proposed budgets for promotion and information must be submitted, along with other information, for the scrutiny and ultimate approval of the various administrative authorities involved in the process of pricing and reimbursement. There are, however, no express rules stipulating what type or level of expenditure is or is not acceptable, and one is forced to conclude that these are matters which are left entirely to negotiation between the various parties.

An additional set of informal, non-binding controls over advertising expenditure made a brief appearance in France during the period of 'contractualization', which was discussed in Chapter 7. Companies were granted price increases if, *inter alia*, they agreed to limit promotional expenditure to a predetermined level, negotiated for each company. This policy was abandoned shortly after its introduction and is generally considered to have had little impact on the promotional strategies of the contracting parties.[84]

The failure of the contractualization policy to curb either promotional activities in general or the more particular problem of con-

trolling medical representatives led the Socialist Minister of Social
Security and National Solidarity, Bérégévoy, to introduce a special
publicity tax in January 1983.[85] This tax was to be applicable to
each company's entire promotional and informational budget; in
other words, there would be no attempt to distinguish between
'useful' and other forms of expenditure.[86] The proceeds were paid
to the health insurance funds to help finance budget deficits.

The industry protested vehemently against the new tax, not only
because it hit at what they regarded as legitimate expenditure, and
particularly the costs of employing medical representatives, but also
because the amounts paid under this special tax could not be offset
against general corporation tax. In addition, the tax had been introduced at a time when relations between government and the
French-based industry over pricing policy were deteriorating
rapidly. The companies argued that the various price freezes
imposed on their products had already caused serious damage to
their profitability. The medical profession were also critical of the
new tax, which they claimed would threaten the viability of a
number of important journals.[87] Government ministers, who were
able to raise an average of 200 million francs per annum from the
tax, were not impressed. In May 1983 the SNIP challenged the
decree implementing the tax as being an abuse of power. The constitutionality of the measure was a matter of doubt, and the enabling law had in fact been referred to the Conseil constitutionnel,
which held that there was no legal principle restricting the transfer
of tax revenue to the health funds.[88]

Conclusion

It is perhaps in the regulation of the quality and content of promotional literature that the persistent contrast between the British and
French approaches is at its most stark. Even with the abolition of
the system of a priori controls, the French legal requirements and
monitoring techniques remain a much stricter alternative to the
British self-regulatory mechanisms. In its initial conception,
however, the system of a priori control did not seem to fit well into
the passive administrative style of regulatory implementation
which, as was argued in earlier chapters, characterized product-
safety licensing and price control. It might be argued that a strict
set of controls was seen as necessary at the time to compensate for

the weaknesses in the product-safety regime, or to act as a disincentive to the proliferation of medicines, itself encouraged by the price-
control regime. This divergence is more apparent than real,
however, in that two important qualifications must be added. First,
in practice the a priori system was administered with a flexibility
which belied the formal nature of the regulatory framework;
second, and more importantly, it had little impact on the most
important form of promotion in France, the activity of medical
representatives. In large firms such as Roussel-Uclaf almost one-
tenth of the total full-time staff are employed in this capacity.[89] In
fact the aim of the publicity tax introduced in 1983 was as much to
penalize the employment of representatives as to raise money for
the health funds.

In the UK formal statutory controls over advertising content
remained very much in the background, and indeed a continued
reliance on self-regulation appears to have prevented the Department of Health from prosecuting what appear to be blatant
breaches of the regulations.[90]

Advertising control is of crucial importance to the regulation of
an industry where product differentiation is a paramount concern.
In consequence, it is perhaps inevitable to find that in terms of styles
of implementation, these controls closely reflect the techniques
employed in the regulation of prices, profits, and product safety in
each of the two countries. A continued governmental commitment
to self-regulation of promotional material by British-based industry
in turn buttresses industry's commitment to an otherwise non-
binding PPRS. At the same time, the British system of advertising
controls intrudes very little upon industry's commercial freedom,
while simultaneously holding down aggregate NHS expenditure on
promotion. The French system is equally unobtrusive: it leaves the
most important aspects of promotion almost totally unregulated,
while attempts to regulate the levels of promotional expenditure
within the overall system of price control have been a singular
failure.

Given the crucial role of advertising in product-based competition, it comes as no surprise to find that this is an area where
national governments have been markedly reluctant to surrender
sovereignty to the European institutions. The member states have
now failed to agree on two separate proposals for directives on
pharmaceutical advertising, in 1968 and in 1978. This in itself is

indicative of the way in which advertising regulation is treated as a safety-valve. Although the White Paper on the internal market[91] indicates that the Commission will take action on the provision of prescribing information to consumers, there is nevertheless a conspicuous silence on the matter of advertising control. The Commission has indicated, somewhat diplomatically, that it is content to wait and review the impact of the general directive on misleading advertising[92] before launching any new initiatives in this field.

Notes

1. A. Herxheimer, *The Lancet*, 3 Jan. 1987, 338.
2. CES Report, *L'Industrie pharmaceutique*, p. 71.
3. Ibid, p. 50.
4. L. Hancher, 'Regulating Drug Promotion: The British Experience', in *Journal of Consumer Policy*, 10 (1987), 383–407.
5. The DHSS employ regional medical officers who may investigate the prescribing patterns of individual doctors. The doctors in turn may be disciplined by the FPS. In France this task falls to the regional health officers.
6. Lord Sainsbury, *Report of the Committee of Enquiry into the Relationship of the Pharmaceutical Industry with the NHS* Cmnd. 3410 (London: HMSO, 1967), recommended that its proposed medical commission should exercise such powers, while the Vernejoul Report in France proposed the creation of a special commission to produce and distribute information to doctors.
7. 'Initial Report of the Informal Working Group on Effective Prescribing', unpublished DHSS report, 1983. In France the Rapport Jean (1982) found that students received an average of 50 hours in 7 years on therapeutics. (Quoted in CES Report, *L'Industrie pharmaceutique*, p.72).
8. P. Jean, *Rapport sur la visite médicale* (Paris: Inspection générale des affaires sociales 1982); Sainsbury Report, Cmnd. 3410, 1967; R. E. A. Swapes and W. O. Williams, 'Prescription Drug Advertising', *Journal of the Royal College of General Practitioners*, 26 (1976), 76–82.
9. Rapport Jean.
10. House of Lords Science and Technology Committee, 1987, reported in the *Financial Times*, 12 Apr. 1988.
11. J. Collier, 'What the Doctor Ordered', *The Times*, 16 Oct. 1984.
12. Decree 87-772 of 23 Sept. 1987 in JO, 24 Sept. 1987, 11144, which substantially amends the system of a priori controls, will be considered in detail below.

13. *Guardian*, 17 Dec. 1986.
14. In 1986 thirty-five non-member companies had agreed to be bound by the Code. ABPI, *Annual Report 1985–86*, (London: ABPI, 1987).
15. DHSS, *Medicines Act Consultation Letter* (MLX, no. 61C, 1976).
16. 'Code de bonnes pratiques d'information', *Bulletin d'information et de documentation publié par l'Ordre national des pharmaciens*, 253 (1982), 277.
17. Sect. 20(i)(b).
18. Arts. L.601, R.5128, and R.5143 CSP.
19. Sect. 103.
20. Sect. 65(3).
21. Arts. R.5108 and R.5110 CSP.
22. Arts. R.5050 CSP.
23. ABPI, 'Report of the Code of Practice Committee', Case 2/81.
24. *Scrip*, 1145, 13 Oct. 1986, 4–5.
25. *Scrip* 1104, 12 June 1987, 3.
26. J.-M. Auby and F. Coustou, *Droit pharmaceutique*, (Paris: Librairies techniques, 1980) fasc. 38, 9–10.
27. A. Melville and C. Johnson, *Cured to Death: The Effects of Prescription Drugs* (Sevenoaks: New English Library, 1983), 41–60.
28. A. Herxheimer, *The Lancet*, 3 Jan. 1987, 338.
29. C. Maurain, 'Publicité et droit de la santé', thesis (Université de Bordeaux II, 1981), 123.
30. Arts. R.5045–R.5055 CSP.
31. Decree 76-807 of 24 Aug. 1976 in JO, 26 Aug. 1976.
32. Art. L.551 CSP.
33. Decree 69-104 of 3 Feb. 1969 in JO, 4 Feb. 1969.
34. Arts. R.5045 and R.5047 and arts. L.551 and L.552 of the CSP.
35. Assemblée générale, 15 Mar. 1979, section sociale no. 324; In addition, in an earlier judgment, the Cour de Cassation held that the question of intention was irrelevant to deciding whether material was promotional or not. It was its result or effect which was important.
36. SNIP, circular 8487, Dec. 1980.
37. Maurain, 'Publicité et droit de la santé', p. 243.
38. Art. R.5047 CSP.
39. Art. R.5050 CSP.
40. Sect. 96. The concept of the 'data sheet', is not unlike that of the summary of product characteristics now required by EEC directive 83/570 on proprietary medicinal products (art. 4(9)).
41. Medicines (Advice to Medical and Dental Practitioners) Regulations 1978, S. I. no. 1020/1978.
42. Sect. 93.
43. DHSS, MLX no. 94, 1979.

44. C. Medawar, *The Wrong Kind of Medicine* (London: Consumers Association, 1984).
45. Herxheimer, *The Lancet*, 3 Jan. 1987, 338.
46. DHSS, MLX no. 144, 1983.
47. DHSS, Medicines Act Leaflet, 57, Aug. 1983, 3.
48. Maurain, 'Publicité et droit', p. 345.
49. Medicines (Advertising of Medicinal Products) (no. 2) Regulations 1975, S. I. no. 1326/1975.
50. Arts. R.5050 and R.5128 CSP.
51. Art. R.5050.
52. See, for example, *Que Choisir?*, (1981) and *L'Impatient*, 48 (1981).
53. Art. R.5052 CSP.
54. However, in a letter to the president of the SNIP dated 11 Oct. 1976 the Minister of Health indicated that these restrictions could be relaxed in certain circumstances. See M. Tisseyre-Berry and G. Viala, *Législation et déontologie de l'industrie pharmaceutique* (Paris: Masson, 1983), 154.
55. A. Langlois, 'Les Comités d'éthique locaux en France', *Revue française des Affaires Sociales*, 3 (1986), 91–103.
56. ABPI, 'Report to the Chief Executives', Case 490/1/84.
57. Hansard, Jan. 1983, vol. 36, col. 465W.
58. ABPI, 'Report of the Code of Practice Committee', *Annual Report 1983–84*.
59. I am grateful to Dr J. Collier for providing me with copies of his correspondence with the DHSS on this matter.
60. CES Report, *L'Industrie pharmaceutique*, p. 51; Commission du contrôle de la publicité, *Rapports des présidents des commissions 1981–5* (Paris: DPHM, 1986).
61. EEC Council directive 84/450, OJ 1984, L250/17.
62. A summary of the judgment is reported by Collier and Herxheimer in *The Lancet* 10 Jan., 113–14.
63. J. Braithwaite, *Corporate Crime in the Pharmaceutical Industry* (London: Routledge & Kegan Paul, 1984).
64. M. Brazier, *L'Industrie pharmaceutique et la publicité* (Paris, 1984), 13.
65. Non-illustrated advertising material sent by direct mail, illustrated and non-illustrated adverts appearing in medical and pharmaceutical journals, and prescription guides and catalogues were exempted from the full visa procedure on two grounds. First, if they included the so-called sixteen *mentions legales* or obligatory items as stipulated by the CSP. These consisted of the generic name and basic prescribing information, including warnings on side-effects and 'undesired' effects, precautions in usage, and any other warning or special condition

contained in the AMM. The Minister of Health and the Publicity Commission expanded this list informally to include a requirement that the daily cost of treatment be specified and that the generic name be clearly displayed next to the brand name.

66. Commission du contrôle de la publicité, *Rapport annel* 1983–4 (pp. 132–3) and 1984–5 (pp. 72–3). (Paris: DPHM, 1986).

67. This situation was altered by the impact of the general law 79-587 *relative à la motivation des actes administratifs*, in JO, 12 July 1979, 1711.

68. Letter of 15 Sept. 1976 reproduced in *L'Industrie pharmaceutique et la publicité*, p. 41.

69. Decree 87-772 of 23 Sept. 1987, in JO, 24 Sept. 1987, 11144.

70. Art. R.5054-3 CSP. See further C. Maurain and G. Viala, 'La nouvelle réglementation de la publicité pharmaceutique', *Gazette du Palais*, 31 (1988), 12–14.

71. *Le Monde*, 8 Apr. 1989.

72. Committee of Public Accounts, 'The VPRS', *Third Report for the Session 1967–68* (London: HMSO, 1968), 11.

73. Banks Committee on Patent Reform, Cmnd. 4467 (London: HMSO, 1970).

74. Reproduced as appendices to the Sainsbury Report, Cmnd. 3410.

75. Ibid.

76. Hansard, June 1968, vol. 767, col. 46.

77. R. Lang, *The Politics of Drugs* (Farnborough: Saxon House, 1974), 285.

78. Cmnd. 7710 (London: HMSO, 1971).

79. DIISS, 'The Pharmaceutical Price Regulation Scheme' (London: DHSS, 1986).

80. Committee on Public Accounts 'NHS Supplies and the PPRS', *Twenty-third Report for the Session 1984–85*, (London: HMSO, 1984).

81. Paras. 10.5 and 10.6 of PPRS, 1986.

82. Opren Action Group, press release, 1985.

83. J.-P. Dupuy and S. Karsenty, *L'Invasion pharmaceutique* (Paris: Seuil, 1974), p. 151.

84. Interview, May 1986.

85. Law 82-35 of 19 Jan. 1983, in JO, 20 Jan. 1983.

86. A decree of 17 Mar. 1983 spelled out the details of this tax.

87. CES Report, *L'Industrie pharmaceutique*, p. 52.

88. JO, 20 Jan. 1983. A decree of 17 Mar. 1983 spelled out the details of this tax. It was subsequently modified to exempt smaller firms and to exclude the costs of salaries and social charges from the basis of calculation (law 87-588 of 30 July 1987, amending L.245-2 CSS).

89. See *Le Figaro*, 28 Sept. 1987 for a description of the number of

medical representatives employed by the largest firms and of the nature of their qualifications.

90. See correspondence between Dr J. Collier and the Minister for Health referred to above.

91. Commission of the EC, *White Paper on the Completion of the Internal Market*, Com (85) 310. (Brussels: Commission of the EC, 1985).

92. EEC directive 84/450, OJ 1984, L.250/17. The Commission has now announced that it plans to submit a draft directive on pharmaceutical advertising to the Council by the end of 1990.

9

Competition Law and Policy: An Alternative Strategy?

A study of the interaction of regulation and competition would be incomplete if general competition law and policy were ignored. This chapter has two objectives. In the first place, it examines the application of competition law and policy in France and the UK to pharmaceutical pricing. Competition or antitrust law may be used as an alternative to specific pricing regimes, and indeed certain countries, such as the USA and, until recently, West Germany, rely solely on antitrust law to control excessive drug prices.[1] Both France and the UK have gradually abandoned their *general* price-control regimes in favour of a more selective control through strengthened mechanisms of competition law. The first section of this chapter considers whether competition law could provide a feasible alternative to price control, given the oligopolistic structure of the market. The application of competition policy to the pharmaceutical sector is further complicated by the impact of the patent system on the structure of the market. As we have seen in Chapter 2, the temporary monopoly provided by patent protection may allow manufacturers to monopolize a particular therapeutic submarket. The second section examines in detail the development of the two national systems of competition law and the influence of European law upon them. The third section goes on to examine the way in which these two sets of controls have in practice functioned as an adjunct to the specific controls on prices discussed in earlier chapters, given the shortcomings of these regimes. It also examines proposed adjustments to the patent system as a means of compensating for the impact of other forms of regulation affecting the process of product competition in the sector.

As in earlier chapters, the intention here is to draw out the major differences in the legal style of policy implementation rather than to compare the two systems in detail. Although competition law is an area where European law has had a significant impact, substantial differences in the national systems remain. The following review of competition and patent law therefore serves a second objective: it offers additional insights into the divergent nature of regulatory traditions in the UK and France.

Competition Law and Policy

The meaning of competition policy

The term 'competition policy' must be used with caution and should not be taken to imply the existence or pursuit of a single, coherent set of objectives. In reality France, the UK, and the European Commission, which is responsible for European competition policy, pursue a variety of objectives in the name of competition policy. At the risk of over-simplification, several different goals can be discerned in *national* competition law.[2] The first is to safeguard the consumer against the abusive exercise of market power, either by a single monopolistic firm, or by a number of firms acting in agreement. Such practices might include excessive pricing or imposed prices. A second, related objective of competition policy is to ensure an efficient allocation of resources. Where powerful firms refuse to supply rival manufacturers or distributors with raw materials or other products, thus preventing them from undercutting their own product prices, this could lead to inefficiency.[3] European competition policy, however, fulfils the distinctive function of promoting single-market integration. Its aim is to prevent firms from dividing up the Common Market on national lines—for example through export bans or market-sharing agreements.

Competition policy, Oligopoly, and Pharmaceuticals

At the theoretical level, the application of competition policy to the pharmaceutical sector is problematic for two reasons. In the first place, as Chapter 2 indicated, the market is predominantly *oligopolistic* in structure, i.e. it is characterized by the presence of a few suppliers, none of which is in a position of overall market

dominance, but each of which is relatively large. The main argument against oligopoly *in general* is that the structural conditions of
the market operate as a disincentive to compete, because firms are
interdependent: the actions of one firm will be invariably matched
by similar action by its rivals.[4] Through parallel conduct which
does not necessarily involve overt agreement, oligopolists can
charge prices which tend towards a monopolistic level. The two
main instruments of competition policy common to the three
systems examined here—that is, controls over the abusive
behaviour of a monopolist and controls over cartel-like agreements
between independent firms—are not easily applicable to an oligopolistic situation. By definition, the antimonopoly provisions as
such rarely apply. A major problem for competition authorities
seeking to utilize controls over illicit cartels is to distinguish
between conscious parallel conduct by oligopolists that is aimed at
earning high profits, and parallel conduct that may be objectively
justifiable for reasons of *market structure*.[5]

   In the second place, the pharmaceutical market exhibits certain
distinctive peculiarities. Whereas under normal oligopolistic conditions, products are assumed to be relatively homogeneous, or substitutable, so that rivals are considered interdependent and are
therefore constrained to match each other's marketing strategies,[6]
this is not necessarily the case with medicinal products. A combination of the low levels of substitutability within therapeutic submarkets and the temporary protection provided by the law on
intellectual property allows some firms to enjoy a temporary
monopoly within a specific therapeutic submarket. For this reason,
the third section of this chapter includes a discussion of controls on
the abuse of patent privileges and on the interaction of controls
with competition policy, it being generally acknowledged that there
is a 'grey area' where the concerns of competition law and policy
and intellectual property overlap and even conflict, a conflict which
is especially problematic at the European level. Typically, rights
relating to intellectual property have a territorial dimension, so
that, for example, a patentee has exclusive rights to manufacture
and market the patented product within the territory of the state by
which the patent is granted. As mentioned in Chapter 5, patent
rights may restrict free movement of goods within Europe by parti-
tioning the Common Market along national lines.

European law and national law

The contrasting approaches which the national competition authorities take to these problems must be understood in the context of the specific role which competition policy assumes in each country and of the legal character that policy assumes. Recent developments in national law and policy have not occurred in a vacuum but rather are influenced by changing attitudes to competition in general and to administered price-controls in particular, as well as by the impact of European competition law. The 'infiltration' of European competition law and policy has occurred along three routes.

In the first place, in 'internationalized' sectors such as pharmaceuticals the activities of firms often transcend national markets, affecting trade between the member states and therefore triggering off the application of Community rules. The Commission and the Court of Justice have consequently been required to assess alleged anticompetitive practices on the part of pharmaceutical firms on a number of occasions. The directorate-general on competition policy, DG IV, has a special section which deals with the chemical and pharmaceutical sector.

The so-called interstate trade clauses contained in Articles 85 and 86 of the EEC Treaty, which regulate, respectively, restrictive agreements and the abuse of a dominant position, are of central importance in EEC competition law. These clauses define 'the boundary between the areas respectively covered by Community law and the law of the Member States'.[7] Both the Commission and the Court have interpreted the phrase liberally, enlarging the range of Articles 85 and 86 at the expense of national law.[8] As Community law is superior to the latter, where a clash occurs, it takes precedence.[9]

Two tests have been developed to determine whether Community rules apply. In a series of cases on Article 85, the Court has examined an agreement to establish whether it influences, actually or potentially, directly or indirectly, *patterns of trade* between member states.[10] A second, *structural* test has been applied to determine the applicability of Article 86; the Court has examined whether a firm's dominance could result in an alteration in the structure of competition within the Common Market. This test was applied in a case involving the monopoly supply of an intermediate medicinal product, aminobutanol, used for the manufacture of a tuberculosis drug, world supplies of which were controlled by the Commercial Solvents Corporation (CSC). The latter's Italian subsidiary refused to supply the product to another Italian firm, Zoja, which complained to the Commission that CSC had abused its dominant position.[11] Since there was no alternative source of supply, Zoja, which actually sold almost all of its production outside the Common Market, was liable to be driven out of business. The argument that intra-Community trade would not be affected was rejected: the elimination of a major producer would impair the competitive structure of the EEC.

A second source of the influence of European law derives from the principle that Articles 85 and 86 are directly effective and may be enforced by the national courts. As the Court said in *BRT* v. *SABAM*[12] 'the provisions of Articles 85 and 86 tend by their very nature to produce direct effects in relations between individuals . . . which national courts must safeguard'.[13] These directly effective rights can be exercised 'offensively', to challenge particular practices, as well as 'defensively'. The availability of remedies for their enforcement is a matter of national law. The possibility of using private remedies under EEC law give individuals the opportunity to circumvent the administrative bias which, as we will see below, attends the enforcement of British competition law. British courts may grant injunctions and damages to the victims of infringements of EEC competition rules.[14] Similar developments have occurred in France, where the civil courts have traditionally been more receptive to EC law than their administrative counterparts.[15] The impact of EEC competition law was an important stimulus to the reforms of French competition law in 1985 and 1986.

A third source of influence has been the application of the substantive provisions of EC law on the methods of analysis adopted by the national competition authorities. In particular, the flexible, effects-based approach adopted by the Commission and the Court to restrictive agreements is regarded as an important yardstick by which to assess national law and policy, and, as the next section illustrates, this has featured as a point of reference in recent proposals to reform national policy on competition.

The Development of National Competition Policy

France

The promotion and regulation of economic activity through competition did not feature among the principal instruments of French economic or industrial policy until comparatively recently, even if France can lay claim to one of the oldest sets of legislative prohibitions against restrictive practices in Western Europe. Formulated during the French revolution, the *Loi Chapelier*,[16] the legislation designed to suppress the power of the guilds, was gradually deprived of any real efficacy by a series of court rulings and statutory exceptions, so that controls over cartel-like practices were virtually non-existent by the end of the nineteenth century. Although Articles 412 and 419 of the Napoleonic Penal Code, as amended by a law of 1926, rendered parties to price cartels liable to criminal sanction, the courts imposed such a high standard of proof of intent[17] that the provision was seldom used.[18] Restrictive practices also fall within the provisions of Article 1382 of the Civil Code, enabling anyone who can prove that they have sustained a loss from such practices to claim damages in the civil courts.[19]

Post-war governments preferred to rely on the planning process and various forms of administered price-control as the principal instruments of a *politique de persuasion constrainte*.[20] Indeed, the very purpose of economic planning and of the implementation of its goals through contracts between government and industry was to displace competition between firms as an efficient method of allocating resources.[21] The prolonged absence in France of a coherent competition policy and an effective set of legal controls for its implementation is hardly remarkable.

Restrictive practices and monopolies

Administrative controls over restrictive practices were first introduced by Article 59 of ordinance 45-1483. Their purpose was not to promote competition, but to secure the implementation of price control and counter the effects of rationing and of severe shortages in supply in the immediate post-war period. Further detailed provisions were introduced in 1953, in the face of intense opposition from Parliament and the business community.

These cartel controls have been described as 'an uneven blend of severity and leniency'.[22] On the one hand, the law attached criminal penalties to the so-called *per se* or absolute prohibitions against certain practices such as refusal to sell, loss-leader selling, and misleading advertising, thus setting France apart from its European neighbours (Article 37). These practices were condemned where a firm had acted individually or collectively. On the other hand, a commitment to the enforcement of these prohibitions as a means of promoting competition was almost entirely absent. The 1953 decree created an advisory body, the *Commission technique des ententes*,[23] to examine agreements referred to it and make recommendations to the Minister of Finance, who in turn could instruct the criminal prosecutor to pursue an action in the criminal courts. However, Article 59(3) of the decree provided that agreements which were beneficial to economic development would be exempted. The Commission was charged to examine the implications of agreements which might have an adverse effect on prices; the wider concept of 'anticompetitive practice' did not make an appearance on the statute book until 1967.[24] Competition policy was therefore implemented by the Ministry of Finance initially as an adjunct to price regulations and later as a means of ensuring that the prohibition against the fixing of minimum prices was properly enforced. Few resources were devoted to policing restrictive practices: the majority of the civil servants seconded to deal with matters relating to competition were redeployed to deal with the enforcement of price control.[25] Although the legislation required the Commission to publish an annual report, prior to 1960 the Minister refused to allow it to do so, nor were any details made public of the undertakings which he was empowered to obtain from enterprises as an alternative to prosecution.[26] In 1959 the Rueff-Armand Report on barriers to economic expansion concluded that 'although restrictive practices are forbidden by law, they are frequently applied, insufficiently hunted out and very rarely repressed'.[27]

A further flaw in the 1953 legislation resulted from the fact that neither the exact scope of the prohibition against restrictive practices nor the exemptions to it were clearly defined. A ministerial circular issued in 1953 advised that beneficial cartels could be distinguished from 'bad' cartels on the basis of the substantive provisions of any agreement between them.[28] The Technical Commission preferred, however, to compile an 'economic balance sheet' (*bilan économique*), in order to assess the overall effects of the agreement. If the net effect was considered beneficial, the cartel was exempted in its entirety under Article 59, even, as in one infamous case, where the agreement pertained to the whole of the relevant national market. For the most part, the few restrictive agreements which were referred to the Commission[29] were tolerated as long as some benefit to their participants, as opposed to the consumer, could be discerned.[30] Agreements did not have to be registered, and the Commission was reluctant to use its own powers to investigate possible restraints. It was forced to acknowledge its own failure:

After fifteen years . . . we are entitled to be surprised and even disappointed to find that firms still erect 'pure' price cartels, backed by pecuniary sanctions . . . without the slightest preoccupation as to their contribution towards economic progress.[31]

Provisions to control the abuse of a monopoly or dominant position were introduced in France in 1963.[32] Only national, as opposed to local or regional, monopolies were covered by this legislation, which did not invest the Commission with any new powers of control. Key concepts such as 'abuse' and 'dominance' were left undefined.[33] Although the legislation extended to groups of firms, the government was meanwhile actively promoting mergers and joint ventures between individual firms through a variety of tax incentives, as well as through the promotion of economic interest groupings (*groupements d'intérêt économique*), a loosely knit company structure which allowed firms to pool financial and administrative services.[34] As several commentators have observed, the major governmental preoccupation of this period was with size; larger firms were seen as a prerequisite to effective competition on international markets.[35]

In consequence, administrative controls over mergers appeared belatedly in France, in 1977,[36] and only then as a result of political opportunism. Not only was the government anxious to pre-empt the impact of a draft European directive on mergers,[37] but it also wished to appear as a champion of the interests of the smaller firm in the forthcoming legislative elections. The 1977 law, and the ministerial circular on its application,[38] were, however, seen as essentially favourable to increased concentration.[39] Between 1977 and 1984 only eight mergers were referred to the competition authorities, and these gave an unfavourable opinion in only one instance.[40]

The United Kingdom

In the UK, competition law 'has developed in the most extraordinarily haphazard way with little consistent thought being given to the formulation of policy'.[41] It is characterized by two features: the superfluity of predominantly administrative institutions involved in its implementation, and the essential pragmatism which these institutions bring to their task.

Modern British competition legislation also dates from shortly after the end of the Second World War, when a major part of the UK economy was subject to restrictive agreements, many of which involved restrictions on prices. Cartels were looked on as generally benign:[42] centralized intervention would merely inhibit growth.[43] This view prevailed until the publication of the 1944 White Paper on employment policy, committing government to the promotion of full employment by preventing the artificial dampening of demand via restrictions on output.[44] A number of official committees reported on the scale of internal restrictions on manufacturing,[45] and their recommendations culminated in the passing of the Monopolies and Restrictive Practices (Inquiry and Control) Act 1948. This Act set up the Monopolies and Restrictive Practices Commission (MRPC), which was empowered to advise government on agreements referred to it. The 1948 Act was suffused with political discretion. The Secretary of the Board of Trade had discretion to refer a monopoly to the Commission; the Act contained no presumption against any particular anticompetitive practices; its conception of 'public interest' was extremely broad, and in common with early French legislation, the term 'anticompetitive' was not even mentioned.[46] The supply requirements of the NHS did, however, lead to a number of references to the Commission—for example, those relating to the supply of dental goods[47] and insulin.[48]

Monopolies and restrictive practices

The jurisdiction of the MRPC was extended to mergers in 1965, and the body itself was reconstituted as the Monopolies and

Mergers Commission (MMC).[49] In 1973 the Fair Trading Act transferred many of the duties previously carried out by the Board of Trade to a new quango, the Office of Fair Trading (OFT), headed by a director-general. It has been remarked that 'the conduct of monopoly firms, ever since the legislation of 1948, has been open to economic inquiry . . . but not subject to any rule of law'.[50] The Monopolies and Mergers Commission (MMC) has itself described its antitrust policy as one which reflects 'the traditional UK pragmatic approach . . . of treating each case on its merits.[51]

The role of the MMC has been carefully circumscribed in the relevant legislation: it cannot open an inquiry on its own initiative, and for the enforcement of its recommendations it must rely on other government bodies. A reference to the MMC may only be made where a firm or group of firms accounts for at least 25 per cent of the relevant market.[52] The Secretary of State or the director-general of the OFT have discretion to make a reference to the MMC, to define the relevant market which forms the basis of its inquiries into monopoly situations, and to decide whether to initiate further action. The concepts of 'monopoly situation' or 'dominance' are in no way related to those terms as used by economists: the real issue is whether the firm is acting contrary to the public interest, and it is at this stage that the question of market power becomes relevant.[53]

In 1955 the MRPC published a general, industry-wide report, *Collective Discrimination*, recommending direct action against horizontal agreements. The 1956 Restrictive Trade Practices Act (RTPA), which set up the Restrictive Trade Practices Court, introduced a judicialized procedure for examining cartels, while the MRPC retained power to investigate abuses by dominant firms. The former's jurisdiction was extended to vertical resale price maintenance by the Resale Price Maintenance Act 1964 (RPM), which was in turn amended by the RPM Act of 1976. Prior to the passing of this Act, minimum resale-price maintenace was operated on an extensive scale.[54] The 1964 Act, as amended, outlawed collective[55] and individual[56] RPM. RPM for pharmaceutical products was, however, exempted from prohibition.[57] Resale price maintenance in the drugs industry appears to have been abandoned *de facto* by the firms in 1978.

The 1956 Act required that certain kinds of cartel-type agreements be registered with a Registrar of Restrictive Trading Agreements and should remain in force only if the Court decided that they did not operate asgainst the public interest, but it did not impose penalties either for failure to register or on restrictive practices in general.[58] The Act was eventually amended in 1968 to render unregistered agreements void and unenforceable.[59]

While French competition legislation prohibits restrictive agreements and provides for certain exemptions in very general terms, depending on their economic *effects*, British legislation has always been characterized by its *form-based* approach. The 1956 Act, as amended, applies to agreements which take a particular technical form. The criteria for evaluating their economic impact are expressed in closely drafted 'gateways'. The formalistic approach was a direct result of the decision to involve the judiciary in the control of restrictive practices, itself designed to allay industry's fear of loosely drafted political controls.[60] The present law on restrictive practices, consolidated in the 1976 RPTA, has built on these foundations and is now considered inflexible, unnecessarily complex, anomalous, and, in many respects, redundant. Following several highly 'procompetitive' decisions[61] in the early years of the Court, firms have tended to devote their energies to devising forms of collaboration which fall outside the scope of the legislation.[62] Very few agreements currently reach the Court.

Recent developments in national competition law

The recent, if partial, dismantling of administered pricing in France has been accompanied by major reforms in competition law. In the UK the Competition Act 1980, which abolished the Prices Commission, also aimed to strengthen existing controls on competition. In their attempts to improve their national controls, both governments have looked *inter alia* to European law for guidance.

France

In France initial disillusionment with the inadequacy of the 1977 merger controls deflected attention from the increased administrative powers attributed to the new Competition Commission (*Commission de la concurrence*) created by Articles 1 to 3 of the 1977 Law. The Barre government, reluctant to set up either a fully

independent economic court or an independent cartel agency modelled along the lines of the German Cartel Office,[63] opted for a
compromise solution. The new competition authority was endowed
with wider powers, including the power to recommend maximum
fines and to suggest alterations to potentially restrictive agreements,
but the final decision to condemn practices and impose sanctions
fell to the Minister.[64] In particular, the Commission's independence
from the administration was theoretically enhanced. It could
recommend the imposition of administrative sanctions where it
discerned an illegal restrictive practice or an abuse of a dominant
position. Its decision, although advisory, was binding on the Minister to the extent that the latter could not impose higher fines or
condemn a firm for any activity not considered as prohibited by the
Commission.[65] The Minister's power to reach informal agreements
without consulting it was suppressed. Finally, it was empowered to
publish its own opinions.

These reforms met with only moderate success. The Commission
dealt with an average of eight referrals per year, although the
standard of its opinions was considered high.[66] Having no budget
or staff of its own, it was still dependent on the DGCC at the
Ministry to carry out its inquiries, even although it could now
initiate its own investigations, as well as respond to complaints
from parliamentary deputies and consumer organizations. The
Commission itself complained of a lack of co-operation from the
DGCC where investigations had not been demanded by the Minister, and indeed the competition staff at the DGCC was actually
reduced in this period.[67] In addition, the provisions of the decree
implementing the 1977 law ensured that the Ministry played an
influential role in the Commission's deliberations, in particular
through the participation of its *Commissaire du Gouvernement* at
almost every stage.[68] The Minister was also free to permit, in the
interests of the national economy, any practice which the Commission had found anticompetitive.[69]

Further reforms were introduced by the Socialist government in
1985.[70] These aimed to increase the independence of the Commission from the administration, but without granting it full autonomy, and to align the principles of French competition law on
individual anticompetitive practices with European law. The provisions on mergers were also reformed and simplified.[71] The Commission was designated an 'independent administrative authority',

provided with its own budget and empowered to appoint its own rapporteurs to investigate complaints, although the final decision to condemn a restrictive practice or abuse of a dominant position remained the prerogative of the Minister.

In this period the number of references, in particular from consumer organizations, increased steadily from 30 in 1984 to 39 in 1986. Although the substantive reforms of 1985 were generally welcomed as a step towards modernizing the concepts on which competition policy was based, as well as introducing a much-needed degree of flexibility into the law,[72] criticism switched to the absence of procedural guarantees afforded to firms at the various hearings before the Commission and to the unbridled investigative powers of its rapporteurs. In addition, a firm still risked cumulative exposure to the administrative penalties imposed under the competition legislation, civil damages under Article 1382 of the Civil Code, and, conceivably, criminal penalties under Articles 412 and 419 of the Penal Code.[73]

To meet these criticisms, and to strengthen competition law in general, legislation introduced in 1986 finally depenalized much of French competition law,[74] divorced it from price control, and abandoned the distinction between individual and collective anti-competitive practices.[75] Ordinance 86-1243 abrogated the 1945 ordinances and with it the power to fix prices, except in certain exceptional circumstances.[76] A new, autonomous sixteen-member Conseil de la concurrence, (Competition Council), with its own power of decision, greater resources, extended competences, and enhanced powers to impose pecuniary sanctions was created. Only administrative control over merger policy remains vested in the Minister of Economic Affairs, who may consult the Council. Individuals may now bring a case directly before the Council, provided that they have locus standi (Article 11). In addition, the Council must be consulted by the government in relation to proposed regulations which will directly affect competitive practices in certain sectors of the economy (Article 6). As a counterpart to these enhanced powers, procedural rights have been greatly strengthened (Articles 16 and 18), so that an aggrieved party may now appeal against the Council's findings in the ordinary civil courts.

The substantive provisions of the law essentially re-enact and codify the earlier legislation and decisions of the Commission. The concept of a 'dominant position' has, however, been refined to include condemnation of anticompetitive practices which harm an 'economically dependent' business partner, a concept borrowed from German law (Article 8).

It is too early to assess the impact of these reforms.[77] It might be noted that there is no provision for the possibility of informal reference to the new Council to seek its views on the potential application of the new controls to a proposed agreement. French competition law appears to have turned a full circle from a system based almost entirely on administrative discretion to a fully judicialized, formal set of procedures.

The UK

In the UK Sections 2 to 10 of the Competition Act 1980 closely follow the recommendations of the Liesner Committee, which had reported in 1978 on the various problems and inadequacies of existing competition policy and machinery. Although the Committee endorsed the essentially pragmatic approach to monopoly control in the UK, it recommended a number of procedural improvements to speed up investigations and to extend the reach of competition law. The 1980 Act strengthened the powers of the director-general of the OFT to control anticompetitive practices by individual firms — that is, conduct which had the effect of restricting, distorting, or preventing competition.[78] Although rather illdefined and general, this definition, which concentrates on company practice and not product markets, has been welcomed by the industry as a move towards an 'effects-based' approach to competition, which approximates more closely to EC law. At the same time, the Act's vague terminology has been criticized,[79] and it does not go so far as the recent French reforms in establishing an independent authority to deal with competition.

The latest set of reform proposals, published in 1988, which are closely modelled on Article 85 of the EEC Treaty, aim to shift the basis of legal control away from the traditional 'form-based' approach towards an 'effects-based' system. Anticompetitive agreements will be prohibited *ab initio*, and agreements which are not submitted for approval to the proposed new competition authority will be subject to large fines. The term 'anticompetitive practice' is closely modelled on EEC law and will include all 'agreements and concerted practices between undertakings . . . which have the object or effect of preventing or restricting or distorting competition in the UK'.[80]

It is perhaps in recognition of the difficulties of applying the general provisions of competition law to the complexities of the pharmaceutical sector that, despite the abolition of general price controls in the United Kingdom in 1980 and in France in 1986, special regimes have been retained to control profits and prices of medicinal products.

European competition law

The philosophy which informs EEC competition policy, its substantive provisions and style of implementation, differ markedly from the French and British systems. EEC competition policy is concerned to promote market integration first and allocative efficiency second.[81] As a result, economic analysis of the *effects* of cartel-like agreements, prohibited by Article 85, and abuses of dominant positions, sanctioned under Article 86, are central to the approach taken by the Commission, which is entrusted with the enforcement of competition policy, and by the Court, which may review Commission decisions. Its judgments are, of course, the most authoritative statement of the law.

The substantive provisions of EEC competition law are quite original; they differ considerably from antitrust regulation in the USA, which, as a mature, pro-competitive system would perhaps have provided the most obvious antitrust model for the framers of the EEC Treaty to emulate. Under EEC law there is only a very limited role for absolute or *per se* illegal practices, i.e. certain types of practices which can never be vindicated or justified even when they might have beneficial effects, which are a prominent feature of American law.[82] If an agreement falls *per se* within the prohibitions of Article 85(1) of the Treaty of Rome, it is always theoretically possible that it will qualify for exemption under Article 85(3). However, this is not to say that the Commission has followed the 'rule of reason' approach which has developed in American antitrust law. This would imply that certain forms of beneficial agreement should fall outside the scope of Article 85(1) altogether. In certain circumstances, the Court has shown some sympathy for this approach, in particular with respect to licences for rights relating to intellectual property, where certain restrictive terms are often considered necessary to promote research and innovation,[83] or in the absence of Commission action.[84] However, as we shall see in the third section of this chapter, which deals with patent licensing, the Commission has preferred to maintain its powers in full and to proceed by way of exemption under Article 85(3).

A comparison of the different systems

It is beyond the remit of this chapter to engage in a detailed appraisal of these different approaches to competition policy, but several comparative features of the three systems must be considered further. These are of general relevance to understanding recent moves towards a convergence of European law, and of more particular relevance to the understanding of the application of competition law to the peculiarities of the pharmaceutical market. Two substantive issues of antimonopoly policy—the concept of the 'relevant market' and the control of oligopolies—are examined first, and a comparison is then made of the different approaches taken to monitoring and enforcement of competition law.

Delimiting the relevant product market

A distinctive aspect of the Community's approach to monopoly control is its emphasis on the delimitation of a relevant product market. A firm's economic strength is assessed in relation to the position it occupies within a certain product market. The crux of this test is the notion of the interchangeability of one product for another. In other words '. . . the possibilities of competition must be judged in the context of the market comprising the totality of the products which, with respect to their characteristics, are particularly suitable for satisfying constant needs and are only to a limited extent interchangeable with other products'.[85]

The concept of interchangeability is nevertheless difficult to apply, particularly to the pharmaceuticals market, where medical and commercial views as to whether one product is substitutable for another will vary. This case can be seen in the problem of the proper definition of the relevant market for two groups of vitamins which could be used for bionutritive purposes in animal feed and health products as well as for technological purposes. This problem arose in the case of *Hoffmann-La Roche* v. *EC Commission* and involved allegations of excessive pricing for vitamin products.[86] Roche, in an attempt to show that the relevant market was larger than that established by the Commission, claimed that vitamins C and E were part of a wider market because purchasers of anti-oxidant products did have substitute products to which they could turn. On this occasion the Court ducked the issue by simply stating that the Commission's decision was not incorrect, and it did not go on to specify how the 'relevant market' should have been identified. In later cases the Court has insisted that the Commission carefully define the relevant market and back up this definition with a reasoned decision.[87]

In the UK and, until the reforms of 1986, in France, the preferred approach has been to grant a discretionary power to enable the activities of monopoly firms to be investigated where there is a prima-facie case for supposing that market power exists. The identification and measurement of market power has never been accorded any particular legal significance in the British system: the MMC is simply required to confirm that a monopoly situation within the meaning of the Act exists, but not to identify the market in economic terms.[88]

This pragmatic and flexible approach has not been without advantage in applying monopoly controls to the pharmaceutical market. Thus in a reference concerning alleged excessive pricing on the part of Hoffmann-La Roche for its products valium and librium, the MMC did not inquire into the nature of the market for antidepressants as a therapeutic class, but only into the market for a particular category of antidepressants, which it nevertheless drew more widely than the market for Roche's two patented products.[89]

The former French Competition Commission chose to employ a method of analysis of the existence of a dominant position similar to that used by the EC Commission,[90] establishing firstly the nature of the relevant market and then proceeding to an examination of potential abusive conduct. Given the largely administrative and discretionary nature of the legal structure within which it functioned, the market-power test did not assume any independent significance, and hence, in the opinion of some commentators, it was able to confound the two tests with relative impunity.[91] Thus in a 1978 opinion on the abusive conduct of the pharmaceutical company Boehringer in respect of the prices it charged for its intermediate product dipyridamole, the Competition Commission began by establishing that the company had continued to charge abnormally high prices for its products even after its patent had expired, and had continued to charge these prices despite competition from new suppliers. It concluded that Boehringer enjoyed a dominant position on the relevant market and recommended that a fine be imposed.[92]

Oligopolistic behaviour

The French and British authorities have taken a similar flexible approach in their application of antimonopoly controls[93] to oligopolistic behaviour. The British system provides for the referral of *complex monopoly situations*[94] to the MMC, which may then investigate whether a market structure itself might operate against the public interest. The MMC has in fact condemned excessive pricing by oligopolists on a number of occasions.[95] French antimonopoly controls also extend to groups of firms,[96] and the former French authorities devoted a considerable amount of their investigative effort to oligopolistic practices.[97]

By way of contrast, it would now seem that Article 86 of the Treaty of Rome cannot be used to attack the structure of an oligopolistic market itself.[98] In the past the Commission attempted to apply Article 86 to joint monopolization,[99] but in *Hoffmann-La Roche* v. *EC Commission* the Court, in its explanation of the meaning of the concept 'dominant position', held that it 'must be distinguished from parallel courses of conduct which are peculiar to oligopolies'.[100] As one commentator has observed, this 'means that there is a gap in the armoury of EEC competition law, since it is not possible to do anything where it is the structure of the market alone which is the problem'.[101]

Article 85(1) undoubtedly catches deliberate co-operation between firms, but a particular problem with the application of this article to the pharmaceutical sector is that it will only apply to co-operation between independent companies. Thus it is settled law that Article 85 does not apply to an agreement between a parent company and a subsidiary where the latter enjoys no real freedom to determine its course of action on the market, even if there is a market-sharing agreement in operation.[102] The element of 'consensus' between independent participants in the market is missing. If, however, the subsidiaries can act independently of their parent company, then an agreement between them to restrict competition is likely to be caught under 85(1). Thus in its 1980 decision relating to an agreement between three European subsidiaries of the American Johnson and Johnson Inc. to restrict exports of Gravindex pregnancy tests from the UK to Germany, the Commission imposed fines amounting to US $270,000.[103]

The Commission has recently imposed a fine of 800,000 ECU on Sandoz Italia, the Italian subsidiary of the Swiss company, for displaying the words 'export prohibited' on its sales invoices for pharmaceutical products. Sandoz brought an action before the Court of Justice on the basis that there was in fact no agreement between it and its customers, but that it had acted unilaterally. If the Commission had wished to attack its behaviour it should have used Article 86 and attempted to establish that Sandoz had abused a monopoly position. The Commission in its original decision held that the prohibition on exports was a contractual clause forming an integral part of the agreement between supplier and customer, which by its very nature and purpose insulated the national market and distorted competition. The Court has now upheld this decision, although it reduced the fine.[104]

Monitoring and enforcement

The contrasts between British, French, and European practice in the field of competition are at their most obvious at the level of monitoring and enforcement.

Whereas the former French competition authorities were heavily dependent on the DGCC at the Ministry of Finance, the British authorities have enjoyed far greater independence. The MMC is supported by a staff of 110 civil servants, while the director-general of the OFT has a staff of some 300. The EC Commission's specialist directorate-general on competition, DG IV, which comprises a staff of some 290 economists and lawyers, is far too small in itself to ensure enforcement of Articles 85 and 86 throughout the twelve member states. The Commission has stressed that it would favour more private enforcement in the national courts.[105]

Under current British law, unlike French law, anticompetitive practices are not offences in themselves.[106] In the case of monopolization, for example, it is only where the MMC has concluded that the public interest has been, or is likely to be, adversely affected that the Secretary of State or the director-general of the

OFT are empowered, but not required, to take action.[107] Unlike in EC law or, since 1978, French competition law, there is no power to impose administrative sanctions or fines; nor do injunctions, interim measures, or cease-and-desist orders play the central role which they do in EC law, and have come to do in France following the latest reforms. The key instrument of enforcement in British law is the voluntary undertaking, given by the individual firm or firms either to the director-general of the OFT or to the Secretary of State for Trade and Industry. Voluntary undertakings and informal settlements may be solicited at almost every stage in the enforcement of the various competition acts. The usual procedure following the completion of an MMC report under the Fair Trading Act is for the Secretary of State to ask the director-general, in the light of the MMC's recommendations, to discuss with the parties concerned the action needed to remedy adverse effects. Under Section 21(2) of the RTPA, the director-general has discretion not to refer various restrictive agreements to the Court in cases where, following negotiation, the offending terms have been removed. The majority of agreements are now dealt with in this way.[108]

Once the director-general of the OFT has obtained outline agreement on the terms of the undertaking, the precise wording of the agreement will then be negotiated with government, that is with the Department of Trade and Industry. It is the duty of the director-general of the OFT, however, to ensure compliance.[109]

The Competition Act 1980 added a further layer of discretionary controls to the existing law, again implemented by informal settlements. Section 3(1) of the 1980 Act allows the director-general of the OFT to carry out a preliminary investigation to determine whether the conduct in question is in fact anticompetitive, following which he or she may either refer the case to the MMC for a full public-interest inquiry or obtain undertakings on such conditions as he or she may determine.[110]

The EC Commission's approach to enforcement, particularly with regard to restrictive agreements under Article 85, is much more bureaucratic, even if the method of approving notified agreements is 'editorial'.[111] Agreements are subject to a process of formal notification, and negative clearance involves the deletion or amendment of restrictive clauses and the insertion of pro-competitive ones. This cumbersome decision-making procedure resulted in a huge backlog of work at DG IV, and in considerable legal uncertainty for the parties to agreement or for a large firm which might find itself subject to Article 86.[112]

As its procedural powers are more closely circumscribed by law, the Commission does not enjoy the same scope as the British authorities to reach informal settlements, but to overcome the backlog of work, the Commission has resorted to the informal device of 'comfort letters', that is 'administrative letters' signed by a DG IV official indicating that there are either no grounds for applying Article 85(1) or Article 86 or that the agreement is considered eligible for exemption under Article 85(3). For the addressee, the comfort letter is said to create a legitimate expectation that the Commission will take no further action, unless there is a material change of circumstance.[113] Comfort letters are not binding on national courts.[114] Unlike the French or British competition authorities, however, the Commission has a duty to hear interested third parties when granting clearances and exemptions,[115] and if it fails to discharge this duty in informal settlements it could theoretically be exposed to an action for failure to act.[116] The Commission has recently adopted the practice of publishing prior notice of its intention to issue a comfort letter, thus giving third parties the opportunity to be heard.[117] In addition, the Commission's final decision can be challenged in the Court of Justice, not only by the parties to the agreement but also by a third party who considers itself adversely affected by it.[118]

To save parties to qualifying agreements the uncertainty and delay of seeking individual exemption, a system of block exemptions has been developed.[119] For the pharmaceutical sector, the most relevant of these is the block exemption on patent licensing, considered below. It is argued that the gain in legal certainty is paid for in the acceptance of a degree of *dirigisme*, as parties are required to order their affairs to attract block exemption.[120] A combination of extensive enforcement powers and the 'effects-based' nature of controls has allowed the EC Commission to fashion powerful and wide-ranging instruments of antitrust control, and this is perhaps reflected in the fact that many informal complaints about anti-competitive practices in the pharmaceutical sector are directed first to this body. Even if the Commission may be slow to set in motion its cumbersome formal machinery, the mere threat of investigation can have a deterrent effect. A number of British-based firms, for example, stopped warning pharmacists not to purchase parallel-imported products as soon as they became aware that the Commission was planning an investigation of these practices.[121] The British and particularly the French systems of control have remained relatively weak in comparison, although the flexible and pragmatic nature of the British system can, as we have seen, offer certain advantages over the more legalistic European framework.[122] Before turning to an assessment of the way in which competition policy has served as an *adjunct* to these regimes, however, it is necessary to analyse the availability of a further general set of controls over monopoly abuses, under patent law.

Patent Protection, Competition, and Pharmaceuticals

The objectives of the patent system

The patent has played a significant role in economic policy for over 650 years. Originally conceived in the form of inventor's privileges, it became an important instrument in promoting industrial development, especially with the passing of the British Statute of Monopolies in 1623. The notion that the inventor should be rewarded with a time-limited monopoly to exploit his or her invention was also incorporated into the laws of antimonopoly nations like France, which introduced its first patent law in 1791. Modern patent legislation retained four classic objectives[123] as justifying patent protection. These are:

to recognize the intellectual property of the inventor
to reward the inventor for services to technology
to encourage investment and innovation
to further the early disclosure and wide dissemination of technical knowledge

In other words, the patent system is based on a form of trade-off: the inventor is accorded a time-limited, exclusionary right as consideration for his or her contribution to the enrichment of technology. This requires that the patentee disclose or reveal his of her invention to the public with the patent application. Disclosure is meant to perform three legal functions:

to prevent any person from inadvertently infringing the patent right during the term of the monopoly

to put the public in possession of the patentee's secret on the expiry
of the patent term   ·
to prevent patents being granted for known inventions

Disclosure as 'exchange for secrets' serves a number of additional
technical functions:

to supply the public with a complete survey of the most recent state
of technological development
to provide the necessary information and stimulation for continuing development on the basis of the patented invention
to direct those interested in the exploitation of an invention to the
relevant source of technology

Approaches to patent protection

Although these objectives are common to most systems of patent
law and are undoubtedly shared by the UK and France, each takes
quite different approaches to the questions of disclosure and protection. In particular, certain countries such as West Germany, the
USA, and, to a lesser extent, the UK have a 'strong' patent tradition.
Patent protection is only conferred after a detailed examination of
the prior state of the art has been completed by a specialized
administrative authority. The patent holder's rights, although not
immune from challenge from third parties, are difficult to attack.

Although it is hard to establish a link between the rate of innovation and the degree of patent protection, in recent years both
French and British governments have introduced measures to
strengthen their patent systems, to promote the dissemination of
technical knowledge, and to make patents more accessible to small
and medium-sized firms.[124]

The French tradition has been one of 'weak' patent protection.
Patent rights in France were first recognized by a law of 7 January
1791 and reformed by a law of 5 July 1844, which gave the patent
holder an exclusive monopoly for 20 years, extending to all the
described usages of the patented good. In other words, unlike the
English, German, and American systems, where patent specifications were based on the detailed *claims* made for an invention, the
French system required only a description of the invention.
Whereas most other patent systems required that the subject-matter
constituted 'an inventive step' according to the state of the art, the

French system merely demanded novelty and industrial application. As a consequence, French patents were issued without a prior examination, by a specialist administrative agency, of the existing state of the art in order to substantiate the novelty claimed. Thus the scope of the patent holder's monopoly was unclear: because he or she was only obliged to describe the product, the limits of the monopoly were adjustable.[125] French patents were therefore rather easily obtained but were eminently challengeable by third parties willing to embark upon costly litigation in the ordinary courts.

This system was eventually overhauled by the law of 1 January 1968,[126] the aim of which was to strengthen the patent system and to bring it closer into line with other national systems following France's signature of the Strasbourg Convention in 1963.[127] Patent protection was available for a period of 20 years as before,[128] but the 1968 law introduced four major reforms: the notion of the 'inventive step' was incorporated into French law,[129] enhancing the value of the patent; the extent of patent protection was now based on the claims made for the invention;[130] an *avis documentaire* (documentary opinion) on the prior state of the art, prepared by the administration, was published together with the patent;[131] and the penalties for infringement of patent rights were overhauled. The *avis documentaire* represented a compromise solution to demands for the introduction of a full prior examination into French patent law. This document assesses the nature of the claims made for the product in the light of the existing state of the art but does not purport to evaluate the product in that light; it merely lists the factors which might lead a third party to oppose the claims made for it. At the time of the passage of the 1968 law it was considered that the French patent administration had insufficient resources to carry out a full prior examination.[132]

The 1968 law was amended in 1978,[133] implementing the European Patent Convention (EPC) of 1973, but the *avis documentaire* remains, although it has been modified to allow the director of the *Institut national de la protection industrielle* (INPI) to assess the novelty of the invention and to reject an application where the claims made for it are not justified.[134] As a consequence, industrialists still complain that French patents are insufficiently strong and that France should adopt a system based on the full prior examination.[135] In the meantime, an increasing number of French-based drug firms have opted for the European patent.[136]

Until the reforms introduced by the 1883 Patents Act, which also overhauled the administration of the patent system, British patent law was also based on a description of the patent specification, as opposed to claims made for it. The adoption of the claims-based system, followed in 1905 by the introduction of an administrative search for novelty, considerably strengthened the attractions of the British patent.

Modern British patent law dates from the Patents Act 1949, which streamlined patent administration and rationalized the procedures for granting patents. Under this Act, patent protection was available for a period of 16 years, but this period was extended to 20 years by the Patents Act 1977, which incorporated *inter alia* the provisions of the EPC into British law.[137]

Pharmaceutical patents

Within the general systems of patent law, pharmaceutical inventions have been singled out for special treatment. Most countries have been reluctant to allow complete monopoly rights over products which are considered of vital public interest. The French and British patent systems have adopted different approaches to the problem of reconciling considerations of public health with the desire to promote innovation. In the UK, comprehensive patent protection for medicinal products and chemical substances has been available, subject to certain limitations, since 1909.[138] The conferring of full patent protection was seen as an important means of developing a home-based chemical industry to compete with Germany.[139] The position in France remained much more complex, however.

Nineteenth-century French governments were notably hesitant to allow patents for drug-based products. Although the 1791 Patent Act applied to all discoveries or inventions, the law of 21 Germinal, outlawing secret remedies, effectively excluded medicines from patent protection. Medicinal products were also excluded from the 1844 law on patents[140] on two grounds: first, that it was against the public interest to allow pharmacists to exercise a monopoly over these products; and second, that the public might consider the award of a patent as a form of quality guarantee. It was unclear from the terms of Article 3 of the 1844 law whether *process* patents were available for drug manufacture. This is a relatively weak form of protection, since a number of routes to a particular product normally exist, but process patents were considered to be of increasing value as the industrial manufacture of drugs expanded in the inter-war period.[141]

As noted in Chapter 3, the product 'visa', introduced in 1944, was granted only for novel products and in effect functioned as a surrogate, if somewhat inadequate, form of patent protection. Following the reform of the visa system, in 1959, a special form of protection for medicinal products, the *brevet spécial du médicament* (BSM) was introduced by an ordinance of 4 February 1959.[142] It would appear that the government of the period was reluctant to include drugs within the scope of the general patent regime precisely because of the ease with which patents could be obtained under it. Instead, the 1959 ordinance provided that a BSM could only be issued in conjunction with an *avis documentaire*, and it was only on the extension of this latter procedure to all types of patents by the law of 1968 that medicinal products were finally integrated into the general patent regime. However, as a number of commentators have pointed out, this integration was only partial.[143] In effect Article 10 of the 1968 law only provided for an 'application' or 'usage' patent, as opposed to a full product patent, for medicinal products.[144] Whereas under the general rules of French patent law, each and every novel industrial application of a product is patentable, Article 10 restricted patent protection of a medicinal product, defined in accordance with Article L.511 of the CSP, to its first therapeutic application. If a new therapeutic application for the product, or its active substance, were subsequently to be discovered, this could not be protected and therefore fell into the public domain.

This restriction on the patentability of 'second applications' appears to have been a distinct feature of French patent law and was at variance with the British approach to the patentability of new uses of a known substance under the 1949 Act.[145] The French government was sufficiently convinced of the utility of the restriction as a means of protecting the legitimate needs of public health to influence the drafting of Articles 52 and 54 of the 1973 EPC, which preclude the patenting of a method of treatment. The provisions of the EPC were subsequently incorporated into Articles 6 and 8 of the law of 1978, Article 5 of which abolished Article 10 of the 1968 Law and therefore incorporated medicinal products fully into the general system of patent protection.

Controls on the use of patents

As the protection afforded by full product patent was extended to medicinal products, a number of specific restrictions on their exercise were developed, to supplement the general controls applying to all types of patents. The subsequent operation of these special restrictions has been influenced by wider regulatory developments affecting the process of product competition in the pharmaceutical sector. There are basically three types of controls over the potential abuse of patent monopolies common to each system. These are: the award of compulsory licences of right to third parties to use the patent; the taking of compulsory licences so that the patent may be worked for the benefit of the state; and the award of compulsory licences of right to third parties to use a patent on a medicine.

General compulsory licences of right in national law

To prevent patentees from abusing their monopoly rights by not exploiting an invention, the patent-law regimes of each country allow the relevant patent authorities to grant compulsory licences of right to third parties deemed capable of exploiting the invention after the elapse of a specific period of time. Under the French law of 1844, penalties for non-exploitation were severe: the patent was declared void if its holder did not put it to use, and such non-use could be considered an abuse of the patent holder's monopoly rights.[146] The law of 1968,[147] however, modified this regime in line with international law, to provide that compulsory licences of right (*licenses obligatoires*) could be issued if, within a period of three years from the issue of the patent, the patent holder had not worked the patent effectively.[148] The patent must be worked on French territory; importation of the goods in question does not amount to exploitation.[149] Whereas the decision to award a licence of right, to set the conditions and terms on which it is granted, and to fix the level of fees payable to the original patent holder are within the discretion of the patent authorities in the UK, these matters are for the determination of the ordinary civil courts in France, before which the director of the INPI has a special right of audience.[150]

In the UK the Comptroller General of Patents (CGP) has power to grant compulsory licences at the end of 3 years after the original patent was granted.[151] The CGP enjoys a wide discretion to settle the terms of the licence as he or she sees fit,[152] provided that the applicant can make out a case based on the specific grounds set out in Section 48(3). Section 53(2) permits the CGT to treat, where relevant, any views expressed by the MMC as prima-facie evidence of any matter to which they relate.[153]

There has been little use of these compulsory licensing provisions in either country,[154] for a number of reasons. First, in British law there is no a priori principle that once one of the grounds is made out by an applicant, a licence should be granted. The CGP will usually only exercise his or her discretion in exceptional circumstances.[155] Second, the British and French courts have taken the view that the patentee, as the owner of a proprietary right, enjoys considerable freedom to set prices and royalties.[156] Third, the award of a compulsory licence does not include the licence of the know-how which is usually required to work the patent effectively.[157] Fourth, if the original patent-holder chooses to contest the award of a compulsory licence, litigation will prove both costly and time-consuming, particularly in France, where the courts play a key role. More often than not, the economic benefit of a compulsory patent will have been lost by the time a final decision is reached, as the market situation may well have altered. Nevertheless, it is generally concluded that the mere existence of compulsory procedures acts as an incentive to patent holders to negotiate licences voluntarily.[158]

Compulsory licences for the benefit of the state

Whereas the former category of compulsory licences will be available only at the end of a three-year period and are entirely dependent on the initiative of private third parties, compulsory patents to be worked by the state are available at any time and are activated by a separate procedure.

In France the 1968 law, as amended, provides that the minister responsible for industrial property matters may award compulsory licences to ensure the exploitation of an invention in the interests of the national economy.[159] The procedures attending the award of these licences are complex and byzantine and appear never to have been used.[160] Articles 40 and 41 of the 1968 law provide that in the interests of national defence, the state may at any time obtain a licence to work a patent.

Sections 55 to 59 of the British Patents Act 1977, replacing Section 46 of the Patents Act 1949, also lay down special procedures by which rights under patents may be appropriated by the government for Crown use, on payment of compensation as deemed appropriate by the CGP. Third parties may then be authorized to exploit the patent. This form of compulsory licensing has played an important role in the UK, as an adjunct to the informal methods of profit control reviewed in Chapter 3.

Faced with high prices for antibiotics, and in the light of continued intransigence over pricing negotiations on the part of a number of foreign multinationals, the Conservative government in 1961 made use of Section 46, when it introduced new procedures for central buying of hospital drugs by tender. This action was undoubtedly stimulated by the report of the Kefauver Committee in the USA, which revealed the excessive profits earned by certain manufacturers of antibiotics. Importers, whose prices averaged one-tenth of those charged by the patentees, obtained cheap unpatented supplies of antibiotics from Italy and elsewhere and were awarded Section 46 licences.[161] In view of the savings realized by the NHS, the Sainsbury Report recommended the extension of Section 46 to include general practitioner and pharmaceutical services. Perhaps in view of industry's protests at the earlier, unprecedented use of Section 46 and the precedent which these compulsory patents had set in a number of Commonwealth countries, the government initially ignored these suggestions. They were, however, eventually adopted by way of an opposition amendment to the Health and Social Services Act 1968.

Compulsory licences for medicinal products

Special procedures for obtaining compulsory licences for patents on drugs were incorporated into both French and British law along with the extension of full patent protection. In France a special form of compulsory licence (*licence d'office*) for medicinal products, as defined by Article L.511 of the CSP, was initially introduced by the 1959 ordinance creating the BSM.[162] Articles 37 and 38 of the 1968 law, as amended,[163] provide that, in the interests of public health, patents for medicinal products, for the processes of obtaining a drug or any substances relating to its manufacture, may be subject to a special form of compulsory licence where the medicinal products in question are not made available to the public in sufficient quality or quantity, or are sold at abnormally high prices. The procedure for awarding this type of compulsory licence is again highly complex: the Health Minister must request the Ministry of Industry, who is responsible for intellectual property, to issue an *arrêté* submitting a patent to compulsory licences. The latter is required to consult a special commission constituted for this purpose[164] and, having obtained its approval, may award licences to interested third parties under such terms and conditions as he or she determines. However, it should be noted that in default of amicable settlement between the parties, patent royalties are fixed by the ordinary civil courts.

Given the complexity of these procedures, it is hardly surprising that they have never been used. It is also unlikely that they would be used as an adjunct to price control. Given the extensive powers which the French administration already possesses in this respect, there seems little occasion for the use of the procedure for compulsory licences in relation to abnormally high prices. That said, however, it was rumoured that the Minister of Health was considering using these powers against Hoffmann-La Roche if the company did not agree to lower voluntarily the price of its Valium products.[165] Although the Minister of France might have used his or her powers to impose price reductions for the products in question, the company could simply have refused to supply the French market. Had the Minister chosen to use the powers under the patent legislation, a rival firm could have been authorized to import valium into France—from Italy, for example.

The use of special compulsory licences for drugs has been far greater in the UK. Encouraged by their success under Section 46, unlicensed importers attempted to expand their market to general practitioners, seeking to rely on Section 41 of the Patents Act 1949.[166] In contrast to Sections 48–51 of the 1977 Act, Section 41 of the 1949 Act *obliged* the CPG to grant the licences unless there were good reasons for not doing so.[167] This procedure was therefore more favourable and more accessible to third parties than the general provisions on compulsory licensing discussed above. Consequently, it was the smaller firms and importers who relied primarily upon Section 41.

These licences were nevertheless subject to substantial litigation by the larger multinationals, which tried to delay, if not prevent, their use by rivals.[168] Despite these limitations, the Sainsbury Report[169] estimated that Section 41, while a very marginal and indirect means for governments to influence pharmaceutical prices, should nevertheless be retained. If any part of the industry should be taken into public ownership in the future, Section 41 would be a useful way of building up the product profile of the nationalized sector, a prospect which evidently alarmed the ABPI.

In the meantime, the Banks Committee, which had investigated the reform of patent law[170] recommended that, in the light of the extension of Section 46 powers under the 1968 Act, Section 41 licences should be abolished.[171] The White Paper on the reform of patent law, published in 1975 by the Labour government, advocated their retention, much to the ire of the industry. The fate of Section 41 licences was eventually sealed during the lengthy negotiations over the introduction of advertising regulations, discussed in Chapter 8. The Lord Chancellor made it clear during the second reading of the patents bill that the government would consider dropping the licences altogether in return for industry's co-operation on the introduction of advertising regulations. Special compulsory licences were subsequently dropped from the 1977 legislation.

Competition law and patents

The terms on which patents are licensed *voluntarily* by the patentee to third parties may be subject to the general rules of competition law. There are substantial differences in the British and French treatment of patent licensing as compared to EEC competition law. Compulsory licensing is a matter for national law, and so there is little scope for its use in EC law. Article 85(1) may in certain cases prohibit the grant of an exclusive licence, but it cannot be used to force the patentee to issue a competing licence, nor can a third party resist a patent infringement action on the basis that an existing exclusive licence has been found to contravene Article 85(1).[172] Article 47 of the Community Patent Convention, which has not yet entered into force, provides that compulsory licensing will remain governed by national law. In its jurisprudence on Article 36, which grants a limited derogation from the Treaty's rules on free movement in favour of industrial property right protection, the European Court has ruled that the exhaustion principle does not apply to compulsory licenses.[173]

Voluntary patent licences, which are a grant of rights rather than a restriction on their use, are prima facie exempt from the British RTPA 1976.[174] The terms of a licence, but not the refusal of a licence, are also subject to the Competition Act 1980,[175] although there has been no case-law to date.[176]

A distinctive feature of British competition law is its direct link with patent law. Where the MMC concludes adversely that a course of conduct by a patentee is against the public interest, the powers in Section 51 of the Patents Act 1977 may be exercised. Section 51(2)(a) provides that the Minister may apply to the CGP to cancel or modify certain conditions in the licence, or subject the patent to licence of right, a power which has not as yet been used.[177] No equivalent positions exist in France.

Although there are no special provisions on patent licensing in French competition law, the authorities have followed the European Court's distinction between the *existence* of intellectual property rights and their *exercise*. The former Technical Commission considered it within its jurisdiction to investigate whether the exploitation of patent rights conformed to the provisions of ordinance 45-1483.[178] More recently, the former Competition Commission, in a case involving phytosanitary products, recommended that price fixing and market sharing could not be imposed by way of patent licensing agreements.[179]

Trans-frontier patent-licensing and European law

In contrast to these rather indulgent national approaches, patent licensing has been regarded with some suspicion by the EC Commission and, to a lesser extent, by the European Court. While patent licensing may promote the diffusion of technology throughout the Common Market and promote interstate trade, it may also lead to the division of markets on territorial lines. The use of patent licences to compartmentalize international markets has been reasonably well documented in the pharmaceutical sector.[180] It is alleged that in order to keep competition within tolerable limits, the large firms trade licences between themselves with territorial restrictions which neatly carve up the world market and foreclose competition. Smaller firms, which cannot afford extensive research and so have little to offer by way of trade, tend to be shut out of the market. For example, by constructing a network of protective patent agreements for antibiotics and penicillins in the 1950s, the American TNCs not only established and consolidated their market strength in Europe but effectively precluded the threat of competition in their home markets. The American company Parke Davis had obtained a patent on the antibiotic chloramphenicol in 1949. In 1950 it signed an agreement with its French licensee, *Laboratoire français de chimiothérapie*, which not only limited the French company to sales in France and French territories but also isolated the French market from all the others. The *Laboratoire* pledged not to buy or sell the product outside its assigned territory and to ensure that none of its customers would so resell it. Further, the drug could only be sold in its finished form, not in bulk, and the *Laboratoire* agreed to 'refrain from shipping in any parts of the territory quantities ... notoriously above its needs'. The agreement also contained a no-challenge clause and a grant-back clause, which stipulated that the French firm had to share new discoveries with Parke.[181]

European companies have not been slow to follow suit. In 1968 the US Justice Department filed a suit challenging the limits on patent licences granted by two of the UK's largest producers, ICI and Glaxo, to three of the largest American companies, American Home Products, the Schering Corporation, and Johnson and Johnson. ICI and Glaxo had pooled their US patents for an antifungus drug—griseofulvin. They then licensed the patents to the American companies on condition that the drug was sold only in finished form. Sales in bulk to third parties were prohibited except with the express consent of ICI and Glaxo. In 1973 the Supreme Court upheld the Justice Department's ruling that these restrictions amounted to a restriction on trade.[182] In 1976 Beecham, another of the large British firms, granted to Hoechst a similar licence for the sale of ampicillin, restricting sales by Hoechst to finished forms in two countries.[183]

If the terms of the licences granted by the major firms to each other can be restrictive, those granted to independent small firms, particularly those situated in developing countries or countries with weak patent-systems, may be even more so. Such agreements may not only impose export restrictions but may often also withhold essential technology and know-how. This pattern of licensing is also found in countries such as Spain and Portugal, where product patents on drugs have not always been available. Local firms are often forced to import the active ingredients in intermediate form if they want to manufacture and sell a drug. This pattern of trade has been especially problematic in France, where, as we saw in Chapter 3, the system of price control, together with the absence of patent protection, already acted as an incentive to import intermediate products.

The application of EEC competition law

The Commission first took the view that Article 85(1) did not apply to the voluntary granting of a patent licence: licensing was a desirable process which spread technology.[184] Taking its cue from the Court's judgment in *Consten and Grundig* v. *EC Commission* in 1964,[185] where the Court made it clear that vertical restrictions could fall within Article 85(1), as could, by analogy, the *exercise* of intellectual property rights, the Commission adopted a stricter attitude towards patent licences.[186]

In a case involving the restriction of imports of unpatented drugs from Italy to the Netherlands, the Court ruled that while the *existence* of rights granted under national law relating to patents is not affected by Articles 85 and 86, the provisions of these articles may in principle be invoked to prevent the abusive exercise of patent rights.[187] The application of the competition rules to agreements concerning intellectual property rights should therefore take place in two stages. In the first stage the provisions of an agreement will be assessed in order to determine whether they form part of the subject-matter of the property right. The possibility of exploitation through licences was explicitly recognized by the Court in *Centrafarm* v. *Sterling Drug*[188] as an element in the subject-matter of a patent. If, however, the terms merely regulate the exercise of the property right, they may be prohibited under Articles 85 and 86. Thus the grant of sole or exclusive rights to a licensee is not regarded by the Commission or the Court as coming within the specific subject-matter of the patent, on the ground that contractual terms which fetter the exercise of an intellectual property right by its owner cannot be regarded as necessary incidents of the existence of that right.[189] The distinction between the exercise and existence of an intellectual property right has not always been easy to apply and is not always clearly marked in the reasoning of either the Commission or the Court.[190]

In a series of subsequent decisions, the Commission applied Article 85(1) to various clauses in patent licensing agreements, granting exemption under Article 85(3) to those which met certain conditions. The severity of this approach, however, subsequently met with the disapproval both of the Court[191] and of academic commentators.[192] It also contributed to the backlog of notified agreements awaiting individual exemption, so that by 1983 over 60 per cent of the cases pending concerned patent licences. In fact in 1979 the Commission published a special draft block-exemption for patent licences,[193] but its restrictive proposals met with such devastating criticism[194] that they were substantially modified and revised in line with the more liberal approach then being developed by the Court. As far as patent licensing for pharmaceuticals is concerned, the Commission now seems prepared to accept that the high costs involved in developing and marketing a new drug justify a more lenient approach, in particular to exclusive manufacturing rights. Without protection from competition, licensees will have no incentive to undertake the considerable financial risk involved.

The new block-exemption, finally adopted at the end of 1984,[195] reflects this new lenient attitude. Article 1(1), which lists the various types of clauses benefiting from block exemption, includes clauses which allow the patentee to impose an obligation on the licensee not to manufacture or use the patented product in territories of other licensees. Furthermore, exemption is also given to an obligation on the licensee not to pursue an *active* sales policy in another licensee's territory so long as the product is protected there by a parallel patent: licensees may not therefore advertise or establish a branch in another territory, although they may respond to unsolicited orders by parallel importers (Article 2(2)). However, the block exemption also allows a ban, during the first 5 years after the launching of the protected product on the Common Market, against all sales in the territories of other licensees (Article 1(1)(b)). In other words, where the product is new, full protection may be given against competition from fellow licensees, *passive* as well as active. Sales by licensees to customers established in their own territories who intend to export the goods for resale, i.e. parallel importation, cannot be banned, however. These provisions seek to strike a compromise between the need to safeguard property rights and promote innovation while ensuring that their exercise does not unduly restrict competition and free movement within the Common Market.

The restrictions on abuse of a patentee's monopoly privileges which form part of the national patent regimes appear too blunt and cumbersome as instruments to control the particular problems which arise in the regulation of pharmaceutical prices and profits, as their infrequent use would appear to testify. This is not to say that national patent law, like competition law, has not functioned as an important complement to the more specific regimes designed to regulate the process of product competition, reviewed in earlier chapters of this book. This process of interaction is assessed in the final section of this chapter.

The Interaction of Competition Law and Pharmaceutical Regulation

In assessing the interaction of competition law and patent law with the specific regulatory regimes discussed in earlier chapters, I return to one of the principal themes of this book: the cumulative impact of regulation on the process of product competition, and its implications for relations between government and industry. In the first place, I have argued that, in reality, the techniques adopted in the context of the regulation of prices and profits have not always proved effective as mechanisms for the promotion of product competition. Governments may turn to the instruments of competition law to remedy this failure. Competition law and, more particularly, patent law may also serve to supplement the process of product competition in another sense. Impressed by industry's contention that legislation on product safety has impaired the process of innovation, both governments are considering ways to restore or extend the industry's temporary monopoly over the fruits of its research. The final part of this section deals with the current debate over 'effective' patent term.

The legal context

Obviously, given the different legal character which legislation on pricing and product safety has assumed in each country, the process of interaction between the different regulatory regimes will vary. This is especially evident with respect to price control. Chapters 3 and 6 emphasized the voluntary and informal nature of the British approach to pharmaceutical price regulation. In Chapter 3 it was suggested that voluntary compliance was to a certain extent secured by the threat of resort to supplementary controls, including patent law and competition law. In 1971, following the company's persistent refusal to participate in successive VPRSs, the British Secretary of State for Trade did in fact refer the Swiss multinational Hoffmann-La Roche to the MMC. This case offers a useful example of the interaction of the informal system of profit regulation in the UK with the pragmatic approach to antimonopoly, as discussed above.

Inevitably, competition controls have not played a similar complementary role in France, where the separate, formal regime of legal controls kept prices low. For example, as mentioned in the third section of this chapter, the French authorities never made use of their powers to issue compulsory licences for medicinal products. This is not to say that competition law has had no role in the process of promoting product competition, but rather that its role has been different. Indeed, it was argued in Chapters 3 and 7 that the French system of price regulation has, to a certain extent, suppressed product competition and has also prevented the emergence of price competition from generics and OTC products. It is in the attempt to promote this form of competition that competition law as such has come to play a role in France, and I will now go on to look at these developments.

The Hoffmann-La Roche saga

Following Hoffmann-La Roche's persistent refusal between 1966 and 1970 to enter into negotiations on its prices for Valium, officials at the DHSS were prompted, within the limits of their legal powers, to take a closer look at the element of group profit in the price charged by the Basle-based parent company to its British subsidiary for imported bulk materials.[196] Roche was informed that, according to the Ministry's estimates, at least 20 per cent of these so-called costs represented profits.

Hoffmann-La Roche justified its refusal to participate in the VPRS on the basis that its products were currently subject to competition from companies which had applied for Section 41 compulsory licences to import Valium from Italy.[197] In reality, however, Roche, in a series of skilful tactical manœuvres, had neutralized this competitive threat. In the first place, it had refused to supply any detailed information on its prices to the Patent Office. In order to determine the royalties payable by the licensee, the CGP based his calculations on Roche's current selling prices, which he mistakenly assumed to have been subject to VPRS procedures and therefore reasonable, even if, as he acknowledged, they were monopoly prices.[198] The applicant company, DDSA, which alleged that it could import its base products in Italy for some £20 per tonne, was forced to pay a further £20 per tonne in royalties, making their final selling price much less competitive.[199] In the second place, Roche proceeded to assert trade-mark rights in the 'get-up' of the green and black oblong capsule in which DDSA had attempted to market its products, thereby frustrating the latter's marketing campaign. Trade marks in pharmaceutical products are, of course, a particularly effective form of monopoly right. Doctors become more readily familiarized with a trade or brand name and patients more familiar with a particular get-up. Unlike patent rights, trade-mark rights are not limited in time, and the owner's exclusive rights may be terminated only in restricted circumstances. In the third place, Hoffmann-La Roche forestalled the possibility that the government might attempt to use the Crown's right to work patents under Section 46 of the 1949 Act by supplying voluntarily its products free to civil and military hospitals.

Following the company's refusal to participate in the fourth VPRS in 1970, the government took the unusual step of referring the whole issue of pricing to the MMC. Roche remained firm in its resolve to supply only the minimum of information to the inquiry unless the latter would accept additional information on cost calculations, based on world prices and average costs as opposed to national figures. The MMC declined and on the basis of its own calculations—extrapolated from the accounts of competitors— reported that Roche had made grossly excessive profits at the expense of the NHS between 1969 and 1972. Capitalizing on the NHS's monopsonistic position, it further recommended that these past profits should be recouped by way of price ceilings on *current* sales of Valium. In this way the absence of a power to impose fines on errant companies could be circumvented.[200]

Hoffmann-La Roche was reluctant not only to create a pricing precedent which might have expensive repercussions in other jurisdictions but also to forgo its monopoly profits while the patents on Valium and Librium remained extant. In a major departure from the traditional approach to the resolution of disputes about competition, it refused to give a voluntary undertaking on future price ceilings to the Secretary of State, forcing the latter to make a rare use of the statutory order procedure to give effect to the MMC's recommendations. At that time such orders required the approval of both Houses of Parliament, a time-consuming process which Roche attempted to prolong by extensive lobbying in both houses. Three months later however, the necessary order was finally approved.[201]

The company then sought a declaration in the courts that the order itself was illfounded as the MMC, by failing to afford the company an opportunity to comment on its price calculations, had not observed the rules of natural justice when it compiled its report. The Secretary of State meanwhile sought an interim injunction to prevent Roche from exceeding the prices stipulated in the Order, but Roche counter-claimed that it would only comply with the interim injunction on the condition that the Crown gave a financial guarantee of compensation should the company's earlier case succeed. The sole issue which eventually reached the House of Lords in 1974 was whether the Secretary of State was required to give financial guarantees to indemnify Roche, as defendant, should the injunction prove not to have been justified at full trial. This issue was finally resolved in the former's favour,[202] and Roche conceded defeat.

The use of competition law on the one hand and of the statutory order on the other marked a significant departure from the traditional style of British government relations with its home-based pharmaceutical industry. This was to have wider repercussions on the informal approach to profit regulation. Roche refused to come back into the VPRS to negotiate its prices on its other products, and it made threatening noises about the future of its British-based investments. Finally a compromise was reached: Roche agreed to repay to the NHS £3.25 million instead of the £13 million recommended by the MMC, so that increases which would have been allowable under normal VPRS guide-lines would have to be taken into account. The prices of Librium and Valium were halved, and the company agreed to withdraw all legal action against the government. It should be noted, however, that by the time the settlement was announced, the patent on Librium had expired. The government persistently refused to disclose what the price of

Valium would have been under normal VPRS rules, and in any event the price was allowed to rise by some 45 per cent in the following year. Furthermore, the final sum was repaid only in late 1975, allowing the company 5 years to reap the benefits of its excess profits and to take advantage of a 30 per cent depreciation in sterling against the Swiss franc.

Tangentially, it might be mentioned that in order to ensure the completion of the company's proposed vitamin-plant in Scotland, the Labour government provided subsidies totalling some £100 million for a factory which was estimated to have cost some £140 million to construct.[203]

Competition law and generics in France

As I have noted in Chapter 7, the French government chose to place its faith in the promotion of generic competition as a mechanism for reducing public expenditure on drugs in the late 1970s. The manufacturers of branded products were able, eventually, to manipulate the reimbursement system to scuttle this policy, but in the interim the pharmacists also mounted their own campaign. As their fees are calculated at a fixed percentage of a product's price, they were understandably reluctant to stock and to sell cheaper products. Clin-Midy, the parent company whose affiliate LFPG was the target of a nation-wide boycott by pharmacists, lodged a complaint with the Ministry of Finance in early 1980. The Minister was reluctant to risk rendering his government unpopular with a politically powerful profession, and the complaint was taken no further until the issue was revived by the National Federation of Consumers. The Competition Commission[204] finally delivered its opinion in mid-1981, several months after LFPG was put into liquidation. In the light of the overt nature of this boycott, which had been orchestrated by the pharmacists' organizations at national and regional level, the Commission had no difficulty in establishing the existence of a series of concerted agreements whose object and effect was to distort competition within the meaning of Article 50 of the 1945 ordinance. It was required to consider further, however, whether the boycott was justified by the provisions of Article 51(i) which exempted agreements which (i) resulted from the application of a legislative or regulatory text or (ii) had the effect of promoting economic and technical progress. The contention of the pharmacists' organizations that they were prohibited by their professional code of conduct from engaging in competition with one another did not, in the opinion of the Commission, come within the scope of the exemption. It recommended the imposition of a fine of 2 million francs on the national association and fines ranging from 100,000 to 20,000 francs on the regional organizations. It further instructed the national association to complete a full report on the generic market in France within 18 months of the Minister's final decision.[205] These fines, which were duly imposed by the Minister,[206] were the subject of review by the Conseil d'État. The latter confirmed the Commission's opinion that the requirements of the pharmacists' professional code did not justify the boycott.

This ruling has been an important precedent in later cases involving the exercise of exclusive selling arrangements by pharmacists for the sale of parapharmaceutical products and certain 'borderline products' such as milk products for infants, vitamins, and cosmetics.

The effective length of intellectual property rights

As we have seen in the third section of this chapter, the imposition of various forms of 'negative' discrimination against full patent protection for pharmaceuticals has been the rule in the UK and France. The pharmaceutical industry world-wide, however, is now actively seeking 'positive' discrimination in terms of patent rights. The industry protests that because of the increased length of the development phase of a new chemical entity and of the time taken to comply with stricter regulatory requirements, the effective lifespan of a patent for a drug product—that is, from the date of marketing the protected drug until patent expiration—is shorter than its nominal life, which begins with the grant of the patent. Drugs are normally patented at a stage when the commercial potential of an active substance is apparent, but several years may elapse before the various analytical, toxicological, and clinical tests now required by the regulatory authorities have been successfully carried out. A further period of time must elapse before the product clears the administrative hurdles involved in securing a marketing authorization. In France administrative delay prior to marketing is prolonged by negotiations over the price at which a product will be reimbursed by the health funds and, until recently, by the need to obtain prior official clearance for promotional materials. It is generally estimated that the effective life of a patent has been reduced from 20 to between 13 and 8 years, depending on the therapeutic class of product. The firms contend that this is an insufficient period in which to recoup sufficient monopoly profits to support the spiralling costs of innovation. Furthermore, controls on product price prevent the manufacturer's charging high prices when the product is under patent.

These claims have to be examined in the context of the cumulative protection afforded by the various forms of intellectual property rights, which apply not just to a particular product but to its major ingredient or active substance. Even if the proportion of the market protected by patent is shrinking, manufacturers may extend the period of effective monopoly protection either by patenting new presentations or combinations of an active substance or by careful manipulation and extension of their other intellectual property rights, including monopoly rights in brand names, trade-mark rights in a product's get-up,[207] and copyright in package inserts. In addition, national courts[208] and the Enlarged Board of Appeal of the European Patent Office[209] are increasingly disposed to grant 'second application' patents for a new use of a known substance.

The European industry's protestations are perhaps not unrelated to the overall decline in the number of drugs still in patent. In the UK in 1973, for example, about 70 per cent of the sales revenues generated by the top 100 medicines on the British market were protected under current patents. A decade later, and despite the extension of the patent term from 16 to 20 years in 1978, the equivalent proportion had fallen to about 35 per cent.[210] In France the proportion of products which have been on the market for more than 10 years has increased from 32 per cent in 1970 to 50 per cent in 1986.[211]

The French and British governments are broadly sympathetic to the industry's case, as is the EC Commission. The latter recognizes that the problem of effective patent-life will probably increase with the commercialization of products derived from biotechnological processes, and that European innovators will be afforded less protection than their American or Japanese rivals.[212] In the USA the Patent Term Restoration Act 1984 (or Waxman-Hatch Act)[213] extends patent protection to 17 years from the date at which the drug obtains FDA approval.[214] This development not only increases the attractiveness of the USA as a location for research and development but puts US-based firms at a competitive advantage. In the light of the jurisprudence of the European Court of Justice on exhaustion of property rights, an extension of patent term can be meaningful only on a Community-wide basis. Thus if the patent term is extended in the UK but not in Italy, where the product is already on the market, the manufacturing company cannot prevent its importation as it would have already exhausted patent rights.[215]

However, national governments as well as the Commission have limited room for manœuvre when it comes to extending patent term. France and the UK, along with other members of the Community, are parties to the EPC, which restricts the patent term to 20 years.[216] The Commission hopes to secure ratification of the Luxembourg Convention, which provides *inter alia* for a unitary Community patent. The EC would be treated as one country for the purposes of the EPC.[217] Denmark, Ireland, and Greece, however, are not in favour of the strong patent protection which the Community patent offers and have refused to ratify the Luxembourg Convention and the EPC. Any attempt to amend the EPC would be likely to provoke considerable political controversy and would further delay harmonization at EC level. Initially there was also a general reluctance to create a special, exceptional regime for pharmaceuticals, but in autumn 1989 the Commission announced that it was, in fact, considering ways of extending protection for newly patented products.

National law

Other possibilities do exist at national level, however, as the EPC does not regulate the *date* from which protection will run. In France for example, the Socialist government considered varying the patent term by providing that it should run from the date on which the product's AMM was issued, as opposed to the date on which application for the patent was made.[218] This proposal was revived in a private member's bill and was considered, but not adopted, by the Chirac government in December 1987.[219] The obvious difficulty with this approach is that technical and scientific information relating to the product would be kept absolutely secret until marketing authorization had been granted. This would frustrate the disclosure and dissemination of technical knowledge, which is one of the essential roles of the patent system. In addition, scientists who want, and often need, to publish their inventions would be prevented from doing so.

Alternatively, patent term might be calculated from the date at which the patent is granted, and not, as is usual in most EPC countries, from the date at which application is made. This could extend protection by between 18 months and 2 years.[220] A final approach would be to vest the courts or the patent authorities with a discretion to extend the patent term in cases where patentees could make a convincing case that, due to circumstances beyond their control, such as delays in obtaining product licences, they had not been adequately remunerated or rewarded. This possibility in fact existed under the British Patents Act 1949[221] but was not re-enacted in the 1977 legislation as it was considered at the time to be cumbersome and too expensive to be of practical significance for the patentee.[222]

Legislation on product safety

Viewed against the perspective of these constraints, the provisions of EEC directive 87/21, discussed in Chapter 5, which restrict access to the data contained in the original supporting file for a marketing authorization, are recognized as an important compromise solution to the problem of effective patent-life. Access to data may be restricted for a period of 10 years in the case of high-technology products and for 6 years in the case of all other categories, restrictions which will apply after the patent has expired. Most governments think that the additional protection provided by directive 87/21 is sufficient, and both France and the United Kingdom have opted to apply the ten-year period of protection to *all* medicinal products. The recent Dangoumau-Biot inquiry into the French pharmaceutical industry has, however, suggested that the issue of the extension of patent life should be seriously considered as a means of improving the competitive position of French firms.[223]

'Transitional' licences of right and patent life in the UK

Although somewhat idiosyncratic, the extension of patent term for certain patents issued under the 1949 Act is a useful illustration of the British government's reluctance to use patent law as an instrument to control prices or costs. It will be recalled that the Patents Act 1977, which assimilated British patent law more closely to the European systems, extended patent protection from 16 years to 20 years for all patents granted after 1 January 1978. At the time of the 1977 Patent Bill's passage through Parliament, the ABPI actively lobbied for the new provisions to have retroactive effect. The Labour government of the time was initially reluctant to strengthen the industry's oligopolistic structure, especially so soon after the public outcry over Hoffmann-La Roche's profits on Valium and Librium. Extensive negotiations followed, and the Patents Bill was eventually amended to allow the extension of patent term for patents which had more than 5 years to run.[224] Patents subject to these transitional provisions are subject to a compulsory endorsement of licences of right. This procedure allows rival firms, in default of agreement with the patent holder, to apply to the CGP to settle the terms of the licence and the royalties payable. The latter has a wide discretion, subject to considerations of EEC law, to set these terms.[225]

A significant number of patents on market leaders which would otherwise have expired in the period 1984 to 1993 have now been extended, subject to the procedures for compulsory endorsement. Compulsory licences of right have proved an attractive means for parallel importers and generic manufacturers to extend their product range, undercutting the original manufacturer's prices by up to 50 per cent. It is estimated that exploitation of these licences of right will yield savings for the NHS of between £8 million and £200 million per annum in the years from 1988 to 1993.

The possible abolition of these transitional provisions surfaced on the government agenda shortly after the introduction of the Limited List. Once again, adjustment of patent protection was held out as a quid pro quo for the acceptance of new regulatory restrictions. The second Thatcher government subsequently gave its backing to a private member's bill aimed at abolition, but this measure was lost when Parliament dissolved in June 1987. The new government, however, renewed its pledge to the industry, and Clause 266 of the Copyright, Designs and Patents Bill, introduced in the House of Lords in late 1987,[226] provided for the abolition of compulsory endorsement for all patents with more than 15 years to run from the date of commencement of the Act.

The slow progress of this massive bill coincided with renewed debate over health spending and the restructuring of NHS financing. An independent research report, commissioned by several generic manuf.cturers, which estimated the costs of abolition of the compulsory licences to be as high as £200 million per annum, provoked a reconsideration of the issue of patent-life. At one point it seemed that the government would accept an amendment to the bill, tabled by a Labour peer, which would have allowed the continued availability of licences for products which obtained a *product licence* more than 10 years ago. Given the less onerous procedures which obtained at this time, this was felt to be a reasonable compromise, but following further consultations with the ABPI, government backing was withdrawn and the amendment lost. Significantly, the government was unable at any time during the prolonged debates on this issue to produce consistent or convincing estimates of the costs of abolition of special licences of right. The Minister of Health presumed the cost to be modest and went on to argue that it would be more than offset by 'the likely widespread gain in confidence of major pharmaceutical companies prepared to invest in research and manufacture' in the UK.[227] The generic manufacturers failed to win support for a further amendment to the bill in the House of Commons, and the endorsement procedure was duly abolished.[228]

'Transitional' licences of right and European law

Prior to this legislative amendment, the major companies resorted to the courts to try at least to delay generic manufacturers' attempts to exploit compulsory licences. Initially, the latter had attempted to argue that endorsement should be automatic, at the end of the patent's sixteenth year, a view not upheld by the courts.[229] The licence became operative only when CGP had settled its terms. This in effect allowed the companies to drag out negotiation over terms for up to a year after the first application for a licence was made.[230]

Under Section 46(3) of the 1949 Act, the CGP could prohibit importation. The original patentee could in theory obtain an injunction to prevent importation by a compulsory licensee.[231] This issue was of some economic importance to companies who wished to import cheaper products from Italy, where products marketed prior to 1978 did not benefit from patent protection. If the patentee had effectively exhausted his rights under European law and had already placed the product on the market in another country, importation could not in any event be prevented.[232] Where the product had not been marketed by the patentee but manufactured in another country without consent, importation could be restrained as long as the patentee's rights under national law remained extant.[233] But to what extent was the substance of the patentee's exclusive rights modified when the patent was endorsed 'licence of right'? This was the question which the House of Lords put to the European Court of Justice in the long-running case of *Allen and Hanbury Ltd. v. Generics Ltd.*[234] The case concerned Generic's application to import from Italy the highly profitable anti-asthmatic drug Salbutamol, manufactured in the UK by Glaxo and its subsidiary Allen and Hanbury. Generic's selling price would have been considerably reduced if it had not been obliged to buy its raw materials from the patentee, and if the royalty payable had been based on a percentage of the price of the imported material. The Court of Justice held that where an injunction was not available against a domestic manufacturer who applied for a licence of right, 'an injunction against an importer-infringer . . . would constitute arbitrary discrimination prohibited by Article 36 of the Treaty and could not be justified on grounds of the protection of industrial and commercial property'.

The CGP is also required, in default of agreement, to settle the royalties payable by the licensee. The Patents Act 1977 provides little guidance on this matter. Section 50(1)(b) and (c) require that the patentee shall receive reasonable remuneration having regard to the nature of the invention, and that the patentee's interests and those of others working the invention shall not be unfairly prejudiced. The courts have therefore taken the view that it is appropriate to have regard primarily to any existing agreements entered into by the patentees.[235] In consequence, some of the large companies have attempted to set 'reference rates' by voluntarily granting licences to their own subsidiaries with substantially high royalty rates.[236] In addition, the courts have looked at the methods used to calculate royalties under the former Section 41 licences, which required that

the patentee's expenditure on research and development and promotion, as well as basic costs of raw materials, be taken into
account.[237] Obviously, this information can only be supplied by the
patentees, and it is difficult for either the CGP or the applicant to
contest its accuracy. The preferred approach has been to calculate
royalties at a rather high rate of 20 to 25 per cent of the patentee's
selling price.[238] However, where the patentee has failed to supply
sufficient information on costs, the CGP has been prepared to fix
royalties on the basis of the applicant's selling price.[239] For the most
part, the generic companies faced an uphill struggle in attempting
to use the provisions relating to the transitional licences of right to
their full competitive effect.

Conclusion

A combination of the difficulties of applying the general rules of
competition law to the pharmaceutical sector, together with the
rather diffident and pragmatic approach which has characterized
British and, until very recently, French monitoring and enforcement, has meant that controls over cartels and monopoly practices
have played a relatively minor role in this sector. The few instances
where competition laws have been used cannot be described as a
resounding success. On the one hand, restrictions relating to patent
law, particularly the provisions on compulsory licensing, have not
in reality offered third parties the effective means of competing with
the large firms who hold the original patent. Lacking the considerable financial and legal resources of their larger rivals, smaller firms
have usually been discouraged from using the route offered by
compulsory licensing. There appears to be little political will, at
least on the part of the British authorities, to facilitate this form of
competition. Indeed, at least as far as the 'transitional' compulsory
licences are concerned, the intention appears to be to suppress it,
thus reinforcing the emergence of the two-tiered market discussed
in Chapters 2 and 6.

On the other hand, controls provided for in competition law
have not been deployed with any great effect as a supplementary
form of control, to bolster up or counter the weaknesses of the
French and British systems of control on pharmaceutical prices and
profit, as described in Chapters 3, 6, and 7. Indeed, as the brief
account of the Hoffmann-La Roche saga has illustrated, the British

government was forced to abandon its attempts to use legal mechanisms to enforce price reductions on the company and was instead constrained to return to the usual voluntary, bargained approach to control on prices and profits. Until the mid-1980s competition law and policy in France has remained very much the handmaiden of the system of administered price-controls, even although in theory extensive interventionist powers are available to counter anticompetitive practices on the part of pharmaceutical firms.

One possible explanation for the weaknesses of both the French and British system as 'support' mechanisms with which to reinforce product competition in the pharmaceutical sector might lie in the fact that their implementation has followed the dominant patterns observed in the implementation of the specialist price-control regimes. In the UK, competition policy has assumed a pragmatic, *ad hoc* form, implemented in a highly discretionary style through essentially self-regulatory or voluntary agreements with the industries concerned. In France legal controls abound, but, until the reforms of 1985 and 1986, powers to regulate anticompetitive practices were dispersed over a number of institutions, including the Ministry of Finance, the civil, the penal, and the administrative courts. In theory the former Competition Commission might have acted as a co-ordinating institution, but in reality it was too under-staffed and underresourced to fulfil such a role. These themes will be examined in greater depth in the final chapter.

In conclusion, the practical impact of competition law and policy has done nothing to disturb the dominant patterns of product com-petition discussed elsewhere in this book, and the general rules of national law on competition are unlikely to offer a realistic sub-stitute for the present, albeit flawed, system of regulating prices and profits. This chapter has also indicated that, despite the more exten-sive and formal nature of the powers over anticompetitive practices under European law, their practical application to an oligopolisti-cally structured industry is problematic. It was argued in Chapter 5 that the economic position of the large research-based firms in the Community is likely to be strengthened on the completion of the internal market in 1992. The Commission will be required to be increasingly vigilant if the interests of manufacturers in the other tier of the market, the generic tier, are to be at least safeguarded, if not actively promoted. In the following, concluding chapter, and in the light of this foregoing analysis, I will return to the more general problem of regulating for competition.

Notes

1. L. Hancher, 'Regulating Drug Prices in Britain and West Germany', in L. Hancher and M. Moran (eds.), *Capitalism, Culture, and Economic Regulation* (Oxford: OUP, 1989), 79–108.
2. V. Korah, *Competition Law of Britain and the Common Market*, (The Hague: M. Nijhoff, 1982), 1–10.
3. The anticompetitive effects of refusal to supply is a matter of some debate between lawyers and economists alike. See R. Bork, *The Anti-Trust Paradox* (Harvard: Harvard University Press, 1978).
4. P. Hall and J. Hitch, 'Price Theory and Business Behaviour', *Oxford Economic Papers*, (1939), 12–45.
5. Bork, *The Anti-Trust Paradox*, chap. 8.
6. See generally F. Scherer, *Industrial Market Structure and Economic Performance*, 2nd edn. (Cambridge, Mass.: Harvard University Press, 1980), chaps. 5–8.
7. Case 22/78 *Hugin Kassaregister AB* v. *EC Commission* [1979] ECR 1899.
8. See generally A. Dashwood and D. Wyatt, *The Substantive Law of the EEC*, 2nd edn. (London: Sweet and Maxwell, 1987), Part VII.
9. Case 14/68 *Walt Wilhelm* v. *Bundeskatellamt* [1969] ECR 1.
10. This is often known as the STM test, after the Court's decision in Case 56/65 *Société Technique Minière* v. *Maschinenbau Ulm* [1966] ECR 235, and developed in Case 107/82 *AEG-Telefunken* v. *EC Commission* [1983] ECR 3151.
11. Cases 6/73 and 7/73 *Istituto Chemioterapico Italiano and Commercial Solvents Corporation* v. *Commission* [1974] ECR 223.
12. Case 127/73 1974] ECR 62.
13. The doctrine of provisional validity, however, prevents the application of the prohibition in art. 85(1) to, and consequential nullity of, certain agreements, pending a decision by the Commission on the availability of an exemption under art. 85(3).
14. See in particular *Garden Cottage Foods* v. *Milk Marketing Board* [1984] A.C. 130.
15. *Syndicat général des fabricants de semoules de France* v. *Direction des industries agricoles* [1970] CMLR 395.
16. See generally C. D. Edwards, *Trade Regulations Overseas*, (New York: Oceana, 1966), 5–33 for a history of the early legislation.
17. See, for example, the reasoning of the Cour de Cassation in Case 1902, *Comptoir Métallurgique*, approving the activities of a cartel which

controlled over half of France's steel production. (Paris: La Documentation française, Notes et Études, no. 1735, 1955).

18. Although there was speculation that art. 419 might enjoy something of a renaissance after it had been successfully relied upon in the so-called 'Marseilles petroleum cartel case'. See P. Selinksy, 'L'Affaire des pétroliers: la reconquête judicielle du contrôle des ententes', *Cahiers du droit de l'entreprise* (1983), 1.

19. J. G. Castel, 'France' in W. Friedman (ed.) *Antitrust Laws* (London: Stevens, 1956), 112.

20. W. C. Baum, *The French Economy and the State* (Princeton: Princeton University Press, 1958), a report commissioned by the Rand Corporation, described French business as 'something resembling a private corporate state', in which market forces were impaired by 'the pronounced weakness of competitive pressures' and the lukewarm enforcement of laws against restrictive practices.

21. G. Farjat, *Droit économique*, 1st edn. (Paris: PUF, 1974).

22. Baum, *The French Economy and the State*, p. 54.

23. Decree 54-97 of 27 Jan. 1954, as amended by decree 59-1004 of 17 Aug. 1959.

24. Ordinance 67-835 of 28 Sept. 1967, arts. 2 and 3.

25. La Commission technique des ententes et des positions dominantes, *Rapport annuel 1968*, JO Handbook, DA no. 1193/71.

26. Decree 54-97, art. 17.

27. J. Rueff, *Rapport sur la situation financière*. (Paris: La Documentation française, 1959).

28. Circular 65 of 31 Mar. 1954: 'Instruction portant commentaire des dispositions du décret no. 53-704 du 9 août 1953 relative aux ententes professionelles'.

29. Farjat, *Droit économique*, p. 256, notes that whereas the Commission issued about one hundred opinions in the first 14 years of its existence, experts calculated that at least 3,000 restrictive practices were in current use.

30. Ibid. 255.

31. *Rapport annuel 1968*, JO Handbook, DA no. 1193/70.

32. Theoretically, the preamble to the Constitution of 27 Oct. 1946 provides that all firms enjoying a monopoly over the supply of any good or service should be taken into public ownership. The law of 2 July 1963 appended art. 59(2) to ordinance 45-1483 and prohibited the activities of a firm or group of firms which occupied a dominant position on the national market where such activities threatened to prevent the normal functioning of the market.

33. V. G. Venturini, *Monopolies and Restrictive Trade Practices in France* (Leiden: A. W. Sijthoff, 1971).

34. This company form was introduced in the ordinance of 23 Sept. 1967. For an appraisal of its impact on competition policy see F. Jenny and A. Weber, 'Groupement d'intérêt économique et allocation des resources', *Revue française de gestion*, 5 (1976), 69–76. The Technical Commission did, however, critically examine the formation of a number of GIEs, and was prepared to condemn those which it found to be anticompetitive. *Rapport annuel* JO, DA no. 66/74, 2604.

35. F. Jenny and A. P. Weber, *L'Entreprise et les politiques de concurrence* (Paris: Les Éditions d'organisation, 1976).

36. Law 77-806 of 19 July 1977, JO, 20 July 1977, art. 4 provided for an optional notification system for all mergers or take-overs which would result in an enterprise's enjoying more than a 40 per cent share of the national market for substitutable goods and 25 per cent for non-substitutable goods.

37. A. Lyon Caen, 'Le contrôle des concentrations: étude de loi française', *Revue trimestrielle de droit européen*, 15 (1979), 440–65.

38. Circular of 14 Feb. 1978 'relative au contrôle de la concertation économique et à la répression des ententes illicites et des abuses de position dominante', BOSP 6, 17 Feb. 1978.

39. C. Bolze, 'L'Ineffectivité du Titre II de la loi du 19 Juillet 1977 sur le contrôle des concentrations ou le naufrage du droit anti-trust français', in *Études dédiées à Roblot* (Paris: Librairie générale de droit et de jurisprudence, 1984), 181 ff.

40. Commission de la concurrence, *Rapport annuel*, 1984, (Paris: La Documentation française, 1984).

41. R. Whish, *Competition Law* (London: Butterworths, 1985), 18.

42. D. C. Elliot and J. D. Gribbin, 'The abolition of Cartels and Structural Change in the UK', in A. Jacquemin and H. de Jong (eds.), *Welfare Aspects of Industrial Markets* (Leiden: Leiden Publishing Company, 1977). D. Swann, D. P. O'Brien, P. Maunder, and B. Howe, *Competition in British Industry* (London: Allen & Unwin, 1974).

43. See, for example, the conclusions of the Balfour Committee on Trade and Industry, Cmd. 3282 (London: HMSO, 1932).

44. Cmnd. 6527 (London: HMSO, 1944).

45. C. K. Rowley, *The British Monopolies Commission*, (London: Allen and Unwin, 1966), 21–34.

46. See further Whish, *Competition Law*, pp. 36–40.

47. (1950–51) H.C. 18.

48. (1951–52) H.C. 296.

49. The Monopolies and Mergers Act 1965.

50. A. C. Neale and D. Goyder, *The Anti-Trust Laws of the USA* 3rd edn. (Cambridge: Cambridge University Press, 1981), 494.

51. *A Review of Monopolies and Mergers Policy*, Cmnd. 7198 (London:

HMSO, 1978), para. 3.46.
52. Reduced from 33 per cent in the Fair Trading Act of 1973. Sects. 6–11 of the Fair Trading Act 1973 provide the statutory definition of monopolization.
53. Whish, *Competition Law*, pp. 50–5.
54. See further *A Review of Restrictive Trade Practices Policy*, Cmnd. 7512 (HMSO: London, 1979), 20.
55. Sect. 1(1) RPM Act 1976.
56. Sect. 9 RPM Act 1976.
57. *Re Medicaments Reference (No. 2)* [1971] All E.R. 12, R.P.C.
58. Sect. 10(1) of the Act provided that 'particulars of agreements shall be furnished to the Registrar', but stipulated no penalty for failure to do so.
59. Sect. 7 of the Restrictive Trade Practices Act 1967. A cause of action was also conferred on parties claiming to be harmed by the operation of any such agreement.
60. On the background to the 1956 Act, see Allen, *Monopoly and Restrictive Practices*, 89–92. In his autobiography, Lord Kilmuir, who was Lord Chancellor at this time, describes the problems he experienced in overcoming the judges' anxiety about their becoming involved in complex economic problems. *Political Adventure*, 1964.
61. The most celebrated of which is *Re Yarn Spinners' Agreement* [1959] All E.R. 299, R.P.C.
62. For a review of the possible routes of escape, see J. Lever, 'Bipartite Agreements and the Restrictive Trade Practices Acts', *Law Quarterly Review*, 85 (1969), 177–91.
63. See JO, Débats, Assemblée nationale, 10 June 1977, 3617 ff. and JO, Débats Sénat, 29 June 1977, 1838 ff.
64. In a letter of 31 May 1978 M. Barre, the Prime Minister, contended that the new Commission was 'une autorité administrative de type quasi-jurisdictionnel, puisque chargée d'exercer une véritable magistrature économique', on which the law conferred 'des pouvoirs propres d'investigation et prévoit qu'elle peut se saisir d'office'.
65. Art. 53(3) of ordinance 45-1483 as amended by the law of 1977.
66. M. Glais, 'Six ans de répression des ententes illicites et des abus de position dominante: un bilan de l'activité de la Commission de la concurrence', *Revue trimestrielle de droit commercial*, 2 (1984) 420–54.
67. F. Bloch-Laine, *La France en Mai 1981. Commission du Bilan*, 2. *Les Grands Équilibres économiques* (Paris: La Documentation française, 1982), 19–25.
68. Art. 7 of decree 77-1189 of 25 Oct. 1977 in JO, 26 Oct. 1977. Certain provisions of this decree were annulled by the Conseil d'État in its

decision of 13 Mar. 1981. 'Ordres des avocats et autres', *Gazette du Palais* 21 May 1982, note Gohin.

69. For example, in a case concerning collusive tendering by cable manufacturers for contracts put out by the PTT (Postes, Télégraphes, Téléphones), the Minister considerably reduced the fines recommended by the Commission on the grounds that the concerted practices in question had not adversely affected prices (decisions 1239 and 1249 BOSP, Dec. 1984). In the famous 'perfumes' litigation, the Minister, contrary to the advice of the Commission, found that the selective distribution agreements in question were not anticompetitive. (decision 1189 BOSP, Nov. 1984).

70. Decree 85-909 of 28 Aug. 1985, in JO, 29 Aug. 1985; law 85-1408 of 30 Dec. 1985, in JO, 31 Dec. 1985.

71. Art. 4 of the law of 30 Dec. 1986 abolished the different thresholds applicable to horizontal, vertical, and conglomerate mergers. The new threshold is 25 per cent of the relevant market, whether national or local. The former distinction between substitutable and non-substitutable goods also disappeared.

72. J. Azéma, 'Droit français de la concurrence', *La Semaine juridique*, 15185, 20 Feb. 1986, 72.

73. D. Achach, 'La Nouvelle Législation de la concurrence', *Revue de la concurrence*, 5 (1986), 7–11.

74. Art. 17, however, allows fines and/or prison sentences to be inflicted in cases where a natural person has wilfully engaged in a concerted practice with fraudulent intent. The Conseil de la concurrence is empowered to transfer such a case to the public prosecutor. Art. 31–5, regulating the types of practices which were formerly known as individual prohibitions, provides for the imposition of fines by the civil courts.

75. Art. 36, however, allows certain discriminatory practices, practised by an 'isolated economic agent', to be the subject of an action in the ordinary civil courts. It would seem that an individual company could fall within art. 7 of the ordinance, which prohibits certain forms of restrictive agreement or collusive behaviour, if the firm has collaborated with others. In addition the firm could be sued for damages in the civil courts.

76. Art. 1.2. Art. 61 also provides that certain sectoral price controls would remain in force for a transitional period. Hence *arrêtés* 83-9/A of Feb. 1984, 84-55/A of 29 June 1984, and 86-31/A of 10 July 1986 on the price of pharmaceutical products reimbursed by the social security institutions remain in force.

77. A number of commentators had suggested that greater certainty might have been introduced into French law on restrictive practices if the EC

practice of notification and exemption had been adopted. Instead, the 1986 law only provides for the possibility of block exemptions (art. 10(2)).

78. Sect. 2(1). The Liesner Committee had noted in chap. 6 of its report that various practices by single firms were often outside the remit of either the Fair Trading Act, which required that the firms had to hold a large degree of market power, or the RTPA 1976, which only condemned *horizontal* and not *vertical* restraints.

79. T. Sharpe, 'Refusal to Supply', *Law Quarterly Review*, 99 (1983), 37–67.

80. Cm. 331, para. 4.2.

81. The classic expression of this philosophy is to be found in the Commission's *First Report on Competition Policy* (Luxembourg, 1972).

82. Sherman Act, sect. 1.

83. Case 258/78 *L C Nungesser KG* v. *EC Commission* [1982] ECR 2015, and Case 262/81 *Coditel* v. *Cine Vog Films* [1982] ECR 3381.

84. Cases 202-213/84 *Ministère Public* v. *Lucas Asjes and others* [1986] ECR 1425.

85. Case 31/80 *L'Oréal* [1980] ECR 3793.

86. Case 86/76 [1979] ECR 461.

87. Case 3232/81 *Michelin* v. *Commission* [1983] ECR 3461. The narrow approach to market definition has met with considerable criticism, and some commentators have suggested that the proper approach to the issue is to recognize that firms can face competition from within and from outside the relevant market. See further V. Korah, 'The Concept of a Dominant Position within the meaning of Article 86' C.M.L.Rev., 17 (1980), 395–411; L. Gyselen and N. Kyriazis, 'Article 86: The Monopoly Power Issue Revisited', E.L.Rev. 11 (1986), 134–49.

88. Fair Trading Act 1973, sects. 48(d) and 54(2).

89. MMC, *Chlorodiazepoxide and Diazepam*, (London: HMSO, 1973).

90. *Rapport annuel 1978*, p. 11.

91. Glais, 'Six ans de répression', p. 425.

92. Decision 83-4 DC, BOCC, 31 Aug. 1933, 249–53.

93. The application of controls on cartels to cases of collusive conduct, in the absence of any overt agreement between oligopolistic firms, is more complex and cannot be considered here. See further Whish *Competition Law*.

94. Sect. 6(1) of the Fair Trading Act 1973 defines a complex monopoly situation.

95. *Breakfast Cereals*, (1972–3) HC 2; *Household Detergents* (1965–6) HC 105; *Tampons* Cmnd. 8049, 1980; See also its special report on *Parallel Pricing*, Cmnd. 5330, 1973.

96. Art. 50 of ordinance 1483 of 30 June 1945, as re-enacted in art. 7 of

ordinance 86-1243 of 1 Dec. 1986.

97. Glais, 'Six ans de répression', p. 422.

98. Case 48/69 *ICI* v. *Commission* [1972] ECR 619; Case 40/73 *Suiker Unie* v. *EC Commission* [1975] ECR 1663; Case 35/83 *CRAM* v. *Commission* [1984] ECR 1679.

99. *Re European Sugar Cartel* OJ 1973 L 140/17.

100. Case 85/76 [1979] ECR 461.

101. Whish, *Competition Law* p. 401.

102. Case 22/71 *Béguelin Import* v. *G.L. Import Export* [1971] ECR 959.

103. Commission decision of 25 Nov. 1980, OJ 1980, L 377.

104. Commission decision of 13 July, OJ 1987, L 222; Case 277/87 *Sandoz* v *Commission*, judgment of 11 Jan. 1990.

105. See the Commission's *13th Annual Report on Competition Policy* (Luxembourg, 1984), points 217 and 218. It has also stressed that authorities in member states may enforce the competition rules by virtue of art. 9(3) of regulation 17/62, *Journal officiel des Communautés européennes* (1962), 204: OJ (special edn.) 1959–62, 87.

106. The government's recent Green Paper on restrictive practices does, however, make provision for fines to be levied on parties to anti-competitive agreements. (DTI, *A Review of Restrictive Trade Practices Legislation*, Cm. 331 (London: HMSO, 1988), para. 6.1.)

107. Fair Trading Act sect. 56(1) and Competition Act sect. 10(1) empowers the Secretary of State to exercise by order any of the powers listed in sched. 8 to the Fair Trading Act. The most extreme measure is divestiture, countenanced by para. 14 of sched. 8, a power which has never in fact been used.

108. See D. P. O'Brien, 'Competition Policy in Britain: The Silent Revolution', *Anti-Trust Bulletin*, 27 (1982), 218–38; and the rejoinder by G. Borrie, 'British Competition Law', *International Journal of Law and Economics*, 2 (1983), 139–49.

109. Fair Trading Act sect. 88(4); Competition Act sect. 9(1).

110. Sects. 4(1) and 5(1) of the Competition Act.

111. A. Boyer, 'Form as Substance: A Comparison of Antitrust Regulations', *International Comparative Law Quarterly*, 32 (1983), 904–29.

112. Regulation 17 of 1962, as amended. On average about sixty formal decisions are handed down each year, and at the end of 1983 the Commission had over 4,100 cases pending, 62 per cent of which concerned patent licensing agreements, 25 per cent distribution agreements, and 13 per cent horizontal agreements. See *13th Annual Report on Competition Policy*, (Luxembourg, 1984), point 80.

113. See the opinion of Advocate General Reischl in Case 31/80 *L'Oréal* v. *De Nieuwe AMCK* [1980] ECR 3803.

114. Although they are entitled to take the letters into account in reaching

their own conclusions on the applicability of arts. 85(1) or 86. Joined Cases 253/78 and 1-3/79 *Procureur de la République* v. *Giny and Guerlain* [1980] ECR 2327.

115. Arts. 19(3) of regulation 17.

116. However, the Court has held that the complainant cannot insist on the Commission's reaching a final decision, Case 125/78 *GEMA* v. *EC Commission* [1979] ECR 3173. Furthermore the Commission's final decision would not be addressed to it, as is required for action for failure to act under art. 175(3). Case 246/81 *Bethell* v. *EC Commission* [1982] ECR 2277.

117. See *12th Report on Competition Policy* (Luxembourg, 1983), point 72, and the Commission's practice note, OJ 1982 C 343/4.

118. Case 26/76 *Metro* v. *Commission (no. 1)* [1977] ECR 1875.

119. The earliest block exemption measure, regulation 67/67 (*Journal officiel des Communautés européennes* (1967), 849; OJ 1967, 10), applied to exclusive distribution and exclusive purchasing agreements. This was replaced by two regulations which came into force on 1 July 1983. Exclusive distribution agreements are regulated by regulation 1983/84 (OJ L 173/1) and exclusive purchasing by regulation 1984/84 (OJ 1984 L 101/2). Regulation 417/85 applies to specialization agreements. (OJ 1985 L 53/1) and regulation 418/85 to research and development agreements. (OJ 1985 L 53/5). Regulation 2349/84 on patent licensing agreements and know-how came into force on 1 January 1985 (OJ 1984 L 219/5).

120. Whish, *Competition Law*, p. 354.

121. *Pharmaceutical Journal*, 20 Apr. 1984, 2.

122. K. Hopt, 'Restrictive Practices', in G. Teubner (ed.), *The Juridification of Social Spheres* (Berlin: De Gruyter, 1987), 291–332.

123. F. Machlup and E. Penrose, 'The Patent Controversy in the Nineteenth Century', *Journal of Economic History*, 10 (1950), 1–29.

124. The recent interest in patent reform in France appears to have been stimulated by the provisions of the Law on the Orientation and Planning for Research and Technical Development (*Loi d'orientation et de programmation pour la recherche et le devéloppement technologique*) of 15 July 1982, which aimed to promote the industrial use of scientific research. This was followed by the Minister of Industry's announcement of 3 Aug. 1983, in the Council of Ministers, of twenty measures designed, *inter alia*, to improve access to patents, to promote the utility of patent protection to scientists, and to secure wider diffusion of the technical contents of patents. (The text of this announcement is reproduced in the *Bulletin de droit et pharmacie*, (Vie Juridique), 2 (1984), 17.) In the following year reforms to the 1978 Patent Act were implemented strengthening

rights to oppose patent infringement. Law 84-500 of 27 June 1984, in JO, 28 June 1984.

125. P. Mathely, *Le Droit français des brevets d'invention* (Paris: Journal des notaires et des avocats, 1974), 228.

126. Law 68-1 of 2 January 1968 'sur les brevets d'invention', in JO 3 Jan. 1968.

127. See the debates on the introduction of the 1968 law and the statement of M. Herzog, JO, Débats parlémentaires, Sénat, 1 Dec. 1967, p. 1997.

128. Art. 3.

129. Art. 6. Art. 9 defines the inventive step (activité inventive) as follows: 'une invention est consoderée come impliquant une activité inventive si elle ne découle pas d'une manière évidente de l'état de la technique'.

130. Art. 8.

131. Art. 19.

132. Mathely, *Le Droit français des bievets d'intervention*, p. 187–89.

133. Law 78-742 of 13 July 1978, in JO, 14 July 1978.

134. Art. 19, in conjunction with arts. 16b bis and 8.

135. See, for example, Rapport du Conseil Économique et Social, *La place et l'importance des transferts techniques dans les échanges extérieures*, JO, 19 Aug. 1982.

136. Institut national de la propriété industrielle, *Rapport annuel 1984* (Paris: INPI, 1985).

137. Convention on the Grant of European Patents, Munich, 5 Oct. 1973, Cmnd. 5656 (London: HMSO, 1974).

138. Patents and Designs Act 1909.

139. L. F. Haber, *The Chemical Industry, 1900–1980* (Oxford: Clarendon Press, 1981).

140. Art. 3 excluded 'compositions pharmaceutiques et remèdes de toute espèce'.

141. Legal debate over their potential application to drug manufacture in France was brought to an end by the enactment of a law of 27 January 1944 which explicitly granted process patents for such processes. In a number of countries such as Denmark, Greece, and Spain patents remain available only on the processes for manufacturing the product and not on the product itself.

142. As applied by a decree of 30 May 1960. Art. 1 of this decree provided that a medicinal product was patentable in accordance with the terms of the law of 1844, subject to certain exceptions. In particular, art. 3 provided that a product would be considered 'novel' only if it was presented for the first time as having therapeutic qualities. Thus if a product had already been patented as a treatment for one form of disease, its application as a treatment for another type or category of

diseases was not patentable.

143. See, for example, R. Lemay, 'Les Médicaments: particularités du brevet', *Droit social* 1 (1971), 7–25.
144. Art. 12 of the Strasbourg Convention, to which France is a signatory, provides that medicines should become fully patentable in all contracting states after a ten-year transitional period.
145. *Schering's Application* [1971] R.P.C. 337.
146. Arts. 32 and 53.
147. Codifying amendments introduced by decree 53-970 of 30 Sept. 1953.
148. Arts. 32 and 33 of the law of 1968, as amended by arts. 17 and 18 of the law of 1978.
149. TGI 6 June 1973 *Dalloz Sirey* 1974 J., 179, note J. Azema.
150. Decree 69-975 of 18 Oct. 1969 'relatif aux licenses obligatoires', JO, 18 Oct. 1969.
151. Sect. 48(1) Patents Act.
152. *R.* v. *Comptroller General of Patents, ex parte Gist Brocades NV* [1986] 1 W.L.R. 62, 63 (H.L.).
153. Sect. 51 of the Patents Act 1977, which provides for a special procedure for remedying particular matters relating to licensing found to be contrary to the public interest by the MMC, will be discussed below.
154. From 1977 to 1983 there had been twelve applications, one of which had been granted. See Cmnd. 9917, *The Reform of Intellectual Property Law*, (London: HMSO, 1984), 28.
155. See further W. R. Cornish, *Intellectual Property Law* (London: Sweet and Maxwell, 1981), 252.
156. *Kambourian's Patent* 1961] R.P.C. 403; *Robin Electric Lamp Co's Petition* [1915] 32 R.P.C. 202.
157. See further Cmnd. 9917, (London: HMSO, 1984), pp. 28–30.
158. See, for example, the MMC's discussion on this point in its report *Ford Motor Company Ltd.* Cmnd. 9437 (London: HMSO, 1985), para. 6.70.
159. Art. 39 as amended by art. 21 of the 1978 law.
160. Chapter III of decree 69-975 requires a decision of the Council of State.
161. One of the largest companies affected, Pfizer, sued the Ministry of Health—unsuccessfully—for infringement of its UK patent rights. *Pfizer Corporation* v. *Minister of Health* [1965] R.P.C. 261.
162. Hence a *licence spéciale obligatoire* was provided for by decree 53-971 of 30 Sept. 1953, in JO, 1 Oct. 1953, which governed the issue of process patents for drug manufacture, and by the ordinance of 4 Feb. 1959 establishing the BSM.

163. Art. 20 of the law of 1978.
164. Art. 38 of the law of 1968, as applied by arts. 7 and 9 of decree 69-975 of 18 Oct. 1969.
165. *Le Monde*, 6 Sept. 1975.
166. Activity under sect. 41 was fairly slight. Between 1958 and 1968, forty-one applications were filed, twenty-three of which were in the years 1963–4. A further twenty-two applications were filed in 1969–70. C. Taylor and Z. A. Silberson, *The Economic Impact of the Patent System*, (Cambridge: Cambridge University Press, 1975), 17.
167. *Hoffmann-La Roche* v. *DDSA* 1965 R.P.C. 1.
168. *ICI* v. *Berk* [1963] R.P.C. 302.
169. Lord Sainsbury, *Report of the Committee of Enquiry into the Relationship of the Pharmaceutical Industry with the NHS*, Cmnd. 3410 (London: HMSO, 1967).
170. Report of the Committee of Inquiry into the Patent System, Cmnd. 4467 (London: HMSO, 1970).
171. Ibid. pp. 112–18.
172. *Kalwar/Plast Control* v. *Kabelmetal*, Twelfth Report on Competition Policy, 1982, point 87. However the *effect* of compulsory licensing may be achieved by virtue of the direct effect in national law of art. 85(1). In *British Leyland* v. *T. I. Silencers*, the Court of Appeal ruled that if an exclusive licence is found to contravene art. 85 at full trial in the UK, an injunction may not be granted against any person whose use is unauthorized, but that further use will be permitted only on payment of a reasonable royalty to the patentee ([1981] F.S.R. 213). Some commentators argue that it may therefore be presumed that the same principle would operate where the patentee is found to be in breach of art. 86 by not issuing licences at all. (R. Merkin and K. Williams), *Competition Law* (London: Sweet and Maxwell, 1984), 320.
173. Case 19/84 *Pharmon* v. *Hoechst* [1985] 3 CMLR 775.
174. Sched. 3, para. 5 expressly exempts licences. In addition, the licensing of a proprietary right has been considered by the courts not to amount to a supply of services or goods for the purposes of the RTPA: *Ravenseft Properties* v. *Director General of Fair Trading* [1977] 1 All E.R. 47.
175. See ministerial statement on clause 16 of the Competition Bill, Hansard HC Committee Report 13 Dec. 1979, cols 673–5. Clause 16 became Sect. 14 CA 1980.
176. See the ministerial statements made in connection with the Competition Bill, HC Committee Report 22 Nov. 1979, cols. 383–5.
177. See MMC, *Chlorodiazepoxide and Diazepam*, pp. 58–9.
178. Avis du 17 Octobre 1955 *Entente dans l'industrie du Magnesium*;

avis du 17 mars 1971, *Casiers à bouteilles en matières plastiques*, quoted in Farjat, *Droit économique*, p. 254.

179. Avis du 26 mai 1983, BOSP 8 Nov. 1983, and Commission de la concurrence, *Rapport au Ministre de l'économie et des finances pour l'année 1983* (Paris: Direction des Journaux Officiels, 1984), 21.

180. K. R. Mirow and H. Maurer, *Webs of Power* (Boston: Houghton Mifflin, 1982); J. Braithwaite, *Corporate Crime and the Pharmaceutical Industry* (London: Routledge & Kegan Paul, 1984).

181. Mirow and Maurer, *Webs of Power*, p. 126.

182. *Wall Street Journal*, 23 Jan. 1973.

183. *European Chemical News*, 9 July 1976, quoted in Mirow and Maurer.

184. Commission's Patent Notice; this Notice has now been withdrawn: OJ 1984 C 220/4.

185. Cases 56/64 and 58/64 [1966] ECR 299.

186. *Re Davidson's Rubber Co*, [1972] OJ L 143/31: [1972] CMLR D52.

187. In Case 24/67 *Parke, Davis and Co. Ltd* v. *Probel* [1968] ECR 55, the Court made it clear that the doctrine of exhaustion may apply equally to patent licences.

188. Case 15/74 [1974] ECR 1162.

189. For the Commission's view, see its decision in *Re AOIP/Beyrard* OJ 1976 L 6/8 and for the Court, Case 258/78 *Nungesser*, [1982] ECR 2015. See further Dashwood and Wyatt, *The Substantive Law*, 504.

190. R. Guy and D. Leigh, *The EEC and Intellectual Property*, (London: Sweet and Maxwell, 1981).

191. Case 258/78 *LC Nungesser KG* v. *EC Commission* [1982] ECR 2015, and Case 198/83 *Windsurfing International* v. *Commission* [1986] CMLR 489.

192. J. Venit, 'The New Block Exemption for Patent Licensing' *Anti-Trust Bulletin*, 31 (1986), 1–45; R. Stone, 'The Block Exemption for Patent Licences' *European Intellectual Property Law Review*, 5 (1986), 21–7; J. S. Venit, 'The Community's Opposition Procedure' C.M.L.Rev. 22 (1985), 167–202.

193. OJ 1979 C 58/12.

194. V. Korah, 'Proposal for a Group Exemption for Patent Licences', E.L.Rev. 4 (1979), 206–12.

195. OJ 1984 L 219/15.

196. Initially, the DHSS had accepted a series of one-off cash repayments as well as free supplies of Valium and Librium for hospital and army use.

197. Patent protection for pharmaceutical products was unavailable in Italy until 1978.

198. A series of legal actions over whether a compulsory licence could be

extended to *imported* products as well as products manufactured by the applicants delayed the award of the licence for 5 years.

199. *Hoffmann-La Roche's Patent* [1969] R.P.C. 517.
200. Monopolies and Mergers Commission, *Chlordiazepoxide and Diazepam* (London: HMSO, 1973), 21.
201. Regulation of Prices (Tranquillising Drugs) (No. 3) Order 1973 S.I. 1093/1973. Under the 1948 Act any order presented to Parliament would lapse unless positively approved within 28 days. Sect. 134 of the Fair Trading Act 1973 changed the procedure so that the order automatically comes into effect unless voted down within 40 days.
202. *Hoffmann-La Roche* v. *Secretary of State for Trade* [1974] 2 All ER 1128.
203. This sum included £46 million under the Industry Act 1972, sects. 7 and 8, an additional £1.4 million under the Railways Act 1974, plus further subsidies from the Scottish Development Agency to meet the cost of site development. See further Hansard, 12 Dec., vol. 975, col. 658 and M. Sharp and M. Brech, *Inward Investment* (London: Routledge & Kegan Paul, 1984), 118.
204. The 1977 legislation empowered certain interest groups to refer anti-competitive practices to the Commission.
205. BOCC, Avis de la Commission de la concurrence, 17 July 1981, 191–8.
206. Décision no. 81/07/DC du ministre relative à des pratiques concertées de pharmaciens pour s'opposer à la commercialisation de médicaments génériques.
207. *Smith, Kline & French's Applications* [1976] R.P.C. 511.
208. For example, the Federal Supreme Court in Germany recognized patents for a new use in *Hydropyride*, (15 IIC 215 (1984)), and the British courts have been prepared to interpret sect. 14(2) of the 1977 Patents Act to allow patentability for a new use: *Re Schering's Patent* [1985] R.P.C.
209. In its decision in *Bayer* (5 Dec. 1984, *Official Journal of the European Patent Office* (1985), 60, 64, 67; 16 *International Review of Industrial Property and Copyright Law*, 83 (1985)) the Board ruled that a European patent may be granted with claims directed to the use of a substance or composition for the manufacture of a medicine for a specified new and inventive therapeutic application. See generally K. Bruchhausen, 'The Second Medical Use of Medicaments in European Patent Law' 16 *International Review of Industrial Property and Copyright Law*, (1985), 306–18.
210. *The Economist*, 7 February 1987.
211. P. Weisenhorn, 'Rapport au nom de la commission de la production et des échanges sur la proposition de loi no. 982 tendant à assurer

aux médicaments une durée de protection identique aux autres produits', Assemblée nationale report 1092, 1987–8.

212. EFPIA, *Biotechnology and the European Pharmaceutical Industry*,
(Brussels: EFPIA, 1984).

213. Sect. 156.

214. Research in the USA contended that the extensive tests required
under the 1962 amendments to the Food and Drugs Act had reduced
the effective patent life of new chemical entities introduced in the
years 1966 to 1973 to 13.1 years. See D. Schartzman *Innovation in
the Pharmaceutical Industry* (Baltimore: The John Hopkins University Press, 1976), 180 ff.

215. The European Court has, however, recently decided, in a case concerning divergent periods of copyright protection in different member states, that the importation of products from a country where the
duration of protection is shorter can be prohibited 'if the protection
period is inseparably linked with the existence of the exclusive rights
themselves'. Case 341/87, *EMI Electrola v. Patricia Import and
Export GmbH* [1989] 2 CMLR 413, 423.

216. Art. 63.

217. The Convention for the European Patent for the Common Market,
Luxembourg, 15 Dec. 1975, Cmnd. 6553, 1976 (HMSO: London,
1976), arts. 1 and 2.

218. See the declaration of M. E. Hervé, then Secretary of State for Health,
to the Assembly on the International Federation of the Pharmaceutical Industry, 18 Oct. 1984.

219. Proposition de loi 982, M. B. C. Savy (Journal Doc. Sénat, 1987).

220. See L. Osterborg, 'Patent Term à la Carte' *International Review of
Industrial Property and Copyright Law*, 17 (1986), 60–80.

221. Sect. 23.

222. See T. Blanco White, *Patents for Inventions*, 4th edn. (London:
Stevens, 1974), 604.

223. *Le Monde*, 15 Apr. 1989.

224. Sect. 46 of the Patents Act 1977: sched. 1, para. 4(2).

225. In *Re Gist Brocades NV*, Court of Appeal, Times Law Reports, 8
June 1985.

226. House of Lords Bill 12, 1987.

227. House of Lords Debates, 12 January 1988.

228. *Financial Times*, 21 June, 1988.

229. *In Re Gist-Brocades NV and Another*, Financial Times Law Reports,
29 Mar. 1985.

230. It would seem, however, that the applicant is *not* obliged first to
negotiate with the patentee before applying to the CPG to settle the
terms of the licence. See the application for a licence of right by

Harris Pharmaceuticals, Patent Office decision 0/169/86, 25 Nov. 1986.

231. Sect. 61 governs the right to bring proceedings for infringement. Sect. 60 lays down what constitutes infringement for the purposes of the Patents Act 1977.

232. Case 15/74 *Centrafarm* v. *Sterling Drug* [1974] E.C.R. 1823.

233. Case 187/80 *Merck* v. *Stephar* [1981] E.C.R. 2063.

234. Case 434/85, judgment of 3 Mar. 1988, not yet reported.

235. This was the approach adopted by the High Court in *Generics* v. *Allen and Hanbury* [1984] CMLR 621.

236. *The Guardian*, 8 Apr. 1986, 3.

237. *Geigy's Patent* [1964] R.P.C. 391.

238. An approach recommended by Whitford J. in the *Allen and Hanbury* case. The normal royalty rate for non-pharmaceutical products appears to be between 5 and 7 per cent, but the patent office and the courts justify the higher rate for pharmaceuticals as a necessary reward for past R. & D.

239. *In the matter of an application by Harris Pharmaceuticals for a licence of right*, decision of the Patent Office O/140/86, 16 Sept. 1986.

10

Regulating for Competition: An Impossible Goal?

In this concluding chapter I return to a discussion and evaluation of the three major themes of this study, outlined in Chapter 1 and developed in the subsequent chapters. The first subject to be examined was the impact of regulation on competitive processes and market structure, and the persistence of recurring tension between regulation and competition. Secondly, it was contended that national variations in the way in which the public–private divide is conventionally drawn in the practice of regulation should form a major focus for comparative study. In particular, it was hypothesized that these variations find expression in the diversity of mechanisms, instruments, and techniques of regulation present in each country under study. The third and related theme was the contribution of legal factors to the creation and institutionalization of patterns of relations between government and industry.

I argued in Chapter 1 that regulation must be understood and analysed above all as a dynamic process. In approaching its study from this perspective, I have attempted to establish the links between these three themes. The relationship between regulator and regulated, I have stressed, is in a constant state of change. As market structures have altered, regulatory goals have undoubtedly grown more complex in the 40 years since price controls were first adopted by the British and French governments. Despite this growing complexity and the various tensions between regulator and regulated induced by it, one particular dilemma has remained constant throughout this period: the regulator's persistent quest to design suitable mechanisms with which to promote and secure efficient competition within the sector. This task has found a new expression in the last decade in the context of a more complex market structure, as governments strive to formulate and implement more effective techniques of cost control.

Chapter 1 suggested that it is the dynamic aspect of regulation which sets in motion a continual process of interest intermediation between regulator and regulated, as new issues are forced on to the regulatory agenda. The changing forces of competition within the market can also offer regulators the opportunity to develop new techniques of control or to refine existing ones. In the pharmaceuticals sector the ability of regulators to resolve new conflicts, as well as the potential to fashion new techniques of control, has, however, been constrained in several ways. Firstly, it must be acknowledged that the impact of regulation on competitive processes has not been identical in the two countries studied here. One striking contrast to emerge here between the UK and France is the extent to which strict regulatory control has for many years insulated the French-based firms from competition and from the gradual changes taking place in the European market; the French domestic market appears to have been sealed off from the processes of adjustment taking place in the UK. Whereas emergent competition from generic manufacturers and parallel importers has provided the UK government with some leverage with which to bargain with British-based firms over policies of profit control, the French government has been denied similar opportunities; the industry had no incentive to bargain and negotiate. This is not to say that successive French governments have been able to neglect the competitive dimension of regulation. Indeed, as has been argued in Chapters 3, 4, and 7, there has been a consistent concern over the decline in the international standing of the industry. This has become more acute with the impending impact of the industry's greater exposure to competition as the EC forges ahead with its plans to complete the internal market for pharmaceutical products by 1992.

A second constraint on adjustment, discussed in Chapters 3, 4, 6, and 7, is related to the very different techniques of control and regulation in the UK and France, and is reflected in the divergent attitudes to the exercise of public authority, and to the participation of private interests in the regulatory process. The ability of government regulators to respond rapidly to new opportunities, to exploit changes in the market, and consequently to refine or reform their existing interventionist tools depends in part on the nature and extent of the powers which they have generally enjoyed in the past. In this respect, a common feature of government intervention in both France and the UK has been the extensive discretionary powers vested in the executive and the relative exclusion of Parliament from this sphere of government activity. Nevertheless, there are important differences in the legal form in which these executive powers have been couched, and this in turn has had an important impact on the extent of the discretion which bureaucrats have enjoyed in practice to adjust to changing market situations.

Where regulatory mechanisms are expressed in formal legal rules, as, for example, in the case of the former system of pharmaceutical price control in France, the process of regulatory adjustment, reform, and even refinement has proved complex, requiring protracted and often public negotiations between the relevant government ministers, even if the French Parliament has had no formal role in the process. In the UK, on the other hand, profit control has always assumed a non-legal, voluntaristic form. This has allowed the DHSS officials who are responsible for its implementation enormous discretion to renegotiate, and to alter fundamentally, the terms of the Pharmaceutical Price Regulation Scheme on several occasions in the last 30 years. Moreover, it has accomplished this in almost complete secrecy.

The third constraint is the related but arguably more powerful one imposed by the relationships of interdependence which these divergent techniques of control have engendered in each country. The absence of effective formal legal controls over the exercise of discretionary power by government was discussed in Chapters 6 and 7. The scope for disgruntled firms and their representative associations to challenge the legality of new cost-containment measures in their respective national courts was seen to be minimal. Legal challenges to the introduction of the Limited List in the UK, for example, or to the French government's nationalization programme, were of little avail. It cannot, however, be assumed that regulators are completely free to respond to changes in market structure in whatever manner they choose, refining their techniques of control accordingly. Indeed, it has been emphasized at numerous stages in this study that the various techniques of regulation discussed in the preceding chapters have engendered relationships of different degrees of interdependence between regulator and regulated. To a varying extent, governments in the UK and France have co-opted industry into the process of implementing regulation. Consequently, the former are rarely free to respond to change, if and when it arises. Adjustment is usually negotiated, and this has functioned as a far more effective constraint on the regulator's room for manœuvre. Nor has this process of negotiation and bargaining necessarily been confined to any single regulatory regime; policy trade-offs can be accomplished across the broader spectrum of the entire regulatory relationship between government and industry.

While this book may be read primarily as a comparative study of regulating for competition in the British and French pharmaceutical sectors, it is hoped that by stressing the broader legal aspects of these constraints on government intervention in industry this book will serve the wider purpose of drawing attention to the complex interplay of regulation and competition in other sectors of the economy.

It might, of course, be contended that, from a regulatory perspective the pharmaceutical industry is perhaps unusual, and even *sui generis*. The extent and density of regulation sets it apart from most other productive sectors. At the same time, however, the primary aim has not been to provide a detailed comparative analysis of pharmaceutical regulation but to examine its implementation from the perspective of its impact on market structures and competitive forces. Many of the observations on the impact of national regulation on globally organized firms in other sectors, and on the relationship between regulation and competition, should therefore be of relevance to understanding and analysing the persistence of regulatory tensions which are undoubtedly present in other sectors of the economy where government intervention takes place. Comparative analysis of the legal dimensions of state intervention undoubtedly presents a useful opportunity to explore a somewhat neglected aspect of governmental relations with regulated industries.

The preceding analysis of two separate legal traditions on changes in the regulation of an economically important and politically powerful industrial sector has highlighted some striking contrasts in the French and British approaches to state intervention. In this concluding chapter I will therefore draw upon some of the comparative evidence presented in previous chapters on the operation of two distinctive legal traditions or 'legal cultures' and on the impact of those traditions on the regulation of this particular industrial sector, in order to offer some more general and tentative conclusions about the role of law in the process of institutionalizing relationships between regulator and regulated. Given the absence of similar research on the legal aspects of government relations with firms in other industrial sectors, one can only speculate about the role which law might play in other areas of the economy.

Such speculation would nevertheless appear justified for two reasons. In the first place, as we have seen at various points in this study, precisely because this legal dimension of economic intervention and its consequences has remained relatively unexplored in the European context,[1] an American perspective on regulation has predominated, or at least features as a point of departure in much of the recent literature. In the second place, there is currently considerable governmental, as well as more general public interest in the concept and nature of regulation. As many governments, and particularly the present British administration, embark upon large-scale privatization programmes, control based primarily on regulation, as opposed to ownership, of a number of key sectors of the economy has increasingly come to characterize the relations between government and industry in each country. In this context, a recent remark by a British parliamentary select committee to the effect that, at least in the UK, there is no 'tradition of regulation or regulatory culture', appears apposite. In the preceding chapters of this book I have sought to establish that such a tradition does in fact exist in at least one important sector of the economy, but it is precisely because of its voluntaristic and predominantly non-legal form that it has remained a largely hidden culture.[2]

The Impact of Regulation on Competitive Processes

Before turning to a comparison of regulatory traditions and the patterns of institutionalized relations to which they can give rise, it is appropriate here to draw a number of general conclusions about the overall nature of the relationship between regulation and competition, and to consider whether national regulatory regimes will remain a valid topic of study, given the drive to harmonization within the member states of the EC. In this section I will examine three aspects of the relationship between regulation and competition discussed in detail in this book: the problem of designing adequate regulatory tools to promote effective competition in 'problematic' sectors of the economy, where the traditional forces of competition are considered weak; the continuing relevance of national regulation in the light of EC developments; and finally the relationship between regulation and changing competitive forces.

Regulating 'problem sectors'

I argued in Chapter 2 that the three important distinguishing features of the pharmaceutical industry were its increasingly globalized or multinational organization, its oligopolistic structure, and, lastly, the absence of price-based competition within the market for prescription drugs. Should this imply that the interaction of regulation on competition discussed in previous chapters raises issues which are peculiar to the pharmaceutical sector? There are a number of reasons to suggest that this is not necessarily so.

In Chapter 9 I discussed the problems of applying the norms of general competition law to a complex sector and contended that particularized forms of price control were necessitated, at least in part, by the perceived ineffectiveness of the former method of control. The pharmaceutical industry cannot, of course, claim the dubious distinction of being the only sector of the economy where the standard mechanisms of competition policy are hard to apply. Oligopolistic market structures are after all, not uncommon, and one can point to numerous other sectors of the economy where a few large firms predominate. The oil industry, the telecommunications industry, the car industry, the consumer electronics industry, and the chemical industry all spring readily to mind. It is perhaps the centrality of patent protection, and the potential for near-monopolistic control of therapeutic submarkets that it facilitates, which accentuates the problem of applying competition norms to the pharmaceutical sector. These problems are in turn exacerbated on the one hand by the special conditions of demand for prescription drugs, and on the other by the high barriers of entry into the market. Price competition is effectively displaced by product competition, and the recurrent task which has confronted both governments over the past 40 years has been to design suitable mechanisms, whether legal or non-legal, to promote and monitor effective product-competition in this sector.

Even if the predominance of product competition and the attendant problems for regulators is perhaps a feature peculiar to the pharmaceutical market, this study's findings are not without relevance to the more general dilemmas facing those governments which are presently searching for methods to secure effective competition in 'problem' sectors, where price-based competition is weak and price elasticity is generally low. Arguably, the task of designing suitable regulatory instruments to supplement or augment general rules on competition is a more urgent one than ever, given the general trend towards privatization, and more especially the UK's extensive programme of privatizing 'natural monopolies' including telecommunications, gas, and now water and electricity, hitherto the preserve of publicly owned firms.

In the current economic debate about the possible role for regulation in these monopolistic or oligopolistic markets the theory of *contestable markets* has been given considerable prominence. According to this theory, even where an industry enjoys a monopolistic position, it is conceivable that it would be deterred from monopolistic behaviour by the threat of entry: in other words, its behaviour is influenced by potential competitors. 'A contestable market is one into which entry is absolutely free and exit is absolutely costless.'[3] Hence a contestable market is one in which there are no sunk costs—that is, all costs are recovered when the firm exits or leaves the market. The theory has several implications for the application of competition and regulation to 'problem' sectors. In the first place, if a market is contestable then there is no real need for regulation, because the threat of entry disciplines the existing firm or firms. In the second place, the same should be true if the market can be made contestable—for example, by the dismantling of entry barriers and other liberalization measures.[4] According to this theory, government intervention through regulation should be confined to dismantling entry barriers.

In the context of competition in the pharmaceutical industry, government attempts to deal with one particular barrier to entry— product differentiation—are illustrative of the fact that even if the focus of regulation is shifted away from the direct regulation of profits or prices, towards regulating entry barriers, the problem of designing suitable regulatory instruments will not disappear. Product differentiation through advertising promotion, it was noted in Chapter 2, can be set apart both from patent grants and regulatory requirements, which come from government, and from certain scale economies, which may be technically imposed. Product differentiation originates as a set of policies on the promotion of brand loyalty and advertising which firms themselves adopt and which subsequently create a structural barrier.[5] I have noted in Chapter 8 that where competition is treated as primarily product-based, the regulation of industry's promotional activities poses particular dilemmas for regulators. If, in the interests of a better allocation of public resources, restraints are imposed on promotional expenditures, companies must still be able to promote new products to doctors to break into new markets. The problem, like so many problems of regulating the process of product competition, was seen as one of demarcation—that is, to establish a method of determining the point at which promotional expenditure perpetuates and strengthens rather than weakens market concentration. In consequence, the regulation of advertising and promotion is one of the most sensitive areas of pharmaceutical regulation.

The inherent problems of regulating complex sectors are unlikely to disappear merely because the focus of regulation is altered: the problem of demarcating desirable activity from that considered undesirable will remain, as will the problem of designing the requisite controls. Nor is there any reason to suppose that the patterns of interdependence which have acted as a constraint on reform of other forms of regulation are absent in entry regulation. I suggested in Chapter 8 that neither France nor the UK had succeeded in implementing adequate controls over pharmaceutical promotional activities and that, despite the emergence of detailed statutory controls, each regulatory system in its own way allows the industry a considerable amount of commercial freedom.

The diminishing importance of national regulation?

Despite the global level on which the pharmaceutical industry's activities are now organized, it is evident that national regulation has been of central importance to its economic well-being. Although in world terms the French and British markets for prescription drugs are small, both countries are host to some of the world's largest drug companies. Furthermore, prices and other regulatory practices adopted in both the UK and France are taken as important reference points in numerous other countries, particularly former colonies, which are themselves lucrative markets for home-based firms.

I have also stressed that the industry is a relatively mobile one. If one country's regulatory climate is perceived as unfavourable to a firm's commercial interests and strategies, it can set up business elsewhere. In the past, national legislation on product safety has operated in such a way that companies found it easier to satisfy regulatory requirements if they carried out at least secondary manufacture and Phase III clinical trials in the country where they sought licensing approval. This situation is unlikely to be a permanent one, however. In Chapter 5 the European Commission's intensified efforts to complete a single European market for pharmaceuticals by 1992 at the latest were critically examined. The Commission has already issued a large number of directives on the subject of product safety, directives which are, of course, binding on the member states to which they are addressed. In 1988 it turned its attention to the harmonization of price controls, a development which undoubtedly marks a further erosion of national sovereignty.

These developments will have several important consequences, particularly for countries like France, where the present regulatory climate is perceived by the industry as inimical to its interests. If national pricing controls are not reformed, the larger firms are likely to be tempted to locate an increasing proportion of their activities outside France. Once automatic mutual recognition of product licences is established within the EC, the companies will no longer have any incentive to remain within the jurisdiction of the French licensing authorities. Hence developments at the European level, or at least impending developments, will undoubtedly generate pressure for national reform. In view of the repeated failure by a succession of French governments to rationalize the system of price control, the current administration's ability to respond to the changing European environment does not look promising.

Similar pressures could manifest themselves in countries where the implementation of standards on product licensing, even if these are formally harmonized, is considered particularly onerous by industry. Once again, faced with threats of relocation from such an important and profitable sector of the economy, governmental authorities could embark upon 'a regulatory race for the bottom' and attempt to ease regulatory requirements in practice—for example, through a more flexible approach to their implementation and administration.

There is no reason to suppose that these types of regulatory developments will be confined to the pharmaceutical sector. Although in 1989 one can hardly confirm or rebut predictions that the 'regulatory focus' in numerous sectors of the economy will shift from national governments to the European Commission in Brussels by 1992, one need only look to the example of the highly mobile financial and investments industry which is presently re-establishing itself in countries such as Luxembourg, where the regulatory climate is perceived as extremely benign. The European consumers' associations have expressed widespread concern about the impact of the completion of the internal market in 1992 on general standards as regards the protection of consumer safety in Europe.

If at the same time the European Commission continues to adopt an increasingly strict stance on state aids and other forms of subsidy and special privileges for nationally based firms, national governments will find themselves unable to 'sugar the pill' of strict safety and other forms of consumer legislation with generous incentives for firms who establish themselves within their territories.

In conclusion, I would suggest that national regulation will not necessarily become less important to industry in the future but that it will be viewed from a different perspective: highly mobile firms will increasingly compare the advantages of one national regulatory climate with another, and make their future investment decisions accordingly.

Changing forms of regulation and changing competitive forces

In Chapter 2 it was suggested that in many cases the impact of regulation on competitive processes was often incidental rather than deliberate. The general argument that regulation designed to deal with one market imperfection, such as monopolistic pricing, is likely to introduce secondary distortions in decisions about the allocation of resources is, of course, well known to economists.[6] As the latter have stressed, this is not to say that regulation is undesirable, but simply to point out the inevitable trade-offs involved.[7] The outcome of negotiations over such trade-offs is, of course, a function of the bargaining strengths and resources available to each side. In Chapter 2 the centrality of regulation both as a mechanism for controlling the pharmaceutical industry's performance and as a crucial determinant of market structure was repeatedly stressed. Many of the main barriers to entry into the industry are in fact a result of legal and regulatory factors. In consequence, the trade-offs which regulatory distortions can necessitate will invariably have legal implications. The relevance of this cumulative economic impact of legally distinct regulatory programmes was evident in two ways. Firstly, it enabled us not only to understand the protracted *failure* to introduce reform, as for example in French price-controls, but also to understand why the apparent inadequacies and irrationalities of one set of regulations were 'tolerated' by regulator and regulated, as long as the operation of a related regime, in this case product safety control, functioned as a protectionist façade, shielding a large number of small to medium sized firms from direct foreign competition. In the second place, it allowed us to discern an underlying logic of seemingly unrelated incidents and pressures for reform. This study has produced numerous illustrations. Where, for example, stricter regulation of one aspect of the industry's activities raises barriers to entry, countervailing adjustments in another field of regulation may be required. Concern over the possible structural impact of more severe regulations on product safety, for example, has prompted demands for adjustments in the system of patent protection, to extend 'effective' patent life. In other words, because the operation of legally distinct regimes of regulation have a cumulative impact on the structure of the pharmaceutical market, and consequently on the performance of the industry, considerable scope for bargaining between regulator and regulated over the future direction of reform exists.

A further aspect of the cumulative impact of pharmaceutical regulation on competitive forces should also be discussed in the context of the problem of regulating or promoting product competition. In Chapter 3, which compared early attempts to regulate the prices of the new branded medicines whose marketing coincided with the socialization of health care, I concluded that neither system had established satisfactory ways of determining whether competition was effective, and therefore whether the NHS or the health insurance funds were obtaining value for money from the products they purchased or reimbursed. The introduction of legislation on product safety, based on the three criteria of safety, quality, and efficacy, in theory offered regulators an alternative mechanism of assessing the pharmaceutical products. If either system had evolved a *comparable efficacy* test, then economic criteria would have found their way into the implementation of legislation on product safety: at least some of the deficiencies of the instruments deployed in the regimes for controlling prices and profits might have been offset. In Chapter 4 I offered some explanations as to why this has not occurred, and I will return to this issue in the final section of this chapter. It should also be noted that the question of product efficacy has reappeared on the regulatory agenda once again, this time with the adoption of new techniques of cost containment, reviewed in Chapters 6 and 7.

The point that must be stressed here is that the conflicts and tensions between regulation and competition are recurring ones, conflicts which not only re-emerge within the context of the implementation of individual regulatory programmes but which constantly reappear across the entire spectrum of governmental relations with home-based industry. It could be argued, furthermore, that despite the fact that they have had 'several bites at the regulatory cherry', governments have consistently failed to realize their desired objectives.

The impact of European law and policy on the interaction of regulation and competition is complex. At the time of writing, an internal market for pharmaceuticals, as for many other sectors of the European economy, is by no means complete. In Chapter 5 it was contended, however, that as a result of the Community's efforts at harmonization so far, the European market for pharmaceuticals has become more complex in structure. Although the Community has yet to achieve its ultimate goal of securing the free movement of pharmaceuticals, unhindered by national rules and regulations, some progress has been made in streamlining and speeding up the administrative aspects of national regulations on product safety. As a consequence, different rules apply to different categories of drugs. Whereas the Common Market was previously compartmentalized along national boundaries, the current efforts at harmonization have produced a new form of market stratification, between products as opposed to countries. National governments must give effect to different regulatory procedures for generic products, parallel imports, and high-technology goods.

These developments at the European level have coincided with, and probably exacerbated, the gradual growth of national markets for generic products, given that a large number of patents on major drug products have expired. This in turn has had important implications for the structure of the pharmaceuticals market, and therefore for the interaction of regulation and competition. In Chapter 6 I suggested that in the UK at least, a two-tiered market for research-based and generic pharmaceutical products had emerged. Initially, the British government was able to capitalize on the informal nature of the PPRS and use the threat of increased exposure from generic products, marketed at lower prices, to win important con-cessions on prices from the research-based firms. In France, however, we have seen that a legacy of regulatory protectionism has effectively insulated the national market from these structural changes. In many respects, the French government is hostage to its own past. On the one hand, it has been unable to exploit the changing situation in regard to patents to its own advantage and utilize an emergent generics market as leverage to modernize the system of administered price-controls; on the other hand, the widening gap between average European drug-prices and 'regulated' French prices have caused French regulators to exercise considerable caution in moving towards a more liberal regime.

As I have already argued, at this point in time the primacy of national regulation has not been displaced by the European Com-munity's efforts in the direction of harmonizing the regulation of product safety and pricing. As long as the locus of decision-making both on the safety of individual products and on the price at which they may be sold or reimbursed by the national health systems remains at national level, then the impact of the emergent forms of market stratification and the new tensions it creates within the pharmaceutical market will be played out and resolved at the national level.

This essentially legal dimension to regulatory change is particu-larly important in the market for pharmaceuticals, where, I have argued, many of its structural determinants, including the barriers of entry to it, are in fact legal in origin. Economic growth, techno-logical innovation, and structural change all magnify the com-plexity of issues which arise in the process of regulation. The dynamic nature of the market economy inevitably disturbs the routine processing of issues and problems by national regulators and in consequence imposes a strain on existing patterns of established relations between governments and their regulated industries. The complex but changing legal environment in which government and industry negotiate over regulatory reform and policy trade-offs is perhaps as important in the pharmaceutical market as other forms of change in different sectors—for example, the impact of technological change in the telecommunications market,[8] or changing methods of doing business in financial markets.[9]

An analysis of the processes through which relations between regulator and regulated develop into standardized practices must always strive not to overstate the consensual and stable character of regulatory practice. Bitter struggles may be generated by the changing nature of competitive forces. In Chapter 6 I suggested that this changing legal environment has had a number of important consequences on the direction of regulatory policy on product safety as well as profit control in the UK. New actors have entered the regulatory arena. The British authorities must now negotiate not only with the powerful research-based firms, as represented by the ABPI, but also with parallel importers and generic producers. In other words, the dynamic of regulation is such that one can no longer assume that the interests of the regulated group have remained homogeneous. Indeed, these interests are often conflictual, as the recent controversy over the use of the abridged licensing procedures in the UK, also discussed in Chapter 6, demonstrated.

Similar conflicts will undoubtedly occur in other sectors where, in the slipstream of 1992—the target date for the completion of the internal market—the European Community's attempts to liberalize trade and to harmonize national legislation will generate a variety of economic opportunities and cause new actors to enter the regulatory arena at national level. This may well result not only in challenges to established methods of bargaining between regulatory authorities and their 'clientele' but also in reduced scope to negotiate trade-offs within and across regulatory regimes.

Diversity in Regulatory Techniques and Styles of Intervention

If the interaction of regulation and competition has been an important variable in the generation of conflict and change, we must look elsewhere for an explanation of the processes of resolution and adjustment. In Chapter 1 I suggested that regulatory regimes may well play a role as vehicles in the process of accommodation to changing market structures. There are two aspects to this potential function of regulation. The first relates to the instruments used in regulation: does the instrument itself facilitate compromise? The second relates to the techniques or styles of implementation which attend their usage: how are the roles of public and private actors in the regulatory process to be distinguished, what are the roles assigned to private actors and can we identify major differences in the way in which the public–private divide is conventionally drawn in national systems? In Chapter 1 I argued that capture theory tended to imply a continued dominance of the regulatory process by one set of actors, whereas in practice an understanding of the complexities and dynamic nature of the regulatory process requires a more nuanced approach, which identifies the mechanisms by which each set of actors seeks to maintain its existing bargaining strengths and positions within the regulatory process.

The obvious starting-point for this type of analysis is to be found in a comparison of the techniques of regulation deployed in each country. The divergent political, legal, and economic traditions of the UK and France seemed, prima facie, to offer ample scope for a useful comparison of the impact of divergent traditions of public authority and attitudes to the legitimate exercise of power, and of their implications for the participation of private interests in the regulatory process. It is beyond the scope of this book to engage in a detailed investigation of the origins of these distinctions, or to enter into the theoretical debate about their relevance to an understanding of the nature and direction of modern economic and industry policy in countries with different state traditions.[10] As Sulieman has suggested, 'state power or autonomy varies across sectors', so that the influence of state traditions of intervention cannot be approached in a formalistic manner 'without the necessary empirical investigations'.[11] On the basis of the material discussed in the preceding chapters, some of the principal differences in the regulatory techniques deployed in the UK and France will be highlighted here, with the aim of offering, in the third section of this chapter, some indication of their consequences for relations between firms and government in this particular sector.

The public–private divide and early attempts at regulation

The different attitudes to public authority in the UK and France, and to the way in which the public—private divide was drawn both in the early regulatory regimes governing the control of prices and products and in their subsequent modification, are evident in two particular respects: in their stated objectives, and in the means selected to achieve them. In this section I will compare and contrast firstly the divergent objectives pursued in each country, and secondly the techniques adopted to secure them, with a view to establishing to what extent differences in the patterns or style of intervention are consistent across the various regulatory programmes in each country. I will go on to examine the extent to which these original objectives have altered over the years, and whether this in turn has prompted corresponding adjustment to the existing regulatory mechanisms.

We have seen in Chapter 3, for example, that the objectives embraced by the early British and French pharmaceutical regulatory regimes were notably distinct. In the UK, the Voluntary Price Regulation Scheme (VPRS) was adopted at a time when the political and economic legitimacy of administered price-controls was in doubt.[12] While the need to find some means of limiting growth in public expenditure on drugs was acknowledged by the government of the time, direct state intervention in the process of price formation was not considered desirable or practical. A compromise form of control, the object of which was primarily to regulate each company's aggregate profits, as opposed to its individual product prices, was therefore preferred. In France, however, in the immediate post-war years the legitimacy of administered price-control and direct state intervention in the process of price formation was not widely questioned. In consequence, the French system of price controls began with a very different set of objectives: to regulate the price of each individual product which would eventually be reimbursed by the health insurance funds.

Similar divergences in objective were evident in the early systems of control on product safety. The French 'visa' system served primarily protectionist ends; its role as a mechanism for securing the safety and quality of pharmaceutical products was minimal. It provided a convenient shelter behind which the large number of small French pharmaceutical firms could operate. This form of protectionist regulation was firmly within the French mercantilist tradition.[13] The British system of safety control, however, was adopted some 20 years later, in the light of greater awareness of the potential risks, as well as benefits, of modern synthetically based drug products. Its stated objective was to protect the public interest by attempting to establish that drug products were reasonably safe under normal conditions of use. Furthermore, the British regulatory regime governing pharmaceutical product safety was adopted at a time when the protection of the consumer and the regulation of health and safety in general were viewed as legitimate objects of state intervention.[14] Its goals were therefore more ambitious than those of its French counterpart, and the values it embraced were quite distinct: the regulator was expected, via the statutory licensing process, to guarantee the safety, quality, and efficacy of individual drug products.

These divergences in the objectives or goals of legitimate state intervention and regulation found expression in the regulatory techniques selected for the realization of those goals in each country. The contrasts between the early instruments used to control prices and profits in the UK and France, for example, could not have been more marked. In the first place, price control in France was exercised through a theoretically exhaustive set of formal legal controls which invested government officials with extensive discretionary powers, not only to require information on pricing from French companies but also unilaterally to impose prices for individual products and to implement compulsory rounds of general price reductions or price freezes. French manufacturers were also subject to an additional set of formal controls, through the mechanisms of reimbursement approval.

In the UK the essentially self-regulatory system of profit control lacks any legal foundation in either statute or private law. Although the informal VPRS and its successor, the PPRS, were underpinned by indirect, formal legal powers, these have rarely been used. As observed in Chapter 3, officials at the Ministry of Health found it difficult to utilize these powers in the absence of formal price controls.

The instruments of modern product-safety regulation are less markedly divergent, and this is perhaps unremarkable, given that both systems have essentially been shaped over the last 20 years to reflect the requirements of EC law. Thus each system is based on a formal statutory system of licensing, and product licences in the UK, or AMMs in France, are only granted after the relevant authority is satisfied, on the basis of specified documentation, that an individual product's safety, quality, and efficacy is assured. And yet, as Chapter 4 indicated, there are substantial divergences in the methods of evaluation used in each country. In France control of product safety is still assured by means of a decentralized mechanism. As we have seen in Chapter 4, the expert, nominated and remunerated by the individual pharmaceutical firm, has remained pivotal to the French system. The independence of the expert from the interests of the firm was never a serious issue until the mid-1970s, when increased European competition and the requirements of European law made it necessary to upgrade the quality of product-safety regulation and led to the overhaul of the system. In the UK the industry's suggestions that some sort of voluntary system of self-regulation for product safety should be introduced were rejected, and a relatively rigorous and, above all, centralized statutory scheme of controls was enacted. Its routine application to individual products is entrusted to a permanent Medicines Division, while new NCEs and 'problem' applications are considered by advisory committees comprising outside experts.

Styles of intervention

On the face of it, it would appear that both the UK and France adopted quite separate and distinctive techniques to secure the implementation of their respective policies, first on price regulation and later on safety control. Is it then possible to talk in terms of established or dominant patterns of intervention in the affairs of the pharmaceutical industry in each country? I would argue that this question can be answered in the affirmative when we look more closely at the methods by which the regulation of prices and product safety has been implemented, and the extent of the industry's participation in that process.

In Chapter 4 we noted that the operation of the early regimes for the control of product safety was, in fact, not markedly distinct from that already established for control of prices and profits. On the one hand, the preferred approach in the UK was to enlist industry's co-operation, not only in the design but also in the implementation of an essentially voluntary system of product-safety control, administered by an informal body, the Committee on the Safety of Drugs. Even when the voluntary system was replaced by the formal statutory licensing regime in 1971, a certain flexibility and pragmatism was purposely maintained. Again, as with the system of profit control, the ABPI played an important role; it co-operated in the formulation of the technical standards to be incorporated both into licences for clinical trials and into product licences; it policed compliance with certain statutory provisions, including advertising, on the basis of its own codes of practice. Mutual trust and co-operation are therefore the twin pillars on which most aspects of the British system of pharmaceutical regulation continues to rest. This is firmly reflected in the proliferation of self-regulatory mechanisms which, as we have seen, characterize the regulation of many aspects of the industry's activities.

In the case of the French pharmaceutical industry, however, it is very rare to find any single aspect of the regulatory relationship between government and industry which is not expressed in formal legal rules. The French system of safety control, on the other hand, while not particularly onerous in its requirements, was nevertheless one of the first state-imposed sets of controls on pharmaceutical marketing in Europe. These controls have since flourished and developed into a comprehensive, if not exhaustive, public health code, which impinges on virtually every aspect of pharmaceutical manufacture, distribution, and marketing.

What is perhaps more difficult to explain in the French context is the apparent divergence between the extensive co-operation between regulator and regulated which has been established over implementation of safety legislation and its complete absence in the control of prices and profits. Which of the two could be described as more typical of the French regulatory tradition? This is a rather difficult question to answer given the paucity of research on regulation in modern France, but two tentative explanations will be offered, one organizational, the other legal.

From the perspective of the organization and operation of the French bureaucracy, a number of writers have pointed to the close relationships which can develop between industry and the highly autonomous divisions or *directions* within ministries. Regulators are said to identify closely with the interests of their 'client' group.[15] In matters of safety legislation, the DPHM undoubtedly has considerable autonomy, whereas as far as the control of prices and reimbursement is concerned, it was, and remains, only one of several divisions involved. There was not, therefore, the same potential for the closer relations and identification of interests to develop over policy on price control.

From a legal perspective, one might draw a further distinction between the subject-matter of these different sets of regulations and the way in which regulatory power is perceived to have been traditionally administered in France. It has been remarked of other jurisdictions that while a government's regulatory authority may be extensive, it is not necessarily *intensive*. In other words, government may be able to purport to exercise jurisdiction in a number of areas precisely because it does not regulate very intensively in any of them.[16] As we have mentioned in Chapter 4, some writers characterize the dominant tradition of French regulation as an *administration de police*—that is, as an essentially passive and reactive approach as opposed to an active or executive one. In other words, the dominant practice of the administration has been to refrain from too close an involvement with the enforcement of the detailed technical aspects of regulation. This is a task which is invariably delegated to the professional or trade associations of the regulated subjects. The role of the administration is confined to policing this form of enforcement.

The centrality of the expert in the process of product licensing is a good example of this approach. The technical aspects of safety regulation were initially the responsibility of the pharmacy profession, but once the pharmaceutical industry was given its 'own statute' in 1945, these functions were transferred to the industry-appointed experts, who, as we have seen in Chapter 4, were responsible for preparing a critical assessment of the individual firm's compliance with safety regulation. The expert carried out the necessary tests to establish the safety and efficacy of the product in question: the role of the administration, at least until 1976, when a standardized test protocol was introduced, was confined to one of checking the qualifications of the expert to carry out this task.

To a certain extent, a similar approach to the exercise of formal regulatory powers was also evident in the enforcement by the Ministry of Finance of the former price-framework system. As we have seen in Chapter 3, the Ministry continued to rely on industry's own estimates of its manufacturing costs in its pricing calculations. Although it possessed interventionist powers to check their accuracy, it rarely used them as a direct instrument of pharmaceutical price-control policy, even when confronted with evidence that these costs were frequently manipulated. The Ministry of Finance preferred to use the blunter instrument of the *baisse autoritaire* as one of its many tools to control inflation, and hence to keep the general level of pharmaceutical prices under control. As long as prices were held low, there was little concern over the quality of the industry's economic performance. A more activist approach to the promotion of effective competition would have demanded a far more discriminating approach on the part of the administration.

In conclusion, it might be said that a consistent feature of French pharmaceutical regulation has been the formal enactment of detailed, and even ambitious, regulatory objectives, objectives which are all too frequently not backed up with the provision of the necessary administrative resources, in terms of personnel, to secure their effective implementation. A related distinguishing feature of French regulation is the non-implementation of certain controls. In the regulation of Phase I and II clinical trials, for example, the existing controls are plainly out of date and inappropriate to industry's needs but have nevertheless proved impossible to reform. They remain on the statute book but are simply ignored in practice.

Whether these observations might be generalized to the regulation of other sectors of the French and British economies remains an open question, given the paucity of research. In this context, however, one might note that in certain important respects the administration of French patent law and competition law appears to have conformed to this overall pattern. In Chapter 9 I suggested that the French system of patent protection is a comparatively weak one. The French patent administration has traditionally lacked the necessary powers and resources to support a full 'claims-based' system of patent registration. In other words, the administration of patent law has been essentially passive in nature.

The implementation of competition law has been similarly hampered in the past by a lack of available administrative resources and personnel to conduct the necessary inquiries to establish the existence of an anticompetitive practice. The competition authorities, although theoretically endowed with a battery of extensive interventionist powers, rarely used them prior to the reforms of 1977, and even after this date, the Competition Commission frequently complained that it had insufficient resources to conduct independent investigations of its own.

One can also point to the predominance and persistence of certain techniques of regulatory intervention elsewhere in the British economy. As we have seen in Chapter 9, the British approach to competition policy is both pragmatic and suffused with discretion. Voluntary undertakings are preferred to statutory controls. One can also identify a frequent preference for self-regulation, or 'soft law' as it is sometimes called, in many other areas of state intervention in the economy. Pertinent examples here include the regulation of the insurance industry,[17] and financial services[18] and the regulation of product safety for numerous consumer goods.[19] Similarly, the control of advertising for most consumer goods and services—and not just pharmaceutical products—is assured mainly through self-regulatory mechanisms in the UK.[20] Indeed, the recent proliferation of various instruments of 'soft law', including codes of guidance and other methods of industry self-regulation, has prompted a certain amount of concern over the ability of the courts and Parliament to wield meaningful control over the exercise of discretionary power by the executive.[21]

The persistence of divergence?

If, as this book has contended, regulation is to be considered a dynamic process, one cannot afford to assume that the objectives of regulation have remained static. Indeed, in the previous chapters I have identified several separate sets of factors which have generated pressure for change. Firstly, the threat of increased exposure to competition from other countries, especially as the prospect of the completion of the single European market draws closer, has forced governments to pay closer attention to the competitiveness of their home-based firms. Secondly, however, heightened concern over public expenditure on health, especially in the context of a generally ageing population, has forced both the French and British governments to pay closer attention to ways of seeking savings in their respective drug bills. Thirdly and finally, the structure of the pharmaceutical market has itself changed, and new forces of competition are emerging, as Chapter 2 established in some detail. As we have seen in previous chapters, these various developments have not been without influence on the goals of product safety and price regulation. At the same time, as regulators become more expert in administering complex regimes, one might expect to see more exacting standards being set for the regulated firms. Nor can one afford to ignore more general changes in governmental attitudes towards regulation itself as an instrument of economic intervention. As we have seen in Chapters 6, 7, and 9, for example, Conservative-led governments in both countries have gradually abandoned their general regimes of administered price-control in favour of a more rigorous policy on competition.

We have seen in the previous chapters that, as a result of this changing regulatory environment, both governments have in fact attempted to adjust their respective regulatory regimes and to modify their techniques of regulation, but their endeavours have met with varying degrees of success. This brings me to one of the central themes of this study: have the original patterns of regulatory intervention remained constant within and across the separate fields of regulation, and if so, have the various regulatory techniques deployed in each country themselves contributed in any way to the maintenance of this established pattern? I will deal with the first of these questions in the remaining part of this section and return to the second question in the final part of this chapter.

The regulation of product safety

As the two systems of product safety have 'matured', standards of product safety have become substantially more onerous, with different consequences in each country. As we have seen in Chapters 4 and 6, because the British licensing system is a centralized one, administered by a relatively large specialist staff at the Medicines Division of the Department of Health, the British pharmaceutical industry has not been co-opted into the actual processes of decision-making on the licensing of individual products to anything like the same extent as its French counterpart. In Chapter 4 it was argued that the latter's participation in the deliberations of the Committee on Marketing Authorizations and in various ad hoc committees for formulating policy strategy, as well as the continued decentralized nature of product-safety control, with its continued reliance on the industry-appointed expert, has allowed the French-based industry to influence the direction of policy on product safety. Following the introduction of standard test protocols in 1976 and their frequent modification since then, the administration has undoubtedly become more directly involved in the technical aspects of product licensing. The small staff at the Ministry of Health's medicines division, the DPHM, lack the necessary resources and have not accumulated the technical knowledge to act independently of industry's interests. The 'modernization' and improvement of the operation of the licensing system has inevitably led to the proliferation of decrees and *arrêtés*, but without visible protest from industry. This can very probably be attributed to the fact that the improved acceptability of French products on international markets is a shared goal of regulator and regulated in France, and this is a goal which can only be achieved if the regulatory regime appears to be more rigorous and thoroughgoing than in the past.

It is perhaps for these reasons that the implementation of product-safety regulation has not generated the tensions and conflicts which have appeared in recent years in the implementation of product-safety licensing in the UK. Three particular periods of 'tension' were discussed in earlier chapters: the attempted implementation of stricter standards for clinical-trial certificates; the so-called 'product licence review process'; and, more recently, the controversy over the handling of the abridged procedures for obtaining licences. Arguably, the centralized and more formalistic approach to product licensing in the UK has allowed regulators unilaterally to develop stricter safety standards, independently of the industry. At the same time, constraints on the implementation of stricter standards must be acknowledged. In the case of clinical-trial certificates, we have seen that in fact the government accommodated the industry's demands and introduced a new exemption scheme which substantially relaxed the regulatory burden. As for the review process for product licences, those aspects of the scheme to which the industry objected were eventually removed when firms withdrew their co-operative attitude towards the licensing process in general. Finally, discontent in regard to the overall direction of licensing policy, and in particular the industry's dissatisfaction with the speed at which licence applications were being processed, was dealt with by directly co-opting industry representatives on to a general review body.

Pricing control

Although in the UK compliance with what is little more than a gentleman's agreement is now no doubt reinforced by the potential use of indirect statutory controls—including the reserve powers to compel the provision of information and to set prices, or the power to issue compulsory patents or to refer a firm to the competition authorities—in practice these indirect controls have rarely been used. Indeed, we have noted in Chapter 6 that the Conservative government succeeded in persuading industry to lower its prices voluntarily and to accept a price freeze without a single threat of recourse to its indirect powers. It was argued that the government could instead use the threat of exposing the research-based firms to greater competition from generic manufacturers and parallel importers if their demands for price cuts were not met.

The introduction of the Limited or Selective List in April 1985, did, however, mark a significant departure in regulatory style in the UK, as this was the first time the Minister of Health had assumed statutory powers to evaluate medicines for reimbursement under the NHS. There was never any indication, at least on the government's part that a voluntary or self-regulatory approach might have been taken; indeed, such an approach would in all probability have proved impractical, as it was surely unlikely that competing firms would reach agreement on whether or not their products should continue to be available for NHS prescription purposes. At the same time, however, I have argued that the seventh PPRS has reinforced and expanded the scope of existing voluntary agreement on profit control to include extensive industry co-operation in the formulation and implementation of future cost-containment measures. The dominant style of regulation appears, therefore, to have been reaffirmed and reinforced.

There remained comparatively little scope within the French system of price control for the industry to participate in the formulation of policy on an equivalent basis. As we have seen in Chapters 3 and 7, despite numerous reforms to the system of price control and reimbursement control, formal powers over various aspects of pricing control are still dispersed between several ministries. Proposals for reform have always been debated, at least in the first instance, in a series of *ad hoc* interministerial committees, the primary purpose of which is to secure a consensus between the different *directions* of the various ministries which take an interest in the industry's affairs. The industry is usually excluded from this phase entirely, and its role has been confined to the subsidiary one of bargaining with government officials over the rate and frequency of annual increases in price. The various attempts to reform the system of price control have been largely incremental, and in practice the system remains to a large extent unaltered. It is noteworthy that, despite attempts by a succession of governments to introduce more flexibility into the system, thus aligning it more closely with the British approach to profit control, regulatory rigidity has remained the norm in France.

Advertising

The persistence of divergence in regulatory style is confirmed by the different approaches which have been adopted for regulating the industry's promotional activities. As we have seen in Chapter 8, both governments attempted to introduce reforms to the existing systems of advertising control in the mid-1970s. In France this resulted in the introduction of a strict set of a priori controls over all forms of advertising material relating to pharmaceutical products. Although this system was substantially modified in 1987, the Chirac government was not prepared to replace formal regulation with self-regulatory mechanisms. In the UK, however, the Labour government of the day was less successful in its attempts to exercise stricter controls over the industry's promotional activities. Although statutory regulations were eventually adopted in 1975, it was made clear that the powers made available to the Minister of Health would be viewed very much as 'reserve' powers, and that primary responsibility for policing promotion would remain with the ABPI.

In conclusion, I would contend that the general divergences in the objectives and techniques of pharmaceutical regulation in the UK and France have in fact persisted—despite adjustments necessitated by changing market structures and the growing importance of EC directives—for most of the forty-year period under study in this book. The enduring structural aspects of these very different regulatory frameworks, the different objectives which they serve, and the instruments of intervention which typify each system, undoubtedly reflect the different traditions of public authority and private participation in each country. To confine analysis of the impact of legal cultures or traditions to the structural features of regulatory intervention, however, can be dangerously misleading. It has led some writers, for example, to ascribe to the French bureaucracy an autonomy, and therefore a capacity for policy innovation and direction, which is not necessarily true for all sectors of the French economy.[22] One has to take a much closer look at the legal traditions or cultures which inform the practical application of these regulatory edifices. I have argued in this section that one must also look closely at the dominant styles of sectoral intervention in each country. This approach, however, raises further questions. Why have these 'styles' persisted and what are their consequences for government–industry relations? The concluding part of this chapter develops this theme in the context of a comparative discussion of the institutionalization of certain patterns of government's relations with its home-based firms.

Institutionalization: Interdependence and Fragmentation

I have suggested that despite the changed market context within which government–industry relations now operate, there has been no really fundamental change in the dominant patterns and styles of regulation in each country. In the preceding chapters I suggested that divergent regulatory practices can forge very different linkages between government and industry, which in turn can lead to considerable variations in both the emergence and role of bargaining frameworks within which adjustment can be negotiated in each country. These factors have been of fundamental importance in maintaining an overall status quo. The concept of linkages brings me to the third and final theme of the study: the contribution of legal factors to the institutionalization of certain patterns of relations between regulator and regulated. Throughout this study the notion of institutionalization has been used to refer to routinized patterns of relations, not only through time but also across the implementation of regulatory programmes.

Arguably, the so-called capture theory of regulation has obscured one of the most important features of economic regulation under advanced capitalism, namely that the most important actors in the regulatory process are organizations. The preceding chapters have concentrated on the influence of two sets of organizations: government regulatory agencies or departments and large firms, represented by powerful professional associations. Large firms and their representative associations are not 'takers' of regulation; they participate to a greater or lesser extent in the rule-making process.

Concepts of institutionalization have been developed and applied primarily in organizational theory. Selznick, in his work on American public corporations, analysed institutionalization as a means of instilling value, supplying intrinsic worth to a structure or process that, before institutionalization, had only instrumental utility.[23] As Hall expresses it, 'organizational structures tend to impose certain perceptions, responsibilities and interests on actors'.[24] For some institutional theorists these perceptions, obligations, and values may take on a rule-like quality.[25]

It will be evident that a primary aim of these versions of institutional theory is to examine and analyse the 'internal' production of standardized ways of doing things, both within organizations such as state agencies and in the relations between such agencies and their client groups. These rules are in turn viewed as important types of resources: those who can shape or influence them possess a valuable form of power. As Burns has commented, 'rule systems ... become resources and stakes in social interaction and the strategic structuring of social life. Thus they cannot be viewed as simply 'neutral' or 'technical means' of realizing certain purposes ... [They constitute] a power resource which social agents utilize in their struggles and negotiations over alternative structural forms'.[26]

To subject formal legal regulation to a similar form of analysis, it might be argued, is misleading; regulation is by definition a process of rule formation and application. There are additional problems. In the first place, regulatory rules, especially formal legal rules, may also reflect 'external' norms, in the sense that their form and character are a function of the general legal and constitutional order. They are not simply a product of an institutionalized process of dealings between regulator and regulated but are shaped by the norms of each country's general legal environment or legal culture. In the second place, legal rules are subject to a variety of pressures and sources of change which are not necessarily contingent on developments pertaining to the implementation of the particular regulatory programmes which they express. The general impact of European law on national legal systems is a good example of this type of development. European law is capable of creating rights which individuals can enforce directly in their national courts. In Chapter 6 it was argued that, traditionally, judicial review of ministerial decisions in the UK has been restricted essentially to the procedural aspects of the decision-making process. Where questions of European law are at issue, however, the English judiciary has been prepared to expand the scope of review to examine the substantive aspects of the decision. Hence the potential scope for legal challenge to the Limited List was widened. This in turn prompted one American firm, which considered itself adversely affected by the decision to introduce the list, and which had failed to persuade the government to change its minds by means of informal negotiations, to seek a remedy in the courts.

Two dominant features of the regulatory process analysed in this book nevertheless suggest that, if used with care, an analysis of the institutionalization of certain regulatory techniques or styles of intervention remains a valid exercise. On the one hand, as the preceding chapters have demonstrated, there is a persistent dichotomy between the preference for non-legal, informal intervention in the UK and the formal nature of the French interventionist style. This in turn has had important implications for the role which private 'actors', including the pharmaceutical firms and the relevant business associations, may assume in the regulatory process.

It would, however, be a mistake to assume that formal legal regulatory arrangements are the only kind of institutionalized relationship. The longevity of the British PPRS is eloquent testimony of the durability of informal relationships. Indeed, formal arrangements may not be institutionalized at all, and formal powers and rights may never in fact be mobilized. Our analysis of French regulation provides a number of examples of this phenomenon. We can also point to formal rules which make provision for 'interdependent' structures which fail to materialize. In Chapter 7, for example, we noted that a statutory consultative committee on reimbursement on which the SNIP and the health insurance funds were to be represented never actually met.

On the other hand, even where regulatory rules are expressed in formal legal terms, we have seen that in many cases these rules are general and open-ended, leaving regulators considerable discretion as to their implementation. Discretion, it would seem, is embedded in the process of economic regulation, but, as we have seen throughout this study, various routine constraints, legal as well non-legal, on its accepted use by government officials have evolved into 'rules of the game' in both countries.

To understand the processes of institutionalization at work in regulation we must therefore attempt to understand the interrelationship of formal legal rules and the informal 'rules of the game' or standard operating procedures which have developed either in the course of the implementation of the formal powers or, indeed, in the absence of such powers. At this point it is necessary to return to the nature of the rules establishing the various regulatory frameworks, and to examine the processes of what institutional theorists refer to as 'power dispersal' between regulator and regulated which those frameworks have facilitated. In this way the question of how certain 'rules of the game' have been established and persisted in the process of regulation may be addressed.

I have argued that the distinction between public and private power has always been much more blurred in the British system of pharmaceutical regulation. This fusion of public and private power appears to have become more complete because of the very nature of the various self-regulatory techniques deployed. In chapters 3, 4, and 6 I argued that the Department of Health has repeatedly failed to fashion adequate mechanisms to determine whether product competition is in fact effective, thus leaving each firm to determine the type of products it will develop and market. In all versions of the PPRS, the Department has been forced to rely on industry's own data and its own estimate of its profitability. In the absence of alternative methods of controls, this has inevitably led to a relationship of interdependence between regulator and regulated, and to a commitment on both sides to a consensual approach to profit and to even more formal safety regulation. The sheer volume of technical information required to support applications for product licences necessitates a co-operative approach on the part of the applicant firm which is vital to the efficient processing of a licence. Hence the broad 'rules of the game' in British pharmaceutical regulation are as follows: a commitment to mutual co-operation through prior consultation on proposed amendments to regulatory regimes; informal negotiation on the desired objectives of regulation and the instruments to achieve them; a preference for self-regulation over formal regulation; and a commitment to informal resolution of conflicts and problems arising from the application of these various rules. As argued in earlier chapters, this has created a distinct informal and flexible bargaining framework in which the research-based industries and the authorities can negotiate over various issues and from which the 'newcomers', including parallel importers and generic manufacturers, are largely excluded.

Commitment by both sides to these rules of the game has been reinforced by the very constraints which are a consequence of their operation. These may be divided into two categories: practical and legal. As to the former, absence of detailed knowledge about the industry has effectively prevented government from assuming stricter regulatory powers on a number of occasions. Perhaps the most clear evidence of the practical consequences of this interdependent relationship was the Labour government's attempt to introduce stricter controls over promotional activities in 1968. As we have seen in Chapter 8, these plans were abandoned when civil servants protested that they did not have sufficient information to put detailed controls into operation. More recently, plans to introduce stricter controls over transfer pricing into the seventh PPRS were dropped, in part because of the absence of resources to secure their effective implementation and in part because of the practical difficulties of drafting effective formal controls over such a complex matter.

Similarly, a co-operative attitude on the part of industry is required if the existing system is to work with its present limited resources and personnel. The attempt, discussed in Chapter 4, to use the procedures to review licences of right to impose what amounted to a comparative efficacy test had to be abandoned when the industry withdrew its co-operative approach to the licensing process in general. If the government had persisted with this strict interpretation of its legal powers under the Medicines Act, the industry might have retaliated by using its formal legal rights of appeal under the Act, causing the administration of the entire licensing system to fall into disarray. The only option open to the government would have been to devote more resources to product licensing—a costly exercise—or to comply with industry's demands. Unsurprisingly, it chose the latter course of action.

As to the legal implications of these 'rules of the game', where the British government has attempted to depart from its essentially consensual approach to regulation, the interdependent nature of its relationship with industry has acted as a further significant constraint because of the narrow basis of legitimacy on which key regimes, most notably the entire edifice of profit control, rest. This was especially evident in the aftermath of the referral of Hoffmann-La Roche to the MMC in 1973, as discussed in Chapter 9. Although the government initially attempted to impose the lower prices recommended by the MMC by means of a statutory order, it was eventually compelled to return to the tried and tested methods of negotiation and bargaining when Hoffmann-La Roche refused to participate in the fourth VPRS to negotiate the prices of its other NHS products. As a consequence of the voluntary nature of the scheme, the government had no powers available to force a recalcitrant firm to the negotiating table.

The constraints on the exercise of formal legal powers have also become manifest in other ways. Recent attempts by the British government to reinforce or extend the ABPI's self-regulatory mechanisms—as in the case of the proposed introduction of codes of practice for the use of licensed products in clinical trials and for controls over the selection of trade marks, as discussed in Chapter 8—were firmly and successfully resisted by industry. There is, of course, no question that from a formal point of view, the government could unilaterally impose the requisite controls on industry. It might be contended, however, that in the course of 40 years of intervention in the affairs of industry, the British government and the industry have implicitly 'demarcated' certain areas which are considered best suited to particular forms of regulation. Advertising is of fundamental importance to the process of product differentiation, and therefore to the profitability of individual firms. It is perhaps for this reason that the present government was prepared to accede to the ABPI's views on the undesirability of these proposed controls. This demarcation might also explain why its predecessor was prepared to surrender one of its few formal legal powers over the process of product differentiation, namely the power to issue special compulsory licences for patented drug products in return for industry's acceptance of some statutory controls over the content of its advertising material.

There are broadly two sets of predominantly 'legal' factors that explain the British-based drug industry's commitment to maintaining a consensual approach to regulation. In the first place, the alternative to this form of control in the field of price regulation would either be a greater use by the NHS of its monopsonistic purchasing powers or the introduction of statutory controls. The industry has already been obliged to accept, as in 1983 and 1984, compulsory price freezes and occasional price reductions, and, following the introduction of the Limited List, it must now live with one of the largest generic markets in Europe.

In the second place, as I have argued in Chapter 6, past reliance on informal non-legal arrangements for profit control have effectively limited the potential for aggrieved firms to seek meaningful challenge to government policy in the courts; co-operation has been a much more fruitful route, although there are signs of a greater use of the courts to review the implementation of safety controls.

Furthermore, as argued in Chapters 4 and 6, a good record of co-operation with, and support for, governmental regulators has yielded high returns for the research-based industry and has offered it opportunities to counter adverse regulatory developments. We noted in Chapter 4, for example, that from time to time the British regime governing product-safety licensing has operated in a manner which appears to depart from the more consensual approach of its predecessor to product safety. Having acquired the necessary skill and the resources to impose strict safety-testing requirements on industry and even, in the context of the review of licences, to construct a surrogate 'comparative efficacy' test, the British licensing authority has occasionally acted in a way contrary to industry's interests. At the same time, however, a combination of self-regulation over significant aspects of safety control, including clinical trials and the quality and content of promotional material, and a well-established tradition of consultation over, as well as participation in, evaluation studies of licensing policy, has assured British-based industry a considerable influence over the general direction of licensing policy, if not in its routine implementation. Thus we have seen that in early 1988 and ABPI executive has jointly chaired a major review of the operation of the Medicines Division, which is now perceived to be incapable of meeting the demands made upon it by parallel importers, generic manufacturers, and the research-based industry. Important concessions have been made to ensure a greater input from the ABPI into the direction of licensing policy.

In France the picture is quite different. Whereas the British industry association, the ABPI, has actively participated in all aspects of policy formulation, revision, and implementation, the French industry's involvement in the regulatory process has been marginal, and has been generally limited to participation at the implementation stage of a specific set of regulations-product safety and to negotiations over the value of the annual rounds of price increases. There are undoubtedly established links between the French DPHM and the industry in regard to the implementation of controls on product safety, where the regulatory rules themselves make provision for industry's active participation in the licensing of individual products. This in turn has allowed the SNIP to exercise considerable influence over more general policy discussions, as in the formulation and implementation of the process of product review, discussed in detail in Chapter 4.

It might well be asked why participation and co-operation at this level has not been sufficient in itself to allow industry to cultivate the confidence of successive governments in other areas of regulation, including advertising and price control. A possible response to this question is to be found in the nature of the French legal and administrative traditions. As we have seen throughout this book, almost every aspect of the relationship between government and the pharmaceutical industry is expressed in formal regulatory mechanisms. Furthermore, regulatory power over prices has remained dispersed over a number of ministries or has been allocated to a large number of advisory committees. The former have repeatedly failed to agree between themselves on a coherent strategy for the promotion of research-based industry, and there is no reason to presume that industry's past record of co-operation with the Ministry of Health should impress the Ministry of Finance. The firms have therefore little to gain from co-operating with one ministry when the fruits of its efforts may be negated by another ministry availing itself of its own regulatory powers. This fragmentation of regulatory power has prevented the development of mutual trust, which, it has been argued, is the foundation on which British pharmaceutical regulation has been built.

It cannot be assumed, however, that fragmentation is entirely dysfunctional from industry's point of view, and indeed the industry has, on certain occasions, endeavoured to maintain as well as exploit it. In other words, regulatory fragmentation has been institutionalized in the French pharmaceutical regulatory system. Two examples can be offered to illustrate this point.

First, in the absence of opportunities and incentives to co-operate constructively in the regulatory process, as we have seen in Chapters 4 and 7, the French-based pharmaceutical industry has instead successfully exploited the rigidities of the system to its own advantage. In this way, the larger firms managed to defeat the implementation of the government's pro-generics policy. The paradoxical result of the general failure to arrive at a consensus on price control has been to force regulators to bargain and negotiate directly over individual product prices with that segment of the industry over whose activities they have arguably least control or leverage—the multinational firms. The various attempts to 'graft' consensual regulatory mechanisms on to the formal system, as the Socialists attempted to do in their contractualization policy, have only met with failure, and as a result both sides have reached stalemate over the future direction of policy.

Second, we have seen that the French industry exploited regulatory fragmentation to prevent the emergence of comparative efficacy tests. Arguably, this could easily have been accomplished in the French system, given the nature of existing controls over reimbursement. Nevertheless, once efficacy criteria were included among the conditions to be met for the award of a marketing authorization, the SNIP obtained the assurance of the government that the application of these same criteria would be the exclusive task of the Committee on Marketing Authorizations; questions of product efficacy would not be dealt with in the course of the procedures for reimbursement approval. These various 'rules of the game' in the French system have therefore led to the creation of a bargaining framework, albeit one which is more specific and circumscribed as compared to its British equivalent. Adjustment and reform in France has also been of a more limited nature.

The persistence of these very different 'rules of the game' in government–industry relations has been strengthened by their interaction with more general aspects of each legal environment or legal culture. Divergent traditions of public authority in each country have had a marked impact on attempts to reform or overhaul existing regulatory practices. The traditional French deference to the élite civil servant, for example, has had significant implications for the attempted reform of price controls. Policy reviews have invariably been conducted by senior civil servants from the *Conseil d'État* or the *Cour des Comptes* or, more recently, by the President's senior scientific advisers. The resultant recommendations have tended to reflect certain assumptions about what an ideal, rational system of control should look like, and the distortions which inevitably arise in the policy process have been ignored. Hence one system has tended to replicate the faults of the predecessor, and in the process has perpetuated the very fragmentation which has contributed to the failure of meaningful reform in France.

I have suggested that in the UK the mechanisms for the renewal of the PPRS function as an established stable forum in which pragmatic reform of controls on pricing and profit can be negotiated between industry and government. Within that forum, it is the interests of the large research-based firms which are paramount. The very informality and discretionary nature of the PPRS have allowed industry to reinforce its position. In other words, there has always been an implicit assumption that industry should be actively involved in, or incorporated into, the process of reforming or modifying the system of profit control to meet new demands upon it. This assumption has now been made explicit in the latest version of the PPRS, which accords a privileged role to both the ABPI and research-based firms in the formulation of general cost-containment measures. The twenty largest suppliers to the NHS now actively assist the Department of Health in monitoring costs and other trends by furnishing information about projected annual sales. In return the Department supplies the industry with spending projections, and if the prices of NHS medicines are increasing at a rate higher than general inflation, the industry will participate actively in the formulation of cost-containment measures and will assist the Department in monitoring costs and other trends by furnishing information about projected annual sales. It is highly unlikely that these deliberations will ever be made public, since their subject-matter will be treated as commercially sensitive. A combination of the extensive discretion vested in officials at the Department to negotiate with industry and the blanket operation of the wider constitutional convention of ministerial responsibility prevent public scrutiny of their content in any detail. Significantly, other groups whose interests are also directly affected by the adoption of new cost-containment measures, including the generic manufacturers, the medical and pharmacy professions, and the consumers are completely excluded from this privileged bargaining forum.

The only independent review of the industry's relationship with the NHS, conducted by the Sainsbury Committee, which reported in 1967, was chaired not by a civil servant but by an industrialist from another sector: in the final event, the majority of the Committee's recommendations were not incorporated into the renegotiated pricing scheme in 1968.

Conclusion

This brief summary has suggested ways in which the different techniques of regulation developed over the forty-year period during which the British and French governments have sought to intervene in the affairs of their home-based drug industries have led to contrasting patterns of relations between regulator and regulated and to the institutionalization of certain 'rules of the game' in the regulatory process. For the reasons discussed above, these rules have become almost self-sustaining. They have played an important part in determining the fate of various initiatives for reform and in the resolution of the continual conflicts which arise in the process of regulation.

I do not intend to suggest, however, that regulatory outcomes or the fate of attempts at policy innovation can be attributed solely to factors such as legal culture or tradition in a deterministic manner. The French-based industry's comparatively weak competitive base, for example, may have a variety of causes, the independent influence of any one of which is difficult to isolate.[27] Nevertheless, the divergent legal traditions discussed at length here have played a significant role both in mediating the conflicts generated by changing market structures and in shaping the regulatory response to them, and they cannot therefore be ignored.

While there remains a considerable amount of work to be done on the influence of distinctive national legal traditions on the nature and direction of state intervention in the economy, it is hoped that a detailed analysis of one key industrial sector has explored one particular approach to the legal dimension of government–industry relations, and that it has in the process offered some useful insights into the more general problems facing governments who embark upon the complex task of regulating for competition.

Notes

1. See, however, the collection of essays edited by T. C. Daintith entitled *Law as an Instrument of Economic Policy* (Berlin: De Gruyter, 1988), which examines, from a comparative legal perspective, the implementation of selected economic policies. The essays do not, however, look at the consequences of these policies, or the legal form in which they were executed, for any individual sector of the economy.
2. Select Committee on Energy, 'The Structure, Regulation and Economic

Consequences of Electricity Supply in the Private Sector, *Third Report for the Session 1987–88*, (London: HMSO, 1989), xlix.

3. W. Baumol, 'Contestable Markets: An Uprising in the Theory of Industry Structure', *American Economic Review*, 72 (1982), 1–15.

4. See further W. Shepherd, 'Contestability vs. Competition', *American Economic Review*, 74 (1984) 572–87.

5. Chap. 2, pp. 51–4.

6. The classic study is H. Averch and L. Johnson, 'Behaviour of the Firm under Regulatory Constraint', *American Economic Review*, 52 (1962) 1052–69.

7. J. Vickers and G. Yarrow, *Privatization and the Natural Monopolies* (London: Public Policy Centre, 1985).

8. See further J. Hills, *Privatization and Telecommunications* (London: Gower, 1986).

9. See further M. Moran, 'Investor Protection and the Culture of Capitalism', in L. Hancher and M. Moran (eds.), *Capitalism, Culture, and Economic Regulation*, (Oxford: OUP, 1988), 49–69.

10. See generally A. Gamble, *Britain in Decline* (London: Macmillan, 1985); and K. Dyson, *The State Tradition in Western Europe* (Oxford: Martin Robertson, 1980).

11. E. N. Sulieman, *Private Power and Centralization in France* (Princeton, NJ: Princeton University Press, 1987), 303.

12. R. K. Middlemass, *Competition, Power and the State* (London: Macmillan, 1985), 18.

13. A. Shonfield, *Modern Capitalism* (London: OUP, 1965), W. C. Baum; *The French Economy and the State* (Princeton: Princeton University Press, 1958).

14. See generally R. Cranston, *Consumers and the Law* (London: Weidenfeld & Nicolson, 1984).

15. A. Cawson, P. Holmes, K. Morgan, and A. Stevens, *Hostile Brothers* (Oxford: Clarendon Press, 1990).

16. M. K. Young, 'Structural Adjustment of Mature Industries in Japan: Legal Institutions, Industry Associations and Bargaining', paper presented to the Economic and Social Science Research Council Conference on Government–Industry Relations, Oxford, Mar. 1988.

17. R. Lewis, 'Regulating the Insurance Industry', *Modern Law Review*, 48 (1985), 275–92.

18. A. Page, 'Self-Regulation: The Constitutional Dimension', *Modern Law Review*, 49 (1986), 141–67.

19. T. Bourgoignie and D. Trubek, *Consumer Law, Common Markets and Federalism* (Berlin: De Gruyter, 1987). See particularly pt. III.

20. J. J. Boddewyn, 'Advertising Self-Regulation: Organisation Structures in Belgium, Canada, France and the United Kingdom', in W. Streeck

and P. Schmitter (eds.), *Private Interest Government: Beyond Market and the State* (London: Sage, 1984), 34.

21. House of Lords debate on codes of practice, H.L. Deb., vol. 469, cols. 1075–104 (15 Jan. 1986).

22. See, for example, M. M. Atkinson and W. D. Coleman, 'Strong States and Weak States: Sectoral Policy Networks in Advanced Capitalist Economies', *British Journal of Political Science*, 32, who draw on the work of John Zysman and Peter Hall to suggest that where individual bureaux administer a corpus of law and regulation that defines their responsibilities, and where those rules are not subject to negotiation, these agencies will be more autonomous from their clientele, and therefore 'stronger'.

23. P. Selznick, *Leadership in Administration* (New York: Harper and Row, 1957).

24. P. Hall, *Governing the Economy: The Politics of State Intervention in Britain and France*, (Oxford: Blackwell, 1986), 265.

25. J. W. Meyer and B. Rowan, 'Institutional Organizations: Formal Structure as Myth and Ceremony', *American Journal of Sociology*, 83 (1977), 340–63.

26. T. R. Burns, 'Actors, transactions and social structures' in U. Himmelstrand (ed.), *Sociology: From Crisis to Science?*, 2 (London: Sage, 1986) 8–37.

27. For an explanation based on the failure of French governments to encourage the development of an adequate 'cumulative technical cycle', see J. H. Dunning, *Multinationals, Technology and Competitiveness* (London: Unwin Hyman, 1988), esp. chap. 6.

Bibliography

ABEL-SMITH, B., *Cost Containment in Health Care: The Experience of Twelve European Countries (1977–1983)* (Luxembourg: Commission of the European Communities, 1984).

ABEL-SMITH, B., and GRANDJEAT P., *Pharmaceutical Consumption*, Social Policy Series, 38, (Brussels: Commission of the European Communities, 1978).

ABEL-SMITH, B., and MAYNARD A., *The Organization, Financing and Cost of Health Care in the European Community*, Social Policy Series, 36 (Brussels: Commission of the European Communities, 1979).

ACHACH, D., 'La Nouvelle Législation de la concurrence', *Revue de la concurrence*, 5 (1986), 7–11.

ALLIES, P., GATTI-MONTAIN, J., GLEIZAL, J. J., HEYMANN-DOAT, A., LOCHAK, D., and MIAILLE, M., *L'Administration dans son droit* (Paris: Publisud, 1985).

ASHFORD, N. A., and HEATON, G. R., 'Regulation and Technological Innovation in the Chemical Industry', *Law and Contemporary Problems*, 46 (1983), no. 3, 109–46.

ATKINSON, M. M., and COLEMAN, W. D., 'Strong States and Weak States: Sectoral Policy Networks in Advanced Capitalist Economies', *British Journal of Political Science*, 18 (1988), 47–67.

ATKINSON, M. M., and COLEMAN, W. D., 'Corporatism and Industrial Policy', in A. Cawson (ed.), *Organised Interests and the State: Studies in Meso-Corporatism* (London: Sage Publications, 1985), 21–33.

AUBY, J.-M., 'Les essais de pharmacologie clinique sur l'homme sain sont-ils dorénavant licites?', *Labo-pharma*, Mar. 1981.

——'Les essais de médicaments sur l'homme sain: l'état actuel du problème', *Revue de droit sanitaire et sociale*, 3 (1985), 316–27.

AUBY, J.-M., and COUSTOU, F., *Droit pharmaceutique* (Paris: Libraires techniques, 1980).

AUBY, J.-M., and DUCOS-ADER, R., *Institutions administratives* (Paris: Economica, 1973).

AVERCH, H., and JOHNSON, L., 'Behaviour of the Firm under Regulatory Constraint', *American Economic Review*, 52 (1962), 1052–69.

BAECQUE, F., and QUERMONNE, J.-L., *Administration et politique sous la République* (Paris: Presse de la Fondation nationale des sciences politiques, 1985).

BAILY, M. N., 'Research and Development Cost and Returns: The US Pharmaceutical Industry', *Journal of Political Economy*, 80 (1972), 70–85.

BALDWIN, R., and McCRUDDEN, C., 'Regulatory Agencies', in Baldwin and McCrudden (eds.), *Regulation and Public Law* (London: Weidenfeld and Nicolson, 1987).

BARDACCO, J., *Loading the Dice* (Boston, 1984).

BARTLETT, C. A., 'How Multinational Organisations Evolve', *Journal of Business Strategy*, 3 (1982), 22–53.

BAUM, W. C., *The French Economy and the State* (Princeton: Princeton University Press, 1958).

BAUMOL, W., 'Contestable Markets: An Uprising in the Theory of Industry Structure', *American Economic Review*, 72 (1982), 1–15.

BEIER, F. K., CRESPI, S., and STRAUSS, J., *Biotechnology and Patent Protection* (Paris: OECD, 1985).

BEL, N., *Revue Marché Commun*, (1975), 506–11.

BIRNBAUM, P., *Les Sommets de l'État* (Paris: Seuil, 1977).

BLANCO WHITE, T., *Patents for Inventions*, 4th edn. (London: Stevens, 1974).

BLOCH-LAINE, F., *La France en Mai 1981. Commission du Bilan, 2. Les Grands Équilibres économiques* (Paris: La Documentation française, 1982).

BODDEWYN, J. J., 'Advertising Self-Regulation: Organisation Structures in Belgium, Canada, France and the United Kingdom', in W. Streeck and P. Schmitter (eds), *Private Interest Government: Beyond Market and State* (London: Sage, 1984), 34.

BOLZE, C., 'L'Ineffectivité du Titre II de la loi du 19 Juillet 1977 sur le contrôle des concentrations ou le naufrage du droit anti-trust français', *Études dédiées à Roblot* (Paris: LGDJ, 1984).

BOND, R. S., and LEAN, D. F., *Sales Promotion and Product Differentiation in Two Prescription Drug Markets*, Staff Report to the Federal Trade Commission (Washington, 1977).

BORK, R., *The Anti-Trust Paradox* (Harvard: Harvard University Press, 1978).

BORRIE, G., 'British Competition Law', *International Journal of Law and Economics*, 2 (1983), 139–49.

BOURGOIGNIE, T., and TRUBEK, D., *Consumer Law, Common Markets and Federalism* (Berlin: De Gruyter, 1987).

BOUTET, J., *L'Industrie pharmaceutique* (Paris: La Documentation française, 1975).

BOYER, A., 'Form as Substance: A Comparison of Antitrust Regu-

lations', *International Comparative Law Quarterly*, 32 (1983), 904–
29.

BRAITHWAITE, J., *Corporate Crime and the Pharmaceutical Industry*
(London: Routledge & Kegan Paul, 1984).

BRICKMAN, B., and JASANOFF, S., *Regulating Chemical Hazards* (Ithaca:
Cornell University Press, 1985).

BUREAU OF THE EUROPEAN UNION OF CONSUMERS, *The Consumer and
Pharmaceutical Products in the EEC*, BEUC Report 258/84 (Brussels,
1984).

BURNS, T. R., 'Actors, Transactions and Social Structures', in U. Himmelstrand (ed.), *Sociology: From Crisis to Science?*, 2 (London: Sage,
1986), 8–37.

BURSTALL, M. L., *The Community's Pharmaceutical Industry* (Luxembourg: Commission of the European Communities, 1985).

BURSTALL, M. L., DUNNING, J. H., and LAKE, A., *Multinational Enterprises, Governments and Technology: The Pharmaceutical Industry*
(Paris: Organization for Economic Co-operation and Development,
1981).

CARDON, P., and DOMMEL, F., 'Injuries to research subjects', *New England
Journal of Medicine*, 295 (1976), 650–4.

CASTEL, J. G., 'France', in W. Friedmann (ed.), *Antitrust Laws* (London:
Stevens, 1956), chap. 7.

CAWSON, A., HOLMES, P., MORGAN, K., and STEVENS, A., *Hostile Brothers*
(Oxford: Clarendon Press, 1990).

CAWSON, A., HOLMES, P., and STEVENS, A., 'The Interaction between
Firms and the State in France: The Telecommunications and Consumer Electronics Sectors', in S. Wilks and M. Wright (eds.), *Comparative Government–Industry Relations* (Oxford: Clarendon Press,
1987), 10.

CECCHINI, P., *The Benefits of a Single Market* (London: Gower, 1988).

CHAMPET, Y., *Revue Marché Commun*, (1965), 210–19.

CHAPMAN, B., *British Government Observed* (London: Allen and Unwin,
1963).

CHESNAIS, B., 'L'industrie pharmaceutique en France', *Revue d'économie
industrielle*, 31 (1981), 21–38.

CHEVALLIER, J., 'L'intérêt général dans l'administration française', *Revue
internationale des sciences administratives*, 41 (1975), 325.

CHEW, R., SMITH, T., and WELLS, N., *Pharmaceuticals in Seven Nations*
(London: Office of Health Economics, 1985).

COHEN, E., and BAUER, M., *Les Grandes Manœuvres industrielles* (Paris:
Belfond, 1985).

COMANOR, W. E., *The Political Economy of the Pharmaceutical Industry*,
University of California Department of Economics Working Paper
243 (Santa Barbara, 1984).

COMMISSION D'AUTORISATION DES MÉDICAMENTS, Presidential reports 1978–85 (Paris: Ministère de la Santé, 1979–85).

COMMISSION DE LA CONCURRENCE, *Rapport annuel 1984* (Paris: La Documentation française, 1984).

COMMISSION DES FINANCES DU SÉNAT, *Rapport du Sénat*, 8, 1985 (Paris: Journal Doc. Sénat, 1985).

COMMISSION OF THE EUROPEAN COMMUNITIES, *White Paper on Completing the Internal Market*, Com 85 (310) (Luxembourg: Commission of the European Communities, 1985).

——*The State Aid Element in Capital Transfers* (Brussels: Commission of the European Communities, 1987).

COMMITTEE OF PUBLIC ACCOUNTS, *Fourth Report for the Session 1950–51* (London: HMSO, 1951).

——*Third Report for the Session 1951–52*, (London: HMSO, 1952).

——*Third Report for the Session 1952–53*, (London: HMSO, 1953).

——*Third Report for the Session 1953–54*, (London: HMSO, 1954).

——*Special Report for the Session 1956–57*, (London: HMSO, 1957).

——*Third Report for the Session 1956–57*, (London: HMSO, 1957).

——*First, Second and Special reports for the Session 1959–60* (London: HMSO, 1960).

——*Third Report for the Session 1962–63*, (London: HMSO, 1963).

——*25th Report for the Session 1979–80*, H.C.764 (London: HMSO, 1980).

——'Dispensing Drugs in the NHS', *10th Report for the Session 1982–83*, H.C.356 (London: HMSO, 1983).

——'Dispensing of Drugs in the NHS', *Twenty-Ninth Report for the Session 1983–84*, H.C.551 (London: HMSO, 1984).

——'NHS Supplies and the PPRS', *Twenty-Third Report for the Session 1984–85*, H.C.280 (London: HMSO, 1985).

COMMITTEE ON THE SAFETY OF DRUGS, *Annual Report for the year ending 1964* (London: HMSO, 1965).

——*Annual Report for the year ending 1969* (London: HMSO, 1970).

COMMITTEE ON THE SAFETY OF MEDICINES, *Annual Report for the year ending 1972* (London: HMSO, 1973).

——Annual Reports, 1977–82 (London: HMSO, 1978–82).

CONSEIL ÉCONOMIQUE ET SOCIAL, *La Sécurité sociale*, report by R. F. Vernejoul, *Journal officiel de la République française*, Avis et Rapports no. 15, 24 Oct. 1968.

——*L'Industrie pharmaceutique*, report by Bernard Maurize, *Journal officiel de la République française*, Avis et Rapports no. 1, 1986.

CORFIELD, K., 'An Industrialist's View: The Private Sector', in D. Englefield, (ed.), *Today's Civil Service* (Harlow: Longman, 1985).

COUSTOU, F., 'Les pré-essais cliniques', *Rev. Sc. Techn. Pharm.*, Feb. 1983, 47.

CRANSTON, R., 'Regulation and Deregulation: General Issues', *University of New South Wales Law Journal*, 5 (1982), 1–21.

CROUCH, C., 'Sharing Public Space', in J. Hall (ed.), *The State in History* (Oxford: Blackwells, 1986), 210.

CURRALL, J., 'Some Aspects of the Relation between Articles 30 and 36 of the EEC Treaty', *Oxford Year Book of European Law*, 4 (1984), 169–206.

DAINTITH, T. C., (ed.), *Law as an Instrument of Economic policy* (Berlin: De Gruyter, 1988).

DAINTITH, T. C., and HANCHER, L., *Energy Strategy in Europe: The Legal Framework* (Berlin: De Gruyter, 1986).

DASHWOOD, A., and WYATT, D., *The Substantive Law of the EEC*, 2nd edn. (London: Sweet and Maxwell, 1987).

DAVENPORT-HINES, R. P. T., 'Glaxo as a Multinational before 1963', in G. Jones (ed.), *British Multinationals* (Aldershot: Gower, 1986), 137–61.

DE LAUBADÈRE, A., 'Interventionnisme et contrat', *Revue française de l'administration publique*, 12 (1979), 485–93.

——*Traité de droit administratif*, 1, 8th edn. (Paris: Librairie générale de droit et de jurisprudence, 1980), no. 560.

DELETRAZ-DELPORTE, M., 'Les Produits génériques: droit comparé et analyse du droit français', thesis (Université Paris Sud, 1983).

DEPARTMENT OF HEALTH AND SOCIAL SECURITY, *Sharing Resources for Health in England* (London: DHSS, 1976).

——'Pharmaceuticals and the EEC', Symposium Proceedings (London, 1985).

——*Green Paper on Primary Health Care*, Cmnd. 9771 (London: HMSO, 1986).

DEPARTMENT OF TRADE AND INDUSTRY, *A Review of Restrictive Trade Practices Legislation*, Cm. 331 (London: HMSO, 1988).

DE WOLF, P., 'The Pharmaceutical Industry: Structure, Intervention and Competitive Strength', in de H. W. Jong (ed.), *The Structure of European Industry*, 2nd edn. (The Hague: Kluwer, 1988), 211–44.

DUKES, M., *The Effects of Drug Regulation* (The Hague: MTP Press, 1985).

DUNLEAVY, P., 'Some Political Implications of Sectoral Cleavages', *Political Studies*, 28 (1980), 364–83.

DUNLOP, D., 'The Assessment of the Safety of Drugs and the Role of Government in their Control', *Journal of Clinical Pharmacology*, (1967), July–Aug. 184–92.

DUNNING, H. J., *Multinationals, Technology and Competitiveness* (London: Unwin Hyman, 1988).

DUPUY, J., and KARSENTY, S., *L'Invasion pharmaceutique* (Paris: Seuil, 1974).

DURUPTY, M., *Les Entreprises publiques*, vols. 1 and 2 (Paris: PUF, 1984).

DUTHEIL DE LA ROCHÈRE, J., 'Les régimes conventionnels des prix, engagements de stabilité et contrats de programme', *Actualité juridique (Droit administratif)*, (1967), 597–601.

DYSON, K., *The State Tradition in Western Europe* (Oxford: Martin Robertson, 1980).

EDWARDS, C. D., *Trade Regulations Overseas* (New York: Oceana, 1966).

EHLERMANN, C. D., 'The Single European Act', *Common Market Law Review*, 24 (1987), 361–404.

ELIOT, D. C., and GRIBBIN, J. D., 'The Abolition of Cartels and Structural Change in the UK', in A. Jacquemin and H. de Jong (eds.), *Welfare Aspects of Industrial Markets* (Leiden: Leiden Publishing Company, 1977).

EUROPEAN FEDERATION OF PHARMACEUTICAL INDUSTRY ASSOCIATIONS, *Biotechnology and the European Pharmaceutical Industry* (Brussels: EFPIA, 1984).

FARJAT, G., *Droit économique*, 1st edn. (Paris: PUF, 1974).

FAVOREU, L., 'Les Décisions du Conseil constitutionnel dans l'affaire des nationalisations', *Revue de droit public et de la science politique en France et à l'étranger*, (Apr. 1982), 84–98.

FELDMAN, D., 'Rationing Judicial Review', *Public Administration*, 66 (1988), 109–21.

FINER, S. E., *Five Constitutions* (Sussex: Harvester, 1979).

FLEURIET, M., *Les Techniques de l'économie concertée* (Paris: LGDJ, 1974).

FORCH, S., 'Probleme des freien Warenverkehrs von Arzneimittelversorgung in den Europäischen Gemeinschaften', in *Wettbewerb in Recht und Praxis*, (1981), 71–7.

FRIEDBURG, E., 'Administration et entreprises', in M. Crozier (ed.), *Où va l'administration française?* (Paris: Éditions ouvrières, 1974).

GAMBLE, A., *Britain in Decline* (London: Macmillan, 1985).

GLAIS, M., 'Six ans de répression des ententes illicites et des abus de position dominante: un bilan de l'activité de la Commission de la concurrence', *Revue trimestrielle de droit commercial*, 2 (1984), 420–54.

GORMLEY, L., *Prohibiting Restrictions on Trade within the EEC* (Amsterdam: Elsevier, 1985).

GRABOWSKI, H., and VERNON, R., 'New Studies of Market Definition', in R. I. Chien (ed.), *Issues in Pharmaceutical Economics* (Lexington, Mass.: Lexington Books, 1979).

GRANAT, M., JORDAL, B., and SJOBLOM, T., 'The Processing of Applications for the Registration of Medicines in Nordic Countries', *Journal of the Society of Pharmacists*, 1 (1983), 34–44.

GRANT, W., *Business and Politics in Britain* (London: Macmillan, 1987).

GRANT, W., and MARSH, D., *The CBI* (London: Hodder and Stoughton, 1977).

GRIFFIN, J. P., and DIGGLE, G. E., 'A Survey of Products Licensed in the UK from 1971–81', *British Journal of Clinical Pharmacology*, 12 (1981), 453–63.

GRIFFIN, J. P., and LONG, J. R., 'New Procedures Affecting the Conduct of Clinical Trials in the UK', *British Medical Journal*, 283 (1981), 447–9.

GROUPE DE STRATÉGIE INDUSTRIELLE, *Rapport du Synthèse; Situation et Perspectives de la chimie française*, Cahiers de GSI, 5, 1983 (Paris: La Documentation française, 1983).

GUY, R., and LEIGH, D., *The EEC and Intellectual Property* (London: Sweet and Maxwell, 1981).

GYSELEN, L., 'State Action and the Effectiveness of the EEC Treaty's Competition Provisions', *Common Market Law Review*, 26 (1988), 33–60.

GYSELEN, L., and KYRIAZIS, N., 'Article 86: The Monopoly Power Issue Revisited', *European Law Review*, 11 (1986), 134–49.

HABER, L. F., *The Chemical Industry, 1900–1930* (Oxford: Clarendon Press, 1981).

HABERMAS, J., *Communication and the Evolution of Society* (Oxford: Blackwells, 1979).

HALL, P., *Governing the Economy: The Politics of State Intervention in Britain and France* (Oxford: Blackwell, 1986).

HALL, P., and HITCH, J., 'Price Theory and Business Behaviour', *Oxford Economic Papers*, 2 (1939), 12–45.

HAM, C., *Health Policy in Britain*, 2nd edn. (London: Macmillan, 1985).

HANCHER, L., 'Regulating Drug Promotion: The British Experience', *Journal of Consumer Policy*, 10 (1987), 383–407.

——'Regulating Drug Prices in Britain and West Germany', in L. Hancher and M. Moran (eds.), *Capitalism, Culture, and Economic Regulation* (Oxford: OUP, 1989), 79–108.

HANCHER, L., and MORAN, M. (eds.), *Capitalism, Culture, and Economic Regulation* (Oxford: OUP, 1989), 240–69.

HANSARD, 18 May 1953, vol. 515, col. 1726.

——10 Apr. 1954, vol. 527, cols. 887–90.

——17 June 1955, vol. 348, col. 100.

——20 June 1968, vol. 766, cols. 1433–40.

HARLOW, C., and RAWLINGS, R., *Law and Administration* (London: Weidenfeld and Nicolson, 1984).

HASS, A. E., MCCORMICK, L. D., and ASPEL, S., *A Historic Look at Drug Introductions on a Five-Country Market* (Maryland: Food and Drug Administration, 1982).

HAUT CONSEIL DU SECTEUR PUBLIQUE, *Rapport 1984, 92: La Gestion du secteur public* (Paris: La Documentation française, 1984).

HAYWARD, J. E. S., 'Mobilizing private interests in the service of public ambitions: the salient element in the dual French policy style', in J. Richardson (ed.), *Policy Styles in Western Europe* (London: Allen & Unwin, 1982), 111–40.

——*Governing France: The One and Indivisible French Republic* (London: Weidenfeld and Nicolson, 1983).

HELLINGMAN, K., 'State Participation as State Aids', *Common Market Law Review*, 23 (1986), 111–34.

HILLS, J., *Privatization and Telecommunications* (London: Gower, 1986).

HOLMES, P., and STEVENS, A., *The Framework of Industrial Policy Making in France*, University of Sussex Working Paper on Government–Industry Relations, 1986.

HOPT, K., 'Restrictive Practices', in G. Teubner (ed.), *The Juridification of Social Spheres* (Berlin: De Gruyter, 1987), 291–332.

HOWELLS, J., 'Spatial Location and Decision-Making in the Pharmaceutical Industry', Ph.D. thesis (Cambridge, 1984).

HURLEY, R., 'The Medicines Act: Is it Working?', *Journal of the British Institute of Regulatory Affairs*, 2 (1983), 1–3.

INSTITUT NATIONAL DE LA RECHERCHE MÉDICALE/DIRECTION DE LA PHARMACIE ET DU MÉDICAMENT, Le Contrôle des médicaments (Paris: DPHM, 1984).

JEAN, P., *Rapport sur la visite médicale* (Paris: Inspection générale des affaires sociales, 1982).

JENNY, F., and WEBER, A. P., *L'Entreprise et les politiques de concurrence* (Paris: Les Éditions d'organisation, 1976).

——'Groupement d'intérêt économique et allocation des ressources', *Revue française de gestion*, 5 (1976), 69–76.

KATZENSTEIN, P. J., *Between Power and Plenty: Foreign Economic Policies of Advanced Industrial States* (Cambridge, Mass: Harvard University Press, 1978).

KEELER, J. T. S., 'Situating France on the Pluralism-Corporatism Continuum', *Comparative Politics*, 17 (1985), 229–49.

KELMAN, S., *Regulating America; Regulating Sweden* (Cambridge, Mass: MIT Press, 1981).

KENNEDY, D., *A Calm Look at Drug Lag* (Maryland: Food and Drug Administration, 1981).

KLEIN, R., *The Politics of the NHS* (London: Longman, 1984).

——'Health Policy 1979–83: the Retreat from Ideology?', in P. Jackson (ed.), *Implementing Government Policy Initiatives* (London: Royal Institute of Public Affairs, 1985), 118–35.

KOLKO, G., *The Triumph of Conservatism* (New York: Free Press, 1965).

KORAH, V., 'Proposal for a Group Exemption for Patent Licenses', *European Law Review*, 4 (1979), 206–12.

——'The Concept of a Dominant Position within the meaning of Article 86', *Common Market Law Review*, 17 (1980), 395–411.

——*Competition Law of Britain and the Common Market* (The Hague: M. Nijhoff, 1982).

LALL, S., 'Price Competition and the International Pharmaceutical Industry', *Oxford Bulletin of Economics and Statistics*, 40 (1978), 9–21.

LANG, R., *The Politics of Drugs* (Farnborough: Saxon House, 1974).

LANGLE, L., and OCCELLI, R., 'Le coût d'un nouveau médicament', *Journal de l'économie médicale*, 1 (1983), no. 2.

LANGLOIS, A., 'Les Comités d'éthiques locaux en France', *Revue française des affaires sociales*, 3 (1986), 91–103.

LATAILLADE, P., *Report on the Commission's Proposal for a Directive on Pharmaceutical Pricing Transparency* (European Parliament, Document A2-261/87, 1987).

LECOMPTE, T., *La Consommation pharmaceutique: Structure, prescription et motifs* (Paris: Centre de recherche et de documentation en économie de la santé, 1984).

LEGENDRE, P., 'La bureaucratie et le droit', *Revue historique du droit français et étranger* (Paris: Sirey, 1974).

LEGRAIN, M., 'The Medicines Review Process: The French Approach', in BIRA, *Fifth Annual Symposium on Regulatory Affairs: Medicines Review Worldwide* (London: British Institute of Regulatory Affairs, 1984), 28–34.

LEMAY, R., 'Les Médicaments: particularités du brevet', *Droit social*, 1 (1971), 7–25.

LEMBRUCH, G., 'Concertation and the Structure of Corporatist Networks', in J. H. Goldthorpe (ed.), *Order and Conflict in Contemporary Capitalism* (Oxford: OUP, 1984), 60–81.

LEVER, J., 'Bipartite Agreements and the Restrictive Trade Practices Acts', *Law Quarterly Review*, 85 (1969), 177–91.

LEWIS, R., 'Regulating the Insurance Industry', *Modern Law Review*, 48 (1985), 275–92.

LIEBENAU, J. M., 'Marketing High Technology: Educating Physicians to Innovative Medicines', in R. P. T. Davenport-Hines (ed.), *Markets and Bagmen* (Aldershot: Gower, 1986), 118–40.

LINDBLOM, L., *Politics and Markets: The World's Political-Economic Systems* (New York: Basic Books, 1977).

LINOTTE, D., 'Chronique législative', *Revue de droit publique* (1982), 120–5.

LOUGHLIN, M., 'Tinkering with the Constitution', *Modern Law Review*, 51 (1988), 531–48.

LOWI, T., *The End of Liberalism: The Second Republic of the United States* (New York: Norton, 1979).

LYON CAEN, A., 'Le contrôle des concentrations: études de loi française', *Revue trimestrielle de droit européen*, 15 (1979), 440–65.

MACHELON, J.-M., 'Le mise sur le marché du médicament en droit français: aspects de droit administratif', *Annales de la Faculté de droit et de science politique*, Oct. 1980 (Paris: Librairie générale de droit et de jurisprudence, 1980).

MACHLUP, F., and PENROSE, E., 'The Patent Controversy in the Nineteenth Century', *Journal of Economic History*, 10 (1950), 1–29.

MACMILLAN, K., and TURNER, I., 'The Cost-Containment Issue' in S. Wilks and M. Wright (eds.), *Government and Industry Relations in Major OECD Countries* (Oxford: Clarendon Press, 1986).

MATHELY, P., *Le Droit français des brevets d'invention* (Paris: Journal des notaires et des avocats, 1974).

MARENCO, G., 'Public Sector and Community Law', *Common Market Law Review*, 20 (1983), 495–527.

MASSACHUSETTS INSTITUTE OF TECHNOLOGY, Center for Policy Alternatives, 'Environmental/Safety Regulation and Technological Change in the US Chemical Industry' (Cambridge, Mass., 1979).

MAURAIN, C., and VIALA, G., 'La nouvelle réglementation de la publicité pharmaceutique', *Gazette du Palais*, 31 (1988), 12–4.

MAURAIN, C., 'Publicité et droit de la santée', thesis, (Université de Bordeaux II, 1981).

MAZEX, M., 'Les contrats de plan entre l'État et les entreprises publiques', *Actualité juridique (Droit administratif)*, (1984), 101–9.

MEDAWAR, C., *The Wrong Kind of Medicine* (London: Consumers Association, 1984).

MELVILLE, A., and JOHNSON, C., *Cured to Death: The Effects of Prescription Drugs* (Sevenoaks: New English Library, 1983).

MERCEREAU, F., *La Sécurité sociale* (Paris: Fondations Sciences Politiques, 1987).

MERKIN, R., and WILLIAMS, K., *Competition Law* (London: Sweet and Maxwell, 1984).

MEYER, J. W., and ROWAN, R., 'Institutional Organizations: Formal Structure as Myth and Ceremony', *American Journal of Sociology*, 83 (1977), 340–63.

MIDDLEMASS, R. K., *Competition, Power and the State* (London: Macmillan, 1985).

MINISTRY OF HEALTH, *Annual Report for year ending 1950* (London: HMSO, 1951).

——'Safety of Drugs', *Final Report of the Joint Standing Committee on Prescribing* (London: HMSO, 1963).

MIROW, K. R., and MAURER, H., *Webs of Power* (Boston: Houghton Miffin, 1982).

MITNICK, B. M., *The Political Economy of Regulation* (Columbia: 1980).

MONOPOLIES AND MERGERS COMMISSION, *Chlordiazepoxide and Diazepam*, (London: HMSO, 1973).

MONOPOLIES AND RESTRICTIVE PRACTICES COMMISSION, *The British Insulin Manufacturers' Cartel*, (London: HMSO, 1951).

MORAN, M., 'Investor Protection and the Culture of Capitalism', in L. Hancher and M. Moran (eds.), *Capitalism, Culture, and Economic Regulation* (Oxford: OUP, 1989), 49–78.

MOREAU, V. J., 'De l'interdiction faite à l'autorité de police d'utiliser une technique d'ordre contractuel', *Actualité juridique (Droit administratif)*, 1 (1965), 3–15.

MORTELMANS, K., 'The Campus Oil Case', *Common Market Law Review*, 21 (1984), 405–12.

MURRAY, R., (ed.), *Multinationals Beyond the Market* (London: Harvester, 1981).

NATIONAL ACADEMY OF ENGINEERING/NATIONAL RESEARCH COUNCIL, *The Competitive Status of the US Pharmaceutical Industry* (Washington: National Academy Press, 1983).

NATIONAL ECONOMIC DEVELOPMENT OFFICE, *Focus on Pharmaceuticals* (London: NEDO, 1972).

——*Focus on Pharmaceuticals* (London: NEDO, 1986).

NEALE, A. C., and GOYDER, D., *The Anti-Trust Laws of the USA*, 3rd edn. (Cambridge: Cambridge University Press, 1981).

O'BRIEN, B., *Prescribing Patterns in Europe* (London: Office of Health Economics, 1984).

O'BRIEN, D. P., 'Competition Policy in Britain: The Silent Revolution', *Anti-Trust Bulletin*, 27 (1982), 218–38.

OFFICE OF HEALTH ECONOMICS, *Understanding the NHS in the 1980s* (London: OHE, 1984).

OLIVER, P., *Free Movement of Goods in the EEC* (London: ESC Publications, 1982).

ORGANIZATION FOR ECONOMIC CO-OPERATION AND DEVELOPMENT, *Measuring Primary Health Care* (Paris: OECD, 1985).

——*Innovation Policy in France* (Paris: OECD, 1986).

——*Financing and Delivering Health Care* (Paris: OECD, 1987).

OSTERBORG, L., 'Patent Term à la Carte', 17 (1986), 60–80.

PAGE, A., 'Public Undertakings and Article 90', *European Law Review*, 7 (1982), 19–32.

PAGE, A., 'Self-Regulation: The Constitutional Dimension', *Modern Law Review*, 49 (1986), 141–67.

PARKER, J. E. S., 'Regulating Pharmaceutical Innovation', *Food, Drug and Cosmetic Law Journal*, (1977), 163–79.

PEACOCK, A., et al., *The Regulation Game* (London: Anglo-German Foundation, 1984).

PELTZMAN, S., 'An Evaluation of Consumer Legislation', *Journal of Political Economy*, 81 (1973), 1046–91.

PICARDE, E., 'La notion de police administrative', thesis (Université de Paris II, 1978).

PICCIOTTO, S., 'Slicing a Shadow', in L. Hancher and M. Moran (eds.), *Capitalism, Culture, and Economic Regulation* (Oxford: OUP, 1989), 11–48.

POGGI, G., *Law in the Modern State* (London: Macmillan, 1978).

PRIEUR, C., 'L'Évolution historique de l'organisation des relations entre la médecine libérale et les régimes d'assurance maladie 1930–76', *Revue trimestrielle du droit sanitaire et social*, 46 (1984), 301–19.

QUANTOCK, D. C., 'The effect of regulation on international drug development', in A. W. Harcus (ed.), *Risk and Regulation in Medicine* (London: Association of Medical Advisers in the Pharmaceutical Industry, 1980), 99–108.

QUIRK, P., 'The FDA', in J. Wilson (ed.), *The Politics of Regulation* (New York: Basic Books, 1980), 138–69.

RALITE, J., *Retour de la France* (Paris: Éditions sociales, 1981).

REEKIE, W. D., *Monopoly and Competition in the Pharmaceutical Industry* (London: Macmillan, 1969).

——*The Economics of the Pharmaceutical Industry* (London: Macmillan, 1975).

——'Price and Quality Competition in the US Drug Industry', *Journal of Industrial Economics*, 26 (1978), 223–37.

REEKIE, W. D., and WEBER, M., *Politics, Profits and Drugs* (London: Macmillan, 1979).

RHODES, R. A. W., 'Power-Dependence, Policy Communities and Inter-Governmental Networks', *Public Administration Bulletin*, 49 (1985), 18–31.

ROSA, J. J., 'Lois du Marché et innovation', *Prospective et Santé*, 36 (1985/86), 103–8.

ROWLEY, C. K., *The British Monopolies Commission* (London: Allen and Unwin, 1966).

ROYAL COMMISSION ON CIVIL LIABILITY AND COMPENSATION FOR PERSONAL INJURY, *Report*, Cmnd. 7054 (London: HMSO, 1978).

SAINSBURY, A., *Report of the Committee of Enquiry into the Relationship of the Pharmaceutical Industry with the NHS*, Cmnd. 3410 (London: HMSO, 1967).

SANDIER, S., 'Private Medical Practice in France', *Advances in Health Economics and Health Services Research*, 4 (1983), 335–67.

SARGENT, J., 'The Pharmaceutical Price Regulation Scheme', International Institute for Management working paper (Barlin, 1983).

——'The Politics of the PPRS', in W. Streeck and P. Schmitter (eds.), *Private*

Interest Government: Beyond Market and State (London: Sage, 1985), 105–27.

SAVY, R., 'Le contrôle juridictionnel de la legalité des décisions économiques de l'administration', *Actualité juridique (Droit administratif)*, (1972), 6–15.

SCHERER, F., *Industrial Market Structure and Economic Performance*, 2nd edn. (Cambridge, Mass: Harvard University Press, 1980), esp. chaps. 5–8.

SCRIP, *Parallel Imports and the UK Pharmaceutical Market: A Status Report* (Richmond: PJB Publications, 1984).

SEIDEL, M., 'The Harmonization of Laws Relating to Pharmaceuticals in the EEC', *Common Market Law Review*, 6 (1968), 309–26.

SELECT COMMITTEE ON ENERGY, 'The Structure, Regulation and Economic Consequences of Electricity Supply in the Private Sector', *Third Report for the Session 1987–8*, (London: HMSO, 1988).

SELINKSY, P., 'L'Affaire des pétroliers: la reconquête judicielle du contrôle des ententes', *Cahiers du droit de l'entreprise*, (1983), 1–7.

SELZNICK, P., *Leadership in Administration* (New York: Harper and Row, 1957).

SEMELER-COLLERY, J., 'Tous droits de reproduction non réservés: les médicaments génériques', *Coopération*, 6 (1980), 3–8.

SÉRUSCLAT, F., *La distribution du médicament en France*, (Paris: La Documentation française, 1983).

SHARP, M., and BRECH, M., *Inward Investment* (London: Routledge & Kegan Paul, 1984).

SHARPE, T., 'Refusal to Supply', *Law Quarterly Review*, 99 (1983), 37–67.

SHEPHERD, W., 'Contestability vs. Competition', *American Economic Review*, 74 (1984), 572–87.

SHONFIELD, A., *Modern Capitalism* (London: Royal Institute of International Affairs/OUP, 1965).

SIGVARD, J., *L'Industrie du médicament* (Paris: Calmann-Lévy, 1975).

SILVERSTON, M., and LEE, P., *Pills, Profits and Politics* (Berkeley: University of California Press, 1974).

SIMON, P., and SOUBRIE, C., 'Oui à la pharmacovigilance; non à son isolement', *Prospective et Santé*, 7 (1978), 65–88.

SLINN, J. A., *A History of May and Baker, 1934–84* (Cambridge: Cambridge University Press, 1984).

SNELL, E. S., 'The Regulatory Authorisation of Clinical Trials', *British Journal of Clinical Pharmacology*, 15 (1983), 625–7.

SYNDICAT NATIONAL DE L'INDUSTRIE PHARMACEUTIQUE, *L'Industrie pharmaceutique en France: ses réalités* (Paris: SNIP, 1987).

SPIERS, C. J., and GRIFFIN, J. P., 'A Survey', *British Journal of Clinical Pharmacology*, 15 (1983), 649–55.

STATMAN, M., 'The Effect of Patent Expiration on the Market Position of Drugs', in R. B. Helms (ed.), *Drugs and Health* (Washington: AEI, 1981), 140–50.

STIGLER, G., 'The Theory of Economic Regulation', *Bell Journal of Economics and Managerial Science*, 2 (1971), 21–45.

STONE, R., 'The Block Exemption for Patent Licenses', *European Intellectual Property Law Review*, 5 (1986), 21–7.

SULIEMAN, E., *Power, Politics and Bureaucracy* (Princeton, NJ: Princeton University Press, 1974).

——*Elites in French Society* (Princeton, NJ: Princeton University Press, 1978).

——*Private Power and Centralization in France* (Princeton, NJ: Princeton University Press, 1987).

——'State Structures and Clientilism: The French State Versus the "Notaires" ', *British Journal of Political Science*, 17 (1987), 257–79.

SWAPES, R. E. A., and WILLIAMS, W. O., 'Prescription Drug Advertising', *Journal of the Royal College of General Practitioners*, 26 (1976), 76–82.

TAYLOR, C., and SILBERSON, Z. A., *The Economic Impact of the Patent System* (Cambridge: Cambridge University Press, 1975).

TEFF, H., and MUNRO, C., *Thalidomide: The legal aftermath* (Farnborough: Saxon House, 1976).

TESO, B., *The Pharmaceutical Industry* (Paris: Organization for Economic Co-operation and Development, 1979).

TEUBNER, G., 'REFLEXIVE LAW', *Law and Society Review*, 17 (1983), 240–95.

THI DAO, 'Pharmaceutical Competition', in G. Teeling Smith (ed.), *Health Economics* (London: Croom Helm, 1987), 250–69.

THOENIG, J.-C., *L'Ère des technocrates* (Paris: Éditions d'organisation, 1973).

TISSEYRE-BERRY, M., et VIALA, G., *Législation et déontologie de l'industrie pharmaceutique* (Paris: Masson, 1983).

TURPIN, C., *British Government and the Constitution* (London: Weidenfeld and Nicolson, 1985).

UNITED NATIONS, *Transnational Corporations and the Pharmaceutical Industry* (New York: United Nations, 1979).

VELLUZ, L., 'La Recherche pharmaceutique: Rapport de la Commission d'étude', in *Pour une politique de la santé*, A, vol. 5 (Paris: La Documentation française, 1975), 130–67.

VENIT, J. S., 'The Community's Opposition Procedure', *Common Market Law Review*, 22 (1985), 167–202.

——'The New Block Exemption for Patent Licensing', *Anti-Trust Bulletin*, 31 (1986), 1–45.

VENTURINI, V. G., *Monopolies and Restrictive Trade Practices in France* (Leiden: A. W. Sijthoff, 1971).

VICKERS, J., and YARROW, G., *Privatization and the Natural Monopolies* (London: Public Policy Centre, 1985).

VOGEL, D., *National Styles of Regulation: Environmental Policy in Great Britain and the United States* (Cornell: Cornell University Press, 1986).

VON GREBNER, K., 'Pricing Medicines', in G. Teeling Smith (ed.), *Health Economics* (London: Croom Helm, 1987), 229–49.

WADE, O. L., 'The Review of Medicines', in BIRA, *Fifth Annual Symposium on Regulatory Affairs* (London: British Institute of Regulatory Affairs, 1984), 4–12.

WEISS, J., 'Origins of the French Welfare State: Poor Relief in the Third Republic', *French Historical Studies*, 13 (1983), 47–78.

WHISH, R., *Competition Law* (London: Butterworths, 1985).

WILKS, S., and WRIGHT, M., 'States, Sectors and Networks', in Wilks and Wright (eds.), *Comparative Government–Industry Relations* (Oxford: OUP, 1987), 279–91.

WILLIAMS, R. J., 'Politics and Regulatory Reform: Some Aspects of the American Experience', *Public Administration*, 57 (1975), 55–67.

WILSON, F. L., 'Alternative Models of Interest Intermediation. The Case of France', *British Journal of Political Science*, 12 (1982), 173–181.

WILSON, F. L., 'Interest Groups and Politics in Western Europe: The Neo-Corporatist Approach', *Comparative Politics*, 16 (1983), 121–40.

WINKLER, J., 'LAW, STATE AND THE ECONOMY', *British Journal of Law and Society*, 2 (1975), 103–19.

WRIGHT, V., *The Government and Politics of France* (London: Hutchinson, 1983).

ZINSOU, L., *Le Fer du lance* (Paris: O. Orbans, 1985).

ZYSMAN, J., *Government, Markets and Growth* (Ithaca: Cornell University Press, 1983).

Index of Statutes

UK (*arranged in alphabetical order*)

Index of Cases

UK

FRANCE

EEC (Cases and Commission Decisions)

Index